THE OXFORD ILLUSTRATED HISTORY OF

THE REFORMATION

Peter Marshall was born and raised in the Orkney Islands, and educated at the University of Oxford. Since 1994, he has taught at the University of Warwick, and has been Professor of History there since 2006. He is a leading specialist in the history of the Reformation, particularly its impact in the British Isles, and has written seven books and over fifty articles on these themes. A member of the editorial boards of *Sixteenth Century Journal* and *British Catholic History*, he is a co-editor of *English Historical Review*. He is married with three daughters, and lives in Leamington Spa.

CONTRIBUTORS:
Simon Ditchfield, University of York
Carlos Eire, Yale University
Brad S. Gregory, University of Notre Dame
Bruce Gordon, Yale University
Peter Marshall, University of Warwick
Lyndal Roper, University of Oxford
Alexandra Walsham, University of Cambridge

Praise for *The Oxford Illustrated History of the Reformation*

'This is a fine book, beautifully produced, providing an easily accessible distillation of some of the best recent scholarship of the Reformation. A work of this kind is a vital resource for anyone concerned to understand what ideas, events, and convictions compelled the sea changes in Christianity that took place in the sixteenth century, and, no less important, to understand the repercussions of these changes which are still felt today.'

Anne Dillon, *Times Literary Supplement*

'This is a classic *Oxford Illustrated History* volume: its wealth of pictures forms an instructive rather than merely decorative complement to a text from some of the leading experts in the field, who present a fine panorama of current thinking on this formative era for the modern West.'

Diarmaid MacCulloch, University of Oxford, and author of *A History of Christianity: The First Three Thousand Years*

'This short volume does a magnificent job in providing a birds' eye view of the Protestant Reformation, including appropriate maps and illustrations that grip the historical imagination.'

Mark Greengrass, *Huguenot Society Journal*

'a scintillating collection of essays that challenges conventional views of the Reformation . . . This book does a fine job of unfolding the intricately decorated and richly textured fabric of this extraordinary era.'

Lucy Wooding, *The Tablet*

'it bears comparison with the very best studies and compendia . . . a hearty 'bravo' is in order'

Jonathan Wright, *The Herald*

'Wonderful . . . It's a huge achievement by Marshall, and by OUP, that cleverly gets the ball rolling ahead of the 500th anniversary of Luther's posting of his Ninety-five Theses'

Oxford Today

'An outstanding work of church history.'

Paul Richardson, *Church of England Newspaper*

THE OXFORD
ILLUSTRATED HISTORY OF

THE REFORMATION

Edited by
PETER MARSHALL

OXFORD
UNIVERSITY PRESS

OXFORD
UNIVERSITY PRESS

Great Clarendon Street, Oxford, OX2 6DP,
United Kingdom

Oxford University Press is a department of the University of Oxford.
It furthers the University's objective of excellence in research, scholarship,
and education by publishing worldwide. Oxford is a registered trade mark of
Oxford University Press in the UK and in certain other countries

© Oxford University Press 2015

The moral rights of the authors have been asserted

First published 2015
First published in paperback 2017

Impression: 1

Published in the United States of America by Oxford University Press
198 Madison Avenue, New York, NY 10016, United States of America

British Library Cataloguing in Publication Data
Data available

Library of Congress Cataloging in Publication Data
Data available

ISBN 978–0–19–959548–8 (Hbk.)
ISBN 978–0–19–959549–5 (Pbk.)

Printed in Great Britain by
Bell & Bain Ltd., Glasgow

Links to third party websites are provided by Oxford in good faith and
for information only. Oxford disclaims any responsibility for the materials
contained in any third party website referenced in this work.

EDITOR'S FOREWORD

HALF a millennium has now passed since the Augustinian friar Martin Luther nailed a provocative set of questions for discussion—his Ninety-Five Theses against Indulgences—to the door of the Castle Church in Wittenberg. He did not intend it, and no one at the time foresaw it, but his action set in motion the momentous process of religious change which came to be called the Reformation, which gave birth to a new form of Christianity soon to be known as Protestantism, and which created bitter and lasting disharmonies in European (and later, global) social, cultural, and political life—dissonances whose echoes are still clearly audible today. Whether we like it or not, we are all children of the Reformation. But the nature of our collective inheritance has always been a contentious and disputed one.

As an object of historical study, the Reformation is an old topic with a new face. Recent scholarship has not sought to deny or refute some long-held assumptions: that the changes following from Martin Luther's protest in Germany were extremely important ones; that they ended up transforming numerous aspects of European culture and society; and that they mark a kind of boundary between the medieval and modern worlds. But the manner in which these changes were brought about, the roles assigned to particular individuals and groups, the length of time they took, and the question of whether they self-evidently represented 'progress' or 'improvement'— these have all been discussed and debated over the course of the last few decades in ways which would undoubtedly have puzzled or perplexed earlier generations of historians. The aim of the current volume—which brings together a team of scholars at the very forefront of current Reformation research—is to bring out some of the ways in which over recent years our understanding of the Reformation has become more complicated (and therefore more interesting), while retaining a clear and coherent perspective on the balance between continuity and change. The chapters focus on particular themes, with individual stories to tell, and particular interpretative problems to discuss, but collectively they supply both a broad narrative of the key developments, and a cohesive overall assessment of how the Reformation looks as we gear up to celebrate (or at least commemorate) the 500th anniversary of Luther's posting of the Theses in 1517.

What readers will not find in these pages is much suggestion that the religious debates and conflicts of the Reformation era were merely a kind of code—a necessary language (since that was all that was available to contemporaries) for conducting and resolving deeper clashes over political power and economic resources. Our approach is traditional to the extent that we believe that the actual content of ideas mattered, and had the power to motivate individuals to act in ways that were not always in their own material best interests. But, equally, each of the contributors here is fully aware that, in the period we are studying, 'religion' was not what it has since become in much of the modern West: a narrowly defined, discrete realm of action and experience—the occasional reflective column in the opinion pages of a newspaper, the declining habit of church on Sunday. Our subjects inhabited societies where it was (almost) universally believed that God had not only created the world, but continued to take a close, direct, and controlling interest in every aspect of its governance and workings. To study the impact of the Reformation, therefore, is necessarily to pursue the political, the social, the cultural—questions of relations between rulers and subjects, masters and servants, and between women and men, parents and children. Over the longer term, the emergence of something like the modern Western concept of 'religion'—an essentially private matter, the sincere adherence to which was compatible with other loyalties and obligations, and which might take acceptably plural forms—may have been one of the key outcomes of the Reformation. If so, it was a result few at the time foresaw and fewer still would have welcomed. That the Reformation represents a case study in the law of unintended consequences is one of the recurrent themes of this book.

Alongside a Reformation more unpredictable in its course and consequences than earlier generations supposed, we now also have one which was wider (theologically), bigger (geographically), and longer (chronologically) than in the days, not so very long ago, when textbooks on 'the Reformation' largely confined themselves without embarrassment to developments in (western) Europe, to the followers of Luther and Calvin, and to the short period between 1517 and 1559. Luther and Calvin still matter, of course. Without them, and without the challenging and compelling religious ideas they formulated—justification by faith alone, the doctrine of double-predestination—the religious changes of the sixteenth century would have looked very different, and might well bear another name. The chapters by Lyndal Roper and Carlos Eire demonstrate how the spiritual, and physical, journeys of these key individuals, though they began in very traditional places, led and pointed to some truly new destinations. But Luther and Calvin, and the -isms to which they unwillingly lent their names, should certainly no longer define the character of the Reformation for us, as if in some pure and perfected essence. Brad Gregory's chapter highlights the importance of that loose network of reforming individuals and ideas—known variously as radicals or Anabaptists—who have nearly always been seen as marginal or exceptional, and as lying firmly outside a Reformation 'mainstream'. But he warns that this perception owes much to uncritical hindsight, and he argues that those anti-Roman groups and individuals who rejected the interpretations of scripture supplied by Luther and the other 'magisterial' reformers have as much right as anyone to be considered both founders and heirs of a quintessentially Reformation tradition.

A more inclusive approach to the questions of who qualifies as a 'reformer', and what consequently constitutes 'the Reformation', is also now readmitting the Catholics to a central place in the story. That important changes took place in those parts of a once united Christendom that remained in the papal allegiance, as well as in those that rejected it, has never really been in doubt. But the familiar designation (dating from the nineteenth century) of something called the 'Counter-Reformation' suggests a separate, reactive, and essentially negative set of processes. In books on the Reformation it is still in fact not uncommon for 'Reformation' and 'Protestant Reformation' to be regarded as essentially synonymous, and for developments within Roman Catholicism to be entirely omitted from the account, or relegated to an appendical chapter. But if we take as the keynotes of 'Reformation' the range of attempts in the sixteenth and seventeenth centuries—from the top down and the bottom up—to transform the lives of ordinary Christians and point them in a more serious direction, and to create better ordered Christian societies, then what has come to be known as 'Catholic Reformation' deserves to be taken just as seriously as the Protestant variety. By the end of the sixteenth century at the latest, Rome was arguably as much a centre of 'Reformation' as was Wittenberg or Geneva. In his chapter on Catholic Reformation and Renewal, Simon Ditchfield takes this process of 'de-centring' still further, suggesting that to see the (Catholic) Reformation as a purely, or even primarily, European phenomenon is to miss what was, over the longer term, perhaps the most significant development of the entire period. This was the beginning of Christianity's transformation into a truly global nexus of faith, within which, and from the outset, the new territories influenced the religious culture of the old almost as much as vice versa.

Recognizing that Catholics were the agents as well as the objects of constructive religious change should also remind us that reform was older than the Reformation. The once-prevalent (and still surprisingly resilient) idea that the movements spearheaded by Luther, Zwingli, and others were external insurgencies against a corrupt, complacent, unresponsive, and monolithic Church deserves to be finally laid to rest. The predominant impression from Bruce Gordon's survey of late medieval Christianity is of just how diverse, varied, and vibrant the religious culture of Europe was in the century or so preceding Luther's revolt. There were certainly patches of corruption (not least, in Rome itself), as well as pockets of overt dissent, in the communities of Hussites, Waldensians, and Lollards. But impulses towards reform were to be found almost everywhere in orthodox Catholic guise. The idea is increasingly taking hold—in scholarly circles at least—that in its first stages the Reformation was not so much a reaction against the characteristic ideals of late medieval Catholicism, as a radicalized expression of the hopes and aspirations for reform which were universally recognized, but all too often frustrated by various forms of institutional inertia.

Once underway, revolutions follow their own logic, and they adapt to circumstances on the ground over which they are being fought. There is no doubt that Germany, and, more specifically, Electoral Saxony, was the original epicentre of the quake. As Lyndal Roper shows in her chapter, distinctive local and regional features, such as the presence of a developed printing industry, had a decisive impact on how Luther's message was spread. But even here, and from the very earliest days, Luther could not completely control how his teaching was received and understood.

It is in any case somewhat misleading to imagine the German Reformation as the model or archetype, in respect of which all other Reformations are 'variants'. The bifurcation of the Protestant movement into separate Lutheran and 'Reformed' branches was not a later schism breaking out in a hitherto unified body of reformers, but the institutionalization of tensions present among them from the outset. Zwingli at least claimed to have been 'preaching the Gospel of Christ' before anyone in his part of the world had even heard of Luther. In the awareness of contemporaries, Catholic and Protestant alike, of an international struggle against the forces of Antichrist (whose identity varied according to the perspective of the observer), the Reformation was certainly more than the sum of its geographical parts. But the parts should not be regarded as mere case studies serving to facilitate our understanding of a transcendent whole. Whether in small, self-contained Swiss city-states like Geneva, German princely territories, Italian archdioceses, ethnically and jurisdictionally complex lord-ships in eastern Europe, or the thinly populated kingdoms of Scandinavia, the Refor-mation exhibited distinctive—indeed, unique—patterns wherever it took root. Peter Marshall's chapter on the pathways Reformation followed in Britain and Ireland, through the sixteenth century and into the seventeenth, does not presuppose any kind of overt contrast with a notional 'continental' model. But it illustrates the complex and capricious interweaving in these islands of dynastic, political, cultural, and ethnic factors—an interplay that in other places took different forms and produced dramat-ically contrasting results.

In the British Isles, a series of drives to ensure the uniformity of the populace in the practice of the religion authorized by the State in fact ended up producing a marked plurality of belief and religious custom. This was a situation that few welcomed in principle and most learned to live with only reluctantly. The ideal of a population united through collective tenure of a single religious allegiance and identity was not unobtainable—it was more or less achieved in Catholic Spain, for example, or in Lutheran Denmark. But across Europe as a whole it was probably more the exception than the rule, as waves of Reformation, 'Second Reformation', and Counter-Refor-mation left tidal pools of minority religious culture along the shorelines of supposedly homogeneous political entities. In her chapter on the legacies of the Reformation, Alexandra Walsham discusses the paradoxical extent to which confessional coexist-ence and toleration were accidental and unwanted by-products of the Reformation. Only at the very end of our period, and among a restricted group of elite thinkers, was a virtue made out of the necessity of tolerating those whose beliefs were patently 'wrong', and who could not be persuaded or coerced into a different way of thinking.

This raises the question of whether the Reformation, or individual Reformations, should be considered a failure rather than a success, as some scholars have indeed argued to be the case. If the definition of failure is one by which the high aspirations of idealistic clergymen never completely enshrined themselves as societal realities, then the accusation certainly stands. Reformers (particularly, perhaps, the zealous Calvinists discussed here by Carlos Eire) strove towards a vision of a genuinely godly society, purged of superstition, idolatry, and sin. Human nature—or, as reformers of various stripes might have seen it, the consequences of Original Sin—made complete victory in this area a virtually impossible goal. Campaigns of total moral reformation, whether promoted by Calvinist Consistories, Catholic Inquisitors, or Lutheran Church Visitors, almost invariably foundered on the rocks of rural conservatism and deeply ingrained popular custom. Elite investigators found low levels of literacy, and high levels of ignorance of the complex doctrines reformers wanted ordinary people to learn and internalize.

But if lay people across Europe did not all become paragons of piety and understanding, it scarcely follows that the Reformation just passed them by. The contributors to this volume are united in finding evidence of deep, meaningful, and lasting change, not just at the level of church organization and worship, but in the structures and patterns of everyday life. The Reformation created a series of new 'confessional' identities. This was so even for the inhabitants of the parts of Europe remaining loyal to Rome—for a Catholic who knew that he or she was not a Protestant was different from one who had never contemplated such a hypothetical alternative. Increasingly, confessional allegiance determined patterns of work and habits of dress, attitudes towards art and music, choice of marriage partner. Some historians have detected in Lutheran, Calvinist, and Catholic territories parallel and remarkably similar patterns of 'confessionalization', as Church and State worked together to align a sense of political identity and religious commitment, and to mould dutiful, obedient, and pious subjects. But to contemporaries of all stripes, the differences here seemed more important than the similarities, and there is little support in the chapters which follow for any notion of the Reformation as a fundamentally uniform and unidirectional 'process', delivering similar social and political outcomes in societies that differed from each other only in culturally superficial ways.

Counting and identifying the trees is always important work, but it is important that historians keep an eye on the size and contours of the wood. What real difference did the Reformation in the end make? Alexandra Walsham dissects some of the received wisdom on this question, and interrogates a number of long-standing 'myths'. It is much less clear than it used to be that the (Protestant) Reformation was the foundation stone of modern science, a spur to the development of capitalist individualism, or the root cause of a secularizing 'disenchantment of the world'. Yet historians will continue to debate these questions: Carlos Eire actually does see in Calvin's radical disentangling of spirit from matter the thin end of a wedge which would ultimately displace religion itself from its central place in explaining the nature of reality.

The Reformation, as many of us now understand it, and as reflected in these chapters, is a decidedly untidier phenomenon than it used to be: it is a long-term process (or set of processes) rather than an event; it is plural and multi-centred, and frequently paradoxical and unpredictable in its effects. Broadening the scope of enquiry in this way poses some greater interpretative challenges, but there is little doubt that it enhances rather than reduces the significance of the topic under review. Few aspects of life were left untouched by the ramifications of religious change, and if the consequences were multifaceted they were nonetheless profound. One consequence for authors and readers is that complete comprehensiveness is now harder than ever to deliver in a volume of this kind, if it is not to become excessively unwieldy. Ideally, there would be more here on later Reformation confessional culture in Germany, and on the European peripheries (such as eastern Europe and Scandinavia), as well as (following up on some suggestive sections in Lyndal Roper's chapter on Luther) fuller discussion of the effects of religious reform on gender relations, and on the development of Christianity's troubled relationships with Judaism and Islam. The Reformation's momentous impact on art, music, and literature can only be slightly sketched in these pages. But if readers come away provoked by questions to which they are still seeking parts of the answer, and are inspired to delve deeper into some of the issues raised, then the authors of this book on the Reformation will assuredly feel justified in their endeavours.

PETER MARSHALL

CONTENTS

List of Colour Plates   xiii

List of Maps   xv

1. LATE MEDIEVAL CHRISTIANITY   1
   Bruce Gordon

2. MARTIN LUTHER   42
   Lyndal Roper

3. CALVINISM AND THE REFORM OF THE REFORMATION   76
   Carlos Eire

4. THE RADICAL REFORMATION   115
   Brad S. Gregory

5. CATHOLIC REFORMATION AND RENEWAL   152
   Simon Ditchfield

6. BRITAIN'S REFORMATIONS   186
   Peter Marshall

7. REFORMATION LEGACIES   227
   Alexandra Walsham

Further Reading   269

Chronology   285

Picture Acknowledgements   289

Index   293

LIST OF COLOUR PLATES

1. Triptych by Hans Memling, Bruges, 1484
2. Page from the Sherborne Missal, early fifteenth century
3. Interior of the Temple de Paradis, Lyon, 1564
4. *The Spanish Fury at Antwerp* by Franz Hogenberg, 1576
5. Escape of Swiss Anabaptists from the Zurich *Hexenturm*, 21 March 1526
6. Execution by drowning of Hutterite missionaries Heinrich Sommer and Jakob Mandel in Baden, 9 October 1582
7. Portrait of St Ursula, Goa, sixteenth /seventeenth century
8. St Ignatius of Antioch mauled by a lion, Hispano–Philippine ivory, seventeenth century
9. Title page of the 'Great Bible', 1539
10. A preacher in the pulpit, from the Commonplace Book of Thomas Trevilian, 1608
11. *Room in a Dutch House* by Pieter Janssens Elinga, 1668–72
12. *American Gothic* by Grant de Volson Wood, 1930

LIST OF MAPS

1. The states of Europe, *c.*1500   3
2. The Papal States in the early sixteenth century   7
3. Saxony at the time of Martin Luther   52
4. Germany before the Peace of Augsburg   74
5. The Swiss Confederation at the time of Calvin   78
6. Iconoclastic violence in the Netherlands, 1566   102
7. The spread of Calvinism in the German Empire to *c.*1600   107
8. The German Peasants' War, 1525   128
9. Religions of the World, *c.*1500   164
10. Political boundaries in the British Isles on the eve of
    the Reformation   189
11. Plantations in Ireland, 1556–1622   218
12. Religious coexistence and conflict in Europe, *c.*1600   238

1 *Late Medieval Christianity*

BRUCE GORDON

To imagine late medieval Christianity is to enter a world bewildering in diversity of belief and practice, complex in theology, and populated by angels, demons, saints and heretics, nepotistic popes, and Chaucer's Wife of Bath. The faithful believed that the Son of God was present in the upraised hands of the priest. They knew that death led a dance with emperor and peasant alike. Wealthy bankers and merchants, mindful of usurious lives, dispensed their wealth in the hope of being remembered by those who remained in the world while they suffered in the flames of Purgatory. The monks of the Antonine monastery near Colmar treated victims of plague and prayed before Grünewald's crucified Christ, whose sore-infested skin revealed a God who suffered with the afflicted. The Florentine prophet Savonarola perished in flames in the Piazza della Signoria in 1498, repudiated by the people he had once roused to a different conflagration, a bonfire of the vanities. In Rome, meanwhile, the master of ceremonies in the papal palace wrote of a banquet with chestnuts and prostitutes attended by Pope Alexander VI.

The Church in the world, Christ's bride, was everything her contemporary advocates and critics claimed—fervent in worship, devout in prayer, rich in sacramental reverence, fearful of the afterlife, and zealous in pious works and gifts. At times, the Church was poisoned by corruption and venality in her highest offices and drained of life by indolence in her lowest. For aspirational temporal rulers, whether emperors, princes, or civic magistrates, the wealth and lands of churches were the stones of Ophir, and like Solomon they would have them. Noble families understood all too well the material rewards of spiritual authority and wisely invested in the cardinal's hat, the bishop's crozier, and the abbess's staff of office for their offspring. Yet from the chaos and confusion depicted in Hieronymus Bosch's *Garden of Earthly Delights* (c.1500), where Heaven and Hell meet in the present, rose a profession of faith in a Church 'One, Holy, Catholic and Apostolic'.

The true character of Christianity on the eve of the Reformation will never be found in a narrative of irredeemable decay and decline, or in a celebration of a lost golden age. There was something of both, and no single perspective suffices. The Church kneeled before an all-powerful omniscient God who had created

BEHOLD THE MAN. This woodcut from the Low Countries (c.1450) of blood pouring from the dying Christ is an indulgence for 80,000 years' relief in Purgatory for those who know the prayer of the Sacred Heart of Christ. Such single leaves were posted on the walls of churches and homes to stir devotion, reminding the faithful of the suffering of the Son of God, the cleansing power of his blood, and the time they will spend being purged of sin.

Christ, would plead on their behalf for mercy, advocating for the faithful when her Son descended from Heaven at the consummation of time. Christ had told John, the Beloved Disciple, from the cross that Mary was mother to those who followed him, and the devotion of late medieval Christians enthroned her as the Queen of Heaven. Around Mary assembled a chorus of saints who interceded on behalf of penitent sinners. These saints were the intimates of men, women, and children, and their remarkable lives were told in stories, and their images found in churches and homes. They cured, protected, and blessed those who honoured them.

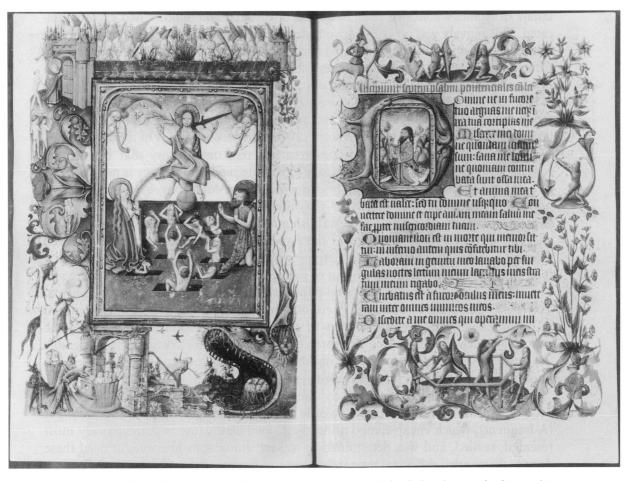

END OF TIME. A Book of Hours prepared for the French noblewoman Yolande de Lalaing, wife of Reinard II van Brederode, presents Christ appearing in glory announced by the angels to judge humanity. Mary, Mother of God, pleads for mercy, while John the Baptist, on Christ's left, demands justice. On the bottom the gaping mouth of Hell consumes the damned. The souls in Purgatory ascend to the blessed company assembled in the heavenly city.

Popes and Councils

Late medieval Christianity was traumatized by the disintegration of papal authority and the humiliation of the Church in the protracted nightmare known as the Great Schism (1378–1417). Rival popes, one at Avignon in France, one in Rome, did incalculable damage to the Church and divided the loyalties of Europe. A brutal resolution was found at the Council of Constance (1414–18) when the Holy Roman Emperor Sigismund strong-armed into submission the by now three claimants to the papal throne. The Council restored unity by electing Martin V, a member of the distinguished Colonna

CHRIST ON LAKE GENEVA. Konrad Witz, a German painter active in Basel, completed this biblical scene in 1444 for the Peter altar in Geneva cathedral. The painting has long been admired as one of the first accurate representations of landscape, as Witz represents Lake Geneva from personal observation. With his portrayal of an oversize Christ on the water with the diminutive disciples in the boat Witz offers a commentary on the contemporary Church. He painted as the Council of Basel deposed Eugenius IV and elected the Duke of Savoy as Pope Felix V. Christ on the calm water is an image of the tranquil Church, while symbols of the House of Savoy in the background assert the legitimacy of Felix.

V, the Duke of Savoy, who had been elected pope. He fought with the increasingly radical leaders of a council that had rapidly dwindled to a rump, abandoned by those with more moderate views. Basel seemed to be reviving the very crisis of schism within the Church that councils had been summoned to resolve.

Basel failed to topple the papal monarchy, but its true legacy did not lie in its failure to reshape the church hierarchy. It marked the cultural transformation of northern Europe. At its height the Council assembled the greatest figures of the age, and a collective desire for reform found articulation in extensive legislation aimed at restoring the Church in 'body and head'. Even conflict seemed to leaven achievement. The late medieval Church was adorned with remarkable men and women of learning, some of whom had visited crumbling Byzantium and returned bearing the intellectual riches of Greek Christianity. Notable was Nicholas of Cusa (1401–64) from the German Mosel valley, a canon lawyer, diplomat, philosopher, ecclesiastical reformer, and eventually a bishop. He travelled across Italy, the Mediterranean, and northern Europe in the service of reform, though often to little applause. Possessed with a mind that saw unity in thought and creation, his *De Docta Ignorantia* (1440) drew together philosophy and theology, while his earlier *De Concordantia Catholica* (1433) reflected the ultimately vain hope that papal and conciliar authority could be reconciled. It is still thought possible that in 1451 he encouraged Johann Gutenberg to begin printing on behalf of the Church, four years before the famous Gutenberg Bible appeared in Mainz.

The Rise of Papal Rome

As the papacy faced down the most serious threat to its authority, Rome was slowly transformed from a fetid, malaria-ridden swamp, full of unregarded ruins, into a city worthy of the successors of St Peter. An ardent patron of the arts and sciences, Nicholas V (1447–55) was the first of what can be called the Renaissance popes, and he planned a new basilica and palace that required the demolition of the thousand-year-old St Peter's. In fact, the basilica was not razed until 1506 under Pope Julius II (1503–13), when the old St Peter's began to be replaced, but change was everywhere. Nicholas's successors, men such as Sixtus IV (1471–84) and Alexander VI (1492–1503), contributed to the building of the Vatican, which in time became the favoured papal palace.

The popes were joined by cardinals in commissioning sumptuous palazzi as suitable residences for princes of the Church and members of influential noble families. The benefits to Rome from these worldly interests were evident, as foreign merchants and entrepreneurs were drawn to the city, among them the leading bankers of Europe, the Fuggers of Augsburg. The interest of the popes in reviving Rome extended to personal involvement in urban planning: they oversaw the repositioning of streets, the building of bridges, and the connecting of piazzas, all in anticipation of pilgrims journeying to the ancient city, the only apostolic See in the West.

Papal authority in Rome extended beyond buildings and roads to encompass ceremony and ritual. At the centre was the Vatican, where the pontiffs resided, papal elections were held, and from where newly elected popes processed to St Peter's to be crowned. The spectacle that was the Renaissance papacy was a heady mixture of sacred and secular. Court jesters danced in front of Alexander VI during a Corpus Christi procession, and the chapel choir performed comedies for Leo X (1513–21). Pope Innocent VIII (1484–92) had his daughters married in the Vatican in great ceremony, and during the reign of Alexander VI upper-class ladies and prostitutes alike had access to the papal palace for events such as the rumoured and notorious 'Ballet of the Chestnuts' of 1501. In the season of oppressive summer heat and plague, popes often retired to rural retreats, where they pursued princely activities such as hunting, leaving behind delegated clergy to see to their liturgical obligations.

POPE AND SAINT. Vittore Carpaccio's *c*.1494 depiction of pilgrims meeting Pope Cyriac before the walls of Rome. The legend portrayed concerns the Roman-British princess Ursula, who kneels before the pope with her betrothed, following a pilgrimage to Rome. Ursula was later massacred with 11,000 virgins in Cologne. The Italian chronicler Voragine records that Cyriac was a pope in the third century who abdicated and had his name removed from the catalogue of successors of Peter because he went to martyrdom with Ursula without informing the clergy of Rome. Carpaccio's painting of this saint-pope is rich with symbols of the authority and glory of the Renaissance papacy.

Such goings-on played large in later, censorious Protestant accounts, but they do not tell the whole story. In spirit, authority, and intellect the popes resurrected the ancient heart of Western Christianity. Over the course of the fifteenth century, the papal court changed from an intellectual backwater to a prestigious centre of learning where scholarship flourished. Rome embraced its Classical and Christian pasts, and successive popes used their patronage to revive Greek and Latin learning, now known as humanism, in the service of the Church. Secretaries such as Flavio Biondo elevated the Latin style of papal correspondence to the standard of leading humanist writers. Nicholas V was a man of vision who, in addition to church building, assembled the papal library, collecting treasures ancient and contemporary. Pius II (1458–64) was more than a patron of learning. He took his name from the great Roman poet Virgil's 'pius Aeneas', and enjoyed an extraordinary career as a distinguished humanist and diplomat, before finally becoming pope. He knew the ends of the earth, having once dined on porridge in distant Scotland—an unhappy memory. Pius was also among the first to see the printed pages of Gutenberg's Bible, which he declared a wonder. The many phases of his life are captured in frescoes in the Piccolomini library in the Siena Duomo.

The success of the popes owed much to a practice repeatedly cited as evidence of their corruption. Nepotism was the granting of offices or favours to members of one's family, not just nephews or nieces, and several occupants of the papal throne had sons favourably placed in the church hierarchy. Alexander VI was unique in fathering children during his pontificate, but others had offspring from earlier in their careers. Such families were not merely an unwanted consequence of a lamentable absence of chastity. In the precarious world of the fifteenth-century Renaissance court, these blood ties ensured stability. Just as the sale of cardinals' hats and of indulgences was a lucrative and necessary source of much-needed income, family ties were essential for success in ecclesiastical preferment, favouring a candidate as he sought high office, including the papacy itself. Such was the level of nepotism that a mere four families attained the papacy on nine different occasions, with the family of Sixtus IV, the della Rovere, leading the field with three elections.

The triumph of the papacy in the fifteenth century owed much to Rome's wooing, most cannily by Pope Eugenius IV, of the temporal rulers of Europe, who found they could gain increased control over the Church in their lands without being required to back the fractious Conciliarists, whose views on monarchical rule were hardly congenial to royal authority. It was easy enough to lend support to a distant pope whose only real power lay in his legal right of appointment to senior ecclesiastical offices. Such largesse did not benefit the supporters of conciliar authority. To bring the schism at Basel to a close, Nicholas V concluded a disadvantageous concordat with Emperor Frederick III in 1448 that curtailed papal influence in appointments to bishoprics in the Holy Roman Empire. Similar agreements were struck with the imperial electors, who were the leading princes of Germany, greatly increasing German control over ecclesiastical offices. These arrangements did much to sever the bonds between Rome and the German lands to the north. Desire for a church free of Rome and the hated papacy found expression in the 'Grievances of the German Nation', a document that circulated among princes and cities after 1450. Frederick III was not the last emperor to be crowned by a pope—that would be Charles V, in 1520—but in 1452 he was the last to journey to Rome to kneel before the Vicar of Christ.

Relations with France were differently configured, largely because of the contentious Pragmatic Sanction of Bourges (1438), which had greatly limited the authority of the papacy by embracing the conciliar legislation from Basel. Although never enforced, the Pragmatic Sanction was deployed by successive French kings to bring argumentative popes to heel. King Louis XI (1461–83) was principally concerned with the establishment of peace in his kingdom, but with the invasion of the Italian peninsula in 1494 by his successor Charles VIII (1483–98), the papacy's relations with France were deeply compromised. By the end of the century, the papal court was the largest in Italy and the centre of diplomatic activity. Its key role in the ever-changing politics of the Italian peninsula ensured that papal Rome would not go untouched by the carnage of the French invasion. Successive popes pursued the abolition of the Pragmatic Sanction, offering the French kings attractive terms, but negotiations dragged on until 1516 and the Concordat of Bologna. In this agreement with the young, vital King Francis I, the popes renounced their right to appoint bishops and abbots in France, as well as to revenue from benefices and taxation. The ensuing decades would see little love lost between Rome and Paris.

Two Spanish popes, Callistus III (1455–8) and his nephew Alexander VI, as well as numerous churchmen and nobles at the papal court, bound Rome and the newly united kingdoms of Aragon and Castile. But relations were uneasy. After the fall of Constantinople in 1453, Callistus pleaded for a crusade by the Christian rulers of Europe, who stopped their ears. The Catholic rulers of Spain were not supplicants to Rome. It was under their authority that the Spanish Inquisition was established in 1480, declaring the intention of Ferdinand and Isabella to secure the faith in their kingdom by dealing with the problem of often superficially conforming former Jews and Muslims, known derisively as *conversos* and *moriscos*. The situation had arisen from the Spanish crown's decision to offer non-Christians the unsavoury options of conversion, expulsion, or death. The vision and ambitions of the Spanish monarchs spread far beyond Iberia, and with the 1494 Treaty of Tordesillas, Pope Alexander VI, a native of Valencia, drew a line down a map of the known world and allocated half each to the conquering forces of Spain and Portugal. Within each sphere of conquest, the monarchs were granted right of 'patronato': control over church appointments and finances.

England's very distance from the hot seat of Italian politics facilitated cooperation with Rome. The Wars of the Roses (1455–85) certainly weakened the position of the monarchy in this relationship, though by the 1470s Edward IV was appointing men to bishoprics as best suited him, an authority gladly assumed by his Tudor successors. The late medieval English Church was monarchical in the sense that it was under the hand of the crown, which tolerated ecclesiastical privileges only as long as they did not impede royal authority. Yorkist and Tudor kings were respectful to the papacy, but invariably put their own interests first. Relations were generally good until the spectre of Henry VIII's divorce.

Theology and Universities

A text from Sebastian Brant's satirical *Ship of Fools* that accompanies Albrecht Dürer's 1511 woodcut *Foolish teachers and foolish students* reads: 'Who never learns the proper things | Upon his cap the dunce bell rings, | He's led by idiot's leading strings.' Brant was in little doubt about the identity of the 'dunces', for the name was derived from the fourteenth-century theologian Duns Scotus. In the view of humanist critics such as Sebastian Brant and Erasmus of Rotterdam, late medieval theology was often little more than a series of obscure answers to non-questions, a word game presided over by the doctors of the Sorbonne in Paris and practised by 'hooded sophists'. Yet although they made for pleasing and amusing reading, caustic assaults by eminent humanist writers ignored the genuine theological energy of the late Middle Ages. In German lands, to take one example, brilliant scholars such as Conrad Summenhart, Johannes Eck, and Jacob von Hogestraten wrote manuals of theology, as well as teaching guides and commentaries that bore witness to creativity and vigour.

Late medieval Latin Christianity possessed no one single theology. Within the bounds of creedal faith numerous schools of thought contested with one another, many associated with different religious orders and the new universities that had sprung up across northern Europe. The female English mystic Julian of Norwich spoke of God as mother and father, and of the divine love that lay behind suffering. Nicholas of Cusa belonged to the revival of Neoplatonism, with its attachment to the mystical hierarchies of the fifth-century Dionysius the Areopagite. The Dominican Girolamo Savonarola in Florence was steeped in the theology of Thomas Aquinas. Augustinianism flourished, finding elegant and profound expression in the sermons of Johann von Staupitz, mentor of Martin Luther.

It was an age of intellectual revolution, in which antiquity became the means for transforming the present. Yet, for all the polemic, older scholastic thought and the new intellectual force, Christian humanism, did not enter the lists as sworn enemies in martial combat. The revival of good Latin enhanced the quality of theological writing, while scholastic forms of argument, notably the syllogism, remained part of the mental furniture of humanist writers. In France, the writing of Jean Gerson (1363–1429) continued to inspire new generations of theologians and reform-minded churchmen. Sometime chancellor of the University of Paris, Gerson combined nominalist philosophy with deep piety, and with a strong interest in mysticism and pastoral care. The extraordinary Jacques Lefèvre d'Étaples (c.1455–1536) was a pre-eminent interpreter of Aristotle, Neoplatonism, and the Apostle Paul, and his commentaries on the Bible for the cultivation of devotion won many admirers. Scholasticism had numerous critics, but it was the only known way of philosophy, and even Erasmus remarked that while it may have been 'frigid and strife-ridden', it 'must be tolerated until some more suitable method is available'.

Diversity brought conflict and controversy. Across northern Europe, the late medieval period witnessed the founding of new universities: from Heidelberg and Budapest to St Andrews and Lund. Among the German universities, in contrast to the Italian, the theological faculties were pre-eminent, so divisions over forms of theological thought were rancorous and fraught with ecclesiastical and political consequences. Most prominent was the division between the so-called Nominalists and Realists, who argued over the existence of 'universals' as realities outside the mind. At stake was

ACADEMIC MACES. Three academic maces from the fifteenth century from the University of St Andrews, founded by papal bull in 1413. The late Middle Ages witnessed rapid growth of universities in northern Europe, from Hungary to Sweden. The maces were the symbols of authority and they were borne before the rector (head), who was usually a cleric, on all ceremonial occasions. The mace commissioned by Archbishop Kennedy for his college, St Salvators, was created in Paris in 1461. The other two are earlier: arts (1416) and canon law (mid-fifteenth century) (right).

what the human mind could know of God, and the nature of divine revelation. The debate was intellectual and Latinate, with obvious and significant consequences for the teaching of theology, yet the legacies of Nominalism and Realism were the profound ways they shaped the thought-world of the Reformation and the rise of natural philosophy (science).

Despite the polemic and occasional fistfights, the two *viae* (ways) drew from a shared well: a commitment to logic, the unassailable authority of Aristotle, and a method of theological argumentation grounded in the *Sentences* of Peter Lombard. The *Sentences*, known to every medieval university student, were a twelfth-century collection of opinions gathered from disparate sources, mostly biblical and patristic, on four areas of theology: God as unity and Trinity; Creation and Sin; Redemption; the Sacraments and Human Beatitude. In the arts faculties of late medieval universities, logic reigned supreme, dominating the curriculum. Peter of Spain, the thirteenth-century author of a highly influential work on logic used in universities for over four hundred years, wrote that logic is 'the art of arts and the science of sciences'. The 'queen of the sciences' was theology, but even she bowed to logic, the 'empress' of all that could be known.

The study of theology was not an end in itself, an independent reality approached through philosophical method. The years of intellectual labour required of those who would obtain a theological degree had but one purpose—interpretation of the Bible. The Bible was everywhere: the two-volume folio Vulgate was the first fruit of Gutenberg's press, all aspiring doctors of theology had to lecture on scripture, and lay men and women eagerly sought vernacular translations for private devotions. Dutch churchman Wessel Gansfort (1419–89) remarked that if a doctor of scripture was a true doctor he would grasp the verity of revelation better than any untrained prelate. Among the most influential voices was that of the fourteenth-century Franciscan Nicholas of Lyra, who was deeply influenced—much to the consternation of his ecclesiastical opponents—by Rabbi Solomon ben Isaac (1030–1105), known as Rashi. He also drew deeply from the *Summa Theologica* of Thomas Aquinas. Lyra's *Postilla Litteralis* and *Postilla Moralis*, completed in the 1330s, were word-by-word explanations of the literal and moral meaning of the Bible. Their influence in the late Middle Ages is testified to by their survival in hundreds of manuscripts, six editions 1471–1509, and translations into German, French, and Italian. Lyra's commentaries were well known to Martin Luther, and their influence was unmistakable, though the reformer often cited them to express disagreement, such as over what the Apostle Paul meant by 'faith' in his letter to the Romans.

Humanism

As the leading churchmen and scholars of southern Europe made their way north to attend the councils at Constance and Basel, merchants from the Low Countries in the north did brisk business across the Mediterranean, notably in Spain and the cities of the Italian peninsula. They traded cloth from Flanders, where Bruges and Antwerp had become major commercial centres, with entrepreneurs growing wealthy on linen, crafts, and luxury goods as well as the ever-profitable business of banking. The opening of mountain passes, and advances in ship design, contributed to the burgeoning trade between north and south in goods and ideas. Books, manuscripts, artwork, scholars, and craftsmen travelled in both directions. From Italy came the revival of ancient Greek, Classical Latin, and even Hebrew, while Flemish painters were welcomed, praised, and emulated in Florence. From 1450, artists from the Low Countries such as Rogier van der Weyden introduced Italians to oil paint and more lifelike representation of persons and nature.

The German scholar Johannes Reuchlin returned from Rome in 1498 with a collection of Hebrew books and knowledge of the Jewish Cabbala, initiating a Christian fascination with the ancient language. In Nuremberg, Augsburg, and Strasbourg, humanist scholars such as Willibald Pirckheimer, Konrad Peutinger, and Sebastian Brant edited Classical texts, translated the works of antiquity into German, satirized the failings of the Church, and advised Emperor Maximilian I in literary matters. Pirckheimer and Peutinger had studied at the Italian universities of Padua and Pavia and spent time in Rome.

German humanism was no pallid reflection of Italian glories. With the recovery of Tacitus' *Germania*, scholars at the imperial court, who had imbibed the revival of Classical learning during sojourns in the south, began to perceive ways in which a distinctive, German culture might be valorized. Tacitus' praise of German virtue underpinned a northern claim to antiquity not dependent on the arrogant Italians, who regarded their unwelcome visitors as barbaric and uncultured. German humanism proclaimed the cause of the Habsburg dynasty, which encouraged a patriotism shaded with hostility to the south and the papacy. The impecunious emperor was generous in patronage, creating poet laureates of the German nation, though he proved less eager to pay them.

Rodolphus Agricola (1444–85), who took the Latin name Phrisius, is often credited as the first great figure of the Renaissance in the north. Born in the Low Countries, he was a model for many. He studied in Pavia and Ferrara, where he learned the classics from the masters, before returning to the north to live the life of an independent scholar, associated with neither religious order nor university. His fame was closely tied to his role in introducing the study of rhetoric, but his formidable linguistic knowledge was not to be overshadowed, for Agricola was among the first in the north to achieve a command of Greek and Hebrew. Among his many friends was Johannes Reuchlin. His more renowned intellectual and spiritual descendant, Erasmus of Rotterdam, wrote of Agricola that he was 'the first to bring a breath of better literature from Italy'.

Erasmus too had spent time in Italy, learning, among other things, Greek and cultivating relations with the great Venetian publisher Aldus Manutius. The experience was not entirely pleasant, but like others before him he was transformed. In Erasmus' case a compelling vision emerged of how ancient pagan literature, philosophy, and history could be 'baptized' to serve the revival of Christianity. In Hans Holbein's 1523 portrait, the ageing Dutchman is at work commenting on the Gospel of Luke; his attitude recalls the image of the church father Jerome (c.347–420), creator of the Latin translation of the Bible known in the sixteenth century as the Vulgate. Erasmus' bond with the greatest of biblical scholars was intentional and intimate. He had edited Jerome's works and written a biographical account that portrayed the church father as the pre-eminent Christian scholar, learned in the ancient languages

ERASMUS, BY HOLBEIN THE YOUNGER. Hans Holbein's portrait of Erasmus shows the Dutch humanist at work on his commentary on St Luke. The portrait in profile is reminiscent of Roman effigies. Erasmus, dressed in warm robes, sits at his desk in deep concentration. His image is set against a rich wall hanging depicting mythical creatures. He appears as the model Christian scholar, the very image of St Jerome, the great translator of the Latin Bible. Erasmus cultivated the comparison.

and Classical culture, and deep in piety. Erasmus saw himself as Jerome to his age, restoring the faith of the Church through his work on the Bible.

The treasure of those labours was Erasmus' *Novum Instrumentum*, a Greek edition of the New Testament begun in 1512. Two years later he had completed his annotations on the whole Bible, and in 1516 the work appeared in Basel from the press of Johann Froben. The Greek text was the result of consultation of numerous manuscripts, while the accompanying Latin translation and extensive notes were the achievement of years of study. They were influenced by the great Italian scholar Lorenzo Valla, whose investigation of the errors of the Vulgate Erasmus had chanced upon in a monastery in the Low Countries. The Dutchman's edition of the New Testament inspired a generation of young scholars, exhilarated by the belief that knowledge of Greek and Hebrew would return the Church to the truth of the Bible.

His Latin translation of the Greek, however, incited rage from those who saw it as a challenge to the Vulgate. For his part, Erasmus insisted that he sought only to improve what he acknowledged as the 'Church's Bible'. Whatever his intentions, there is no doubt that Erasmus revived a debate about the Bible that would preoccupy the Church and scholars for generations. What, many would ask, was the relationship between the manuscript and linguistic correctness of the text and the traditional theology of the Church? This was a question that would resound through the sixteenth century.

Clergy

Away from universities and scholars' studies, almost all men and women in late medieval Europe experienced the Church in parish communities under the care of priests and mendicant friars, such as the Dominicans and Franciscans. Dissent and dissatisfaction was certainly to be found, but in truth, few people separated themselves from the local churches where they worshipped, confessed their sins, and ultimately sought burial. Nonetheless, in local churches, larger towns, and cities, intense anger periodically flared against clergy of every status, from humble parson to worldly bishop, on account of perceived indolence, debauchery, rapacity, and corruption. At its most harmless, discontent with clerics expressed itself in mere mockery and tavern jokes, but violent assaults and even murder were not unknown. In 1523 Niklaus Manuel, Swiss mercenary turned author, political leader, and eventually evangelical reformer in Bern, gave voice to such hostility in his drama *Totenfresser* (Eaters of the Dead), when he asked, 'should one permit the current clergy that which they devise in their proud, stupid noodles?'

Lay resentment of priests, monks, friars, and bishops as lazy, gluttonous, and sexually predatory was widespread. Absent from the unflattering woodcuts, mocking plays, and general ribaldry, however, is anything that helps to illuminate the extreme and often dire conditions in which most priests lived and served. Like the parishioners over whom they had care, they were often poor and desperately vulnerable to the vicissitudes of weather and disease.

English parishes in the late Middle Ages were relatively healthy and well served. In German lands, in contrast, where in many regions hierarchical authority was weak, living conditions of priests often bordered on poverty, forcing them to other forms of work to provide not only for themselves, but for 'wives' and children. Although clerical marriage was formally prohibited by canon law, in German and Swiss dioceses it was unremarkable for bishops and parish priests to have common law wives and a house full of children. Not a few Protestant reformers were offspring of clerical families. In the sprawling archbishopric of Constance, priests could pay the 'cradle tax' and have their children made legitimate. This state of affairs was often decried by reform-minded churchmen, and synods required priests to put aside the 'concubines' with whom they lived and return to priestly celibacy, if they had ever practised it. Where priests were diligent in performance of their duties, however, the laity showed little concern about their domestic arrangements.

PARISH CHURCH. A fifteenth-century church near the York city walls close to Layerthorpe, St Cuthbert Peasholme dates from 1430, when it was restored by the Lord Mayor William de Bowes, member of four parliaments. The church, built on the site of an ancient foundation, is a beautiful example of English late Perpendicular. St Cuthbert's belongs to the flourishing of parish church building in the late Middle Ages. The patronage of new churches by figures such as de Bowes were benefaction for the worship of the community and the commemoration of souls. Remembrance was the heart of the liturgical and devotional life of parishes.

Clerical reform engaged the greatest figures of the late medieval Church, men and women deeply troubled by the venality, greed, and ignorance that afflicted Christ's Church. John Colet, the Dean of St Paul's, addressed the convocation of the province of Canterbury in 1512 to exhort greater moral reformation and defence of clerical dignity. The Church in the fifteenth century heard many voices for reform. Bishops such as Nicholas of Cusa insisted on heightened levels of education for those seeking ordination, with senior posts granted only to men who had studied in cathedral and collegiate schools. Priests were expected to be able to pray the canonical hours, to read and sing well, to know how to confer baptism and extreme unction, and to celebrate the mass by heart.

How effective were such injunctions? At first glance it might seem that most of these noble expectations were little realized. However, education in the theological teachings of the Church, liturgical worship, and pastoral care was not limited to formal institutions. Young men entering the priesthood frequently served apprenticeships to experienced clergy, who might well have been their fathers or uncles. The universities of northern Europe, with their growing number of theological faculties, certainly played their part in preparing clergy, though often in rather haphazard ways. Priests might attend lectures without taking a degree, or be present for university sermons. Mendicant friars, as committed preachers, brought formal theology to the wider Christian body through their preaching and by loaning books to local clergy. The libraries of the monasteries that filled the cities and dotted the countryside were rich in volumes for literate clergy. There were many paths to a theological education, however modest.

Sacraments

For clergy and laity alike, religious life was sacramental. The Catholic Church taught that there were seven sacraments of 'dominical institution' (that is, established by Christ himself): baptism, confirmation, Eucharist, penance, extreme unction, ordination, and matrimony. According to church teaching, what distinguished the sacraments of the New Testament from those of the Old was of the greatest significance: the latter did not convey God's grace, but pointed forward to Christ's Passion, while the former existed not only as a sign of God's grace, but as a conduit for it: sacraments 'effect what they signify'. Within the seven, there were important distinctions: the first five were intended for the spiritual perfection of each man and woman, while the final two (ordination of priests and marriage of the laity) were for the governance and extension of the Church.

The sacraments told the story of the Christian life. Through baptism, an infant was born again in the Spirit, and by confirmation a child was strengthened in the faith. Throughout the years of their lives, Christians were fed by the divine meal of the mass, in which they received the body and blood of Christ sacrificed for their salvation. For those who defiled their body with mortal sin, penance restored grace and justice. Christ's promise to the Apostles, that whatever they bound on earth would be bound in Heaven, was, for the Church, authority and power to forgive sin, but also to cut off those who refused reconciliation. Forgiveness did not come lightly: for the penitent, absolution demanded contrition (genuine sorrow), confession (acknowledgement of sin), and satisfaction (action to recompense for it).

For the sacraments to be effective, the Church required three things: symbols, words, and persons, known as 'material', 'form', and 'ministrant'. Three of the sacraments—baptism, confirmation, and ordination—were thought to leave an indelible mark that could not be removed, rendering repetition unnecessary. Eucharist and penance, in contrast, punctuated the lives of the faithful, sustaining and restoring them in a life of grace. Marriage and extreme unction, depending on circumstance, might be repeated. In the disease-filled conditions of late medieval society, remarriage after bereavement was common, though the church authorities struggled to persuade ordinary lay people that the seriously ill, if they recovered, might be anointed again in the future. Popular belief saw extreme unction as a harbinger of death, and those who received it and survived were sometimes, like lepers, shunned by the truly living.

Lay Christians

The Fourth Lateran Council (1215) held all Christians to a minimum obligation of annual confession and reception of the Eucharist. For most men and women, this remained a peculiarly Easter ritual, with Holy Week confession followed by the Eucharist on Sunday. In the late Middle Ages laypeople were repeatedly exhorted to confession and penance, and vernacular books such as John Myrc's *Instructions for Parish Priests*, composed in the early fifteenth century, aimed to help clergy perform their sacramental role. Confession was not a private, intimate affair in confessionals where all was revealed to a priest in a box with a screen—those would appear later in the sixteenth century. In late medieval parish churches, confession was a public ritual. Men and women knelt before a priest to declare their sins, as neighbours and relatives queued at a discreet distance, admonished not to listen. Gossip was natural, though angry parishioners would round on any priest they suspected of sharing confessions.

The Church expected much of the faithful. In addition to the Apostles' Creed, the Lord's Prayer, and the Ave Maria, the Lambeth Council of 1281 was not unusual in requiring knowledge of the Seven Sacraments, the Ten Commandments, the Seven Deadly Sins, the Seven Holy Virtues, the Two New Laws of the Gospels, and the Seven Works of Bodily Mercy. Standards of knowledge varied enormously, depending, among other things, on the diligence of the local priest. But the faith was not simply about knowing, or even about believing, a series of statements. Late medieval Christianity was a religion of practices, of deeds, in which the faith was performed in community. To know the sins and virtues was inseparable from carrying out works of mercy. It was to aid this religion of good and charitable works that a vast body of written and printed works appeared in the vernacular to engender holy living.

Among the wealthy, there was an insatiable appetite for richly decorated devotional works, exemplified by exquisite Books of Hours. These were themselves precious objects that instructed in prayer, serving the laity as a link between the liturgy of the Church and their own private devotion. Books of Hours contained psalms, portions of the book of Job, the Song of Songs, and other parts of the Old Testament, and were particularly associated with devotion to the Virgin Mary. They were accompanied by a wealth of other works. Sermons, saints' lives, poetry, psalters, collections of prayers, and biblical passages were read aloud in homes, guildhalls, and in the market square. In a world in which few could read, written words came to the people through hearing. Reading was aloud, whether in the scholar's study, among the family or in the village.

The Christian faith was heard and seen everywhere. In city squares, famous preachers hired by the magistrates held forth before great crowds during the holy seasons of Advent and Lent. Bernardino of Siena (1380–1444), said by a contemporary to possess a voice 'soft, clear, sonorous... elevated and efficacious', was the most renowned and sought-after preacher of his day. His audiences gathered in the piazzas of Italian cities to listen to sermons lasting two, three, and four hours, Bernardino leaving them in little doubt why they should hear the Word: 'And if, between these two things—either to hear mass or hear a sermon—you can only do one, you must miss mass rather than the sermon; the reason for this is that there is less danger to your soul in not hearing mass than there is in not hearing the sermon.'

In parishes, less-celebrated priests made use of books of homilies to read the message to the people, while in convents abbesses expounded the Word to their nuns. Even in small, remote communities, sermons contained the same essential elements that attracted the people to the centres of Siena, Nuremberg, and Paris. They were mixtures of daring, heroic, and entertaining deeds of saints, familiar biblical stories, local news and gossip, and imaginative explanations of the painted images that hovered above on church walls, full of examples of how to live the good Christian life. Itinerant mendicants brought tales and reports from distant lands of miracles, wars, and strange happenings, such as monstrous births and comets. Sermons reminded the faithful they were surrounded by spiritual forces, divine and malign, and that they had to choose the path they would follow. The Devil was everywhere and very real. Just being present at sermons was not enough, and certainly no guarantee of salvation. The people were constantly warned of the sinfulness of dozing off, or letting their minds wander from the words of the preacher.

The Laity and the Bible

A Protestant refrain of the sixteenth century was that the medieval Church was without bibles. It was effective polemic, but quite untrue. As we have seen, interpretation of the Bible was the well-spring of scholastic theology. But the Reformation also emerged from a world in which laypeople had grown accustomed to possessing sacred and devotional literature. For educated medieval Christians, the Latin Bible was essential, and following Gutenberg's introduction of the press with moveable type, it became the most printed book in the fifteenth century. Latin bibles were available in all sizes, including copies that would fit easily into a pocket for travel. The elegant images of the Books of Hours were matched by those found in the illustrated bibles of the period, which told the stories of the Virgin Mary and of the Passion of Christ through a typology in which the figures of the Old Testament prophesied the new covenant.

Gutenberg's printed Vulgate of 1455 resembled the beautiful folio manuscript bibles popular with religious houses and wealthy lay people. Those who bought the 180 bibles from Gutenberg's press had them rubricated and illuminated by hand so that no two were the same. They were lectern bibles, not for use in worship but for communal reading in monastic refectories and the private devotions of individuals. Most people encountered the Bible in worship through the Missal, which contained selected readings for the liturgical year.

In German lands, translations of the Bible appeared in large number and the laity were encouraged to possess and read the Word of God. In 1513, one text reminded the faithful that 'All that you hear in sermons and other modes of instruction... should incite you to read with piety and humility the holy Scriptures and Bibles, which are now translated into German, and printed and distributed in large numbers, either in their entirety or in part, and which you can purchase for very little money.' Despite low literacy levels, people clearly heeded the message, though with results displeasing to some in the Church. In 1515 a preacher recounted with horror that his people believed they could interpret the Bible, and learn the path to salvation, without Church and pope. They would declare, 'In my book it is different from what the preacher says.' Late medieval printed bibles seem to have been within the means of many laity, and partial bibles and individual books could be cheaply produced.

In England the situation differed from Germany. The 1408 Constitutions of Oxford, intended to combat the heresy of Lollardy, suppressed vernacular bibles and their reading. The Wyclif Bible, prepared in Oxford at the end of the fourteenth century, was the most notorious of such translations, though it has survived in greater number than any other English-language work of the age, demonstrating that copies were possessed by many orthodox Christians. Originally tolerated, by the early fifteenth century the Wyclif bibles were banned, although it is known that Lollards held furtive readings, and their trials revealed how greatly they valued possession of scripture.

The richness of printing has led to an estimation that by 1519 in the Empire, France, and Italy alone there were 151 printed editions of the Latin Bible. A figure of 20,000 German-language bibles has been reckoned for the end of the fifteenth century. Making that figure even more impressive, the number includes only whole bibles, and not the countless individual books, Bible stories, and devotional literature. Late medieval Europe was awash with the Word of God in every conceivable printed form.

Stories from the Bible appeared on stage in Mystery plays, such as the famous cycles in York or the Passion Plays in Germany, and were memorized in devotional practices like saying the rosary. The bond between the staging of biblical stories and church teaching gave the plays the quality of 'dramatized sermons'. In these entertaining, humorous, and at times ribald and bitingly critical performances, in which the audiences were by no means passive spectators, the plays worked as forms of scripture and were deliberately didactic, seeking to reinforce through spectacle what was taught by catechism and sermon. Pedagogy, however, was but one aspect. Religious and social comment filled the frequent asides by the players to the audience, offering pithy explanations of the faith enveloped in caustic observation. This drama had its roots in the liturgical life of the Church, but by the end of the Middle Ages plays had moved

POCKET-SIZE BIBLE. Johann Froben printed the first pocket-sized octavo Latin Bible at Basel in 1491, the so-called 'Poor man's Bible'. Although in Latin, and therefore intended for the educated, it was affordable for many clergy and laity. This Bible had marginal chapter divisions and references, a subject index, and summaries of the books. This was also the earliest printed Latin Bible to include a woodcut illustration, an image of St Jerome after a woodcut by Albrecht Dürer.

beyond the walls into the community, where they came under the patronage of guilds, fraternities of crafts, and tradespeople whose influence within the civic worlds of the late Middle Ages grew with economic expansion.

Devotion

The Word spoken and read was never separated from what was seen; perhaps the most profound religious experiences of late medieval Christians were visual ones. Although the faithful confessed and received the Eucharist once a year, as required, they attended mass frequently and witnessed Christ's sacrifice and beheld his presence in the host. Although the priest may have been partially obscured from view by the rood screen that separated the laity from the miracle at the altar, the drama of the liturgy was witnessed by all. Bells announced the moment of consecration, the great mystery, and the divine presence was manifest in a range of sensory experiences: the light pouring through the windows, the smell of candles, and the clouds of incense making visible the ascent of the prayer of the faithful to Heaven. Christ's eucharistic presence was not limited to the mass itself. Display containers known as monstrances housed the sacred host for adoration in church and chapel, while on the Feast of Corpus Christi the Blessed Sacrament was borne through the streets, sanctifying the quotidian places of life. In sacrament, prayer, and art, the body of God's Son accompanied Christians through life. In its lacerations and wounds they saw their suffering and misery; in its glory, their salvation.

Parish churches were crammed with offerings from the people, from altar cloths and vestments to beautiful liturgical vessels. Christian prayer and devotion were focused on the crucified Christ, his Holy Mother the Queen of Heaven, and the saints, for whom the people were named and who from Heaven watched over villages, towns, urban neighbourhoods, and kingdoms. The faithful in late medieval society, in their good works, charitable deeds, devotional acts, and intercessory prayers, sought the mercy of God for themselves and their loved ones, living and dead. Yet the rituals of the parish church did not exhaust the devotional and intercessory efforts of the people. In the world beyond the church door and the graveyard was a sacred landscape with roadside shrines, holy wells, and small chapels, where local saints were honoured and shelter from inclement weather found. Symbols of the faith were everywhere, reminders of a truth the people knew and lived: God and the Devil were in the visible and invisible. Prayer and good deeds brought hope of mercy and assistance, while punishment and even sudden death, no one doubted, awaited the wicked. Angels, saints, demons, and ghosts were constant companions, and nothing in the world, from good fortune to the death of a child, happened accidentally. Unsurprisingly perhaps, amulets, spells, wise women, remedies, and other sources of magic all had their place in the enchanted world, intermixed with the blessings of priest and sacrament. The Church on the whole took a relaxed view of such daily magical practices, though things would change with a growing concern with the hunting out of witches.

Visual contact with intercessory powers was made through images, devotional objects, and fragments of the holy, such as bones of the saints, and pieces of the true cross displayed in churches or at sites of pilgrimage. Relics were material forms of the sacred, displayed in reliquaries, whose physicality sustained, inspired, and healed the faithful. One travelled the dangerous roads on pilgrimage not merely to gaze but to venerate, to be blessed by their presence, and to receive reward for a spiritual journey well done.

Pilgrimages to the dwelling places of relics could represent remarkable mass movements: in one day alone the city of Aachen in Germany received 142,000 pilgrims to the bones of Charlemagne. In the north, important centres of pilgrimage were

HOLY RELICS. This Ostensorium from around 1400 was created in Lower Saxony to display to the faithful a beautiful paten—a liturgical plate for the elevation of the Eucharist by the priest during mass—associated with the eleventh-century St Hildesheim. On the paten Christ is surrounded by the four evangelists while the Latin declares, 'The bread which is broken in me is the body [of Christ] itself. He who receives it in good faith shall live in eternity.' Above the paten is a relic of the True Cross.

Canterbury, Aachen, and St Wolfgang in Salzkammergut, in modern-day Austria. Devotion to the relics and sites of eucharistic miracles, such as Wilsnack in Germany, with its bleeding hosts, meant that Europe was traversed by pilgrimage routes that led the faithful in every direction. Piety and commerce were never strangers, and promotion of cults and relics served the interests and pockets of many. Numerous crowns of thorns and rather too many pieces of the cross invited critics, of course, and the

QUEEN OF HEAVEN. The sculpted crowning of Mary from the main panel of the polyptych high altar of the parish church of St Wolfgang im Salzkammergut in Austria. It is the work of Michael Pacher, which he completed in 1481 after ten years' labour in his workshop in the south Tyrol. By the end of the fifteenth century St Wolfgang was among the most visited pilgrimage sites in Europe after Rome, Aachen, and Einsiedeln. Pacher's use of gold creates a stunningly rich scene of Mary kneeling before her son with the Holy Spirit as a dove above. The angels are present for this most sacred moment. In her attitude of supplication Mary intercedes for the faithful while on the right is St Wolfgang, whose relics drew pilgrims in great numbers.

sardonic wit of Erasmus or the satire of Sebastian Brant's *Ship of Fools* testify to a belief that sincere veneration could fall prey to chicanery.

Scepticism converged with virulent anticlericalism, and predatory political interests, in the infamous case of fraudulent apparitions of the Virgin Mary in the Swiss city of Bern in 1507, orchestrated by the lay brother Johannes Jetzer and four Dominican friars. Helpfully, Mary revealed to Jetzer that the Dominicans were correct in denying

ELEGANT MARTYR. This Flemish reliquary of the 1520s contains the skull of St Balbina, a virgin martyr of Rome. Busts as reliquaries were popular in the high and late Middle Ages and greatly prized by owners ecclesiastical and lay. Beauty and craftsmanship combined with the antiquity of the relic to create its spiritual and devotional power. Balbina is portrayed in the sumptuous clothes of the sixteenth-century society in which she was venerated as a saint of the Church.

the doctrine of the Immaculate Conception fiercely defended by the Franciscans. She had, she confirmed to Jetzer, been conceived in sin, and reported that for his false teaching on her birth the Franciscan theologian Duns Scotus was suffering the flames of Purgatory. Jetzer's misdeeds did not stop there. He fabricated tears of blood from an image of the Virgin as a political statement against the money made by wealthy Bern families from the mercenary service. When Jetzer's deception was discovered, he and the

THE VIRGIN AND FRAUD. One of the most notorious scandals of the late Middle Ages took place in the Swiss city of Bern in 1507. Johannes Jetzer, a journeyman tailor, connived with four Dominicans to fabricate appearances by the Virgin Mary. The doctrine of the immaculate conception was hotly contested and Mary reputedly told Jetzer that she had been conceived in sin, confirming the Dominican position against the Franciscans. The four Dominicans were burned at the stake for blasphemy. This woodcut by the Bernese contemporary Niklaus Manuel (c.1484–1530) shows the desperate Jetzer begging to be received into the Dominican house in the city.

four Dominicans were tortured and tried. The mendicants went to the stake while he escaped from prison and fled. The uproar created an audience in Bern for Niklaus Manuel's hostile treatment of Church and clergy in his plays.

Between Cloister and the World

A torrid age living in dread of divine judgement inevitably spawned reform movements: lay, religious, and mixed. In the late fourteenth century the Low Countries saw the emergence of the Brethren of the Common Life, 'converts' who undertook new forms of community to cultivate rigorous prayer and service. The founder was Geert Grote, and his followers sought through reading, meditation, and writing to recast their interior lives with ceaseless self-examination and discipline. At Windesheim a community was founded in 1387 by Florens Radewyns (d. 1400), Grote's successor, and the Christian spirituality professed there, which became known as the 'Devotio moderna' (modern devotion), had a rigour appropriate to the age. It was service to God in the world fired by a 'special interiority'.

The Brethren were between the cloister and the world: laymen and women who lived in religious communities without taking monastic vows, a form of semi-religious life.

Their spiritual discipline reflected growing lay literacy, as they wrote personal notebooks, sermons, prayer books, and spiritual tractates. Even the making of books was a form of devotion. Thomas à Kempis's *Imitation of Christ* emerged from the community at Windesheim to become one of the greatest devotional works of the age, surviving in an astonishing number of manuscript and printed copies in many languages. Its four books, originally separate tracts, were brought together as an instruction in following the example of Christ through disciplined prayer and the taming of the body. Despite its origins in the cloister, the *Imitation* became wildly popular among laypeople, who followed its stress on biblically based conduct and mental prayer in the belief they could live the faithful life in the fallen world. The imitation of which Kempis spoke was more than ethical conduct; through prayer, study of scripture, and good works, a person entered into a unitive relationship with his or her saviour, becoming ever more Christ-like. Following the Reformation, the *Imitation of Christ* would be employed as a model for Christian living by such diverse readers as Jesuits, Lutheran Pietists, and English Puritans.

The aspiration for direct experience of the divine—mysticism—found purchase in many Europeans lands, though the Low Countries and Rhineland were especially prominent, with both men and women writings texts of profound contemplation on the body of Christ and suffering. Christ became the man of sorrows, and through meditation on his Passion a Christian might hope to gain a share of the merit achieved by his suffering. Authors of devotional works on the Passion paid scrupulous attention to each of Christ's wounds, which Ludolf of Saxony numbered at around 5,000. This vivid, visceral adoration of Christ's body found numerous expressions in worship: Christians walked the stations of the cross in churches, meditated on the sorrowful mysteries of the rosary, sang passional hymns, and followed the increasing number of liturgical feasts during the year that marked Christ's suffering.

The Flemish mystic Jan van Ruusbroec (1293–1381), friend and mentor to Geert Grote, and known as the 'Admirable Doctor', was the inspiration for several generations of writers in the Low Countries whose works of Christ-centred devotion were disseminated across northern Europe. Most famous was Kempis's *Imitation of Christ*, but there were others. Franciscans were prominent in this company of mystics, men such as Hendrik Herp (d. 1477), whose *A Mirror of Perfection* was widely translated and read. In his elegant, luxuriant prose and vivid imagery, Herp expressed the human longing for divine healing. The soul renounces all that is not God in its ascent to the life where it will possess 'all the deliciousness, the riches, the knowledge, and all that it can possibly desire'.

Women were prominent. Alijt Bake (1415–55), daughter of an affluent Utrecht family, became a canoness of Windesheim, a female member of the Modern Devotion. Well educated, she read, taught, and copied the works of the German mystics Johannes Tauler and Jordan of Quedlinburg, guided by a series of visions that set before her precisely what she must do. Having been elected prioress, her mystical teachings attracted young women to her house, and she revealed herself a gifted writer. In her *Four Ways of the Cross* (c.1446) she described in vivid detail her spiritual struggles and visions of being forsaken by God and dying again on the cross.

MAN OF SORROWS. A sculpture of the suffering Christ ('Vir dolorum'), naked except for a loincloth, bearing his wounds, and crowned with thorns, was a powerful devotional image in northern Europe. In paintings of this theme Christ is often portrayed accompanied by angels and the instruments of the passion ('arma Christi'). This German pearwood carving from the early sixteenth century presents the Son of God alone. The sculpture served to stimulate men and women to meditate on Christ's Passion and his union with them in agony.

Suffering suffused Bake's astonishing account of ascent to the pure radiance of divine love, a reminder that for late medieval Christians the body remained central to devotion and worship. The powerful bond between women and Christ in medieval culture, personified in the love of the Virgin Mary, owed a good deal to the traditional association of the body with the female. Christ, as God incarnate, was in his flesh deeply spiritually attractive to women, some of whom seemed to experience the divine directly through their bodies. The suffering of God belonged to neither gender exclusively, but so powerful was its force in the devotional lives of men and women that it embraced and transcended all language, spiritual experience, and sexuality.

The Living and the Dead

For late medieval Christians the dead did not entirely depart. The bonds of kinship, marriage, and friendship remained, if rather changed, and the charity that held together the community of the living shaped its relations with the poor souls in the next world. The medieval geography of the afterlife was the subject of much imagining, most famously by Dante in his journey through Inferno, Purgatorio, and Paradiso. It was on Purgatory that the imagination most often fixed, for there people would be cleansed by fire of that which they had left undone in this world. Sins had to be atoned and God's justice satisfied. Purgatory in the medieval world was no pleasant antechamber for those on their way to Heaven, a place of comfortable waiting. The fires of Hell reached Purgatory and Christians could expect to suffer dreadfully in time reckoned in thousands and thousands of years, the precise length determined by the nature and severity of their sins. Once purged, they could anticipate Heaven and its blessed company. Purgatory was a painful journey to God expedited by the intercessory prayers and charitable deeds of the living. Hell was for irredeemable sinners and heretics, those execrable vermin of society who deserved no end to their torment.

Life was preparation for death and eternity. The *ars moriendi* (art of dying) block-books that circulated widely in the late Middle Ages presented woodcut deathbed scenes where demons, angels, Christ, and his mother jostled alongside distraught family members. Image and text were joined to instruct the faithful how to die well. What choice would the dying person make in the final moments? That was the question. The Church offered salvation if sins were confessed and faith in Christ professed, but equally energetic were the Devil's minions who sought to thwart the good death through despair, the ultimate sin and guarantee of eternal loss. At the deathbed a cosmic battle was waged over each and every soul. The comfort was that until one's last breath the door to God remained opened, even if it led first to Purgatory.

Animating the Christian life of remembrance and intercession for the dead, as also of care for the poor, was 'caritas': charity understood as love, a right spirit in which all things should be done well. Far more than modern notions of 'charity', caritas involved justice and reciprocity. The rich were to bring relief to the poor, both spiritual and material, by aiding their journey through the world. The poor in turn, as the more naturally virtuous and closer to Christ, were to pray for those from whom they received. Late medieval wills were full of provisions made by the well-off for the sick and poor, the enactment of charity as part of the culture of intercession. Charity was essential, for reconciliation between individuals made possible an integrated social body and assured the bond between those in this world and the next.

Death did not conceal himself. He had a personality and a recognizable grin that looked down from the walls of churches. At St Mary's in Lübeck, he led a dance of twenty-four men and women from all walks of life: ecclesiastical and secular. This thirty-metre-long painting was lost in the Second World War, but similar representations could be found across Europe, from Estonia to France. In Basel, a Dance of Death painting extended eighty paces along a publicly accessible churchyard, beginning with a painting of an ossuary, a house of bones, and progressing through the orders of society, with cripples, hermits, burgermeisters, cardinals, and kings. The journey commenced with the following words:

> The Prophet Isaiah says
> that all flesh is like hay and grass.
> Its beauty is like the flower in the field,
> the grass withers, the flower fades.
> He compares people with the grass on the heath,
> when the spirit of the Lord blows on them.
> The flower is carried off, the grass withers.
> Yet his word shall stand for ever.

The reminder of the nearness of eternity, and death's lack of sentiment, went hand in hand with ridicule of human vanity, greed, and corruption—foolishness leading to dust.

The dead dwelt among the living in the very real sense that they were buried within the walls of the city in church graveyards—sacred ground that was part of the culture of remembrance and intercession. Apart from the wealthy few who might hope to lie within the church, as close to the altar as possible, the vast majority were wrapped in sheets and placed in mass graves, their bodies covered with lime to aid decomposition. After a period of time, the bones were unearthed and placed in charnel houses so that the grave might be used for the newly dead.

Christians had much to fear, and perhaps nothing terrified more than sudden death, departing this world unprepared, most significantly without confession. Medieval ghost stories were populated with the souls of those who had died badly and wandered unremembered. The forgotten soul was lost, deprived of the intercessory prayers and charitable deeds of the living. Most forlorn of all were suicides, those driven by despair to the worst of deaths and from whom the living had to be protected. In some lands they were buried at crossroads so that, confused, they might not make their way back to the village as revenants, while a German practice was to toss their bodies into rivers in a form of ritual cleansing.

When life ended well, the Office of the Dead was performed in the choir of the church with the body present, if the person was of sufficient means. This sung and spoken service was drawn mostly from the psalter and ended with the *De Profundis* (Psalm 129): 'Out of the depths I have cried to thee, O Lord.' The mass as a votive offering for souls in Purgatory also spoke of rest in Christ. As a celebration of the Eucharist, it was performed communally and privately, with benefits for the living and the dead. Those who could so afford would stipulate in wills that masses, perhaps even a thousand, be said for their souls, both in the time following death and on significant anniversaries.

The profusion of chantries—institutions where masses were to be said for a period of years, or in perpetuity—in the late Middle Ages reflected a culture in which Purgatory, the sacrament of penance, and the power of prayer heightened demand for post-mortem masses for the health of the departed soul. In addition to

DEATH UNOBSERVED. A woodcut by the Swiss artist Urs Graf entitled *Two Mercenaries and Women with Death in a Tree* (1524). In his momento mori, Graf, a soldier-artist, offers a version of the medieval Dance of Death by presenting two mercenaries in a suggestively erotic encounter with a woman while out of sight the skeletal figure of Death watches with evident pleasure. In this satirical representation Graf combines an admonition to consider eternity with bitter observation on the vicissitudes and corruption of war, commerce, and sexuality. Mercenaries as soldiers for hire were widely held by preachers to destroy communities with violence and syphilis.

their liturgical role in ensuring prayer for the dead, the priests attached to the chantry might be obligated by their dead patron to distribute alms and do good works, accruing further benefit. The sheer number of chantries founded in the late medieval Church was astonishing, and their benefit to the welfare of the community was considerable. Only the very wealthy could afford perpetual chantries. For others of more modest means a temporary endowment was an affordable means of relief.

In the next world the fires of Purgatory extracted payment for works of satisfaction left incomplete, and indulgences served a related purpose in this life. Drawn out of the Treasury of Merits, which consisted of the infinite merits of Christ, and the surplus virtues of the saints, all of which were at the Church's disposal, indulgences could be granted to remit the punishment of those who had confessed and been absolved. By the late Middle Ages the practice had in many places degenerated to the hocking of promises of relief to raise money by preachers and the professional pardoner, a figure harshly ridiculed by Chaucer. Peddling comfort they had no right to grant, indulgence sellers played down penitential activity and the doing of charitable works in favour of telling the gullible that they could purchase relief for their loved ones in Purgatory. The Church did allow that indulgences might be acquired to aid souls undergoing purgation but only, and crucially, when the purchaser exhibited the right devotional attitude. Many leading churchmen, including Pope Boniface IX (1389–1404), condemned the commodification of grace. But, as a lucrative source of much-needed revenue, the attraction for senior ecclesiastical figures of the sale of indulgences was considerable.

Dissent and Heretics

Dissent and heresy make for better press than orthodoxy and institutions, yet without doubt late medieval Christianity knew protest, persecution, and forms of belief and practice challenging to the Church. Hostility to clergy, whether verbal or physical, was not uncommon and hardly surprising given the demands placed on priests and laity in times of privation and contagion. Wilful rejection of doctrine, sacraments, and the priesthood itself was, by contrast, sporadic, highly limited, and geographically specific. It was found, for example, among the Waldensians in the Alpine valleys, the Hussites in Bohemia, and the English Lollards. Individuals with heretical, eclectic, or even eccentric views could be discovered in any land, and their treatment at the hands of the Church depended on local circumstances. Deviance in belief or morality found little sympathy from ecclesiastical or temporal authorities, and execution for criminality was an accepted and common part of judicial practice. Failure to prosecute not only denoted weakness and lack of conviction, but risked the opprobrium of God, who demanded the purity of the Church.

The complicated history of the Waldensians illustrates the fluidity of the divide between orthodoxy and heresy. Originating in the twelfth century, and at one time widely spread through Italian and French lands, by the fifteenth century they were largely confined to remote Alpine regions. At times victims of fierce persecution, they rejected the corruption and affluence of the Church rather than its core doctrine, though more radical elements existed. Most Waldensians remained within the Catholic Church, attending mass and retaining devotional rites such as memorials for the dead. Auricular confession was practised, penances assigned, and the authority of the priesthood preserved in a sharp rejection of lay performance of the Eucharist. True to their

SAVIOUR OF THE WORLD. In Erhard Schön's 1515 single-leaf indulgence woodcut a rosary embraces all creation, viewed through the crucifixion of Christ. Angels, figures from the Old and New Testaments, and the whole Church gather in adoration. Central are the Holy Trinity, the majesty of God, and the Father's acceptance of his son's sacrifice. The woodcut was produced by one of the leading indulgence printers of the day and emphasizes the connection between the rosary and Purgatory, and the power of intercessory prayer to relieve poor souls.

Ein grawsamlich geschicht Geschehen zu passaw Von den Juden als hernach volgt.

Hye stylt Cristoff acht partickel des sacraments auß der kirchē. legt das in sein taschē. hat sy darinne drei tag behalte

Hye schuet er die sacrament den juden auff den tisch die vnuerma ligt gewesen sein. darumb sy im ein guldē gaben

Hye tragen die judē vn schulklopffer. die sacrament yn ir synagog. vnd vberantwurtden dye den Juden.

Hye stycht pfeyl Jud das sacrament auff irem altar. ist plut darauß gangen das er vn ander iuden gesehen haben.

Hye teylten sy auß dye sacramēt schicken zwen partickel gen Prag. zwē gen salczpurg. zwen yn die Rewenstat

Hye verprenten sy die sacramēt versuchen ob vnser glaub gerecht wer flogen auß dem offen zwen engel. vn. ij. taubē

Hye vecht man all Judē zu passaw die dy sacramēt gekaufft verschickt gestolen vnd verprant haben.

Hye furt mā sy fur gericht. verurtaylt die vier getaufft. fackel man o. kolman vnd walich. sein gekopfft worden.

Hye zereyst man den pfeyl vnd vettel die das sacramēt behyltē. dz darnach gestochen vnd verprant haben.

Hye verprent man sy mit sampt dē juden. die yn yrem glauben blyben. vnd vmb das sacrament gewyst haben.

Hye wirt der Cristoff des sacramentz verkauffer. auff einem wagē zeryssen mit gluenden zangen.

Hye hebt man an zw pawen. vnserm herren zu lob eyn gotzhauß. Auß der juden synagog ꝛc.

ANTI-SEMITISM. A fifteenth-century woodcut that relates a story of Jewish host desecration in Passau. Christians frequently accused Jews of such defilement, which was a grave offence. In this account the hosts were ritually pierced before being recovered by Christians, who found them to be holy. The Jews are tortured and beheaded. The rest of the Jewish community was driven from Passau in chains, leaving the Christians then kneeling in prayer. Although Jews continued to serve as moneylenders in northern European lands, pogroms became increasingly frequent as rumours spread of poisoned wells and the sacrifice of infants.

tradition, Waldensians were greatly attached to preaching, and an elite clergy, known as 'barbes', brought admonition and instruction in the divine Word. A similar degree of flexibility was to be found in the prohibition of the swearing of oaths. By the end of the Middle Ages, however, persecution and their desire for holiness led to increasing separation from Catholic worship as Waldensians turned to private exhortation, scripture reading, and their own devotional writings.

In England, the Lollards, a disparate collection of laypeople mostly in the Midlands and the south, similarly held a collection of beliefs and attitudes rather than any central or unifying doctrines. The majority were artisans and urban merchants, among whom literacy rates were relatively high, and a commitment to the Bible in English and scriptural reading was a common thread. Their inspiration was the brilliant Oxford theologian and condemned heretic John Wyclif (c.1320–84), who had fiercely attacked the wealth of the Church, rejected scholastic theology and the doctrine of transubstantiation, and played a central role in the translation of the Vulgate into English, producing a Bible that has come to bear his name.

The Lollards faced formidable opposition. Their deep attachment to scripture led to official proscription of translations of the Bible into English, and persecution and executions drove adherents into hiding. Oppression took its toll. As the fifteenth century passed, Lollardy lost much of its intellectual force, with no new literature appearing after the 1480s, and its adherents became dispersed dissidents of little influence. Their connections with the universities were severed; their faith expressed through subterfuge not bold preaching. Although Lollards participated in the outward forms of parochial religion (taking communion once a year, for example), they turned their faces against voluntary forms of devotion, such as pilgrimages, the cult of saints, and the Corpus Christi processions that broadly shaped late medieval orthodox piety. Isolated and contained, they posed no dire threat to the order and worship of the English Church.

More obviously significant were the Hussites, who took their name from Jan Hus, a reforming priest burned at the stake at the Council of Constance in 1415. The movement broke out in Prague in 1419 and five crusades by Emperor Sigismund failed to crush it. However, those who claimed the legacy of Hus were deeply divided, and their fragmentation proved damaging. The moderate Utraquists (mostly nobility and university men) held to the reforms of Hus, most significantly the reception of the Eucharist *sub utraque specie* (in both kinds); that is, the wine from the cup as well as the bread. The Taborites, more militant and apocalyptic, lived in the expectation of the thousand-year reign of Christ. Although not in all details, the Hussites shared many of the teachings of the Waldensians and Lollards, such as communion in both kinds, a stress on preaching, and the repudiation of clerical immorality and corruption within the Church. Of all the so-called heretical groups, the Hussites, despite their divisions, most closely approached the status of a mass movement, largely because they had a strong ethnic and linguistic identity embodied in their martyr Hus. Their beliefs were expressed in song and in the images of the eucharistic chalice that adorned their battle flags. Their redoubtable military might became legend, and their hymns were later to be memorialized in the music of the nineteenth-century Czech composer Anton Dvořák.

The twelfth-century canonist Gratian had taught that heresy was the rejection of the Church's teaching after correction had been offered. Those branded as heretics, however, believed the Church had failed, stained by its sinfulness and mired in false practice and corruption. The heretical movements of the late Middle Ages in many respects drew from changes in Church and society, such as the rise of literacy and the growing desire for lay participation in religion. At the sharp end were those who rejected fundamental teachings such as transubstantiation and Purgatory, notably the Lollards and the more radical Hussites. Most groups designated heretical consisted of men and women desirous of reform, correction, and spiritual renewal; they belonged to the intense religiosity and interiority flourishing across late medieval Europe. That these impulses took forms unacceptable to church officials is certain—one need only look at the deep suspicion cast on female mystics and their profoundly sensuous experiences of Christ. Dissent and diversion, however, rarely amounted to wholesale rejection of the Church.

Christian communities lived in presentiment of judgement, a conflagration that would bring to an end the human history that began in Eden and establish the Kingdom of Christ envisaged in the book of Revelation. Apocalyptic premonitions permeated society, shaping how contemporary events were understood, communities defined, and individuals judged. They coloured, or rather darkened, Christian relations with Jews, the killers of Christ whose conversion would mark the end of time, but whose stubborn and persistent rejection of the gospel justified, in the eyes of many, pogroms against them. Christian attitudes towards Jews were complicated and contradictory. On Good Friday Christians prayed for the 'pernicious Jews', whose failure to believe was understood not as blindness or stubbornness but as a malignant cancer. In German lands they were protected by law, but this could be overlooked at times of heightened tension, such as during the campaign to destroy both Jewish books and religion starting in 1510. Johannes Reuchlin's defence of both the study of Hebrew, and of the Jews, led to the most vicious controversy in the Church in the years before the Luther affair.

Jews were ghettoized, made the object of innumerable mendicant preaching campaigns, vilified in Passion plays, had their Talmuds burned, and were represented visually with hooked noses and bulging eyes: an economy of hatred and suspicion. Ambiguities ran deep. Fascination with Jewish learning and the mysteries of its language, with the place of the Jews in divine history, and even with perceptions of their moral rectitude in a corrupt world, point to a Christian obsession. Hostility to the Jews in word, image, and violence reflected traditional Christian enmity, as well as fears and anxieties about alteration and otherness in a changing and diversifying society.

Deviants were persecuted by forces of authority, temporal and ecclesiastical, and women suffered in large numbers. From the 1430s, witch hunts that would last for several centuries grew in intensity, a reflection not only of the views of elite clerics and scholars but also of wider perceptions of magic and folkloric practices among the common people. Over the course of the fifteenth century, witchcraft came to be seen not only as magical practices directed at neighbour or foe, but as a pact, increasingly sexual, with the Devil. The most famous, or infamous, tract on witch-hunting was the *Hammer of the Witches* (1487) by the Dominican inquisitor Heinrich Kramer, who drew on a growing body of literature concerned with sorcery and the demonic. Belief in malefaction, together with lurid accounts of diabolism, cannibalism, and nocturnal gatherings, was widespread, not simply among inquisitors. The conviction that witches should be rooted out and eradicated grew commonplace among advocates of reform in the Church.

Religious life on the eve of the Reformation was vibrant, diverse, and fragmented, a wide range of beliefs, rituals, and customs local in character and spoken with distinctive accents and variously lived. Yet this palate of many colours was no mere collection of 'Catholicisms', lacking unity of profession or practice. The Church was the body of Christ, its sinews bound by hierarchy and sacraments. The ancient creedal faith of God as Trinity was preached in parish churches, cathedrals, and market squares. The youth, if at times reluctantly, received instruction, and the mass was celebrated in Latin in only mildly variant forms from the Mediterranean to the Baltic. Christ was present in the host, the Virgin was prayed to in the rosary, saints offered protection, and the dead pleaded to be remembered. The Bible was translated and preached, Classical learning was the great hope of Christian renewal, while fraternities and guilds cared for the souls of their departed members and the welfare of those on earth. At the same time, and regardless of what the preachers taught, common people mocked priests as whores and scoundrels, vengeful mobs killed Jews, the faithful combined talismatic practices with devotion, and the dead were thought to haunt the living. If we return once more to Chaucer, we find in his collection of Canterbury-bound pilgrims the humanity, with all that entails, of the medieval Christian world. In the character of his parson, the great poet offers us the spiritual hopes and travails of a faithful Christian: 'a good man was ther of religioun'.

No easy answers explain the emergence of the Reformation in northern Europe. Some will continue to adhere to traditional Protestant narratives: of medieval corruption and venality repudiated, and of spiritual freedom reclaimed. Others will see religious change forced on unwilling Christians by a few reformers in alliance with ruling powers motivated largely by worldly gain. The story is big enough to embrace aspects of both approaches, as well as many more. What it will not support is any notion of historical inevitability that denies the importance of local circumstances, the power of belief and customs, and the force of personalities. One can visit the house in Noyon, France, where John Calvin was born, but the nearby Gothic cathedral reminds us that the Reformation left this ancient city largely untouched after his departure. So why were events so different in Geneva?

The legacy of late medieval Christianity was one of fervency in devotion and practice, vitality in theology and biblical commentary, and of arresting architectural and artistic vision. It was also one of fragmentation and dissent in a diversifying society transformed by population growth, commerce, the printing press, humanist scholarship, and encounters with worlds beyond the seas. The extraordinary fertility of this religious culture was constantly spawning ideas, practices, and literature, and when some of these were transmitted through new means and networks of communication, and found the ears of both the pious and the ambitious in changing political and economic circumstances, novel possibilities abounded. The charismatic early reformers understood this. They sought to persuade rulers and ordinary Christians that the institutional Church was not merely corrupt but false. In a world where discontent with authorities, both temporal and spiritual, mingled with visceral feelings of divine presence, and of impending judgement, opportunities opened for bold voices and new visions.

2 Martin Luther

LYNDAL ROPER

Toasting the Reformation

ON 1 November 1527, Luther and his old friend and fellow pastor Justus Jonas shared a drink in Wittenberg, to commemorate the beginning of the Reformation, when the Ninety-Five Theses were first made public by being nailed to the door of the Castle Church in Wittenberg. They toasted the date, 'ten years after indulgences were trodden underfoot', the biblical echo equating indulgences with a Satanic snake. It would not have been surprising if the glass he raised was the 'Hedwigsbecher' or St Elisabeth's glass, which, as a guest at Luther's table reported in 1541, he passed around the table offering those present a drink. It came from the relic collection that had once been the pride and joy of Luther's old ruler, Frederick the Wise of Saxony himself, and it was reputed to have belonged to St Elisabeth of Thuringia.

There could hardly have been a more tangible demonstration of the depth of the changes the Reformation had wrought. St Elisabeth's glass contained parts of her cloak, dress, hair, and bones and was reputed to have healed a blind person 'and to have raised no fewer than sixteen people from the dead'. When Luther published the Ninety-Five Theses on the eve of the annual display of the relics in the Castle Church at Wittenberg, he was attacking the entire system of indulgences, relics, and pilgrimage that lay at the heart of the late medieval Church. What better way to cock a snook at the pope than to drink from the object that had once been displayed so reverently to pilgrims?

In 1527 Jonas and Luther certainly thought there was something that deserved celebrating, and for centuries after, Luther's reformation has been said to begin with the posting of the Ninety-Five Theses, in 1517. But even that was called into question when in 1966 the Catholic historian Erwin Iserloh pointed out that the only evidence that the theses had been nailed up came from Melanchthon, Luther's co-worker, who had not been in Wittenberg at the time. This was a wonderful piece of debunking of which Luther himself might have been proud. But it has recently been pointed out that Georg Roerer, Luther's secretary, who certainly was present in Wittenberg, does at least corroborate that the theses were put up on the doors of the church; and we know that academic theses were regularly printed and debated in the university, having been displayed in this way.

Certainly the publication of the Ninety-Five Theses seems to have marked a major change in how Luther understood himself. It was about this time that the monk whose name was Martin Luder began to sign his letters as 'Eleutherius', the freed one, from which he eventually designed the new version of his name 'Luther', as if marking a rebirth. Perhaps even more important than the posting of the theses was the fact that Luther sent them to several bishops, including Albrecht of Mainz, from whom they would eventually find their way to Rome, where in due course they were investigated for orthodoxy. It does not seem that Luther ever intended to stage an academic debate, and the Ninety-Five Theses were never debated. But he certainly intended to make his views known. Even at this early date, Luther knew how to stage a Reformation 'happening'. Sending the theses to Albrecht of Mainz and to the Bishop of Magdeburg guaranteed them publicity. Luther chose the date carefully: the eve of the display of the massive relic collection of Frederick the Wise drew pilgrims from far afield who travelled to Wittenberg to gain the indulgences that the relics guaranteed. And if Luther did not post the Ninety-Five Theses, he made up for it a year later, when, after the debate with Cardinal Cajetan at Augsburg, he escaped without taking his leave of the cardinal, making sure to post his appeal to Rome on the doors of the Augsburg cathedral.

On the face of it, the Ninety-Five Theses was a puzzling document to spark a revolution. Written in Latin, in the conventional form of theses put forward for disputation, it looks like a narrowly academic piece. It came from a professor at a new university, founded only the previous decade, a university still being built in a

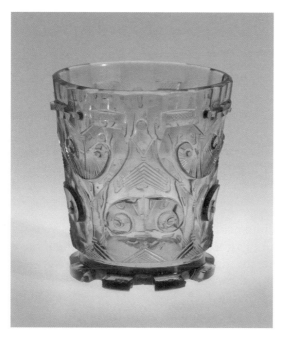

'HEDWIGSBECHER', from the twelfth-century Near East. This or something like it may have been the glass supposedly owned by St Elisabeth which was included in the collection of relics of All Saints, Wittenberg. The ascetic St Hedwig drank only water, which on one occasion miraculously turned to wine. We know that the glass, now at Coburg Castle, was in Luther's possession in 1541.

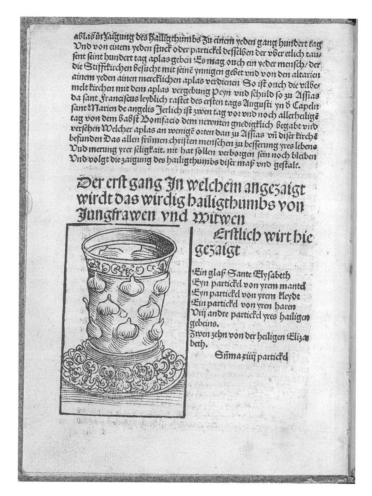

THE WOODCUT ILLUSTRATION OF 'ST ELISABETH'S GLASS' converts the unusual Hedwigsbecher from the twelfth century Near East into something more familiar, depicting it as a luxury 'nipple glass' of the period. This early printed book, with woodcuts by Lucas Cranach, is a complete illustrated guide to the relics collection of the Wittenberg Castle Church, advertising the collection and the indulgences that could be obtained from viewing each relic; and it shows how the new medium of print could be used in the service of late medieval piety.

minor town and with no academic reputation. Ninety-five is a haphazard number—some of the early printings got the numbering wrong, and there is no overall argument or narrative shape to the theses, many of which are very conventional. Even the history of its printing is shrouded in mystery. Luther claimed in a letter to Christoph Scheurl in Nuremberg that he had not had the theses printed himself; but this was in the embarrassing context of explaining to the leading humanist Scheurl, a man whose friendship he had only recently secured, why he had not sent him a copy, as such an important contact would have expected. However they came to be printed, there are copies of the theses from Leipzig, Nuremberg, and Basel; the Leipzig copy as a single broadsheet. Soon there were copies circulating in German—and they spread rapidly.

A set of clearly numbered points, they attacked papal power over indulgences and contrasted it with a different theological understanding of repentance, as something Christians must do their whole life long.

The issue of indulgences—certificates granting a specified period of remission from Purgatory—went to the heart of the nature of authority in the Church and the way in which salvation might be secured. In late medieval Europe, salvation was understood as a collective enterprise, something which you could help others to attain through intercessory prayer, or doing good works to help shorten the time the soul spent in Purgatory. Indulgences (which could be purchased for others as well as oneself) formed part of the whole communal edifice of pilgrimage, monasteries, masses, and brotherhoods which underpinned late medieval spiritual life. So popular were they that indulgences were even printed, some as broadsheets for display, others as simple printed receipts, with spaces for names of the beneficiaries to be filled in. Yet indulgences also had their critics from outside the church hierarchy. Ostensibly sold to fund the rebuilding of St Peter's, the money from indulgences could end up in strange hands. Albrecht was using part of the proceeds to repay the debts he owed the Fuggers, a prominent Augsburg banking family, for money he had raised to gain the wealthy archbishopric of Mainz. Luther's own ruler, the Elector of Saxony, did not permit this particular indulgence to be sold within his territory, perhaps because he feared competition for his own relic collection, which also gave the viewer sizeable remissions from Purgatory. And they raised the issue of papal authority because this indulgence was given directly by the pope; as Luther asked rhetorically, formulating the kind of question he thought pious Christians might rightly ask: 'Why does not the pope empty purgatory for the sake of holy love and the dire need of the souls that are there if he redeems an infinite number of souls for the sake of miserable money with which to build a church?'

Luther's Theology

The Ninety-Five Theses did not, however, contain Luther's whole theology and they are anything but a worked-out doctrinal treatise. Luther's assault on the Church began from an Augustinian understanding of the nature of penance, and of human beings and all their actions as fundamentally sinful. Dour as this anthropology might seem, it was liberating for Luther, because if all our actions are inherently sinful then we cannot strive to reach perfection by doing works, such as fasting, saying prayers, or hearing masses. We cannot earn grace through our works, still less through buying indulgences; rather, God freely gives us the gift of grace. It used to be thought that Luther gained his major theological breakthrough—his famous 'tower experience'—all in one go. Meditating on Romans 1: 17 in despair he realized that God's righteousness as judge, which so terrified Luther the monk, is united with Christ's righteousness, which we receive now through faith. Famously the 'experience' happened in what Luther described as the 'cloaca' tower, which held the privy. As Heiko Oberman has pointed out, there is a dignified way out here: 'by cloaca Luther did not mean the toilet but the study up in the tower above it.' But as Oberman goes on to say, 'That, however, would be to miss the point of Luther's provocative statement. The cloaca is not just a privy, it is the most degrading place for man and the Devil's favourite habitat.'

Throughout his life Luther struggled with *Anfechtungen*, or temptations; and they were so intense during his period as a monk that they defined his religiosity. It is difficult to put one's finger on exactly what these were about. For one of his biographers, Paul Reiter, they were the 'down' cycles of the manic depression from which he believed Luther suffered; others describe them as occurrences of melancholy. Luther saw them as linked to physical suffering—he wrote letters of deep empathy to several people who suffered from melancholy or spiritual crises, and he used the word *Anfechtungen* to describe what they were experiencing. For Luther, the *Anfechtungen* seem to have concerned deep doubts about faith, about the truth of his theology, and about whether or not he was saved; he was aware that for others, they could concern the doctrine of God's providence. The idea that God had already decided who was saved and who was damned remained an intellectual contradiction at the heart of Luther's theology, which he dealt with by saying that even thinking about it was wrong. An aspect that passed human understanding, providence should be left to God to worry about.

Although they made him suffer, Luther clung to his *Anfechtungen*, which were also the emotional anchor of his spirituality. They kept it dynamic. The *Anfechtungen* took both physical and emotional form—he experienced them as headaches, earaches, fainting, and digestive problems. They were the 'buffetings of Satan', an expression which he took from Paul and which was also reminiscent of the physical beatings reported by the saints. But where Catholic saints and mystics might worry that attacks by the Devil meant their visions were diabolically and not divinely inspired, Luther argued the opposite. Their very intensity, he insisted, demonstrated Luther's rightness, because it showed that the Devil was fighting him and so proved he was on Christ's side. For his opponents, of course, this was a gift. Catholic antagonists regularly accused Luther of being the offspring of the Devil, Johannes Cochlaeus also alleging that 'it is the opinion of many, that he enjoyed an occult familiarity with some demon, since he himself sometimes wrote such things about himself as were able to engender a suspicion in the reader of this kind of commerce and nefarious association'. Luther and his followers showed remarkable candour in recounting his experiences with the Devil—and it could also be the source of some of his most pungent humour. Writing about how the Devil would dispute with him at night, he quips that 'when the argument that the Christian is without the law and above the law doesn't help, I instantly chase him away with a fart'.

Historians now agree that, while Luther's central assurance about salvation may have come to him well before 1517, his theology developed in leaps and bounds in the years after the theses were composed. We now think that the key elements of Luther's theology—that man is saved by grace alone, and that scripture is the sole authority, not the tradition of the Church or decisions of the pope or church councils—were not fully developed until 1520, and some came even later. So too with many of the positions he took from this: that there are only two 'sacraments', properly so-called (baptism and the Eucharist); that communion should be given to the laity in both 'kinds', that is, as bread and wine; that the clergy ought to be able to marry; and that monasticism is wrong. What seems to have propelled Luther's theology forward is the opposition he met with from others.

Indeed, the Reformation proceeded by a set of debates and arguments. First Luther had to defend the new theology within his own Augustinian order; then his ruler Frederick the Wise managed to avert a trial in Rome by arranging discussions with Cardinal Cajetan in Augsburg. Cajetan was a convinced Thomist, a follower of St Thomas Aquinas, whose scholastic theology Luther was rejecting in favour of a radical Augustinianism that maintained that humans were so utterly tainted with sin that their works could do nothing to advance salvation. The discussions took place in the Fugger palace, home of one of the richest merchants of the day, in one of the major cities of the Empire—and Luther reacted with fury to Cajetan's attempts to treat the monk in a 'fatherly' manner, writing to Spalatin about how 'almost ten times I started to say something and each time he thundered back and took over the conversation. Finally I started to shout too.' He goes on to describe how Cajetan 'feverishly' rifled through his copy of the bull *Extravagante* of Clement VI for the proof that Christ's merits comprise the treasury of indulgences—only to discover, as Luther delightedly pointed out, that the passage read 'that Christ acquired the treasury by his suffering'— which meant that they are not the same thing. This dramatic description is clearly written with an eye to print, and sure enough, Luther soon published his account of the Augsburg discussions, the 'Acta Augustana' as he titled them. Why was Luther so excited about what looks like a technicality? The point was that the merits of Christ were not the store of good works from which indulgences were drawn, instead, the believer needed to have faith to be saved. Soon, however, Luther began to argue that *Extravagante* itself was not 'truthful or authoritative' because it 'distorts the Holy Scriptures', and he now moved on to articulate his position about the limits of papal power.

But the major public confrontation came when Andreas Karlstadt, another professor at the university and a major supporter of Luther's, provoked a debate with the Catholic theologian Johannes Eck. Karlstadt published a whopping 390 theses designed to refute Eck's critique of the Ninety-Five Theses, adding 26 more for good measure at proof stage. The debate was scheduled for Leipzig, in the territory of Duke George, the sister half of the territory ruled by Frederick the Wise. George had banned the sale of indulgences in his territory and had even seemed inclined to support Luther up to this point, so the debate had major consequences for the future of the Reformation in Saxony. After months of wrangling over the conditions, the debate was held, 'in good hiking weather', and monks and intellectuals from all over Germany made the trip to watch. Karlstadt was not a good debater, and Luther's demeanour left much to be desired. Whereas Eck cannily arrived before the debate, taking part in the Corpus Christi celebrations and hob-nobbing with the Leipzig worthies, Karlstadt and Luther arrived just in time, accompanied by a posse of armed students from Wittenberg—hardly likely to endear them to the Leipzig students. The wily Eck managed to trap Luther into agreeing with the radical position of the fifteenth-century Bohemian heretic Jan Hus that communion should be given in both kinds, with the bread and the wine for clergy and layfolk alike, and Luther, after considering this, not only conceded but by November 1519 had published a sermon in German advocating the cup for the laity. Here again, it was Eck's opposition which radicalized Luther.

This was a very serious development, because Hus had been condemned by the Council of the whole Church at Constance in 1415. Leipzig was not far from Bohemia so the Hussite menace was a real threat, and anti-Hussitism ran in Saxon blood—the Wettins, rulers of Saxony, had been awarded the Saxon lands because of their loyalty to the emperor during the Hussite conflicts. Fighting the Hussites was part of the identity of Luther's own order: it was one of the Erfurt Augustinians, Andreas Zacharias, who had been the leader of the intellectual attack which led to Hus's burning, and when Luther took his vows as a monk at Erfurt, he had to prostrate himself full length on Zacharias's grave. For those who wanted to limit papal authority there was a long tradition of Conciliarism, arguing that the councils were superior to popes and could not err. But now Luther was questioning the authority of councils as well as of popes.

As Luther's Catholic anti-biographer and contemporary Cochlaeus noticed, part of what made Luther such a powerful antagonist was that while you were fighting one heresy, Luther had already moved on to another worse one. In the extraordinary years between 1517 and the publication of the major Reformation treatises of 1520, Luther's theology had widened to embrace an attack on the entire structure of the Catholic Church. Part of the dynamism of the movement came from this intellectual thoroughgoingness: the ability to think things through fearlessly. In his 'On the Babylonian Captivity', Luther denied that there were seven sacraments, arguing that only baptism and communion had scriptural warrant; this meant the end of the idea that the Church accompanies the individual through each stage of life with a sacramental ritual. In the 'Appeal to the Christian Nobility', published in German, Luther begins with a forthright statement that papal power is buttressed by three 'walls', namely that the Church had its own spiritual law, that the papacy alone had the right to interpret scripture, and that only the pope could call a council of the Church. In wonderfully iconoclastic fashion, Luther then demolishes each wall. He sets out a series of financial abuses the Church had engaged in, from the pallium fee paid by new bishops to charging money for matrimonial dispensations—'If this is not the worst whorehouse of all whorehouses', Luther charges, 'then I don't know what a whorehouse is.' He presents Rome as a centre of commercial traffic, sucking Germany dry of money. The conclusion, something of a ragbag as in so many of Luther's works, strung together a series of abuses, attacking the ban on clerical marriage and discussing usury and other moral issues. But there was no doubting the importance of the questions Luther tackled in this passage, which picked up on the long tradition of presenting grievances of the 'German Nation' at imperial diets. And by addressing the 'German nobility', not the pope, emperor, bishops, or towns and villages, as the group who should act to reform the Church, Luther was making an appeal which would have massive historical consequences. As Tom Brady has pointed out, Luther here seems to be creating the basis for the formation of the territorial Church in the future, as secular rulers acted as 'emergency bishops' to implement ecclesiastical reform.

When the bull excommunicating him arrived, Luther again exploited theatre. After the morning lecture Luther took the students in procession to the Elstertor, the east gate of Wittenberg, where the carrion pit was located. There they formally burned the bull, throwing the canon law onto the fire for good measure. As Thomas Kaufmann has shown, the Reformation was driven forward by student involvement. When Luther returned home for lunch, the student carnival continued for the whole afternoon, with students parading around town, blowing trumpets. A cart featuring one of the students dressed as the pope went in procession—his tiara was ceremonially burned, and they sang, 'O you poor Judas,' a reference to the eternal pains of Hell which the pope and his advisers must suffer, because of their betrayal of Christ. The nascent evangelical movement exploited print, too: an anonymous description of the whole event was printed, and a German translation of it circulated, on a single-sided big-format print, ideal for posting up on a wall. The report was careful to mention that none of the professors had taken part in the afternoon's uproarious events. Just as he had done at Leipzig, Luther knew how to make use of student protest whilst keeping a safe distance.

In 1521, in the most dramatic moment of the whole Reformation, Luther was finally called to account at the Diet of Worms. Here, the Emperor Charles V and Luther faced each other. As Heinz Schilling has written in the most brilliant account of the encounter, Charles was a new young emperor, aged just 21, who had his own agenda and who, far from representing 'medieval' backwardness or intransigence, had a different and broader vision of the 'modern world'. Before the assembled estates of the Diet, Luther defended his work, and when asked to retract, said: 'Unless I am convinced by the testimony of the Scriptures or by clear reason...I am bound by the Scriptures I have quoted and my conscience is captive to the Word of God. I cannot and I will not retract anything, since it is neither safe nor right to go against conscience.' A pro-Lutheran account of the events put concluding words into Luther's mouth. But, apocryphal or not, they summarized Luther's attitude of defiance and have resonated down the centuries: 'I cannot do otherwise, here I stand, may God help me, Amen.' Probably nothing Luther wrote made more of an impact than his appearance at the Diet of Worms and defiance of the emperor. And it rapidly took on mythic status. In the account of Worms from the Lutheran side, the Acts, Luther is specifically depicted as a Christ-like figure, one woman in the crowd even exclaiming, in the words of St Luke's Gospel, 'Blessed be the womb that bore you.' For Cochlaeus, who drew on the Acts for his hostile biography of Luther, this was a blasphemous remark he made sure to quote. As he saw it, 'Luther, citing his captive conscience as a cause, was not able to withdraw from the nets in which he was caught; he kept on saying that he could not recant.' Remarkably, Luther managed to have his say at Worms and the Elector ensured that when he left, he remained safe, arranging to have him apparently 'kidnapped' and taken to the castle of the Wartburg where he lived for a time in disguise.

THIS WOODCUT, TAKEN FROM LUDWIG RABUS' history of Luther's life, depicts his appearance at the Diet of Worms and the moment when the titles of Luther's books were read aloud. At the bottom are Luther's apocryphal words 'Here I stand, I cannot do otherwise, May God help me, Amen.'

Luther's Background

Where did Luther come from, and how was a lone individual able to upend the Empire and Church in this way? It used to be thought that Luther's father was a simple miner who worked his way up to become mayor of Mansfeld. As Luther put it, 'in his youth my father was a poor miner. My mother carried all her wood home on her back.' Thanks to the research of Michael Fessner and Andreas Stahl, and to the archaeology undertaken on the house in Mansfeld where the family lived, we now know that this was a piece of image-making. Hans Luder (the form of the name by which the family was known) was part of the local elite of smelter-masters, who ran the mines; the family owned a big house and, as we know from recent archaeology, they ate well, their favourite food being suckling pig, a delicacy in a peasant society because you ate the pig before it was fully grown. His boyhood friends, Nicholas Oemle and Hans Reinicke, were the sons of the leading smelter-masters of the town and they lived on the same street, even if Martin lived slightly less desirably low down the hill. We can trace Luder in the records as he grew more wealthy, and took on positions of local importance, acting as representative attached to the council, inspecting mines, and involved in the local religious brotherhoods. Looking back, Martin may have remembered the family being poorer when he was a child. But Hans Luder could not have gained one of the mine-leases without considerable capital, and he could never have earned the start-up funds through working as a miner. Nor could he have married his wife, a member of the Lindemann family at Eisenach, whose uncle was one of the leading mining officials in the area.

Mining was a booming industry in Saxony, the source of the wealth that allowed Frederick to build up his relic collection, found the new university at Wittenberg, and play a major part in imperial politics. Luther's background was unusual—he understood the new economic forces in a way that those who grew up in the towns in the south with their myriad craft workshops did not. The rough world of the mining town of Mansfeld where Luther grew up was very different from the big imperial cities like Augsburg or Nuremberg, with their fine buildings and traditions of law, commerce, and high-quality artisanal production. It was also a world where friendship mattered, where people had to cooperate to survive, and where it was important to stand your ground—and this too was a lesson that shaped Martin Luther.

Luther's father designed the typical itinerary for his clever son, spending the income of two smelters to send him to study law at Erfurt; but after one visit home, Luther was caught in a terrible storm, and called on St Anna, the patron saint of miners, to save him, promising to enter a monastery. To his father's horror, Martin entered the Augustinian monastery at Erfurt, putting paid to all plans for young Martin to marry into the Mansfeld elite, as his siblings would do, and to bring legal expertise to the mines. This was a huge rebellion, a rejection of his childhood as well as of his father, encapsulated in his later change of name. At the banquet his father hosted to celebrate Luther's first mass, his father wondered publicly whether it had not been the Devil who had tempted him to make the vow, a taunt Luther never forgot. When Luther came to reject monasticism and all its works, he prefaced the work with a letter of dedication to his father. But though this was an ostensible public apology to his father, and set out the theological justification for breaking monastic vows and taking a wife as his father must have wished, it was written in the Latin which his father could not read. Moreover, Luther's 'apology' had limits. Insisting that the vision was not diabolic, Luther now described it as miraculous, reinterpreting the storm as God's summons to him that would in the end bring about the downfall of the papacy. Though Luther broke with saints' cults and Marianism, prophecy remained an important mode for him to convey his authority.

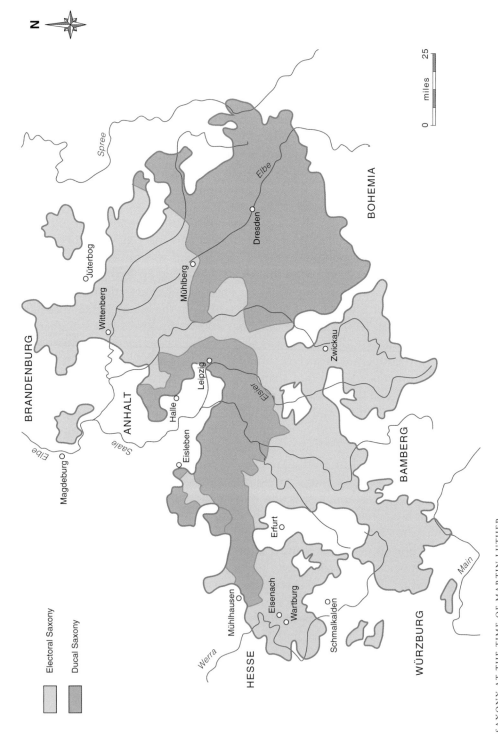

Electoral Saxony

Ducal Saxony

N

BRANDENBURG

Spree

Magdeburg

Elbe

Saale

ANHALT

Jüterbog

Wittenberg

Mühlberg

Elbe

Dresden

BOHEMIA

Halle

Eisleben

Leipzig

Eis[el

Zwickau

Mühlhausen

Werra

HESSE

Eisenach

Wartburg

Schmalkalden

Erfurt

BAMBERG

WÜRZBURG

Main

miles

0   25

SAXONY AT THE TIME OF MARTIN LUTHER
Source: Mark Greengrass, *The European Reformation, c.1500–1618* (Longman, 1998), p. 367.

The Great Escape

How was Luther able to get away with it? In the years after 1517, Luther prepared himself mentally for martyrdom. He knew Hus's fate. The heightened creativity of the years 1519 and 1520 may have had a great deal to do with the idea of impending death: Luther knew that his theological work was putting him in an ever more dangerous position. And yet at the same time he planned carefully to avoid martyrdom. His friendship with Georg Spalatin was key to this. Spalatin was Frederick the Wise's secretary, and he acted as intermediary with the Elector, whom Luther probably never met. Luther corresponded frequently with Spalatin in Latin, and when he wrote to the Elector he did so in German. In Latin, Spalatin and he discussed and planned; and when Luther wrote to the Elector in German, the final policy would be presented. Spalatin brokered the Elector's support: Frederick would not allow his star university professor to be sent to Rome for trial. But that support was possible because of Saxony's political influence, another product of its mining riches. And it sprang from a very particular political situation. The old Emperor Maximilian, who had been trying to secure the imperial title for his son the future Charles V, had just died and elections were being held for the new emperor. Frederick was one of the key electors, even contemplating standing himself though in the end he opted for Charles. The uncertainty maximized Frederick's political influence during the crucial period when policy against the heretic was being devised, and the pope, worried that the election of Charles would imperil his Italian territories, at first courted Frederick; while for his part, the emperor knew what he owed Frederick's eventual support. So it was that the pope had been willing to agree to an informal hearing in Augsburg, and when a hearing at the Imperial Diet was determined upon, Charles provided a safe conduct for Luther, and he was not delivered to Rome.

But the most important reason why Luther did not meet with Hus's fate was technology: the new medium of print. Luther early grasped the possibilities it offered. He used it, for example, to create teaching aids: copies of the texts he lectured on with generous space for students to write in. Print created an academic audience for his work, but it did more. Because Luther's theology moved at such a rapid pace, and because he wrote in German as well as Latin, producing brief, memorable sermons and treatises which addressed the reader directly in powerful prose, there was a huge market for his work—you had to know what Luther was up to now. The result was what Andrew Pettegree has termed a 'pamphlet moment'—an unprecedented increase in the numbers of short writings produced for sale, centred around a set of issues of public debate. Most of them were by Luther himself: between 1518 and 1525, German works by Luther amounted to more than all the seventeen other next most important vernacular evangelical polemicists put together, and he alone was responsible for 20 per cent of all that was printed on German presses between 1500 and 1530—a truly remarkable domination of publishing by one man. Luther's published vernacular works outnumbered those of his Catholic antagonists by 5 to 1. The sheer drama of the Reformation events—the discussions at Augsburg, with Luther thumbing his nose at the papal legate; the burning of Tetzel's counter-theses on the market square at Wittenberg (which Luther claimed to deplore—though somehow he was close enough to events to manage to snatch a copy from the flames); the burning of the papal bull—all these were events that it was impossible to forget, searing themselves into memory and creating 'actions' that would be copied in towns all over Europe. Print and Reformation 'action' went hand in hand to bring about popular pressure for religious change.

Perhaps as important as the printed word was the image, also made newly available by print. Here too friendship played a crucial role. The very first piece of propaganda for the Reformation was produced not by Luther but by Karlstadt, the man who had provoked the Leipzig debate. It was printed in Latin, and then in German, a measure of how important publishing in the vernacular was starting to become—this was before Luther himself had published very much in German. It showed two processional lines of wagons: one containing the scholastic theologians headed for Hell, the other, showing the true believer heading towards Christ. Karlstadt created a partnership with the artist Lucas Cranach, the court painter of the Elector. His workshop was just a short stroll from Luther's monastery and he was among the richest men of the town. In the years that followed, Cranach and other artists learned how to make propaganda that was clear and that attracted its audience. First, in the wake of the Leipzig debate, there appeared a local Leipzig pamphlet prefaced with a crude portrait of Luther himself, shown as a monk: so rapidly has the image been put together that the lettering is around the wrong way. Here it is not Luther's features but his monk's habit, the giant doctor's hat that dwarfs his face, and the rose in the bottom of the roundel that mark this out as 'Luther'. Like many humanists, Luther had early chosen an emblem for himself, the Luther rose; but in his hands it became much more than a humanist fashion statement. It worked rather like a coat of arms, and was later used on his seal as a form of authenticating the letters he wrote. It went on to function as a sign for the whole Reformation movement. (Indeed, in 1530 when the Electoral prince presented Luther with a new specially commissioned signet ring, Luther provided a detailed theological explanation of its meaning.) Cranach soon produced far superior portraits of his friend that were much more sophisticated and emotionally intense than the Leipzig cartoon—and how politically important they were is evident in the effort the Saxon court spent on discussing which design would be better, settling on one that was less provocative, showing a milder, less visionary Luther. It would prove to be a major success: it inspired a series of portraits of the reformer, which were used on the covers of his tracts, and which also formed the model for a series of medals, sold at events like the Diet of Worms in 1521, where Luther's appearance before the emperor and the entire assembly of the Imperial Diet was the highlight of the event. Often they featured Luther in front of a niche, like a saint—and some even included a halo, or a dove suggesting he was directly inspired by the Holy Spirit. These portraits, with their presentation of Luther's deep-set eyes, gaunt face, and intense expression, meant that the reader often encountered Luther's theology through an emotional engagement with him as an individual, so that his dramatic life story was already becoming part of the theological message.

One particular work, the Passional of Christ and Antichrist, exemplifies the Reformation movement's talent for using images. The texts were written by Luther's co-worker Melanchthon and Cranach provided the woodcuts—this time, short and effective, they are clearly separated from the image. In a series of thirteen simple contrasts, they showed scenes from the life of Christ, emphasizing his humility; and on the facing page, a corresponding image of the pope's lust for power and glory. And it was not just artistic techniques that Cranach was developing—Cranach, known as the 'fast painter', was intrigued by the possibilities of multiplying images; his workshop full of patterns and sections of painting that could be endlessly replicated by the journeymen he employed in his workshop. Printing, which offered the same

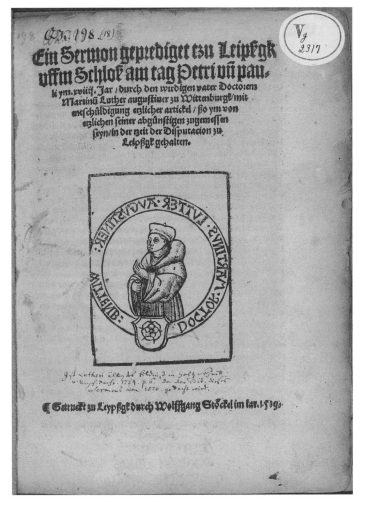

TITLE PAGE OF 'EIN SERMON GEPREDIGET TZU LEIPßGK', printed at Leipzig by Wolfgang Stoeckel, 1519. This is the first depiction of Luther in print. It shows the Luther rose; and it has been put together in such haste that the lettering is partially reversed.

THIS IMAGE OF THE REFORMER in front of a niche and holding a Bible was frequently used as the title page for works of Luther, including editions of his speech at Worms. There were many variants of this kind of image, including ones which add a dove indicating that Luther is inspired by the Holy Spirit. The niche in front of which Luther is standing is reminiscent of depictions of saints, while the patterns on the columns add a fashionable humanist touch.

possibilities of multiplying images, equally fascinated him because it could make an image iconic. In conjunction with the goldsmith Christian Doering, Cranach set up a printing workshop, which (among other things) produced the Passional. It was therefore an experiment in how new technology could be used to convey the same, clear idea in a manner that would reshape the visual environment. It was also, as Bob Scribner pointed out, much more effective in criticizing the Catholic Church than it was in presenting its own positive evangelical message.

Yet print was a medium which could not easily be controlled. Within Wittenberg, the university began to act as censor for books, but it could not prevent material being printed elsewhere. The radical theologian and leader Thomas Müntzer made sure to establish a printing press when he took over the town of Allstedt; and when Luther's erstwhile ally Andreas Karlstadt, no longer welcome in Wittenberg, left to establish a proper peasant reformation, he made sure to create links with a printing press in nearby Jena. The Wittenbergers soon had to fight to be heard above a cacophony of print. Their use of visual devices, such as images of Luther, coats of arms, recognizable print borders, or the Luther rose, show how they were deliberately trying to define a

Paſſional Chꝛiſti vnd

Chꝛiſtus.

So ich ewre fuſſe habe gewaſchen ð ich ewir herz vñ meyſter bin/ vill mehr ſolt yr einander vnter euch die fuſze waſchen. Hie mit habe ich euch ein anzeygung vñ beyſpiel geben/ wie ich ym than habe/ olſzo ſolt yr hinfur auch thuen. Warlich warlich ſage ich euch/ð knecht iſt nicht mehr dan ſeyn herre/ ſzo iſt auch nicht ð geſchickte botte mehr dã ð yn geſandt hat. Wiſt yr das? Selig ſeyt yr ſzo yr das thuen werdent. Johan. 13.

Antichꝛiſti.

Antichꝛiſtus.

Der Bàbſt maſt ſich an itzlichen Tyrannen vnd heydniſchen furſten/ ſzo yre fueß den leuten tzu kuſſen dar gericht/ nach tzu volgen/ damit es waer werde das geſchrieben iſt. Welcher dieſer Beſtien Bilde nicht anbettet/ ſall getödt werden Apocalip. 13. Ditz kuſſens darff ſich der Bapſt yn ſeynē decretalen vnuoꝛ ſcheñßt rümen. c. cū oli de pu. cle. Si ſumnus poſt. de ſat. ercõ.

PASSIONAL OF CHRISTI AND ANTICHRISTI, 1521. This work of thirteen contrasting pairs of images was a brilliant piece of anti-Catholic propaganda, illustrated by Cranach. Here, on the left, Christ humbly washes the disciples' feet, whilst on the right the Pope receives homage from the Emperor and secular estates.

party line in a plethora of different versions of what the Reformation might mean. For example, as Amy Burnett has shown, when in 1524 and 1525 the dispute over the Real Presence in the Eucharist grew increasingly heated, the Wittenbergers produced six treatises that all articulated Luther's line and were published in many editions—the other side published nineteen tracts by ten different authors, which were far more diverse in argument.

Indeed, in the early years of the Reformation it was probably not clear to most people what Luther's theology was. Luther had no monopoly on his 'message', and in the years leading up to the Peasants' War, people took his ideas in new directions. If it is wrong to pay for masses, or for monks to beg, why not put the funds of the old religious donations into new, proper systems of poor relief? If Christians should be free, why should lords own peasants? Evangelical theology gave people concepts through which to reimagine old grievances about their secular lords—and since so many landlords were clerics or monastic institutions, the resentment of tithes, serf-dom, and the failings of the Church could rapidly become a critique of how relations between lords and peasants, and between the clerical and lay estates, should be formed. The 'evangelical peasant', with his hoe and flail, became a Reformation hero, his image prefacing many tracts demanding religious reform.

In 1524–5, the peasants in many areas of Germany rose up against their lords. Their demands mixed religious and secular concerns, many beginning with a call for true Christian preaching to be instituted. In villages and towns across the Empire, peasant bands formed, demanding to 'drink brotherhood' with the lords, uniting with towns, and developing new political models. In 1525 when the peasants appealed to Luther as an adjudicator for their cause he seemed a natural supporter—in retrospect this seems like an incomprehensible error on their part, because he famously condemned the peasants' rebellion as the robbing and raging of 'mad dogs'.

In an age where oral transmission of ideas was probably more important than print, 'evangelical theology' was bound to be a protean thing. For most people, Luther's message was probably understood through key words and sayings, and through actions and events, as much as through complex treatises. For example, the demand for communion in both kinds—the bread and the wine—was something people could unite around and that required action. It was resonant with meaning, encapsulating the idea that clergy should not be a 'special' estate, with privileged access to divine things. Just as the Wittenberg students celebrated the burning of the bull with their own carnival, while in Erfurt crowds including students and journeymen attacked the homes of clerics, Reformation 'happenings' became media events whose significance lay in their drama. They were unforgettable, they could be copied, and they were inspiring in ways Luther probably did not intend. The idea of the good, simple evangelical 'peasant', the notion of 'brotherhood', or the watchword 'freedom' that featured so prominently in Luther's 'The Freedom of a Christian', were on everyone's lips because the attack on the established Church enabled people to rethink relations between the secular and spiritual worlds in new ways.

Luther reacted with horror to what he saw as a disregard for authority and wrote a series of tracts, at first recognizing the justice of some of the peasants' claims, but then, in his infamous 'Against the robbing and murdering hordes of peasants', encouraging the rulers to 'stab, smite, slay' the revolting peasants. It was a brutal piece, and it appeared in print at the point when the peasants had been defeated and repression was underway. Even some of Luther's allies thought he had gone too far, and he later issued a letter of explanation—which, however, did not amount to a recantation.

For Luther's Catholic opponent Cochlaeus, however, Luther was to blame for the Peasants' War, because his message incited sedition:

in every city, the common folk plotted wars and seditions against the Senate, the people against their Prince, and the Princes against their Emperor. And the more each one bandied about the Gospel and desired to appear as an Evangelist surpassing all others, the more he strove for revolution. Why was this so? Because Luther persuaded them that a Gospel was more true, the more revolution it produced.

It is clear that this is a charge Luther felt he had to refute. Though the peasants' defeat of 1525 did not mean the end of the radical Reformation, or put paid to the linking of social grievance with theology, it did mark the end of a remarkable period of social and cultural foment, when the evangelical peasant Karsthans was the hero of the hour and 'evangelical brotherhood' excited thousands of men and women to take collective action. Their defeat made it clear that Luther's sympathy was with the princes, and with a conservative vision of Reformation.

As the Peasants' War made obvious, there was never a single reformation, and Luther's influence on it was always contested as well as sought. Without a formal church structure that reached beyond Saxony, Luther had to rely on a network of personal contacts to police orthodoxy across the many towns, villages, and territories, each with their own preacher. Within electoral Saxony, a system of church visitations was established in partnership with secular authority to oversee the introduction of the Reformation, a model which was replicated in many Protestant lands. Beyond Saxony, one of Luther's main means of influence was through appointments to preaching positions, and much of his correspondence is taken up with recommending individuals for particular posts, many of them students who had passed through the University of Wittenberg. Luther's patronage network was vast, extending even across eastern Europe, though it was far weaker in the rich cities of the south, like Augsburg or Strasbourg. It relied on friendship, and this was always precarious—the closest of friends, like Johannes Agricola, once preacher in Luther's own childhood home of Eisleben, with whom Luther swapped stories about their children, might suddenly succumb to theological unorthodoxy as they articulated theology in their own words. Luther rejected 'Grickel' bitterly, publishing Agricola's assertions himself along with a series of refutations of them, and preventing him from lecturing. The quarrel ground on for years, with Luther writing that 'in sum, Eisleben is our enemy, and he has insulted our teaching and shamed our theologians'. So much did his hostility to his former ally Karlstadt drive his theology that Luther did not finally drop the elevation of the host (the moment in the mass after the consecration where the host is raised for the congregation to see and reverence) until Karlstadt died; as Luther explained, he had retained the elevation because Karlstadt abolished it. Luther spent much of his energy defending the doctrine of the Real Presence, the idea that the consecrated bread and wine are not just symbols but really are the body and blood of Christ.

From the late 1520s onwards his letters are full of warnings against the snakes and vipers of Satan whose poison will undermine the Reformation, and he was not above preventing opponents like the former Lutheran and now Catholic Georg Witzel from getting university positions—unwisely, poor Witzel had even composed his inaugural lecture for Erfurt. Occasionally, Luther's patronage network became dysfunctional. Zwickau, a town which supported the Reformation early on, developed bad relations with a series of preachers Luther had recommended, when they used the pulpit to criticize the immoral behaviour of Zwickau's leading councillors. Luther at first advised the preachers to moderate their tone but increasingly he took their part. As the quarrel grew more heated, Luther became completely alienated from Zwickau, advising one preacher to (in the words of St Luke's Gospel) 'shake the dust off your feet as a testimony against them' and leave. Luther then refused to recommend any preachers, and warned others against taking a job in the God-forsaken town. With no formal power in Zwickau, which lay outside the territory of Electoral Saxony, Luther could do nothing but threaten or cajole. The result was that for a time he lost all influence in a major town.

Marriage

Perhaps the area in which the Reformation had its greatest impact was that of marriage and sexual relations. Here there were two earth-shattering innovations: first, celibacy was no longer required for the priesthood, and the monastic lifestyle of both monks and nuns was rejected. Second, Luther argued that marriage was not a sacrament. This made it possible to take marriage out of the jurisdiction of the Church, and into secular control, and this meant that the regulation of marriage became much more closely aligned with lay people's views.

Marriage was a major social institution, organizing labour, politics, education, and sex. Most people worked within a household, either in a craft workshop or peasant farm, where marital status determined social rank, with unmarried servants and journeymen subordinate to the master and mistress of the household. Only with marriage and masterhood did men become politically part of the community, and the household was a potent metaphor for politics itself. Yet despite its centrality, the sacramental status of marriage had led to endless confusion. Since marriage consisted in the couple's free sacramental 'marital exchange' with each other, astonishingly, a binding marriage could technically be contracted out of doors, or in a tavern, before a couple had sex. It did not require parental permission or a church ceremony to be valid; indeed, the priest was a witness, not the person who administered this sacrament. Once the couple had consummated their union, even a provisional marriage promise became fully binding. Not surprisingly, this system gave rise to endless suits in the church courts, with men and women suing to have a marriage promise recognized, pregnant women demanding compensation for loss of virginity, child support, and fulfilment of marriage promise, and some people remaining uncertain, in conscience, to whom they were truly married in the sight of God.

Meanwhile, social convention was starting to accord more power to parents over their children's marriages. As society became more unequal, marriage strategies were becoming important to all social classes, not just royal households but peasants and miners too—after all, when Luther became a monk, one aspect of his rebellion against his father was his refusal to marry and take a wife who could have advanced the family's mining fortunes. Once jurisdiction over marriage was transferred to secular authority, and marriage was not considered to be a sacrament, the way was open to insist that parental permission was required for a valid marriage, that banns must be read, that marriages must take place in public, and that not just annulment, but divorce could be possible. As anthropologists have taught us, any society's deepest taboos concern incest—and here, too, Luther set to it with a vengeance, using the rules of Leviticus to define minimal biblical prohibitions and throwing out the elaborate system of degrees of kinship. It was fine, he argued to marry 'the sister of my deceased wife or fiancée, as well as the widow of my deceased brother'. It was not long, however, before even he realized this was a step too far, and later, he returned to more conventional definitions of incest.

Luther argued that divorce with remarriage should be possible. If one spouse committed adultery, or deserted the other, the marriage was sundered and the innocent party should be able to remarry; indeed, Luther even contemplated allowing a guilty spouse to marry again, if they had left the area—as we shall see, public reputation continued to be crucially important in how Luther thought about moral issues. Luther's willingness to consider divorce arose from his deeply held conviction about the importance of sex as part of human nature. As he developed his theology of marriage he turned to the story of Creation, arguing that God had made men and women as sexual beings.

Luther also insisted that priests should marry instead of living in sin with their concubines. As he saw it, celibacy was just another vain human work which did not make people more acceptable to God, and it went against nature. Luther also rejected convents for women, though it interestingly proved far more difficult to eradicate convents than it did to close monasteries, in part because he could envisage no other lifestyle for ex-nuns apart from marriage. Yet again, with his flair for the dramatic, Luther was not above getting involved in plans to kidnap willing nuns from nearby convents, sneaking them out hidden in barrels and bringing them to Wittenberg where he spent months looking for suitable husbands for them. Along with this went an insistence on the strength of women's desires, too. As Luther wrote to some nuns in 1524, 'although women are ashamed to admit such things, both Scripture and experience teach that among many thousands there is not one to whom God gives the grace to maintain pure chastity'.

Though Luther originally thought that there were some people who were given the gift of celibacy, marriage soon became a litmus test of orthodoxy for the evangelical clergy. In the early 1520s there was a remarkable series of weddings, as, one after another, the leading reformers took wives—an extraordinary transformation for men who had never expected to be sharing their lives with women. Recent research on evangelicals' wives has shown that two-thirds of those clergy who married in 1521-2 married their concubines; about a third who married 1523-7 did so, and around half between 1528 and 1530. Not everyone wanted to make respectable women of their concubines, however. Bernhard Riet told the Esslingen city council in 1534 that he did not want to marry his maid who was 'old and incapacitated'—she was good only for cooking and cleaning. Men who married their concubines were often allying themselves with women of lower social status, and their wives, once insulted as priests' whores, sometimes had difficulty securing social respect. Many of the marriages did not work, often in spectacular fashion, causing scandal and gossip in their communities. When the pastor Georg Schammer's wife refused to follow her husband to a new parish, and threatened to shack up with a bath-keeper (a very lowly and dishonourable profession), Luther advised his superior Anton Lauterbach to grant Schammer a divorce and free him from 'that vomit'.

Luther himself chose to marry a minor noblewoman and former nun, Katharina von Bora—his Catholic contemporaries were horrified by this double breaking of monastic vows, and published mock exhortations to her to leave her husband and save her soul. Here again Cranach's art proved immensely important in creating a new kind of visual representation of the changed realities, allowing people to imagine the Luthers' marriage in positive terms. The workshop created a series of double portraits of Luther and Katharina, which were mass produced and sent all over Europe; and for those who could not afford the oil paintings, there were printed woodcuts of the couple produced by other artists. Their format is identical, showing the bust of a big, dominant Luther with his instantly recognizable features against a plain-coloured background. Katharina, whose features vary from image to image, is slightly smaller. She is shown against the same block of colour, but in contrast to Martin's shapeless cassock, her bodice (sometimes with an impossibly small waist) emphasizes her femininity. These images adopted the new Renaissance genre of the double marriage portrait, yet they were not commissioned by the couple to commemorate their union, but to make a public statement about married clergy.

The paradox was that while Luther left marriage to secular authority to govern, in practice he was constantly drawn into giving advice on marital cases. Adjudicating on marriage disputes soon began to take up more of his time than anything else, or so Luther complained. The old church courts had been staffed by churchmen skilled in canon law; soon, new ones were established with laymen and theologians, who had to work together to devise new principles—and though Luther had burned the canon law back in 1520, he now had to deal with the views of jurists who applied the principles of both secular and church law. The arguments could be endless. Luther's instincts were deeply patriarchal, and he liked to shoot from the hip, counselling as he felt made pastoral sense. Nearly always he sided with the man's point of view. So for example he took the part of the miller Georg Faber, excoriating his wife, an ex-nun, who—so Faber said—had become a whore and, with her mother's help, had run off with his goods and money. She 'tricked us', Luther wrote, into thinking she was 'pious' and worthy of such a marriage. In the notorious case of Wolf Hornung's wife, who became the mistress of the Elector Joachim of Brandenburg, Luther publicly took Hornung's side, helping him with his defence and publishing pamphlets in his support. Hornung, however, did not deny causing the wounds to his wife's body that she said were still visible, claiming that he was simply 'punishing her', as was his duty; she argued that she had fled a husband who was trying to kill her. And when his old friend Johannes Lang's wife died, Luther wrote in alarming frankness to him that he didn't know whether 'to congratulate or commiserate' on his 'release' from his wife. She was

THESE DOUBLE PORTRAITS OF MARTIN LUTHER AND KATHARINA VON BORA offered a visual representation of the new reality of the married pastor. Produced by the Cranach workshop, they were produced from 1525 until the early 1540s, changing as the couple aged. Katharina, with her impossibly slim waist, does not gaze at the viewer directly; Luther's piercing eyes are unmistakeable.

a rich widow, and the match had caused raised eyebrows at the time, the radical Thomas Müntzer castigating the 'prince's parsons' who 'marry old women with great wealth' instead of earning their own money.

Yet while Luther lauded matrimony, what he meant by it is often disconcerting. As we saw, Luther's theology of marriage was rooted in the idea of Creation, and he saw sex as a fundamental human need, as natural and essential as defecation. Applying scriptural models, he also had to deal with the complicated precedents established by polygamy among the Old Testament patriarchs. And his own emphasis on sex and offspring could mean that his views of marriage are different from modern ones. For example, as early as 1520 he wrote that if a woman could not have a child by her husband then she should take her husband's brother aside and contract a secret marriage with him, an idea which he repeated in his treatise on marriage in 1522, suggesting that she say, 'Look, my dear husband, you are unable to fulfill your conjugal duty toward me. . . . Grant me the privilege of contracting a secret marriage with your brother or closest relative, and you retain the title of husband so that your property will not fall to strangers.' These chickens came home to roost in 1539, when Luther was asked to approve Philip of Hesse, a leading pro-Reformation prince, taking a second wife. Philip had been unhappily married for many years, and had watched the development of evangelical marriage law with keen interest, because he felt unable to receive communion as an adulterer. To have a second wife would therefore allow his natural sexual urges to find expression within the institution God had designed. Luther, who did not refuse to entertain this line of thought, counselled that he could take a second wife but in secret. In the eyes of God the couple would be married and Philip's conscience would be eased, but in public the original marriage would continue to stand. This was all very well, but Philip inveigled Melanchthon and the Strasbourg theologian Martin Bucer into attending the wedding, which was celebrated before a group of invited dignitaries. The news got out, causing a major scandal, with Luther advising the Landgrave to deny that he had taken a second wife and refusing to publish the advice he had given in the matter. Once again, we can see the iconoclastic Luther at work here, willing to rethink human institutions in the light of scripture. He continued to distinguish between what was public knowledge and what one might be allowed to conscience in secret. The bigamy of Philip of Hesse is often treated as a scandalous aberration in Luther's theology of marriage, but it accorded with Luther's long-standing emphasis on the importance of sex in marriage.

Indeed, the early years of the sixteenth century saw a whole range of marital experiments. Some radicals, like Thomas Müntzer, seem to have advocated a new kind of celibacy although he was himself married; others argued that sex itself was a sacrament, and that they must leave their present spouse for the new husband or wife given to them by God. In Münster in 1534–6, Anabaptists gained power and established a godly kingdom. They introduced polygamy, so as to re-create the twelve tribes of Israel—and in order to secure social order in a town under siege where women greatly outnumbered men. The Anabaptists of Münster were defeated, but marital 'experiments' and utopian ways of thinking about sexuality within marriage were central to the foment of Reformation ideas, though they are often forgotten in treatments of the Reformation which credit it with establishing companionate marriage.

Islam and Judaism

Luther's attitude to the Jews is one of the Reformation's most uncomfortable legacies. His stance in relation to the Turks was interestingly different. At first, during the years of Reformation optimism, he objected to crusades against the Turks—far better to fight the true enemy, the pope. He did not believe that force of arms was the way to spread true belief. However, by 1529, when the Ottoman forces had reached the gates of Vienna, Luther began to engage with Islam, writing a tract against the Turks and advising soldiers how to deal with Muslims. He condemned the Turks as murderers, engaging in war against the Christians, as liars who did not accept true religion, and as destroyers of marriage, alleging that men had ten or even twenty wives—though it was easy divorce more than polygamy itself that excited his outrage. But he also thought that Christians who lived in areas ruled by the Ottomans should obey secular author-ity and should not even flee Turkish rule. As part of this engagement he found out what he could about the Turks and their customs, even editing and publishing a tract on the customs of the Turks, knowledge which found its way into much of his writing from the 1530s onwards. His assessment was not entirely negative: he praised their modesty of dress, their abstemiousness in relation to food and drink (so unlike the Germans), as well as their form of government.

Up to this time, however, he had not been able to read a copy of the Koran itself. In 1542, he got hold of a Latin translation; he then embarked on translating a hoary Dominican treatise by Ricoldus, a Refutation of Islam, into German, which he crafted into a work of his own intended to enable Christians to defend the truth of their religion. Later that year, when publication of a Latin Koran was planned by the leading publisher Oporinus in Basel, the city council there banned the work. Luther wrote 'in my own hand' insisting it appear, and he penned a preface for it as well. This was not because he was religiously tolerant, rather, he argued, nothing could be more harmful to Islam than to publish the Koran so that everyone could see what an 'accursed, shameful and desperate book' it is. He added, 'one must open the injury and the wound if one is going to heal it. Covering it up just makes it worse and finally hopelessly impossible'—this from a man who knew what he meant by the metaphor. He himself kept a vein open in his leg to let out noxious humours and heal his headaches. Yet though he here implicitly equates Islam with pus, his writings about Islam were free of the kind of physical, visceral hatred that characterized his attitudes to the Jews. He argued that the Turks were Satan's tools, that their religion was false, and that they were a sign of the Last Days, identifying them with the 'hermaphroditic' 'little horn' of the fourth Beast. But he generally did not equate them—as many writers before him had done—with Antichrist. That was a role he reserved for the pope.

Luther's attitude to the Jews, however, was notably more complicated than his stance on Islam. Because, like many biblically interested humanists, Luther learnt Hebrew, this meant that he had to engage with real Jews—but his attitude towards Jews at the university remained ambivalent, criticizing professors of Hebrew who he thought were not sufficiently Christian. In the early years of the Reformation, when it seemed as if evangelicalism would sweep everything before it, Luther wrote a tract 'That Jesus Christ was born a Jew' (1523), a work which is often treated as if it expressed tolerationist ideas. Luther blamed the Catholic Church for preventing Jews from converting to Christianity, and pointed out that it was Christian repression that forced Jews into practising usury: 'when we forbid them to labour and do business and have any human fellowship with us, thereby forcing them into usury, how is that supposed to do them any good?' Nor did Luther repeat the myth of ritual murder, the commonly held Christian belief that Jews abducted and killed Christian children to use their blood in religious rites, and which was often used to whip up hatred against the Jews. The pamphlet sparked a number of others, some in the 'dialogue' form that was such a favoured means of evangelical propaganda, where a Jew and a Christian would debate; one even had a remarkable cover that showed a rabbi and a pastor breaking bread together, with the rabbi toasting the pastor.

Yet this acceptance was tactical. Most of the pamphlets aimed at conversion or at least discussion with the Jews, but often concluded with a 'stubborn', 'obstinate' Jew refusing to convert, thus reinforcing the idea of Jews as a stiff-necked, proud people. The conversion of the Jews was a sign of the Last Days, and with eschatological fervour high during the early years of the Reformation, friendly attitudes towards the Jews in part derived from an optimism that, with the barriers of the papist Church removed, they would recognize Jesus as the messiah. As Luther put it, Jews should be converted bit by bit: 'Let them first be suckled with milk' and then, when they have recognized Jesus as the messiah, they 'may drink wine, and learn also that he is true God'. If this was toleration, it was strictly conditional on the withering of Judaism. Just as with Luther's positive rhetoric about peasants, which could be picked up and understood to support their cause, so his words about the Jews offered support to Jewish communities—but just as Luther distanced himself from the peasants' cause, so also he repudiated what he saw as the belief amongst Jewish communities that he was their supporter. When Rabbi Josel of Rosenheim wrote asking for his support in petitioning the Elector, Luther responded in a rude letter emphatically distancing himself from the Jewish cause because they would not convert.

As Luther aged, his views became more extreme and in the 1540s he began to push for a change in policy, embarking on a campaign to convince secular rulers of German lands that the Jews should be expelled. Luther's most famous anti-Semitic tract is 'On the Jews and their Lies' (1543), written towards the end of his life. It contains a series of measures Luther recommends should be taken, including destroying synagogues, preventing rabbis from preaching and burning their religious books, banning usury, denying Jews safe conduct on the roads, and encouraging them to become agricultural labourers. He followed it with a tract that was even more violent and contains a gut-level anti-Semitism that comes from a physical revulsion, as Luther describes the sculptural relief that was affixed to the city church of Wittenberg where he preached (and which is still there today). It shows a 'Jewish sow', with Jews suckling from it, while a rabbi looks into its hindquarters in search of true doctrine. The meandering treatise has none of the superficial logic of argument that is evident in 'On the Jews and their Lies' and is highly emotional, describing vomit, excrement, and bodily dissolution in a phantasmagoric orgy of rhetorical excess. Yet it was this tract which headed up the reprinting of his treatises on the Jews in the first centenary anniversary in 1617. Nor was all this just rhetoric: in 1543, a Wittenberg civic mandate banned the Jews and offered half of any confiscated goods to anyone who turned in a Jew to the nearest electoral official, and it explicitly referred to the recent writings of Dr Martin Luther as justification.

The same kind of visceral anti-Semitism emerges in the final letters he wrote to his wife, as he passed through a village where many Jews lived: you would say, he wrote to her, that their breath caused my illness. Luther's anti-Semitism was not unusual, though its physicality was. But it did not stop at personal prejudice—Luther devoted his last energies to persuading the German princes to exile the Jews altogether.

JUDENSAU, WITTENBERG. This anti-Semitic sculpture can still be seen on the outside of the city church in Wittenberg. It shows a rabbi looking for true doctrine in the backside of a pig. The sow suckles the Jews beneath it.

WOODCUT OF THE SCULPTURE ON THE WITTENBERG CITY CHURCH, 1596. Here, the details of the image can be seen more clearly.

Attached to his final four sermons in Eisleben was a special admonition against the Jews, who, he alleged, know the art of poisoning someone so that they die in an hour, a month, a year, or ten or twenty years later. If they do not convert, he went on, be assured they are evil people who will never stop blaspheming against Christ, who will suck you dry, and if they can, kill you—and if you protect them, you share in their sin. Though these sermons dealt briefly with Turks, Jews, and heathens, it was the Jews about whom he was really concerned.

Luther's Death and Legacy

Just how contested Luther remained was evident when he died, ironically on a mission to his birthplace of Eisleben. To the last, Luther remained a public figure, the progress of his death watched by a circle of supporters, doctors, and minor nobility. Two artists painted his body shortly after death, and a death mask and masks of his hands were taken, which are still kept on display in the church in Halle through which the funeral cortege passed. How Luther died mattered, because there was no longer a sacrament of extreme unction. As Luther himself at some level believed, a 'good death' showed that one was saved; a bad sudden death might show that one was bound for Hell. A lengthy description of Luther's death was rushed into print, with moment-by-moment accounts by those who witnessed his passing.

The funeral saw an outpouring of grief, as the procession wound its way from Eisleben all the way back to Wittenberg, the body displayed in leading Lutheran churches along the route. There the funeral sermon was given by Johannes Bugenhagen, and Melanchthon honoured Luther's memory in an oration. There was a flood of commemorative images of Luther, adopting the visual forms that had now become familiar in depictions of the reformer. These were very different from the propaganda that had characterized the early years of the Reformation, reflecting how the movement had changed. It was Cranach and his workshop who made Luther's image iconic. The reformer's face, with his wayward curl of hair on his forehead, his piercing eyes, and heavy jowls, became instantly recognizable—so standardized was the image that the workshop even had traceable designs. So in one such image, produced five years after Luther's death, as the Reformation movement was engulfed in war, the Cranach workshop showed a huge close-up of the reformer, his craggy face seeming almost to weep. There is no halo and, though idealized, it is not an image of a saint—it is a portrayal of a man who radiates authority and personality, a figure with whom the believer can have a relationship. It is also a much more confessional image, produced for people who are already believers, and it was designed for an evangelical movement that was shattering into its different parts.

Luther's authority was conveyed even more powerfully in the monumental Luthers that had become part of how Lutheranism represented itself. These showed a gigantic Luther, his feet four square on the ground, his girth broad, a solid presence very unlike the thin, ascetic saints, whose cadaverous bodies demonstrated their immunity from the temptations of the flesh. In one iconic image produced by the Cranach workshop, a hefty Luther is balanced by an equally weighty Saxon Elector, on either side of a crucifix; this image prefaced the first volumes of Luther's collected works, authorizing them.

For both those who loved and those who hated Luther, there was no denying that he was a towering figure, whose biography mattered. After Luther's death, the movement split between Luther loyalists and those who followed a more moderate Melanchthonian line. The eulogies and funeral sermons began to create a recognized narrative of Luther's life, a process which had begun when Luther himself gave a brief account of his life in the prefaces to the Latin and the German editions of his work. It

D. Martinus Luther.

LUCAS CRANACH THE YOUNGER, 'Wahr-hafftige Abcontrafactur...', 1551. This portrait of Luther, produced after his death, is an idealized image, one of a flood of images of the reformer. His features are immediately recognizable.

took some years, however, before the first biographies were written. First to appear was an anti-biography, penned by Johannes Cochlaeus, Luther's dogged Catholic opponent: it was a brilliant excoriation. And yet in many ways it is an acute portrait of the reformer, by a man who was so obsessed with him that he tried to refute his every heresy—after a time, Luther did not deign even to reply to the many pamphlets he produced. Ludwig Rabus produced an illustrated history of Luther which appeared as a volume in his massive series of Martyrs of the Christian Church, his attempt to provide the new Church with its own tradition, based largely on excerpts from contemporary source material. Johannes Mathesius and Cyriacus Spangenberg published lives of Luther in the same year, 1562, both of which began as series of sermons. They are interesting forerunners to the genre of biography, but these sprawling epics lack an overall narrative structure, eschewing a life story for homilies based on Luther's life. Around the same time, collections of Luther's letters and even of his conversation at dinner, the famous Table Talk, began to appear, and these also served to present Luther's character, warts and all. Indeed, to a remarkable degree, being a

MARTIN LUTHER by the workshop of Lucas Cranach the Younger, c.1560. This huge woodcut portrait measures 1395 mm × 775 mm and it is assembled out of eleven parts. Luther's head could be substituted by other reformers, or you could create a gallery of reformers with matching multi-part woodcuts of other Reformation heroes. Paintings in the same style, nearly life size and using the same iconography, were also produced. Sometimes a near life-size painting of a local reformer would be twinned with a matching portrait of Luther.

Lutheran began to mean engaging with the personality of Luther himself, knowing about him and his private life, and being acquainted with what he looked like. A rich material culture developed around Lutheranism, with glass windows, small medals, tooled leather bindings, and even clay tiles featuring his image; and just about every Lutheran church featuring a portrait of the reformer. Luther himself and his image shaped the emerging Church, for good and ill—the splits after his death had been prefigured in the acrimonious divisions amongst his acolytes during his lifetime, which Luther himself often added to.

The fascination with Luther's life has had an important afterlife in the history of psychology too. Luther has proved irresistible to biographers, including Erich Fromm, Norman O. Brown, Lucien Febvre, and Erik Erikson, whose studies are amongst the classics of psychoanalytically influenced thinking (even if negatively so in the case of Febvre). Erikson's *Young Man Luther* took Luther as a key case of an adolescent

MARTIN LUTHER, by Lucas Cranach the Younger, oil on lime wood, 216 × 94 cm, 1575. Larger than life size, Luther literally towers over the viewer in this late portrait by Cranach's son. In a matching image, Georg III of Anhalt is depicted in the same style, aligning him with the famous reformer.

finding his own identity in rebellion against a tyrannical father. A brilliant study, by a man who understood from the inside the complexities of paternal relationships and was finely attuned to Luther's unconscious, it was also written with the experience of someone from the old world of Europe who was conveying the meaning of Luther to a post-Holocaust America. Along with Fromm and Brown, it pioneered the use of psychoanalytic thinking in writing biography.

Luther remains a paradoxical figure. He is the man whose audacious flouting of Catholic authority made him a symbol of rebellion—and yet who also insisted on obedience to established political authority. An expert propagandist, he used the new medium of print to reach out to new audiences in ways that had not been imagined before—and yet he ended up as the centre of a commemorative cult that was too closely based around himself to appeal to those who were not already Lutheran. He argued that all Christians were 'priests' and that humans had no need of mediators between themselves and God—but he soon affirmed the power of the university-

FREDERICK THE WISE (1463–1525) WITH MARTIN LUTHER. This image from the 1546 edition of Luther's New Testament, published by Han Lufft, was also used in several volumes of Luther's collected German works. Note how, in an intimate detail, Christ's loincloth touches the two figures.

trained pastorate, restoring 'bishops' (called 'superintendents') and using personal networks to establish control of the Church. Politically, he had the brilliance to realize that ecclesiastical matters could be reformed by appealing to secular powers, bypassing the bureaucracy of the Church—but he repeatedly overrated his own political shrewdness, becoming sucked into the morass of Philip of Hesse's bigamy, and making cack-handed moralist interventions against princes he had no need to offend. In the theological realm, Luther brought body, mind, and soul together. For him it was axiomatic that the eucharistic bread remained bread *and* that it was really Christ, at

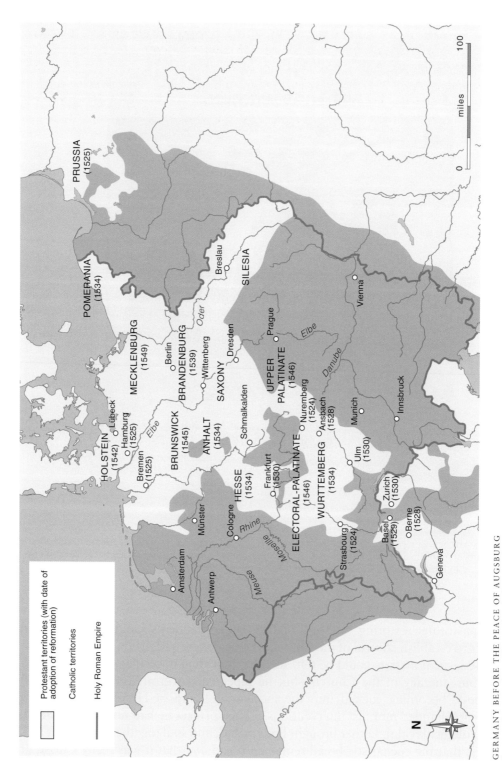

PROTESTANT territories (with date of adoption of reformation)

Catholic territories

—— Holy Roman Empire

PRUSSIA (1525)

POMERANIA (1534)

HOLSTEIN (1542)
Lübeck
Hamburg (1525)
Bremen (1525)

MECKLENBURG (1549)

Berlin
BRANDENBURG (1539)

Breslau

SILESIA

Wittenberg
Dresden
SAXONY

Prague

Elbe

UPPER PALATINATE (1546)

Oder

BRUNSWICK (1545)

ANHALT (1534)

Schmalkalden

Vienna

Danube

Nuremberg (1524)
Ansbach (1528)

Innsbruck

Münster

Cologne

HESSE (1534)

Frankfurt (1530)

ELECTORAL-PALATINATE (1546)

Munich

Ulm (1530)

WÜRTTEMBERG (1534)

Amsterdam

Antwerp

Meuse

Moselle

Rhine

Elbe

Strasbourg (1524)

Zürich (1530)

Basel (1529)

Berne (1528)

Geneva

N

0   100
miles

GERMANY BEFORE THE PEACE OF AUGSBURG

Source: Internet http://hemed.univ-lemans.fr/cours2011/en/co/grain3_4_2.html.

one and the same time. Yet in other areas of life he was a 'splitter': passionately dividing people into friends and enemies. He brought the vernacular into religion, translating the Bible into a German that would resonate for centuries, shaping the German language itself. His radical Augustinianism might look to the modern reader like a gloomy insistence on the utter evil of human nature—and yet it freed him to reject clerical celibacy and celebrate human physicality.

3 Calvinism and the Reform of the Reformation

CARLOS EIRE

'OUR spirit has nothing in common with your spirit.' So said Martin Luther to the Swiss and south German reformers who had come to the Marburg Colloquy in 1529. He was exaggerating, of course. Lutherans had much in common with those other Protestants to the south. But Luther was not wrong either. Those he dismissed as 'others' at that highly charged conference did have a very different take on religion and on what the Reformation should be, and eventually they would come to be known as 'Reformed' Protestants, or simply 'The Reformed'. It was a name generated from within by these non-Lutherans, a self-conscious assertion of the fact that—as they saw it—Luther and his followers had not really reformed much and the Anabaptists had only made things worse: it was a name as anti-Lutheran as it was anti-Catholic and anti-Anabaptist, a way of boasting that they were the only genuine reformers.

Eventually, a new and vigorous branch of this Reformed tradition would arise under the leadership of John Calvin, a French exile. Like their Swiss forebears, Calvin and his followers believed that they were carrying out the purest of all Reformations, nothing less than a reform of the Reformation. Eventually, these newcomers would achieve so much that the term 'Calvinism' became synonymous with 'Reformed Protestantism', much to the chagrin of their Swiss brethren. To fully understand how and why this happened, and what difference it made, one must first trace the genealogy of Calvinism back to its Swiss origins.

Before Calvin

Establishing pure worship and turning citizens into good Christians were the two principal aims of the Swiss reformers, and a key difference between them and the Lutherans up north. Whereas Luther deepened his paradoxical approach to 'good works' and to the relationship between Church and State after 1525, Ulrich Zwingli and his associates in Switzerland and south Germany became wholly committed to building communities in which 'good works' and obedience to the Ten Commandments were stressed, and in which both Church and State joined forces to ensure pure worship and good behaviour. In other words, whereas Luther stressed the pervasiveness of sin and the enduring corruption of the world, the Swiss insisted on the avoidance of sin and the perfectibility of the community. And while Luther spoke of the Kingdom of Christ in apocalyptic terms, and complained that Christian princes were rare birds, the Swiss insisted on having good Christian rulers, and states that endeavoured to build the Kingdom of Christ on earth, here and now. As if these differences were not enough, while Luther reformed rituals and symbols cautiously, and continued to believe in the Real Presence of Christ in the Eucharist, the Swiss revamped worship from top to bottom, rejecting belief in all material points of contact with the divine as 'idolatry', following Zwingli's pronouncement, 'finitum non est capax infiniti', the finite cannot convey the infinite.

Zwingli's Zurich has earned a reputation as a theocracy, that is, a state in which ultimate authority is held by those who represent God. In the case of Zurich and of the other Swiss states that followed its lead, theocratic government did not necessarily mean rule by the clergy, but rather by civil authorities who upheld divine law. Working hand in hand with the city council of Zurich, Zwingli and his clergy helped to create a Reformed community in which Church and State cooperated with one another and corrected one another, without either claiming supremacy. In such a community, all civil laws were ostensibly in accordance with the Bible, and the civil authorities had the power to enforce all discipline. The clergy had a role to play too, beyond their ritual functions. This paradigm would become the hallmark of the Swiss Reformation and of the Reformed tradition as it spread throughout the northern Alpine regions and beyond. In nearly every place where it finally took hold, it was at first a goal rather than an instant realization: a guiding plan with strategies for overcoming the resistance that was always there, everywhere, and for waging war against idolatry.

Eventually, this paradigm would take hold of hearts and minds near and far, spreading like a wildfire across the map: to Germany, France, the Netherlands, England, Scotland, Hungary, Poland, and even America. And one person usually gets most of the credit for this phenomenal expansion: John Calvin.

Calvinism in the Making

When Luther posted his Ninety-Five Theses in 1517, John Calvin was only 8 years old. Needless to say, he and his generation experienced the disintegration of medieval Catholicism in a different way from Luther's. Born in Noyon, in Picardy, on 10 July 1509, this boy then known as Jean Cauvin embodied the ecclesiastical corruption that all church reformers struggled against at that time. His father Gerard Cauvin, a lay administrator for the local bishop, secured him a chaplaincy at the cathedral of Noyon at the age of 12, long before he could even begin to prepare for the priesthood. As was customary, the boy Cauvin collected the income from this sinecure, pocketed the lion's share, and used the remainder to hire some priest who would perform his duties for him. Six years later, his father Gerard was able to trade that benefice for a more

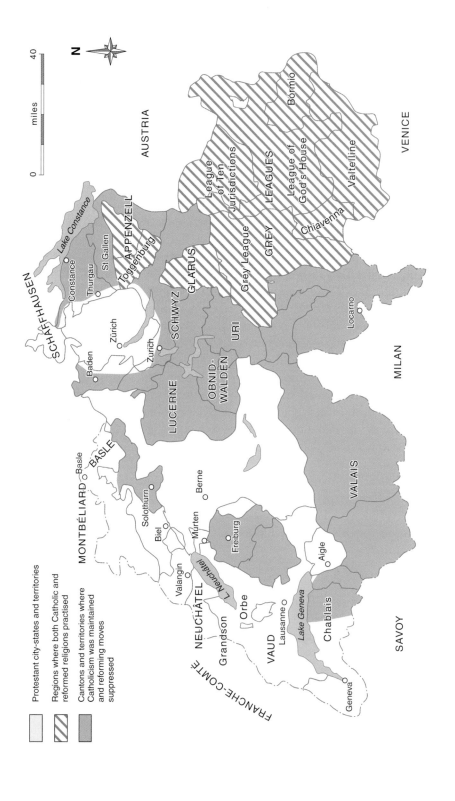

THE SWISS CONFEDERATION AT THE TIME OF CALVIN
Source: Euan Cameron, *The European Reformation* (OUP, 2nd edn, 2012), p. 223.

Protestant city-states and territories

Regions where both Catholic and reformed religions practised

Cantons and territories where Catholicism was maintained and reforming moves suppressed

N

0   40
miles

SCHAFFHAUSEN

AUSTRIA

Lake Constance

APPENZELL

Constance

Thurgau

St Gallen

Toggenburg

Zürich

Zurich

SCHWYZ

GLARUS

League of Ten Jurisdictions

Grey League

GREY LEAGUES

League of God's House

Chiavenna

Valtelline

Bormio

VENICE

Baden

URI

OBNID-WALDEN

LUCERNE

Locarno

MILAN

BASLE

Basle

MONTBÉLIARD

Solothurn

Biel

Murten

Berne

Freiburg

VALAIS

Aigle

SAVOY

Valangin

NEUCHÂTEL

L. Neuchâtel

Orbe

VAUD

Lausanne

Lake Geneva

Chablais

Grandson

FRANCHE-COMTÉ

Geneva

LESS IS MORE. Pieter Janzoon Saenredam, *Interior of St Bavo, Haarlem*, 1628. Dutch Calvinists stripped their medieval churches down to the bone, removing all traces of 'idolatry'. Saenredam was only one of several Dutch painters who celebrated the stark aesthetics of 'purified' church.

lucrative one, and 18–year-old Jean Cauvin became the absentee curate of Marteville, a village near Noyon. It would not be until May 1534, after he had already finished his studies and turned Protestant, that Calvin would resign the post wangled by his father. By then, ironically, his education had provided him with all the tools he would need to wage war against the Catholic Church and reform the Protestant Reformation.

Calvin was very tight-lipped about his early years, so we know little about that period of his life. But we do know that his mother was pious, and that he was constantly exposed to Catholic piety. Years after he left Noyon, writing as a Protestant reformer who despised his idolatrous upbringing, Calvin could not speak about his Catholic past with detachment. In one of his most popular treatises, *The Inventory of Relics*, he heaped scorn on the religion of his mother and fellow townspeople:

I remember what I saw them do to idols in our parish when I was a small boy. On the eve of the feast of St. Stephen, they would adorn all the images with garlands and necklaces, those of the murderers who stoned him to death (or 'tyrants' as they were commonly known), in the same fashion as the martyr. When the poor women saw the murderers decked out in this way, they mistook them for Stephen's companions, and offered each of them his own candle. Even worse, they did the same with the devil who struggled against St. Michael.

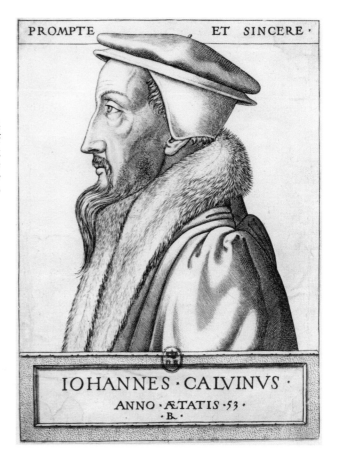

PROMPTE ET SINCERE·

IOHANNES·CALVINVS·
ANNO·ÆTATIS·53·
·B·

AN ICON FOR ICONOCLASTS. René Boyvin, portrait of Calvin at the age of 53, two years before his death, featuring the two key words from his signature motto: *cor meum tibi offero domine prompte et sincere* (my heart I offer to you Lord promptly and sincerely).

It was precisely this kind of condescending observation of Catholics as the 'other'—as primitives of sorts vastly different from himself—that would allow Calvin to formulate a theory of the origins of 'false' religion and of the difference between such falsehood and the 'true' religion he believed he was defending. And it was this detachment, this ability to think of Catholics as pitiable 'others', that made Calvin an inveterate enemy of idolatry and of those who practised it.

In 1523, at the age of 14, Calvin began to train for the priesthood at the University of Paris, but in 1527 his father asked him to change course and take up a legal career instead. Ever the dutiful son, he went straight into law school, first at Orléans, and then at Bourges. However, in May of 1531, when his father died, Calvin switched career tracks again and returned to Paris, to immerse himself in the study of Classical culture.

Back in Paris, he enrolled in the prestigious Collège Royal, newly established by King Francis I, where he morphed from Jean Cauvin to 'Calvinus', as befitted an up-and-coming humanist scholar. Immersing himself in ancient texts and the study of Latin, Greek, and Hebrew, Calvin was also exposed at this time to the work of

Erasmus and Jacques Lefèvre d'Étaples—and to their critiques of Catholic piety—as well as to streams of Reformed Protestant influence flowing in from Switzerland through some of Lefèvre's disciples. Calvin's conversion took place sometime during this period, thanks to these contacts and to reform-minded friends such as Nicholas Cop, a physician and Protestant sympathizer who was appointed rector of the University of Paris. We know this because in December 1533, after Cop preached a sermon thoroughly laced with Protestant sentiments, Calvin fled Paris in a hurry, fearing he would be identified as someone who moved in heretical circles.

Calvin went into hiding for the next few months, but surfaced again in May 1534, in his native Noyon, to resign his benefice and shake the dust from his feet. Five months later, he had to flee France once again when the first large-scale persecution of Protestants was launched by King Francis I, in response to the so-called Affair of the Placards. On Sunday morning, 18 October 1534, residents of Paris, Blois, Rouen, Tours, and Orléans had awakened to find posters plastered throughout their cities that condemned 'the gross, horrible, and unsupportable doctrine of the Popish mass'. Among other things, these placards printed in Switzerland said:

The Pope and all his vermin of cardinals, bishops, and priests, monks and other sanctimonious Mass-sayers and all those who agree with them are false prophets, damned cheats, apostates, wolves, false pastors, idolaters, seducers, liars and wretched blasphemers, killers of souls, renouncers of Christ, of His death and passion, perjurers, traitors, thieves, rapers of God's honour and more detestable than devils.

Astonished to discover that the 'heretics' had been bold enough to post a placard inside his bedchamber while he slept, King Francis called for the immediate punishment of those guilty of such sacrilege. Scores of Protestants were rounded up and burned alive. Though few suspected it at the time, France's inexorable descent into a religious civil war had just begun in earnest, and so had Calvin's unlikely rise to prominence.

The Marrow of Calvinism

Calvin found refuge in Basel, Switzerland, but France and the plight of his brethren remained foremost in his mind. Putting all of his training and talents to use, he wrote a summary of the Reformed Protestant faith, intended for the education of the faithful and also as an *apologia*, or defence, of their cause. This was the first version of his most influential masterpiece, *The Institutes of the Christian Religion*, which he would revise and expand several times between 1536 and 1559, gradually quadrupling its size. And he would write each of these later editions in both Latin and French, making the text accessible to the learned throughout Europe and to his brethren in France. Immediately after its publication in early 1536, Calvin's *Institutes* began to win him acclaim, and for good reason. Hailed as the most orderly and eloquent presentation of Reformed Protestant theology and ethics anyone had ever written, Calvin's text was blessed with a lawyer's penchant for precision, a humanist's love for poetic expression

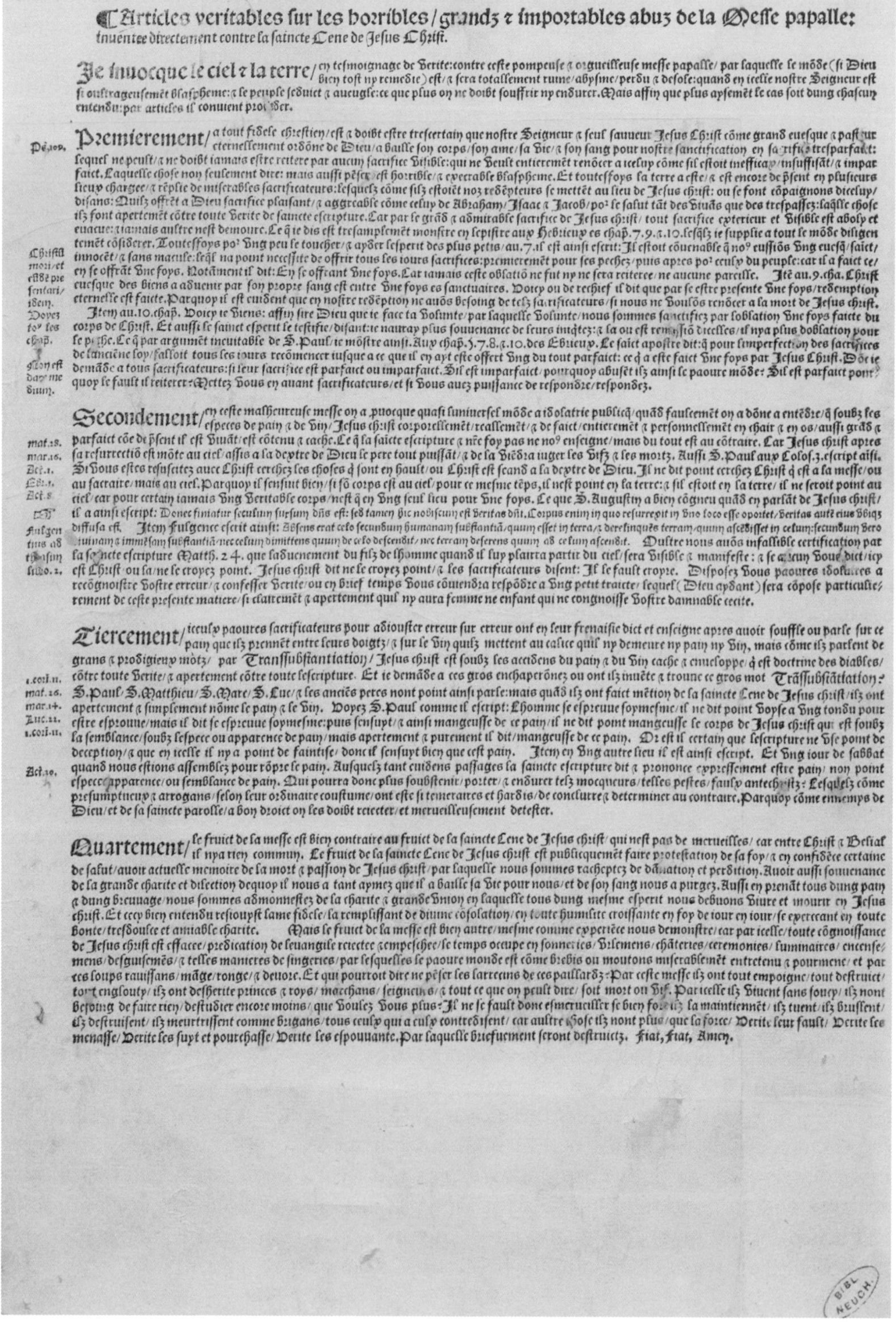

¶ Articles veritables sur les horribles / grandz & importables abuz de la Messe papalle: inuentee directement contre la saincte Cene de Jesus Christ.

Je inuocque le ciel & la terre / en tesmoignage de verite: contre ceste pompeuse & orgueilleuse messe papalle / par laquelle le monde (si Dieu bien tost ny remedie) est / & sera totallement ruine / abysme / perdu & desole: quand en icelle nostre Seigneur est si oultrageusement blaspheme: & le peuple seduict & aueugle: ce que plus on ne doibt souffrir ny endurer. Mais affin que plus aysement le cas soit dung chascun entendu: par articles il conuient proceder.

Premierement / a tout fidele chrestien / est & doibt estre tresertain que nostre Seigneur & seul sauueur Jesus Christ comme grand euesque & pasteur eternellement ordonne de Dieu / a baille son corps / son ame / sa vie / & son sang pour nostre sanctification en sacrifice tresparfaict: lequel ne peult / & ne doibt iamais estre reitere par aucun sacrifice visible: qui ne veult entierement renoncer a icelluy comme sil estoit inefficace / insuffisant / & imparfaict. Laquelle chose non seulement dire: mais aussi penser est horrible / & execrable blaspheme. Et toutesfoys la terre a este / & est encore de present en plusieurs lieux chargee / & replie de miserables sacrificateurs: lesquelz comme silz estoient noz redempteurs se mettet au lieu de Jesus christ: ou se font compaignons dicelluy / disans: quilz offrent a Dieu sacrifice plaisant / & aggreable comme celluy de Abraham / Isaac & Jacob / pour le salut tant des viuans que des trespassez: laquelle chose ilz font apertement contre toute verite de saincte escripture. Car par le grand & admirable sacrifice de Jesus christ / tout sacrifice exterieur et visible est aboly et euacue: & iamais aultre nest demoure. Ce que ie dis est tresamplement monstre en lepistre aux Hebrieux es chap. 7. 9. & 10. lesquelz ie supplie a tout le monde diligentement considerer. Toutesfoys pour vng peu le toucher / & ayder lesperit des plus petis / au. 7. il est ainsi escrit: Il estoit conuenable que nous eussions vng euesque saint / innocent / & sans macule: lequel na point necessite de offrir tous les iours sacrifices: premierement pour ses pechez / puis apres pour ceulx du peuple: car il a faict cela en se offrant vne foys. Notamment il dit: En se offrant vne foys. Car iamais ceste oblation ne fut ny ne sera reiteree / ne aucune pareille. Item au. 9. cha. Christ euesque des biens a aduenir par son propre sang est entre vne foys es sanctuaires. Voicy ou de rechief il dit que par le estre presente vne foys / redemption eternelle est faicte. Parquoy il est euident que en nostre redemption ne auons besoing de telz sacrificateurs / si nous ne voulons renoncer a la mort de Jesus christ. Item au. 10. chap. Voicy te viens: affin sire Dieu que ie face ta volunte / par laquelle volunte / nous sommes sanctifiez par loblation vne foys faicte du corps de Christ. Et aussi le sainct esperit le testifie / disant: ie nauray plus souuenance de leurs iniquitez: & la ou est remission dicelles / il nya plus doblation pour le peche. Ce que par argument ineuitable de S. Paul / ie monstre ainsi. Aux chap. 5. 7. 8. & 10. des Ebrieux. Le saint apostre dit: que pour limperfection des sacrifices de lancienne loy / falloit tous les iours recommencer iusque a ce quil en ayt este offert vng du tout parfaict: ce que a este faict vne foys par Jesus Christ. Donc ie demande a tous sacrificateurs: si leur sacrifice est parfaict ou imparfaict. Sil est imparfaict / pourquoy abusent ilz ainsi le paoure monde? Sil est parfaict pourquoy le fault il reiterer? Mettez vous en auant sacrificateurs / et si vous auez puissance de respondre / respondez.

Secondement / en ceste malheureuse messe on a prouocque quasi luniuersel monde a idolatrie publicque / quand faulcement on a donne a entendre / que soubz les especes de pain & de vin / Jesus christ corporellement / reallement / & de faict / entierement & personnellement en chair & en os / aussi grand & parfaict come de present il est viuant / est contenu & cache. Ce que la saincte escripture & nostre foy pas ne nous enseigne / mais du tout est au contraire. Car Jesus christ apres sa resurrection est monte au ciel / assis a la dextre de Dieu le pere tout puissant / & de la viendra iuger les vifz & les mortz. Aussi S. Paul aux Colos. 3. escript ainsi. Si vous estes resuscitez auec Christ cerchez les choses qui sont en hault / ou Christ est seand a la dextre de Dieu. Il ne dit point cerchez Christ qui est a la messe / ou au sacraire / mais au ciel. Parquoy il sensuit bien / si son corps est au ciel / pour ce mesme temps, il nest point en la terre: & sil estoit en la terre / il ne seroit point au ciel / car pour certain iamais vng veritable corps / nest que en vng seul lieu pour vne foys. Ce que S. Augustin a bien cogneu quand en parlant de Jesus christ / il a ainsi escript: Donec finiatur seculum sursum dns est: sed tamen hic nobiscum est veritas dni. Corpus enim in quo resurrexit in vno loco esse oportet / veritas autem eius vbique diffusa est. Item Fulgence escrit ainsi: Absens erat celo secundum humanam substantiam / quum esset in terra / & derelinquens terram / quum ascendisset in celum: secundum vero diuinam & immensam substantiam / nec celum dimittens quum de celo descendit / nec terram deserens quum ad celum ascendit. Oultre nous auons infallible certification par la saincte escripture Matth. 24. que ladvenement du filz de lhomme quand il luy plaira partir du ciel / sera visible & manifeste: & le aucun vous dict / icy est Christ ou la / ne le croyez point. Jesus christ dit ne le croyez point / & les sacrificateurs disent: Il le fault croyre. Disposez vous paoures idolatres a recognoistre vostre erreur / & confesser verite / ou en brief temps vous conuiendra respondre a vng petit traicte / lequel (Dieu aydant) sera compose particulierement de ceste presente matiere / si clairement & apertement quil ny aura femme ne enfant qui ne congnoisse vostre damnable erreur.

Tiercement / iceulx paoures sacrificateurs pour adiouster erreur sur erreur ont en leur frenaisie dict et enseigne apres auoir souffle ou parle sur ce pain que ilz prennent entre leurs doigtz / & sur le vin quilz mettent au calice quil ny demeure ny pain ny vin, mais comme ilz parlent de grans & prodigieux motz / par Transsubstantiation / Jesus christ est soubz les accidens du pain & du vin cache & enueloppe / qui est doctrine des diables / contre toute verite / & apertement contre toute lescripture. Et ie demande a ces gros enchaperonez ou ont ilz inuente & trouue ce gros mot Transsubstantiation? S. Paul / S. Matthieu / S. Marc / S. Luc / & les anciens peres nont point ainsi parle: mais quand ilz ont faict mention de la saincte Cene de Jesus christ / ilz ont apertement & simplement nomme le pain & le vin. Voyez S. Paul comme il escript: Lhomme se espreuue soymesme / il ne dit point voyse a vng tondu pour estre esprouue / mais il dit se esprouue soymesme: puis lensuyt / & ainsi mangeusse de ce pain / il ne dit point mangeusse le corps de Jesus christ qui est soubz la semblance / soubz lespece ou apparence de pain / mais apertement & purement il dit / mangeusse de ce pain. Or il est certain que lescripture ne vse point de deception / & que en icelle il ny a point de faintise / donc il sensuyt bien que cest pain. Item en vng autre lieu il est ainsi escript. Et vng iour de sabbat quand nous estions assemblez pour rompre le pain. Ausquelz tant euidens passages la saincte escripture dit & prononce expressement estre pain / non point espece / apparence / ou semblance de pain. Qui pourra donc plus soubstenir / porter / & endurer telz mocqueurs / telles pestes / faulx antechristz: Lesquelz comme presumptueux & arrogans / selon leur ordinaire coustume / ont este si temeraires et hardis / de conclurre & determiner au contraire. Parquoy comme ennemys de Dieu / et de sa saincte parolle / a bon droict on les doibt reiecter / et merueilleusement detester.

Quartement / le fruict de la messe est bien contraire au fruict de la saincte Cene de Jesus christ / qui nest pas de merueilles / car entre Christ & Belial il nya rien commun. Le fruict de la saincte Cene de Jesus christ est publicquement faire protestation de sa foy / & en confidence certaine de salut / auoir actuelle memoire de la mort & passion de Jesus christ / par laquelle nous sommes rachaptez de damnation et perdition. Auoir aussi souuenance de la grande charite et dilection dequoy il nous a tant aymez que il a baille sa vie pour nous / et de son sang nous a purgez. Aussi en prenant tous dung pain & dung breuuage / nous sommes admonnestez de la charite & grande vnion en laquelle tous dung mesme esperit nous debuons viure et mourir en Jesus christ. Et cecy bien entendu resiouyst lame fidele / la remplissant de diuine consolation / en toute humilite croissante en foy de iour en iour / se exercant en toute bonte / tresdoulce et amiable charite. Mais le fruict de la messe est bien autre / mesme comme experience nous demonstre / car par icelle / toute congnoissance de Jesus christ est effacee / predication de leuangile reiectee / & empeschee / le temps occupe en sonneries / hurlemens / chanteries / ceremonies / luminaires / encensemens / desguisemens / & telles manieres de singeries / par lesquelles le paoure monde est comme brebis ou moutons miserablement entretenu & pourmene / et par ces loups rauissans / mange / ronge / & deuore. Et qui pourroit dire ne penser les larrecins de ces paillardz? Par ceste messe ilz ont tout empoigne / tout destruict / tout englouty / ilz ont desherite princes & royz / marchans / seigneurs / & tout ce que on peult dire / soit mort ou vif. Par icelle ilz viuent sans soucy / ilz nont besoing de faire rien / destudier encore moins / que voulez vous plus? Il ne se fault donc esmerueiller se bien fort ilz la maintiennent / ilz tuent / ilz bruslent / ilz destruisent / ilz meurtrissent comme brigans tous ceulx qui a eulx contredisent / car aultre chose ilz nont plus / que la force / Verite leur fault / Verite les menasse / Verite les suyt et pourchasse / Verite les espouuante. Par laquelle briefuement seront destruictz. Fiat, Fiat, Amen.

SHEETS OF WRATH. Antoine Marcourt, *Articles veritables sur les horribles grandz et importables abuz de la Messe papalle* (Neuchâtel, 1534). One of the placards posted throughout France in October 1534, printed by Pierre Vingle in Neuchâtel, Switzerland. The text condemns the Catholic mass as idolatrous.

and rhetorical flourishes, and a theologian's respect for paradox. Most importantly, for a people bent on following the scriptures alone, the *Institutes* aimed to complement rather than supplant the Bible. Calvin's goal, in his own words, was to prepare readers for their encounter with the divine Word 'in order that they may be able both to have easy access to it and to advance in it without stumbling'.

The 1536 *Institutes* also included a preface dedicated to King Francis I, which distilled the very essence of Calvin's political theology. In it, Calvin spoke to the monarch directly, to convince him—ostensibly—that the so-called 'Lutherans' he was persecuting were actually the best subjects he could hope for, not at all some seditious cabal, but rather 'an example of chastity, generosity, mercy, continence, patience, modesty, and all other virtues'. But this preface was not merely a brief for the defence, or even directly aimed at the king. Employing all the deference one might expect in a letter to a monarch, but subverting it at the same time, Calvin assumed the role of prophet, preacher, and teacher, not just to the king but to all of France. With consummate skill, Calvin issued a direct yet subtly veiled threat to the king, warning Francis that if he were to continue on the same path, persecuting the godly with 'with imprisonings, scourgings, rackings, maimings, and burnings', then he should ready himself for 'the strong hand of the Lord, which will surely appear in due season, coming forth armed to deliver the poor from their affliction and also to punish their despisers, who now exult with such great assurance'. Summarizing what was at stake, Calvin distilled the message of the Reformed Protestant cause, and the core of his theology, into a tightly packed sentence:

It will then be for you, most serene King, not to close your ears ... especially when a very great question is at stake: how God's glory may be kept safe on earth, how God's truth may retain its place of honour, how Christ's Kingdom may be kept in good repair among us.

Here, neatly condensed, we find the gist of what came to be known as Calvinism: a theologically based political ideology that would brook no compromise with sin, or 'idolatry' and false religion. Reduced to a single formula, this would become the Calvinist battle cry: *Soli Deo Gloria*, 'Glory to God alone.' Calvin's concept of the glory of God and of the honour due to him was derived from Zwingli, but Calvin developed it further, for a flock under the constant threat of extinction, devising a political theology that encouraged active restraint of sinfulness along with passive resistance to 'false' religion and 'idolatry'. Most significantly, Calvin argued that Christians owed their ultimate allegiance to God alone, above all earthly rulers, and especially above earthly rulers who sullied God's glory in any way, whether through laxity or outright affront. In many ways, Calvin revived the jealous God of the Old Testament. Reward and punishment were essential to God's relationship with his people: Calvin's God demanded his proper glory, along with obedience, rewarding those who gave him his due and punishing those who dared not to. This is why Calvinists could seek the total transformation of society into the Kingdom of Christ so passionately, and why they could insist that the civil sphere exclude 'false' religion and be kept 'in good repair'. So, while trying to convince Francis that the evangelicals were obedient, virtuous, model citizens, Calvin delivered a mixed message that contained a serious challenge to any ruler's authority.

That king who in ruling over his realm does not serve God's glory exercises not kingly rule but brigandage. Furthermore, he is deceived who looks for enduring prosperity in his kingdom when it is not ruled by God's sceptre, that is, his Holy Word.

The 1536 *Institutes* also laid out in kernel form two other key distinguishing features of Calvin's theology and of Calvinism in general: belief in the thorough corruption of human nature by original sin, and belief in election and predestination.

   Calvin's theological anthropology was derived from that of St Augustine of Hippo. Like Augustine, Calvin taught that all human beings are deeply warped by the curse of original sin and are thus powerless to overcome their evil inclinations without the aid of God's grace. As Calvin saw it, this corruption made strict social controls and a church an absolute necessity, for all sorts of sins and crimes were an ever-present likelihood in all human communities, and churches were the only conduit to divine grace. Even worse, human depravity was also the source of all false religion, the ultimate insult to God's glory. Espousing a binary concept of religion, as either 'true' or 'false', Calvin argued that false religion was a mere human invention, always focused on the flesh and the material world. In contrast, true religion—which could only be found in the Bible—was derived straight from God, and therefore genuinely spiritual and supernatural. Calvin's binary understanding of religion might have been very traditional, and in keeping with the central message of the Protestant Reformation, but his conception of the origin of false religion was strikingly modern. Whereas most of the ancient and medieval theologians, and even other reformers, had ascribed the creation of false religion to the Devil and to demonic deception, Calvin shifted the blame directly to human beings. False religion was not demonic, therefore, but pure fiction, a twisted projection of human hopes and fears; idolatry was not just the ultimate proof of human corruption but also of self-deception.

   Calvin's take on religion was distinctively modern. By reducing false religion to a purely natural, socially constructed figment of the human imagination, and denying that it issued from the demonic realm, Calvin also denied that all ritual, per se, necessarily connects human beings to some numinous dimension. Banning the Devil from the scene heightened human responsibility, too, giving all false religion an illusory feel, and grounding it in the darkest recesses of the human mind and heart. Further daring steps would have to be taken in order to dismiss the true/false dialectic and call religion itself a delusion sprung from the human mind—steps unthinkable to Calvin—but it could be argued that he opened up that steep trail of doubt. Two centuries later, Enlightenment thinkers such as Giambattista Vico, David Hume, and Julien Offray de la Mettrie would follow that same trail to its summit, reaching more radical conclusions.

   Calvin was equally bold concerning predestination. Luther and Zwingli had paved the way towards this belief with their 'faith alone' principle, and their persistent affirmation of salvation as a gift from God that cannot be earned by human effort.

But neither reformer had dealt with this implicit concept of election thoroughly or systematically. Calvin, in contrast, embraced the logical conclusion of *sola fide, sola gratia*, and made God's overwhelming agency the very structure of his systematic theology, passing on to his disciples a firm, strident belief in election and predestination. This principle, already elucidated in the 1536 edition, would be refined by Calvin many times, but never altered. By 1559, in the final edition of the *Institutes*, Calvin would assert, unequivocally:

No one who wishes to be thought religious dares simply deny predestination, by which God adopts some to hope of life, and sentences others to eternal death... For all are not created in an equal condition; rather eternal life is fore-ordained for some, eternal damnation for others.

Paradoxically, instead to leading to fatalism, this doctrine seemed to have the opposite effect. Calvinists, after all, tended to be very driven communities and individuals who thought of themselves as God's elect. Calvin's own take on predestination was overwhelmingly positive. Stressing the fact that every single event, no matter how small, was expressly willed by God, he offered his followers the hope of believing that anything that came their way, no matter how unpleasant, must be God's will, and therefore good. This gave Calvinists immense resolve, especially in the face of adversity.

Yet when that light of divine providence has once shone upon a godly man, he is then relieved and set free... from every care... His solace, I say, is to know that his Heavenly Father so holds all things in his power, so rules by his authority and will, so governs by his wisdom, that nothing can befall except he determine it.

And that was not all. Election was no passive state for Calvin, but above all a social process, carried out through the agency of the elect and their Church. In other words, God did not reach his elect directly from Heaven, mystically, but only through other human beings on earth: through the preaching of the Word, through teaching, through the sacraments, and through the establishment of godly communities. Whether or not predestination was a great 'comfort' to all Calvinists mattered little in the long run: comforted or not, Calvinists tended to behave as the elect, and often attempted the seemingly impossible, as the elect are wont to do.

Building the Kingdom of Christ

Calvin's own life story is one of the best examples of the way in which this mindset could work. Having published his *Institutes* in 1536, he briefly spent some time in northern Italy at the court of Duchess Renee of Ferrara, who surrounded herself with Protestant refugees. Then he resolved to move to Strasbourg, where he thought he could lead a scholar's life in relative tranquillity. But he never got there. An unexpected roadblock forced Calvin to detour through Geneva, a city that had only recently turned Protestant and declared its independence from the dukes of Savoy. At the helm in Geneva, directing a still chaotic Reformation, was none other than Guillaume Farel (1489–1565), a French disciple of Lefèvre who had become a

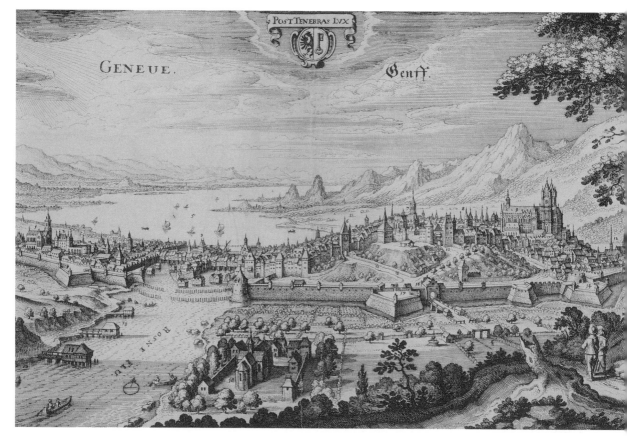

EPICENTRE OF REFORM. Matthias Merian, *View of Geneva*, 1638. A view of Geneva and its impressive fortifications. The 'Protestant Rome' was relatively small, and well aware of its precarious position.

Protestant missionary in French-speaking Switzerland. When Farel learned that the author of the *Institutes* was staying overnight in Geneva, he barged into Calvin's inn and badgered him into staying.

Working closely with Farel, Calvin struggled to bring his vision of Christ's Kingdom to fruition in Geneva, to no avail. Too many Genevans resisted their efforts, and their relations with the civil magistrates were always tense. By May 1538, Farel and Calvin were both expelled from the city for refusing to grant the civil magistrates a say in the process of excommunication. Farel went to nearby Neuchâtel, where he would remain as pastor for many years. Calvin headed straight for his original destination, Strasbourg.

By his own account, the years Calvin spent at Strasbourg, 1538–41, were the happiest of his life. Freed from shepherding an unruly city, Calvin gladly took on the task of ministering to French refugees, and quickly learned to appreciate what made Strasbourg's Reformation unique and so successful an experiment in theocracy.

Calvin also enjoyed the time he spent with Martin Bucer, and learned much from him, including how to find a middle way through the treacherous shoals of eucharistic theology, that most divisive of subjects. Adopting a position about halfway between the Lutheran and Swiss Reformed, Calvin denied the Real Presence of Christ in the Eucharist, but nonetheless affirmed that a real communion with Christ took place, spiritually. This put him at odds with his Swiss brethren, especially those at Bern. On the question of how to reform society, Calvin also owed much to Bucer, whose treatise on Christian political theology, *De Regno Christi* ('On the Kingdom of Christ'), closely parallels Calvin's plan for Geneva.

In 1541, Calvin was invited back to Geneva, after a change in its government. He may have returned reluctantly—'contrary to my desire and inclination', as he put it— but he came back on his own terms. The contract drawn up to secure his return, *The Ecclesiastical Ordinances* of 1541, gave him a greater degree of control than he had enjoyed before, and placed the clergy in a unique position as co-administrators of the city, 'instructing, admonishing, exhorting and reproving, both in public and in private...exercising fraternal correction'. The *Ordinances* gave Geneva a unique political and ecclesiastical structure that would later serve as a blueprint for hundreds of other communities. Asserting that they were derived straight 'from the Gospel of Jesus Christ', the *Ordinances* established four offices in the Genevan Church: pastors, elders, doctors, and deacons. The pastors were in charge of the gospel, and of all discipline, and they selected all candidates for that office, subject to the city council's approval. The doctors, or teachers, instructed the faithful 'in sound doctrine so that the purity of the Gospel is not corrupted either by ignorance or by erroneous belief'. They were to be trained in a *collège*, established in the city for that express purpose. The elders, or presbyters, were men whose office was 'to watch over the life of each person', to admonish all those who were leading 'disorderly' lives, and to report all such delinquents to the pastors. These elders were to be drawn from the various city councils, God-fearing men 'without reproach and beyond all suspicion', representing all quarters of Geneva, 'so that their eyes will be everywhere'. The deacons were given charge of the poor and the sick in Geneva, as stewards of the city's charity. A city hospital was to be established in which medical care would be dispensed to all those who needed it, free of charge if necessary. In addition, begging would be forbidden, and the poor carefully screened, to ensure that only those who truly deserved aid would receive it directly from the deacons.

The Church in Geneva, a city of 10,000, was thoroughly redesigned. First, the number of churches was reduced to three parishes, served by ten pastors. This was a 97.5 per cent reduction in the clerical class: before 1536, Geneva had around 400 clerics. But the numbers alone do not tell the whole story. These ten pastors would be given more power than all of their predecessors ever enjoyed, and they would have to work much harder too. Throughout the week, the three parishes were to offer seventeen sermons, not only on Sunday, but also on Monday, Wednesday, and Friday. Once a month, the Eucharist would be celebrated, and all excommunications strictly enforced. On Sunday at noon, all children had to be brought to their parishes for religious instruction. Attendance at sermons was required of everyone, and so were punctuality and attentiveness. No one was to arrive late, leave early, make noise, or fall asleep. Penalties could be stiff. In 1547, for instance, a parishioner was imprisoned not just for leaving during the sermon, but for not doing it quietly. As if all this were not enough, the clergy were required to visit every parishioner's home twice a year to check up on their morals.

As a capstone to his plan, Calvin established the consistory, a court that would oversee the behaviour of all Genevans, define godly discipline, and impose binding penalties on all those it convicted. The consistory was composed of all of the pastors and one of the city's chief magistrates, along with lay elders elected once a year. Its power was backed by civil law, and it quickly became a formidable and very intrusive institution. Like the Inquisition in Spain and Italy, the consistory relied on informants, and encouraged everyone to report scandalous behaviour. It also kept very detailed records of its cases, and left behind a treasure trove of information for historians to examine. Meeting once a week, nearly always with Calvin present, the consistory handled such a wide range of moral lapses that even a partial listing can seem unduly long: blasphemy, foul language, adultery, fornication, lewdness, quarrelling, gossiping, slandering, showing disrespect for civil and church authorities, not going to church, practising witchcraft or taking part in idolatrous or superstitious rites, and spreading heresy.

Once it was established, the consistory quickly set very high standards, showing little tolerance for misbehaviour, and micromanaging the personal lives of Genevans. Quite often, the consistory was lenient with first-time offenders, and took to admonishing, teaching, and counselling rather than to punishing. This was especially true in cases of marital problems, ranging from loud quarrelling to flagrant adultery. Sometimes the consistory actually advised incompatible couples to divorce. Repeat offenders could expect little leniency, however. Fines and imprisonment on bread and water were common punishments. Banishment from Geneva was reserved for the incorrigible; execution for those convicted of witchcraft, and, at times, also for those who spread heresy. The numbers speak for themselves: between 1541 and 1564, when Calvin served as leader of Geneva's Reformation, 58 people were executed and 76 banished.

The consistory worked on the assumption that it could be the instrument of God's election, reproving sinners, forcing them to find Christ's forgiveness and to mend their ways. It also aimed to make Geneva as pleasing to God and as immune from his wrath as possible. It was a monumentally hard task. Throughout the 1540s, up until 1555, Calvin and his godly elites faced constant opposition from many resentful Genevans, and many of the leaders of this opposition were members of old privileged Genevan families. Among them, the Perrin family was the most prominent. Ironically, Amy Perrin, one of their patriarchs, had been instrumental in bringing Protestantism to Geneva. Calvin took to calling his local opponents 'Libertines', interpreting their love for ancient Genevan customs as unbridled licence. Resistance was both passive and active. Court records provide us with evidence of disputes, riots, and other challenges.

The Libertines—almost always a political minority—were often frustrated. Unable to overturn laws that seemed too strict to them, they simply disobeyed them. And there were a lot of laws to break. Clothing was carefully regulated: all were to dress modestly, shunning loud and expensive fabrics, including velvet and certain kinds of bows, buttons, and lace. Lewd, revealing fashions were strictly forbidden, such as codpieces for men or low-cut dresses for women. Certain hairstyles were declared un-Christian, and so were any banquets or parties with over twenty guests and an 'excessive' number of dishes. Names were carefully regulated too. Genevans were encouraged to give biblical names to their children and forbidden to use 'idolatrous' names linked with local saints' cults, such as Claude and Martin, who had nearby shrines, or names of saints whose existence was unlikely, like Gaspar, Melchior, and Balthazar (the three Wise Men), or 'silly' names such as Dedet, Ayme, Mama, or Pentecost. Enforcement of this law was up to the pastors, who could accept or reject names at the time of baptism. Confrontations between parents and pastors at the baptismal font became endemic: as late as 1552, Calvin reported that a riot had broken out in church when he rejected the name chosen for a child by its parents. Pets were included in all this, too, as one Genevan found out when he was hauled before the consistory for naming his dog 'Calvin'.

Relentless though it was, the imposition of Christian values on the city had its limits. A 1546 law required every inn and tavern to have a French Bible at hand, and to encourage religious conversation and Bible discussions. It seemed like a great idea to the pastors, but, as often happens, the ideals of the clergy proved too lofty for their flock. Admitting that the discussion sessions were a failure, the authorities had to drop that requirement after only three months. But they would not let go of the entire plan: inns and taverns were still required to have a French Bible on hand, for their godly customers. Other rules were designed to prevent contagion from the outside world, too, and innkeepers were placed on the front lines. The rules they were asked to enforce give us a glimpse of Calvinist puritanism at its most extreme:

If anyone blasphemes the name of the God ... or gives himself to the devil or uses ... execrable imprecations, he shall be punished.

If anyone insults anyone else the innkeeper shall deliver him up to justice.

The innkeeper shall be obliged to report ... any insolent or dissolute behaviour committed by the guests.

The innkeeper shall not allow any dissoluteness like dancing, dice, or cards, nor receive anyone suspected of debauchery.

The Innkeeper shall not allow indecent songs.

No one shall be allowed to sit up after nine o'clock at night, except informers.

Calvin's Geneva assumed a siege mentality. Censorship was routine, and applied not just to printed texts, but also to private correspondence. Surrounded as they were on nearly all sides by Catholics, Genevans could be constantly tempted into idolatry at some nearby shrine. Those who entered or left the city were closely watched, and

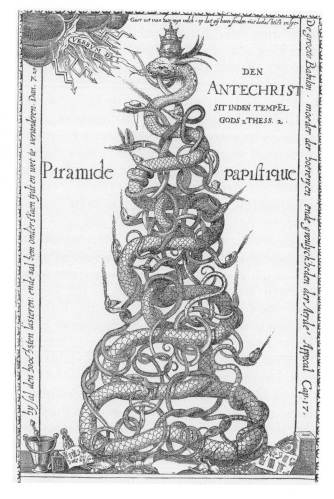

SYMBOLIC DISSONANCE. Hendrik Hondius, *Pyramide papistique*, c.1599. Though opposed to religious imagery, Calvinists sometimes embraced visual propaganda in their struggle against Catholicism. Here, the Catholic hierarchy is depicted as a nest of snakes. The smaller snakes in the bottom and middle parts of the pyramid are the lower clergy, those at the top are identified as higher clergy by their headgear: bishops' birettas and mitres, and cardinals' hats. The large snake around which they all entwine wears the papal crown and is clearly identified as the Antichrist. God's Word flashes forth in lighting bolts at the upper left, striking the pope's forked tongue.

Genevans were encouraged to report all cases of Catholic backsliding to the consistory. And the records of this court reveal that lapses were all too common: visits to shrines, the use of rosaries and Catholic prayers, the invocation of saints, and even the veneration of secretly stashed 'idols' found in homes or brought to the city by visitors. Geneva was far from perfect, but the elect within its walls never stopped trying to make it so. That was what God required of them, according to Calvin.

The Protestant Rome

While taking part in the day-to-day business of Geneva, Calvin continued to write ceaselessly: theological and polemical treatises, biblical commentaries, sermons, and letters—enough output to fill fifty-nine large folio volumes in the modern critical edition. He also kept a close eye on developments in his native France and became deeply involved with its underground network of Protestants, who continued to grow in numbers. Among the most serious problems that Calvin handled among his fellow French Protestants was that of persecution, and of a response to it that came to be known as Nicodemism.

Nicodemites were Protestants or sympathizers who pretended to be good Catholics in order to escape persecution. Many of them argued that their outward behaviour was not a sin or a betrayal of their principles as long as their inner faith was pure. It was a survival tactic that employed a sharp dichotomy between spirit/matter and inner/outer, claiming that what really mattered was inward and spiritual. No one knows for sure how the name came to be applied, but we know its origins: the dissembling was named after Nicodemus, the righteous Pharisee mentioned in John's Gospel, who followed Jesus and believed in him, but only came to see him at night, in secret (John 3: 1–9; 7: 50; 19: 39). Some scholars have argued that the Nicodemites were an international network of elite spiritualists who shared a common theory of dissimulation, but evidence of this remains unconvincing. While it is true that some spiritualist writers such as the Dutchman Dirk Coornherts (1522–90) espoused dissimulation, and practised it, the fact remains that dissembling behaviour had been prevalent among French evangelicals since the 1520s, among reformers who were not avowed spiritualists. Many of the Meaux group, including Calvin's friend Gerard Roussel, were Nicodemites. Calvin had not only rubbed shoulders with Nicodemites, but was probably one of them for a while, which may explain his intense revulsion towards dissembling. From 1537 to 1562, a period that spans his entire public career, Calvin never tired of writing against the phenomenon in letters, sermons, and treatises. His stance was utterly uncompromising: dissembling was always a sin, and an affront to God's honour. 'The Christian', said Calvin, 'ought to honour God, not only within his heart, and with spiritual affection, but also with external testimony.' In 1536, Calvin addressed a long angry letter to his friend Roussel, whose dissembling was extreme. It was published a year later under the title *On fleeing the illicit rites of the ungodly*. Calvin's judgement was as harsh as it was unequivocal:

You deceive yourself if you think you have a place among the people of God, when, in fact, you are a soldier in the army of the Antichrist. You deceive yourself if you hope to partake in the Kingdom of Heaven with the Son of God, when, in fact, you keep company with wretched brigands and take part in their robberies and depredations...Think what you want about yourself: I, at the very least, will never consider you a Christian, or a good man.

Though solidly rooted in theological principles, Calvin's opposition to Nicodemism was an eminently practical one, and its impact should not be underestimated. By telling his fellow evangelicals in France and elsewhere that they could not mingle with Catholics, or camouflage their faith, Calvin was forcing them to become a distinct people, a visible dissenting minority. He was also forcing them to create their own church in hostile territory, since he knew that only a relative few could choose exile. Calvin received many anguished letters from France, asking for his advice about dissembling. His response was always the same: stay there and bear witness to your faith, even to the point of martyrdom, or go somewhere where you can practise your religion openly, in peace. Many found his position unacceptable. In 1543, a friend who was a member of the Paris Parlement wrote to him:

A number of people think your assertions are thoroughly wretched. They accuse you of being heartless and very severe toward those who are distressed; and they say that it is easy for you to preach and threaten over there [in Geneva], but that if you were here you would perhaps feel differently.

Others were even more blunt, complaining that Calvin would only consider as Christians those who came to Geneva and had their ears blasted with his sermons.

Calvin bristled at these accusations and insisted that he admired those who stood their ground in France 'a hundred times more, point for point than we, who enjoy freedom and peace'. Nonetheless, in 1550, he proudly boasted to Philip Melanchthon, 'many, in order to avoid idolatry, are fleeing France and coming here to us in voluntary exile'. The exiles came, indeed, flooding Geneva and altering its social and political structure. But many more remained behind in France and stood their ground, establishing Protestant communities throughout the realm, one by one. Eventually, these Calvinists would come to be known as *Huguenots*. The origin and meaning of the term is uncertain—some have proposed that it is derived from the Swiss term *Eidgenossen*, or 'federated'—but there is nothing uncertain about the cohesiveness of these communities. The Huguenots were tightly knit and disciplined, with their spiritual and moral compass fixed on Geneva. Calvin's opinion held sway, and the advice he had been dispensing since 1536 became inseparable from the gospel for many of them:

Consider it always forbidden to let anyone see you communicating in the sacrilege of the Mass, or uncovering your head before an image, or observing any kind of superstition... through which the glory of God is obscured, His religion profaned, and His truth corrupted.

By opposing Nicodemism and rejecting compromise, Calvin made necessary the establishment of Reformed churches throughout France and Europe, and in doing so he also necessarily provoked social and political conflict. In 1561, the Venetian ambassador to France was able to perceive this. 'Religious affairs will soon be in an evil case in France,' he wrote home. Throughout much of France the followers of Calvin met 'without any respect for the ministers of the king or the commandments of the king himself'. Having penetrated every province and 'every class of persons', and having gained total control of many areas, he continued, the Huguenots were shunning the mass as if it were the plague, turning their back on king and Church. The ambassador could only see two possible outcomes, both deadly: either France would split into two separate societies, or civil war would ensue. And he laid the blame for this crisis directly on Calvin:

Your Serenity will hardly believe the influence and the great power which the principal minister of Geneva, by name Calvin... possesses in this kingdom; he is a man of extraordinary authority, who by his mode of life, his doctrines, and his writings rises superior to all the rest;

and it is almost impossible to believe the enormous sums of money which are secretly sent to him from France to maintain his power.

In his own day, Catholics saw Calvin as a 'grand master' of sedition, and his uncompromising stance as a shrewd political strategy. Even Lutherans could agree. Duke Christoph von Württemberg (1515–68), was blunt: 'Calvinism is seditious in spirit, and wherever it enters it is determined to usurp dominion, even over magistrates.' Whether or not Calvin's intransigence caused the French Wars of Religion is debatable, but one point seems beyond question: speaking of Calvin's political motivations and his theology as distinct from one another, or as mutually exclusive, is not only pointless, but foolish. Calvin's vision of the proper order of things was always shaped as much by his religious convictions as by the harsh realities of politics, and he was painfully aware of the fact that opposition to idolatry could very easily evolve into resistance to an idolatrous ruler. Though Calvin would never go that far, some of his followers did. He would have shuddered at the thought, but those Frenchmen who said in 1577 that 'the Gospel is the seed of rebellion' probably had Calvin in mind, and with good reason.

As refugees poured into Geneva in the early 1550s, the conflict between Calvin and his opponents intensified, especially because some native Genevans felt that foreigners had taken over their city. Tensions finally exploded into a riot in 1555, after which the fate of the so-called 'Libertines' was sealed. Tried for treason, some were executed, the rest expelled. Amy Perrin and his family were not only forced to leave Geneva, but also had their property seized. Unhindered by local opposition, Calvin intensified Geneva's international role. Property taken from the Perrin family was funnelled into the creation of the Geneva Academy, a school that opened its doors in 1559. This Academy was both a preparatory school for local Genevan youths and a seminary for the training of pastors. Its first rector, the French émigré Theodore Beza (1519–1605), was Calvin's right-hand man and anointed successor. Under his direction, the Academy quickly became a veritable factory of Reformed clerics, and especially of scores from France, who returned home as missionaries. Full of zeal, well trained in Reformed theology, and intimately familiar with the Genevan model, they set about creating a tight, growing network of Huguenot churches throughout France. And so it was, oddly enough, that Geneva came to play a role in sixteenth-century France more significant than any other French city, save Paris.

Calvin's Geneva would also figure prominently in the history of many other nations and earn itself the nickname of 'the Protestant Rome': Italians, Spaniards, Germans, Scots, Englishmen, Netherlanders, Poles, Hungarians, Moravians, and others took up residence, or passed through. Those who returned home, like the French clergy trained in the Academy, brought with them Calvin's theology and reform plans based on Geneva. In 1556, the Scottish refugee John Knox described the city in ecstatic terms as: 'the most perfect school of Christ that ever was in the earth since the days of the Apostles. In other places I confess Christ to be truly preached; but manners and religion to be so seriously reformed, I have not yet seen in any other place besides.'

THE GRAND MASTER OF SEDI-
TION. Crimes of Calvinism:
Murder, sacrilege, and war by
land and sea, *c.*1585. Catholics
pin the blame on Calvin for religious violence.

John Bale, an English refugee, concurred: 'Geneva seemeth to me to be the wonderful miracle of the whole world; so many from all countries come thither, as it were into a sanctuary, not to gather riches, but to live in poverty . . . [to] . . . dwell together like a spiritual Christian congregation.'

The growing renown of Geneva made Calvin all the more influential. His success and Geneva's became a myth larger than history, and the myth became a paradigm. Half a century after Calvin's death, John Winthrop, an English disciple of his, would have Geneva in mind as he prepared to sail across the Atlantic to establish a Puritan outpost in the New World. The city he spoke about was not just a figure of speech in a Gospel passage (Matt. 5: 14) or an apocalyptic dream, but a real place, on earth. 'We must consider that we shall be as a city upon a hill. The eyes of all people are upon us,' he told his congregation. So it was that Calvin's spirit sailed to America, long after he was dead; and so it was that Geneva became embedded in the American consciousness.

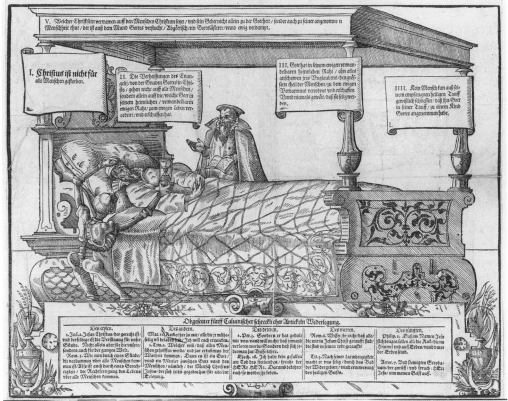

A HOUSE DIVIDED. Jacob Lederlein, *Five Calvinist Articles*, 1590. Lutheran contempt for Calvinists could match that of Catholics, especially when it came to the doctrine of predestination. In this satirical broadside, a Calvinist minister who looks like Calvin himself drives a dying man into despair by reminding him that baptism does not ensure his salvation, that Christ did not die for everyone, and that God has predestined the vast majority of the human race for hell.

What made Calvin's Geneva appealing to his followers, however, was also exactly what repelled all others. Calvin and his adopted city acquired a reputation for coldness, intolerance, and cruelty. And nothing seemed to exemplify the dark character of Calvin's Geneva more vividly than the 1553 trial and execution of Michael Servetus, the Spanish spiritualist and anti-Trinitarian. To this day, no one knows for sure why Servetus went to Geneva. He knew very well that Calvin detested his work, for he had been sending Calvin copies of his writings for years and Calvin had consistently condemned them all. Servetus had also just escaped from a Catholic prison in Lyons, and knew he must keep a low profile. Yet, up the Rhône river he went, straight into the lion's den. Some have speculated that he might have been invited by the Libertines to bait Calvin and stir up trouble, or that he might have wanted to join in their fight against Calvin. Whatever his reasons, Servetus made a fatal mistake. In August 1553 he was spotted, immediately arrested, and tried for heresy. Calvin took charge of his prosecution and pressed successfully for the death sentence. So, on 27 October 1553, Servetus was burned alive. Later, in a letter, Calvin would report that Servetus had 'cried like a Spaniard'.

Although the burning of heretics had become all too common by 1553, the plight of Servetus attracted the attention of Calvin's enemies. Catholics showcased the incident as proof positive of Calvin's cruelty, megalomania, and hypocrisy. How dare a heretic burn anyone else for heresy? Lutherans expressed dismay, over both Servetus and Calvin. Anabaptists and Spiritualists, as one might expect, cried the loudest. A former colleague of Calvin's at Strasbourg, Sebastian Castellio, published a book in 1554 which condemned the killing of Servetus and pleaded for religious freedom and toleration among all Christians. 'The true fear of God and charity are fallen and grown cold,' he argued:

Although opinions are almost as numerous as men, nevertheless there is hardly any sect that does not condemn all others and desire to reign alone. Hence arise banishments, chains, imprisonments, stakes, and gallows and this miserable rage to visit daily penalties on those who differ from the mighty about things hitherto unknown, for so many centuries disputed, and not yet cleared up.

In retrospect, from the vantage point of an age and culture in which toleration is highly prized, Castellio's protest can seem much more significant than it was in its own day. The sad truth is that hardly anyone paid attention to Castellio, least of all in Geneva. Castellio continued to press for toleration, nonetheless. In 1562, he would publish one of the most impassioned defences ever written for religious toleration, entitled *Advice for a Desolate France*, in which he begged the French to stop killing one another over religious differences. But his plea fell on deaf ears in blood-soaked France. Castellio was too much of a rationalist and agnostic for his day. His last book, *On the Art of Doubting*, appealed only to later generations, not to his own, and certainly not to Calvinists. One trait above all distinguished Calvinists: their conviction. Doubt may have been part of their lives, but it was viewed as a temptation, as something to be vanquished by God's grace.

International Calvinism

One of the most remarkable aspects of Calvinism is the way in which one man's influence eventually reached way beyond the walls of a cramped city-state at the foot of the Alps. It did not happen overnight, but we can certainly pinpoint when something that could be called 'Calvinism' became an international movement.

The English exiles who came there in the 1550s, fleeing the wrath of their Catholic Queen Mary, would return to their native land after her death full of Reformed Calvinist fervour, ready to purify England and rid it once and for all of its traces of popery. This was also true of the Scots, and especially of John Knox, who would seek to turn an entire nation Calvinist in 1559–60. And the same could be said of Kaspar Olevianus from the Palatinate (Pfalz), in Germany, John à Lasco from Poland, Philips van Marnix Sainte Aldegonde from the Netherlands, and others like them from Hungary and Moravia. Exiles from Italy and Spain, such as Bernardino Ochino and Juan Pérez, either stayed there or carried Calvinism to lands other than their own.

And wherever Calvinists surfaced, established authorities cringed. The most significant question Calvinists raised everywhere was whether or not an idolatrous tyrant had any legal right to force his subjects to dishonour God. As we have seen, Calvin had offered his followers two drastic choices: stay and suffer the consequences of never compromising with 'false religion', or flee to some other place where you can worship God correctly. Calvin was circumspect and very tight-lipped about a third option: armed resistance. Whenever he wrote about idolatrous tyrants, Calvin was careful to point out that private citizens had no right to resist, and cited several biblical texts in support of this position. 'We cannot resist the magistrate without resisting God,' he argued. Even so, towards the end of his life Calvin began to search for loopholes, somewhat feebly. His 1559 *Institutes*, which appeared just before France plunged into thirty-six years of civil war, had one brief paragraph on the subject of resistance. But it was highly equivocal. All that Calvin dared to say was this: under certain conditions, according to some local or national laws, some lower magistrates 'appointed to curb the tyranny of kings' might have legitimate power to resist an idolatrous ruler. Calvin refused to get specific about such magistrates, however, citing only three examples from Greek and Roman antiquity.

Some of his disciples, however, would reach a different conclusion. One of the first to do this was John Knox, who argued that subjects are not only justified in resisting an idolatrous ruler, but are actually duty-bound to do so, by God's commandments. In his 'Exhortation to the Commonality of Scotland', Knox reminded his fellow Scots that idolatry was everyone's business. 'I say all men are equal', thundered Knox, 'and that God requires no less of the subject, be he ever so poor, than of the prince and rich man, in matters of religion.' His argument was as revolutionary as they come:

It will not excuse you, dear brethren, in the presence of God, neither yet will it avail you in the day of his visitation, to say, 'We were but simple subjects; we could not redress the faults and crimes of our rulers, bishops, and clergy; we called for reformation, and wished for the same...' These vain excuses, I say, will nothing avail you in the presence of God, who requires no less of the subjects than of their rulers.

So, now, for Knox, it was not the idols themselves that needed to be removed, but the governments that supported them. This was a huge step. It was also the ultimate strategy in the war against idolatry, and it was eagerly embraced by other Calvinists.

Among the most significant Calvinists who formulated theories of resistance, two were quite close to Calvin. One of the first to speak unequivocally on this subject was Pierre Viret (1511–71), a close friend who ran the Reformed church in nearby Lausanne from 1536 to 1559, and published several influential treatises on idolatry and resistance, aimed at Huguenots in France. Viret was also joined by Calvin's closest friend and successor, Theodore Beza, who argued in his *Rights of Magistrates* (1574) that God alone was to be obeyed 'without exception', and that all 'irreligious and iniquitous' commands issued by earthly rulers were null and void to the Christian. Even so, Viret and Beza defended only the rights of lower magistrates to resist, rather than granting that right to all believers. Others were less guarded. The very same year Beza published his treatise, Phillipe du Plessis-Mornay (1549–1623) argued in his *Vindiciae contra Tyrannos* that all rulers and magistrates who support false religion forfeit their right to rule. Mornay went further, arguing that Christians who refused 'to resist a king who overturns the Law and the Church of God' were 'guilty of the same crime and subject to the same penalty' as the idolatrous king.

The French Calvinist theorists, however, lagged far behind their English and Scottish counterparts. Knox already had his fully revolutionary theory formulated as he travelled through Switzerland in 1558. So did the Englishman Christopher Goodman, whose treatise on the subject spelled out his argument clearly in its title, *How Superior Powers Ought To Be Obeyed By Their Subjects: And Wherein They May Lawfully By God's Word Be Disobeyed And Resisted* (1558). John Ponet also sanctioned resistance in his *Short Treatise on Politicke Power* (1559), a text that would eventually influence John Locke and some of the leaders of the American Revolution.

What made Calvinists formidable opponents was not only their theorizing, but rather their cohesiveness and their eagerness to overthrow 'false religion' even under the toughest of circumstances. Being a minority seemed not to faze them. On the contrary, that obvious disadvantage emboldened them. As had occurred in Switzerland in the 1520s and 1530s, iconoclasm eventually became the hallmark of Calvinist agitation, most notably in France, Scotland, the Netherlands, and England. Calvinist communities in France grew by leaps and bounds in the 1550s, heightening religious tensions wherever they took root. Buoyed by the number of aristocrats that joined their cause, and by the creation of more than 1,750 churches, French Calvinists began to act much less cautiously than Calvin ever had advised. The first cities to experience Calvinist-led iconoclastic riots were Rouen and La Rochelle in 1560. Within a year, image smashing had spread throughout the realm to Angers, Bouvais, Le Mans, Paris, Pontoise, Touraine, and other towns in the Languedoc. By early 1562, riots had also swept through Abbeville, Auxerre, Bayeux, Bourges, Caen, Lyons, Marseille, Meaux, Orléans, Sens, and Tours. This unprecedented wave of image-smashing, which Calvin condemned, proved to be the prelude to even worse violence. By the end of 1562, the entire kingdom had sunk into an orgy of violence. Wherever possible, despite the bloodshed, Huguenots took control of towns and cities in which they established consistories, mirroring the order of Geneva. The blood-letting would come to a halt in

1598, when King Henry IV—a former Calvinist—issued the Edict of Nantes, which granted toleration to the Huguenots. For eighty-seven years, French Calvinists would coexist with their Catholic neighbours and build a thriving church. But in 1685, King Louis XIV would revoke the aforementioned Edict, outlaw Protestantism, and cause the emigration of over 200,000 Calvinists to other countries and continents.

In the Netherlands, the advent of Calvinism would be more sudden and dramatic. Beginning on 10 August 1566, mobs numbering in the hundreds, sometimes in the thousands, made their way into churches all over the Netherlands, destroying sacred imagery, sacking churches, and attacking the Catholic clergy. In the province of Flanders alone, over 400 churches were sacked in a period of two weeks. This outbreak of violence—like the early ones in France—proved to be a mere prelude to greater troubles. King Philip II of Spain, titular ruler of the Netherlands, sent over 10,000 troops to crush the heretics, whom he viewed as 'enemies of altar and throne'. The end result was just the opposite of what Philip intended, for the Dutch began to fight a war of independence, as fuelled by religion as by nationalism, which would drag on for eighty years.

By 1600, Calvinists throughout the northern provinces of the Netherlands had managed to establish themselves as a ruling majority, and to proclaim their independent de facto republic as officially Reformed, even though their war with Spain would not be over de jure until 1648. However, since Calvinists were never able to become an absolute majority in the new United Provinces, their Calvinism was something of a thick veneer, under which one could find a grudging sort of toleration. While the majority of the population attended the officially approved Reformed Church of the Dutch republic—especially in the north—not everyone became a member of that Church. This meant that the establishment of a Genevan model never fully materialized, and that those who attended the Reformed Church but were not members could not be subjected to the same discipline. It also meant that Catholics and Anabaptists were allowed to coexist and to worship freely beneath the veneer, so to speak, in buildings other than churches. Ironically, then, an officially Calvinist state became the most tolerant place in all of Europe, proving that Calvinism was not necessarily intolerant and inflexible, but rather quite adaptable, at least for that day and age.

In Scotland, it was not just images that were attacked in 1559–60, but also the Catholic Church as a whole, which was dismantled under the leadership of John Knox. The establishment of a purely Reformed Kirk of Scotland—as the Church was commonly called—did not happen overnight, however. Nor was its establishment ever complete. Resistance was fierce in some quarters, especially among some of the nobles, or lairds, and in the north of Scotland, where it ultimately proved impossible to abolish Catholicism altogether, despite persecution. The Reformed Scottish Kirk imposed by state fiat was presbyterian in polity; that is, it was a church run by presbyters (elders) rather than bishops, in keeping with the Genevan model. It had relative autonomy from the State, but, true to its Calvinist principles, it worked with the civil authorities to ensure the creation of a godly commonwealth. Its structure was less hierarchical than that of a church run by bishops, and it was governed at four

Het weg vlugten der Gereformeerde uyt Vrankryk.

Verscheyee weg vlugtige Gereformeerde die agter haalt zynde in Gevangenisse, en op de Galyen gebragt verre.

THE WANDERING ELECT. Jan Luyken, *The Flight of the Huguenots from France*, 1696. Up to 200,000 Huguenots fled France in 1685 after King Louis XIV revoked the Edict of Nantes and outlawed their religion. Since no single place could absorb so many refugees, they dispersed to Germany, Switzerland, Holland, and England, and also North America and South Africa. This engraving shows one such group wending their way to the French port of La Rochelle, formerly a Calvinist bastion, now turned into their point of departure.

interlocking levels, from the strictly local to the national level: elders meeting as a Session, and then Presbyteries, and then a Synod, and finally a General Assembly. Tension and disputes about church polity continued to plague the Scots for over a century, due to the fact that their nation's crown became united with that of England, and its kings—who were also the supreme governors of the Church of England— naturally preferred to bring the Scottish Kirk more in line with the episcopal model of the English Church. Eventually, these disputes with England would lead to war in 1639–40, when King Charles I tried to impose bishops and the Anglican liturgy on the Scots and they rebelled. This conflict, in turn, would spark a civil war in England, and a Calvinist takeover of that realm.

The English Reformation was uniquely complex, for the Anglican Church founded by King Henry VIII went through various transformations after 1534, including a

TIS AL VERlBREN GHEBEDN OFT GHESCHETEN
ICK HEB DE BESTE CANSE GHESTREKEN
1566

LAET ONS WEL BIDDEN SONDER OPHELDEN   LÆT ONS RAS KEREN EN WORDEN NIET MOE

OCH DAT ONS HEILICDOM TE MEER MACH GELBEN   WANT ÆLE DEES CREMEKIE HOORT DEN DVYEL TOE

THE 'WONDER YEAR'. Anonymous, *Iconoclasm in 1566*, a Calvinist depiction of the iconoclasm that swept through the Netherlands in 1566. Calvinists topple idols and their trappings, sweeping the land clean, while the Catholic clergy pray to the Antichrist for help. Above them, the devil hovers with his arms full of costly ritual objects, and tells them, 'it's all over; it makes no difference whether you pray or crap in your pants'.

period of intense Swiss-influenced reforms under King Edward VI (1547–53) and a period of Catholic resurgence under his half-sister Queen Mary (1553–8), who earned herself the nickname of 'Bloody Mary' by persecuting Protestants. Under Queen Elizabeth I, who succeeded Mary, Catholicism was abolished once again, and, while the new Book of Common Prayer of the Elizabethan Church skirted around theological precision, the Church itself once more leaned heavily towards the Reformed tradition. Elizabeth's deliberate theological vagueness and the liturgical conservatism of her Church—later interpreted as a *via media* between Catholicism and Protestantism—would elicit opposition from both Catholics and the Reformed. But while the Catholics were relentlessly persecuted and nearly driven to extinction, the Reformed dissenters would gradually grow into the largest and most powerful non-conforming religious community, and they would never cease clamouring for the

Areas of widespread iconoclasm

Towns where iconoclasm took place

Direction taken by main groups of iconoclasts

Winsum (14 Sept.)

Groningen (18 Sept.)

Leeuwarden (6 Sept.)

Elburg (21 Sept.)

Alkmaar (2 Sept.)

Harderwick (22 Sept.)

Amsterdam (23 Aug.)

Leiden (25 Aug.)

The Hague (25 Aug.)

Utrecht (24 Aug.)

Culemborg (14 Sept.)

Vianen (25 Sept.)

Delft (24 Aug. & 5 Oct.)

Heusden (23 Aug.)

Brielle (26 Aug. & Oct.)

Asperen (18 Oct.)

Batenburg (16 Sept.)

's Hertogenbosch (22 Aug.)

Breda (22 Aug.)

Helmond (25 Aug.)

Middleburg (22 Aug.)

Eindhoven (25 Aug.)

Venlo (5 Oct.)

Axel (25 Aug.)

Antwerp (20 Aug.)

Turnhout (23 Aug.)

From England (June–July)

Hasselt (19 Jan. 1567)

Ghent (22 Aug.)

Mechelen (23 Aug.)

Diksmuide (18 Aug.)

Poperinge (14 Aug.)

Menin (16 Aug.)

Maastricht (29 Sept.)

Ronse (19 Aug.)

Ieper (16 Aug.)

Steenvoorde (10 Aug.)

Tournai (23 Aug.)

Bailleul (13 Aug.)

St. Amand (25 Aug.)

Laventie (15 Aug.)

Valenciennes (24 Aug.)

N

0   miles   50

ICONOCLASTIC VIOLENCE IN THE NETHERLANDS, 1566
Source: Courtesy of Geoffrey Parker.

abolition of all traces of 'popery' and the establishment of their Reformed ideals throughout the realm. These nonconformists, better known as Puritans, were not of one mind, however. At one extreme, some sought to reform the Church of England from within; at the other extreme, separatists decided to establish their own church, and some of them, ironically, went as far as to reject infant baptism and create a church composed exclusively of the elect. Though Calvin himself would have

NO MIDDLE WAY. John Foxe, *Acts and Monuments of these Latter and Perillous Days, Touching Matters of the Church* (better known as *The Book of Martyrs*), 1563. Calvinist influence on the reforms of King Edward VI in England, as depicted in Foxe's *Book of Martyrs*. In the top section, 'papists' pack away their 'paltry' and 'trinkets' and sail away in the ship of the Roman Church, while other images burn in a bonfire. In the bottom section, King Edward distributes the Bible to the clergy, and the mass is replaced by a sermon and a communion table.

condemned these Reformed Protestants who so resembled the Anabaptists, they are nonetheless a most significant branch of the Swiss-Genevan family tree. Some of these separatists fled to the Netherlands, and eventually to New England in North America, where they established a string of Puritan settlements, all of which had Geneva in mind as the model.

Eventually, Puritans would become numerous and powerful enough to plunge England into a civil war in 1642. After six years of fighting under the leadership of Oliver Cromwell (1599–1658), they would defeat King Charles I, capture him, try him for treason, behead him, abolish the monarchy and the supremacy of the Church of England, invade and conquer Ireland, and establish a Puritan state in the British Isles that would last until 1660. With the restoration of the monarchy under Charles II, Puritans lost their political control, but not their influence. Not for a long time, anyway, especially in America.

The spread of Calvinism in other lands led to far less violence, but not to any diminution in Calvinist zeal. On the whole, this expansion took place in central and eastern Europe, in areas that were politically fragmented or lacked strong centralizing monarchies. These circumstances led to the creation of Calvinist islands, so to speak, within which local rulers or aristocrats could sponsor and protect their local Calvinist churches. Though often intermingled with or surrounded by hostile Lutherans and Catholics, persecution of these Calvinists was less likely and therefore so were instances of armed resistance or religious warfare. Since local independence was a key factor in many of these areas, local variations flourished within them.

In Germany, as one might expect, Calvinism made inroads in some of the borderlands with Switzerland, France, and the Netherlands, but it also gained a foothold in territories further inside the Empire, such as Anhalt, Hesse, and the Upper Palatinate. Among these territories, the Palatinate rose to prominence after 1561, not just because of its size and power, but also because of a series of rulers in the Wittelsbach dynasty who were committed to the Calvinist cause and the creation of a godly society. The chief contributions of this area to international Calvinism were its intake of refugees and the swift rise in prominence of the University of Heidelberg, which, along with the University of Leiden in the Netherlands, came to rival and eclipse the Geneva Academy as a centre for Reformed theological study. This region also contributed the Heidelberg Catechism, composed by a team of ministers in 1563, some of whom had spent time in Geneva. Its summary of Reformed Calvinist faith and doctrine would prove to be immensely influential beyond the Palatinate, and would help give shape to international Calvinism for centuries to come. German Calvinism evolved in its own way due to its environment, adapting to local circumstances in the bewildering patchwork quilt of the Empire. Consistories, for instance, developed at a different pace in each German territory, and with different configurations of their function and authority. And in Brandenburg, eventually, there would be the anomaly of a Calvinist ruler, Elector John Sigismund (1572–1619), converted from Lutheranism while studying in Heidelberg, who would have to settle for a bi-confessional state with a Calvinist minority, after his Lutheran subjects stood firm and refused to change churches.

CALVINIST RESISTANCE THEORIES PUT TO PRACTICE. The beheading of King Charles I of England, woodcut 1649. English Puritans execute King Charles I, asserting their conviction that no monarch can disregard their interpretation of God's Law with impunity.

Some areas of central and eastern Europe also proved receptive to Calvinism, each for its own reasons, and each in its own way. In Habsburg-ruled Hungary, which then included Moravia and Transylvania, Calvinism took root in various pockets, always in competition with Catholics and other Protestants, and always under two large shadows: that of Habsburg efforts to promote Catholic hegemony and that of the ever-pressing Ottoman Turkish threat. In Hungary, where the Reformed faith was first introduced from Basel and Zurich rather than Geneva, after Lutherans had already gained a foothold, tensions with the Lutherans often ran high. Eventually internal tensions developed too, as Genevan Calvinism made serious inroads. Despite quarrels among themselves and with Lutherans and Anabaptists, and despite perse-cution, Hungarian Calvinists managed to survive and to play an important role in the development of Hungarian nationalism. Always proud of its independence, the Reformed Church in Hungary would be one of the very few to adopt an episcopal structure.

In Poland–Lithuania, which had a very weak monarchy and a powerful nobility, Calvinism found fertile ground around the mid-sixteenth century and spread quickly among its nobles, many of whom lived in the Grand Duchy of Lithuania and belonged to the Orthodox Church. At that time, Poland–Lithuania was one of the most religiously diverse states in Europe: it had not only a very large Orthodox population but also many Jews and a wide assortment of other Christians, including Lutherans,

ERRAND INTO THE WILDERNESS. Henry Whitfield House, Guilford, Connecticut, 1639. Stone house built for Reverend Henry Whitfield by the Puritan settlers of Guilford, Connecticut, in 1639. The thickly walled house doubled as a fortress for the small Calvinist colony whenever they fell under attack by the local natives. Three of the Puritan judges responsible for the execution of King Charles I fled here in 1660, after the restoration of the monarchy turned them into outlaws with a price on their heads.

Anabaptists, Bohemian Brethren, Armenian Monophysites, Unitarian Socinians, and freethinking spiritualists. Religious toleration was not only observed, but made the law of the land in 1573. For a while, in the late sixteenth century, it looked as if Protestants had the upper hand, with a majority of the seats in the Lower Parliament and nearly half of the seats in the Upper Parliament, and most of the parishes in some areas. This success was relatively short-lived, however, mostly because the Calvinist faith remained a thin veneer among the aristocracy. At its peak, Calvinism claimed about 45 per cent of the nobles, but less than 20 per cent of the total population. Among the peasantry, it was an even smaller percentage. Poland's upper-crust Calvinists could not withstand a very aggressive campaign launched against them by the

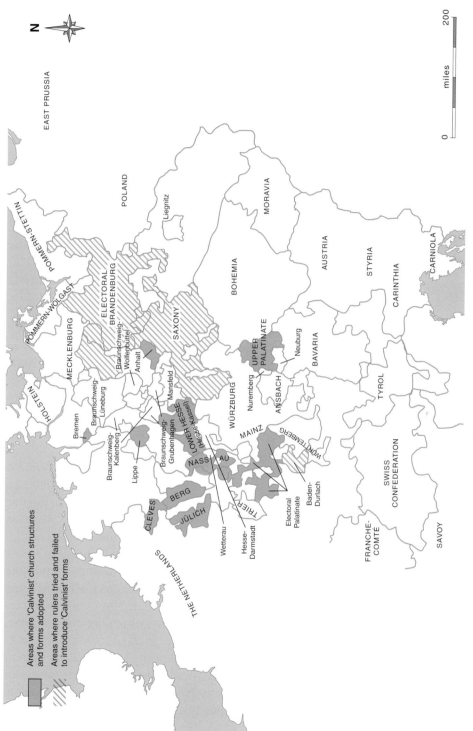

THE SPREAD OF CALVINISM IN THE GERMAN EMPIRE TO *c.* 1600
Source: Euan Cameron, *The European Reformation* (OUP, 2nd edn, 2012), p. 378.

N

Areas where 'Calvinist' church structures
and forms adopted

Areas where rulers tried and failed
to introduce 'Calvinist' forms

0   miles   200

POMMERN-STETTIN

EAST PRUSSIA

POMMERN-WOLGAST

HOLSTEIN

MECKLENBURG

ELECTORAL
BRANDENBURG

POLAND

Braunschweig-
Wolfenbüttel

Anhalt

Bremen

Braunschweig-
Lüneburg

Liegnitz

Braunschweig-
Kalenberg

Mansfeld

SAXONY

BOHEMIA

Lippe

Braunschweig-
Grubenhagen

LOWER HESSE
(Hesse-Kassel)

WÜRZBURG

UPPER
PALATINATE

MORAVIA

THE NETHERLANDS

CLEVES

JÜLICH

BERG

NASSAU

TRIER

MAINZ

Wetterau

Hesse-
Darmstadt

Electoral
Palatinate

Nuremberg

ANSBACH

Neuburg

BAVARIA

AUSTRIA

STYRIA

WÜRTEMBERG

Baden-
Durlach

SWISS
CONFEDERATION

TYROL

CARINTHIA

CARNIOLA

FRANCHE-
COMTÉ

SAVOY

CALVINISM AS COINAGE OF THE REALM. Coin of Gabor Bethlen, seventeenth century. Calvinists in Germany and in central and eastern Europe depended heavily or entirely on the support of secular rulers who had sufficient authority to enact laws and mint coinage. One such ruler was Gabor Bethlen, prince of Transylvania (1613–29), who made possible the establishment of a strong Calvinist presence in eastern Hungary, despite the opposition of the Habsburg emperors and the seemingly unstoppable advance of the Ottoman Turks.

monarchy in the late sixteenth century, with the aid of Jesuit missionaries. Faced with many restrictions imposed by the crown on the one hand, and with the opportunity of sending their children to great Jesuit schools on the other, most of the Calvinist nobility became Catholic. Attrition was further intensified in 1668, when an edict made it a capital crime for Catholics to abandon their faith. From that point forward, winning new converts became virtually impossible for Calvinists. By then, however, it was way too late to hope for new blood: Calvinism in Poland–Lithuania had been reduced to a nearly ghostly presence, with very few churches.

Given such diversity, is it proper to speak of 'Calvinism' at all, as if it were a monolithic tradition? Yes, certainly. But only with caution. Calvinism was above all a very adaptable religion, or, if one prefers to think of it more broadly, a flexible ideology that adjusted to its environments. Yet, when push came to shove, Calvinists always adapted without conforming: they held on to core principles and a certain world-view regardless of local circumstances, whether their churches were run by presbyteries or synods, and whether they had consistories or not. Their uncompromising zeal was the most essential component of their identity and what linked them to Calvin and one another. This is not to say that Calvinists were all of one mind. Not at all. Disagreements were as numerous and as heated among them as in any other religious tradition, and as divisive as those that vexed Calvin in his own day. Of all of the disagreements that shook Calvinist unity, the most intense had to do with the subject of the human will and its relation to God's grace. Adapting predestination to daily life was always a big challenge to Calvinists, and for some, especially New England Puritans, a source of anxiety. Am I one of the elect or not? Can I play any role in my salvation? These were burning questions.

Some Calvinists sought to tinker with Calvin's soteriology, offering milder interpretations of predestination that gave the human will some role to play. Jacob Arminius (1560–1609), a Dutch Calvinist, was the chief architect of such an alternative theology, which came to bear his name: Arminianism. In 1610, his followers summarized their beliefs in a document entitled *The Remonstrance*, which earned them the name Remonstrants. The controversy that ensued was highly divisive, and, as one might expect of Calvinists, the theological brawl spilled over into Dutch politics. It also affected Calvinists elsewhere, especially in England. Ultimately, no compromise was reached, and the dispute led to a schism and to a further clarification of certain points of doctrine. In 1619, at the Synod of Dordrecht (known as Dort in English), the Counter-Remonstrants condemned Arminianism, affirmed double-predestination, and summed up their beliefs in five points. This summation, which came to be known as Five-Point-Calvinism, could be very conveniently memorized in English by means of the acronym TULIP, a very appropriate symbol of Dutch identity:

Total Depravity—(the human is so corrupted by original sin, it cannot avoid sinning)

Unconditional Election—(humans can do nothing to earn salvation: it is all up to God)

Limited Atonement—(Christ's redemptive act applies only to the elect)

Irresistible Grace—(those chosen by God cannot refuse his grace)

Perseverance of the Saints—(the elect cannot lose their salvation)

Not all Calvinists accepted the Synod of Dort or its five points, or its endorsement of the Heidelberg Catechism. Condemned by the synod, the Dutch Remonstrants had no choice but to create their own Church. In England and elsewhere, the pronouncements of Dort led to innumerable disagreements. Eventually, a definitive list of orthodox Calvinist beliefs would be drawn at the Westminster Assembly in 1646. The resulting Westminster Confession was adopted by the Church of Scotland and Presbyterians and Congregationalists in England and America, as was the Westminster Catechism (which was deeply influenced by that of Heidelberg). But this turn towards greater uniformity did not bring an end to disagreements among Calvinists, or an end to Arminianism. Eventually, Arminian theology would be brought to its most dramatic fruition by John Wesley (1703–91), the founder of Methodism.

The Calvinist Legacy

Among his enemies and detractors, Calvin acquired a reputation as a cold-hearted and puritanical tyrant who fashioned a God much like himself. By the eighteenth century, the only portrait that the 'enlightened' could draw of Calvin was one that emphasized the grossest features of this caricature. Take, for instance, what Thomas Jefferson, Deist and third president of the United States, had to say in a letter to John Adams, his predecessor in office:

ORTHODOXY BY VOTE. Synod of Dort, 1619. Dutch divines meet to settle the Arminian controversy at the Synod of Dort in 1619, one of the most important gatherings in the history of Calvinism. Five-point Calvinism is declared the only truly orthodox Christian faith.

I can never join Calvin in addressing his god. He was indeed an Atheist, which I can never be; or rather his religion was Daemonism. If ever man worshiped a false god, he did. The being described in his five points is not the God whom you and I acknowledge and adore, the Creator and benevolent governor of the world; but a daemon of malignant spirit. It would be more pardonable to believe in no god at all, than to blaspheme him by the atrocious attributes of Calvin.

To his legions of followers, however, Calvin remained a sage, a prophet, and a holy man, a model of genuine devotion and Christian sobriety. His emphasis on purity, austerity, restraint, moderation, and hard work as quintessential Christian virtues made his followers a force to be reckoned with. In 1905, the sociologist Max Weber would argue in *The Protestant Ethic and the Spirit of Capitalism* that modern Western civilization owed more to Calvin than to almost anyone else. According to Weber, whose mother was a Calvinist, Calvinism not only 'disenchanted' the West by ridding it of its attachment to miracles, superstition, and magic, but also made possible the upward ascent of reason over faith itself. As if this were not enough, Weber also argued that Calvinist theology and ethics enabled the West to develop its unique capitalist economy and to achieve dominance over the rest of the world. Large claims, indeed, to pin on Calvin, a frail and pious workaholic; so large, in fact, that they still spark debate, a century later. Their brazen political incorrectness makes them a lightning rod of sorts, and an unavoidable subject. As unavoidable as Calvin himself, or Calvinism.

Given the place Calvin has assumed in Western history, it is easy to forget that he was a religious man, above all, and that his particular genius was the ability to link religion to every aspect of life in a logically consistent way. The Calvin of legend is not necessarily the Calvin who inspired countless disciples to unseat tyrants and establish godly societies. Calvin, the man of faith, is easy to miss; so easy, in fact, that some leading scholars have argued that he was not a theologian at all, but rather a shrewd politician. It helps to keep in mind, then, that among Calvin's most enduring legacies, one project is often overlooked: the reform of ritual in Geneva. Ritual should not be underestimated, for it speaks to the whole person, heart and mind, and shapes the consciousness much more effectively than theology. As is the case with most religions, the core messages of Calvinism were communicated and accepted most intensely through ritual, both in an individual and a communal way.

One of the first reforms instituted by Calvin upon his return to Geneva in 1542 was the creation of a psalter, a hymnal composed entirely of psalms from the Bible. Subsequent editions added more psalms to the original Geneva version, culminating with the 1562 edition, which contained all 150 psalms in French, the language of the people, set to simple, singable tunes in poetic metre. Reprinted hundreds of times and translated into many other languages, the Geneva Psalter would come to have an enormous influence on Calvinists everywhere. One should realize, however, that while this psalter sought to ritualize the *sola scriptura* principle by making a biblical text the heart and soul of the liturgy, it was not at all a Protestant invention, but rather a continuation of monastic piety.

In many ways, Calvinists lived up to the Benedictine monastic ideal: *Ora et Labora*. Prayer and work. After all, they sang the psalter on a regular basis, as a community, and sanctified work itself as a holy calling. They also embodied discipline and exclusion. But the parallels end there. Calvinists were committed to transforming the world by living in it, not by setting themselves apart. And there is a world of difference between these two ways of life. Calvinists did not see themselves as new,

THE HEART AND SOUL OF CALVINIST PIETY. Psalms 23 and 24 from the Genevan Psalter, 1562. This French version was supervised by Calvin and Theodore Beza, and based on the poetic renditions of Clément Marot. The words were translated into many languages; the tunes linked Calvinists everywhere.

improved monks, but rather as a new Israel, as God's chosen people, often a minority, and often forced into exile, but always determined to live out their covenant with the divine. And within this conception of themselves, Calvinists accepted one very important difference between themselves and the ancient Israelites: their Promised Land was the whole world, not just some minuscule sliver of real estate at the eastern end of the Mediterranean.

Calvinists were taught to see themselves as the spiritual children of Abraham, as the elect. The covenant, the pact, and the law therefore ruled in Geneva and any spot on earth where Calvinists pitched their tents, even when they were outnumbered. Like the psalmist, Calvin and his followers found great comfort in their election and in the hymns that ratified their convictions, such as Psalm 119: 1–3: 'Happy those whose

DEVOTION TO THE LAW. Anonymous, *Moses with the Ten Commandments*, *c.*1600–25. Decalogue boards that listed the Ten Commandments were installed in many Calvinist churches, to emphasize the centrality of God's revealed Law in the lives of the elect.

way is blameless, who walk by the teaching of the Lord. Happy those who observe God's decrees, who seek the Lord with all their heart. They do no wrong; they walk in God's ways.' As everyone knows, those who do no wrong, or think they can do no wrong, tend to be among those who influence history the most. Especially if they also happen to believe that they are the elect, and on a mission from God.

Calvinists may have disagreed with one another, sometimes vehemently, but they tended to adhere to Calvin's guiding principle: 'soli Deo gloria' (To God alone be the glory). It could be argued that this precept, more than any other, helped shape Calvinism's distinctive ethic, or spirit.

Ever since Weber proposed that Protestants—and Calvinists above all—had caused 'the disenchantment of the world' ('entzauberung der Welt'), his thesis has stirred debate. At issue in this ongoing discussion is the very definition of religion, and how it differs from 'magic' (*zauber*). Also at issue is the question of the secularization of the West, and of the role played by Protestantism and especially Calvinism in engendering the separation of religion and culture. But if we think of 'disenchantment' in non-Weberian terms—that is, not as the eclipse of 'magic', but rather as a drastic redefinition of the metaphysical paradigms governing Western thinking—we encounter what was unique about Calvinism and its legacy: its redefinition of the boundaries between the natural and supernatural, or matter and spirit. It was a new worldview, a major paradigm shift in the West's definition of reality.

This Calvinist redefinition of the sacred was revolutionary on two fronts. First, it was a theological and epistemic upheaval, a cognitive iconoclastic crusade against the medieval worldview, and against the paradigm of mystical union with God that Church and society had promoted for centuries as the ultimate human goal. John Calvin recoiled in horror at the thought that humans might claim any sort of divinization or gain intimacy with the divine, for his God was 'entirely other' and 'as different from flesh as fire is from water'. Calvin had no place in his theology for raptures, trances, visions, and miracles, either. Calvinists, as a whole, followed suit, bringing about a *desacralization* of the world, a 'disenchantment' which made the earth less charged with the otherworldly and supernatural.

This desacralization of the world not only redefined the relationship between humans and God, but also between Church and State, rulers and subjects. When all is said and done, this is why Calvinists can be seen as reformers of the Reformation and avatars of modernity.

4 The Radical Reformation

BRAD S. GREGORY

'Radicalizing' the Reformation

THE Radical Reformation has long been the outlier among the Reformations of the sixteenth and seventeenth centuries. It had nowhere near the early modern influence of the Lutheran Reformation, Reformed Protestantism, the Church of England, or the Catholic Reformation. Some scholars have endeavoured to find an underlying coherence in the religious beliefs and practices, or the social and political attitudes, among those Christians usually grouped under its rubric. But if used inclusively as a term to designate all those Western Christians in the era who rejected not only the authority of the Roman Catholic Church but also the politically protected, magisterial Protestant churches, the Radical Reformation includes a bewildering array of individuals, groups, and churches who espoused and enacted an extremely wide range of divergent claims about what it was to be Christian. We can curb the meaning of 'radical' and apply it more restrictively to denote the ideas and actions of those anti-Roman Christians who challenged political institutions or hierarchical social relationships in overt ways. This has the advantage of narrowing the term and thus lending its referent greater substantive coherence. But it has the disadvantage of excluding those Protestants who were not socially or politically subversive in concrete ways, and yet still rejected magisterial Protestantism and Catholicism. We would then need some additional term to encompass these quiet protestors plus those who were deliberately oppositional in social or political ways—a term to cover all non-magisterial Protestant, anti-Roman Christians. This essay will therefore use the established terms 'Radical Reformation' and 'radical Protestants', but in an inclusive sense to designate all Western Christians in the Reformation era who expressly rejected the claims of Lutheranism, Reformed Protestantism (including the Church of England), and Roman Catholicism. Beginning in the 1520s, the Radical Reformation understood in this sense includes some very different kinds of Christians, from violent revolutionaries to principled pacifists, and from biblical literalists to prophetic spiritualists to critical rationalists. In their common concern to discern and live God's truth, they not only diverged from magisterial Protestants and Catholics but also splintered among themselves.

Even when understood in this expansive and inclusive sense, the Radical Reformation had a relatively minor social, cultural, and political influence in the sixteenth and seventeenth centuries. It has therefore tended to receive proportionally little attention in surveys of the Protestant Reformation, to say nothing of accounts of early modern Christianity as a whole. Even when considered collectively, radical Protestants were comparatively small in number. Future research is unlikely to alter this impression. Because after the mid-1520s radical Protestants were nearly always excluded from (or rejected in principle) the alliances with political authorities characteristic of magisterial Protestant and Catholic regimes, they were not involved in demographically ambitious efforts of confessionalization—the long-term process that has attracted the attention of many Reformation scholars in the past generation of research. This means that radical Protestants had little impact in shaping major historical transformations central to the social and cultural history of early modern Europe. With the exception of certain short-lived episodes such as the so-called German Peasants' War of 1524–6 and the Anabaptist Kingdom of Münster in 1534–5, they had minimal political influence except in the negative sense of alerting authorities to the potential dangers of religious radicalism and inspiring largely successful efforts of political suppression. So it might well be thought that historians responsible for taking the measure of the Radical Reformation within Western Christianity during the era have rightly devoted relatively little attention to it. Radical Protestants merit some mention, insofar as they remind us that small numbers of men and women rejected not only Rome but also the doctrinal claims and reforming programmes of major Protestant leaders such as Martin Luther and John Calvin, and the institutions and communities of faith that they inspired. But, it is often implicitly or explicitly suggested, we should not mistakenly think that they shaped any major long-term historical processes in the period, or bequeathed much of a legacy to the modern era.

It is, however, possible to approach this differently. A contrasting perspective emerges if the Radical Reformation is historically reintegrated with the Reformation as a whole, rather than regarded from the outset as subordinate to, or a deviation from, the ostensibly normative theological claims set out by Luther in Wittenberg, Zwingli in Zurich, or Calvin in Geneva. To be sure, Luther's chronological priority is unquestionable in the events that unfolded between late 1517 and early 1521. He was overwhelmingly the most widely published and prominent anti-Roman reformer in the 1520s, especially through to 1525. Yet although Luther articulated what turned out to be an extremely influential principle—that God's Word in scripture was to be the arbiter of Christian truth—he did not, much to his chagrin, establish anything like a consensus about the meaning or application of God's Word among those who rejected Rome. This is apparent, for example, in his very public dispute with Huldrych Zwingli and the clash of their respective followers over the understanding of the Lord's Supper. Beginning in 1525, this was a divisive disagreement at the headwaters of what would become the socially and institutionally separate traditions of Lutheran and Reformed Protestantism. Yet this lack of agreement about the interpretation of God's Word is still more obvious in the Radical Reformation. Historically and empirically—as opposed to theologically or confessionally—the principle of *sola scriptura* (by scripture alone) did not lead inexorably, clearly, or even at all to *sola fide* (by faith alone) or *sola gratia* (by grace alone) as understood in Luther's terms. Nor did it yield anything remotely approaching agreement about what Christianity purified according to 'the Gospel' actually was, or should look like. Rather, it opened a Pandora's Box about the content and implications of Christian truth. What ensued was an indefinitely wide range of competing claims that began in the early 1520s, persisted throughout the Reformation era, and indeed has endured down to the present day within the very different institutional arrangements of the modern Western world.

The historical reintegration of the Radical Reformation into our understanding of early modern Christianity therefore makes possible a radically different perspective on the Protestant Reformation as a whole. If we consider 'the Reformation' not in the first instance as those forms of Protestantism that turned out to have the most political, social, and cultural influence, but rather as the full range of Christian claims and related practices present among those who rejected the Roman Church, then the Reformation as such appears in a new light. The Radical Reformation then simply becomes a term to denote politically defeated and marginalized expressions of Protestantism, those expressions that lacked sustained bases of support from political authorities anywhere in Europe. Once we distinguish analytically between the sustained exercise of political authority and the interpretation of God's Word—as we should, since there is no intrinsic connection between them—it becomes clear that the vast *majority* of the divergent Christian assertions made by those who rejected Rome in the sixteenth and seventeenth centuries were radical Protestant claims of one sort or another. Just as their beliefs differed widely, so too did their respective convictions about Christian life and how it should be lived out with respect to existing institutions and social relationships.

Seen from the shared perspective of the foundational commitment to God's Word that was taken to justify rejection of the Roman Church, it is Lutheranism and Reformed Protestantism (including the Church of England under Edward VI, Elizabeth I, James I, and more controversially Charles I) which appear as the Reformation era's great exceptions. Only these expressions of Protestantism had a major impact because, like Roman Catholicism in the areas where it continued to hold sway, they were the ones that received lasting political support. 'Scripture alone'—that is, the Bible *without* the power of political authorities standing behind approved interpretative authorities—did not of itself yield the putatively foundational doctrines characteristic of Lutheranism and Reformed Protestantism: justification by faith alone, and salvation by grace alone. These represented only one among many possible readings of God's Word. In this sense, the great outliers of the Protestant Reformation, seen as a whole, were Lutheranism and Reformed Protestantism, including the Church of England. In the sixteenth and seventeenth centuries there were many more radical than magisterial Protestant views of what constituted true Christianity, albeit the authorities' largely successful suppression of radical Protestants kept their numbers small and their early modern influence minimal. At the same time, both because they were politically suppressed and because they usually regarded religious images as objectionable and sometimes idolatrous, radical Protestants produced little in the way of visual expressions of their faith. They appear in written sources, but the Radical Reformation is less visually accessible to us than the Lutheran, the Reformed Protestant, or especially the Catholic Reformation, the last of which lies at the opposite end of the spectrum in this respect.

This perspective on the Radical Reformation affords a different conceptualization of the Reformation era itself. An indeterminate array of conflicting, rival claims about God's Word was what the Reformation's foundational principle of *sola scriptura* by itself produced in the *absence* of control by political authorities. We see this particularly clearly in the early German Reformation, at the outset of the period, and again at its end, in England during the 1640s and 1650s, when the political unrest of the revolutionary years and Civil Wars facilitated a proliferation of radical Protestant groups, including some that were socially and politically subversive. These episodes constitute, as it were, the two bookends of the Reformation era: they are the two periods in which the effects of the Reformation emphasis on scripture alone are most obviously apparent, unconstrained by political authorities' control of the Bible's meaning and application. During the century or so in between the early German Reformation and the English Revolution, a vast range of different radical Protestant beliefs and practices were articulated in different countries throughout Europe. For the most part they were suppressed or otherwise contained by Lutheran, Reformed, or Catholic authorities, as radical Protestants in diverse ways tended to reach various sorts of accommodation with the political circumstances in which they found themselves. No short essay can cover all of the individuals and groups who held these views and sought to live by them; it would be impossible even to treat in brief compass all the various Anabaptist groups, which, notwithstanding their commonalities as a sub-category within the broader Radical Reformation, constitute a wide range of doctrinally diverse and socially divergent Christians in various states of contestation between the 1520s and the late seventeenth century. But some sense of the variety of radical Protestantism, and thus of the variety of the Reformation as such, can be suggested in ways that break down the scholarly wall that usually, but unjustifiably, sequesters the Radical Reformation from its magisterial counterpart.

The Word of God Unfettered: The Early German Reformation

Considering the ubiquity of the late medieval Church, and its pervasive influence in every domain of human life, the principled rejection of its authority in the Reformation era could not have been anything but radical. Such a rejection was bound to strike at the *radix*, the root, of ingrained Christian beliefs, practices, and institutions. More than a millennium in the making, Latin Christianity was embedded in the rest of life, not separate or separable from it as something called 'religion'—this process of separation would in fact occur only as a consequence of the religio-political conflicts of the Reformation age. This interwovenness or inextricability contributed to the Church's objectionable oppressiveness in the eyes of those who spurned it. The

Church, in all its many-layered diversity and uncoordinated complexity, was Europe's most long-standing and important institution, so its repudiation was bound to have far-reaching effects. To regard the pope as the Antichrist rather than the Vicar of Christ, to reject the mass as an unbiblical perversion rather than the sacrificial centre of Christian worship, and to attack devotional images as idolatrous violations of God's commandments—these were not parts of a minor change of outlook or subtle shift in perspective. They belonged to a bid radically to reconfigure an inherited and institutionalized worldview.

In earlier medieval centuries, various groups, defined by ecclesiastical leaders as heretical, from Cathars and Waldensians to Lollards and Hussites, had similarly rejected the Church's authority. But they had been largely stifled, or at least held in check. By contrast, during the early 1520s the Reformation spread explosively in dozens of cities and hundreds of villages in the Holy Roman Empire and Switzerland. Sharply anticlerical and markedly apocalyptic, it was accompanied by impatient calls for 'Christian freedom' and aggressive actions directed against established ecclesiastical institutions. These culminated in the series of uprisings known collectively as the German Peasants' War (1524–6), the largest mass movement in western Europe before the French Revolution. The military suppression of this movement marked the definitive beginning of a differentiation between the Radical and magisterial Reformations: the subversive potential of 'the Gospel', as understood by the 'common man' exercising the 'freedom of a Christian', was made palpably clear to those secular authorities who rejected the Roman Church and offered protection to politically compliant Protestant reformers. With the exception of events at Münster in Westphalia a decade later, alliances between ecclesiastical and secular authorities would be largely effective throughout Europe for more than a century in ensuring that radical Protestantism posed no serious invitation to social or political unrest. It was otherwise in the early German Reformation, which was inherently unsettling and radical, by virtue of its opposition to the established Church, and the unexpected rapidity with which its ideas and imperatives found proactive adherents.

The Reformation was an ongoing and unresolved dispute about God's truth among Christians who rejected the authority of the established, Roman Church. As it first unfolded in the 1520s, the appeal to scripture alone as the authoritative standard for Christian faith and life demonstrated it had the power to break the impasses that had largely frustrated late medieval attempts to reform the Church in any systematic way from within. But 'scripture alone' immediately became an unintended problem of its own by engendering disagreement about the meaning of the Word of God and how its teaching should be applied. This should not be especially surprising, in light of the complex diversity of the texts that comprise the Bible; the fact that all early Protestant reformers insisted in one way or another on the need for the influence of the Holy Spirit in order to interpret God's Word correctly; and the unavoidability of people exercising reason in drawing distinctions and articulating relationships among theological claims. Depending on how one read, how one was moved by the Spirit, and how one employed reason in interpreting God's Word, the results could and did vary dramatically—despite frequent claims that scripture somehow interpreted itself or needed no interpreter. Moreover, the range of issues about which anti-Roman Christians could and did disagree—grace and free will, the sacraments, liturgy, ministry, ecclesiology (doctrines of the nature of the Church), authority, and so forth—ensured that the opportunities for socially divisive exegetical disputes were legion. Interpretative disagreements about the Bible among anti-Roman Christians can be seen even before Luther's formal condemnation in early 1521; hence, arguably even before there was a Reformation movement to speak of. Soon thereafter they became apparent in conflicts about how, and by whom, God's imperatives for Christian worship and life were to be implemented. Luther's case became a cause—that of 'the Gospel'—which far outstripped his or anyone else's control, as the early Reformation, in all its unsettling radicalism, became first a popular and then a mass movement culminating in the Peasants' War. Although it is only with the defeat of the commoners and their allies that the difference between the magisterial and Radical Reformations becomes clear, the distinction had earlier been emerging in the reforming cities of Wittenberg and Zurich.

The earliest 'radical reformers' were simply those who, in urban or village settings, lost out in the contested attempts to define the gospel and to secure support for political control over those attempts. Wittenberg provides the first case in point. By late December 1521, while Luther was in the protective custody of Frederick of Saxony in the Wartburg Castle, following Charles V's condemnation of him in the Edict of Worms, Andreas Bodenstein von Karlstadt (1483–1541) became the leader of the concrete religious changes being implemented in the city. On Christmas day he celebrated the liturgy in Wittenberg without clerical attire, in the German language rather than Latin, and distributed the consecrated wine (traditionally reserved for the clergy) as well as bread to laypeople who in previous weeks had been openly agitating for change. Karlstadt, Luther's colleague in the theology faculty of the city's recently established university, agreed with him that scripture is its own interpreter, the clearer and more Christocentric passages being the presumptive key to understanding more difficult ones. He drew a corollary which was consistent with Luther's view of the priesthood of all believers: that 'the interpretation of scripture will belong to all Christians'. Hence, 'all to whom the Lord bestows that gift of interpreting scripture are able to interpret it, whether they be laymen or clerics, secular or religious'. Yet Karlstadt differed from Luther not, as has sometimes been thought, simply on the pace and timing of reforms to be implemented, but on fundamental issues of biblical interpretation concerning the relationship between God's commandments and Christian life. Some of these divergences were already apparent even before Luther's formal condemnation in the Edict of Worms (May 1521). They became manifest in the liturgical changes, and provision for the removal of sacred images from churches, promulgated in the new ordinances approved by the Wittenberg city council in January 1522. Luther returned to Wittenberg in March, and preached a series of homilies known as his *Invocavit* sermons (from the name for the first Sunday in Lent, taken from the opening word of the introductory prayer of that day's mass). With these he succeeded in reversing Karlstadt's influence. Thereafter, the 'freedom of a Christian' no longer included Karlstadt's freedom to preach or publish in Wittenberg. Just weeks after having been the city's leader of the Reformation, he was marginalized—and thus became a 'radical'. After serving as pastor for a period in Orlamünde in 1523–4, Karlstadt was exiled from Saxony and, despite their earlier congruence on matters of eucharistic theology, he henceforth became Luther's opponent in the rancorous disputes over the Lord's Supper that loomed so large in Germany and Switzerland from late 1524 onwards.

An analogous process unfolded in Zurich, where there was an important initial contestation among reformers concerning the tithe. Prior to the Reformation, in communally minded rural churches, tithes had been for decades the subject of villagers' complaints. They were dissatisfied with the way in which their payments had augmented the income of wealthy religious orders, rather than being used to support local parish worship and pastoral care. The Reformation, with its emphasis on 'the Gospel' and the 'pure Word of God', provided fresh impetus for objections. In June 1523, Wilhelm Reublin, the pastor of Witikon outside Zurich, along with Simon Stumpf of Höngg, petitioned the Zurich city council on behalf of several villages for permission to stop paying the tithe in the customary manner. The city council refused. Huldrych Zwingli, who already in 1520 had denied there was any biblical basis legitimizing the collection of the tithe among elite clergy, sided with the council. He justified its authority to oversee the collection of tithes as part of the proper civic regulation of the city, including control over its surrounding villages. Zwingli thus established a pattern he would follow in subsequent years: he sought to influence the city council, while simultaneously supporting it as the institutional key to the implementation of his understanding of the gospel. It was not how Reublin, Stumpf, and the disgruntled villagers understood matters in 1523. Accordingly, like Karlstadt in Wittenberg, they became 'radicals'.

So too did those who found themselves in dispute with Zwingli over infant baptism, as this issue began to unfold in Zurich the following year. Rebuffed by Zwingli and the civic authorities, Conrad Grebel baptized Georg Blaurock, Felix Mantz, and other adults in Mantz's house in January 1525, the first time any of them, as far as they were concerned, had been truly baptized. They had come to regard infant 'baptism', which had for many centuries been the norm in Latin Christianity, as a meaningless ritual practised on babies who by definition could not have the faith that was the prerequisite for becoming a Christian. Indeed, as they saw the matter, this practice of 'baptizing' infants went a long way toward explaining why so many reforming measures within the Church had so often proved so ineffectual: the very nature of what it was to become a Christian had been radically misunderstood. *First* one had to receive the regenerative power of God's grace as an interior baptism of the Spirit, *after* which one self-consciously accepted external baptism by water as a sign of one's commitment actually to follow Christ as he had commanded in the Gospel. 'Why do you call me "Lord, Lord", and do not do what I tell you?' (Luke 6: 46). Jesus' words in Mark 16: 16 expressed a critically important sequential order that implied a distinctive ecclesiology: 'The one who believes and is baptized will be saved.' Faith had to come first,

REVERENDVS IN CHRISTO D AN

dreas Botenstein Carolstadius, obijt ... anno ætatis suæ quinquagesimoquinto,
In parochiali ... Petri sepultus.

Anno salutis M.D.XLI.

die 24. Decembris.

IN IMAGINEM SEMPITERNAE LAVDIS FOR

tissimi pietatis & diuinæ gloriæ uindicis D. Andreæ Boten...ein Carolstadij Epicedion: olim à
Heinricho Pantaleone Basiliensi, ad opt... spei adolescentem Adamum
Botenstein Carolstadium, in so... paternæ mortis, scriptum.

Huc ades Aonidum cœtus laurumq; superbam
 Temnite, plorantes non decet iste nitor:
Cingite fer ali mox tempora sacra Cupresso
 Addicta hæc uestris luctibus utq; suit:
Inuida Fata simul pergunt extinguere sanctos
 Vt mala grassentur liberiore uia.
Ecce tot annorum studio curaq; paratus
 Ingenij torrens aureus iste cadit.
En CAROLSTADIVS quem olim Franconia misit
 Occidit, Heluetium gloria, fama, decus.
Pro dolor immites crudelia numina Parcæ
 Præstiterat nullas nos habuisse manus:
Nam nos Iudæas uoces & Barbara dicta
 Chaldæo docuit uerba notanda sono
Nouerat Hebræas, Græcas, Musaq́; Latinas
 Magnus erat studijs dogmatibusq; pijs,
Omniq́; diuinæ repetens oracula legis
 Quæq́; fides Christi, quæ pia turba dedit.
Doctrinam Domini docuit resonantia uerba
 Hic docuit quicquid cura salutis habet
Omnibus afflictis peccato ostendere CHRISTVM
 Prodidit, ad cœlos multa trophæa tulit.

Clauiger instructam capitum grege ... nulit Hydram,
 Compulit hic isto durius angue malum.
Scit Romana lues bullarum turba ministri
 Quos Heros fudit sæpius arte sua.
Hinc Medicaq́; legens una cum legibus artes
 Hinc legit Pallas quicquid amare potest.
Explicuit certos nexus, facilemq́; Poesin
 Et uarios orbes pulcher Apollo tuos.
Inde huic plus alijs sæuit Dea cæca nec unquam
 Desijt immeritis exagitare modis.
Sed quanquam Fortuna uiri uirtutibus esset
 Inuida, Fortunam uincere doctus erat.
Hinc patrias nil fecit opes, nil fecit honores
 Quò mel ut posset uiuere Christe tibi.
Donec his quis is lustris Deus addidit unum
 Et noua nix cœpit cœpit inesse suo.
Præscidit atq; uiri uitam: mors falce maligna
 Et rigidus stygio uexit in amne Charon:
Nam tibi ab exequijs uiuat maior imago relucet
 Fama quidem uiuis esse maligna solet.
Teq́; uiri, & iuuenes, uotis plancluq́; requirunt
 Hoc decus ingenij, gloria, fama facit.

Felix ?...issum quem maxima turba bonorum
 Defunctum desiens pectore quemq́; colunt.
Illa dies esset nigro signanda lapillo
 Ni pars restaret maxima uiua tui:
Filius en ADAM superest spes altera turbæ
 Christicolûm, formam, pectora, patris habens.
Sed quorsum hæc? cœlum tenet, isthuc tendimus omnes
 Hoc nos sollicitos nocte dieq; facit.
Omnia nunc nouit, uidet omnia, nec fugit ipsum
 Quicquid habet cœlum, tartara quicquid habent
Lætus enim supra stellatum spiritus orbem
 Incedit, pedibus nubila regna premens.

ADAMI BOTENSTEIN IN sacra paren
tis Carmen,

Laudibus tuebitur permultis pictor Apelles
 Certius at longè carmine cuncta docent
Nam licet ad uiuum referat pictura parentem,
 Hoc tamen elogium rectius arte refert.
Hanc quoties chartam uideo, lætor simul atq́;
 Mœreo, defunctus namq; beatus adest
Vos precor ô superi grates persoluite dignas
 Omnibus, ingenuæ qui sua cuiq́; dabunt.

BASILEAE.

Ex Nr. 1156.323

ANDREAS BODENSTEIN VON KARLSTADT (1486–1541) at age 55 from a Basler Gedenkblatt (1541/2). Karlstadt was senior to Martin Luther in the Theology Faculty at the University of Wittenberg and the leader of the Reformation movement in the city prior to Luther's return from the Wartburg Castle in March 1522. He was soon prohibited from preaching or publishing in Wittenberg because of his disagreements with Luther.

baptism after. The earliest Anabaptists—in this case, members of the group that historians have come to call the Swiss Brethren—insisted that the Bible alone was the basis for their beliefs and practices. They correctly claimed that scripture included no direct mandate for infant baptism; Zwingli defended it by analogy to the Jewish practice of circumcision. But however biblical their view, it was defined as illegal by local authorities and thereby became a 'radical' position, their insistence on believers' baptism a 'radical' practice.

The examples of Wittenberg and Zurich show how, viewed retrospectively, the early Radical Reformation is a phrase describing those evangelicals whose interpretations of God's Word were politically marginalized. At the time, however, as anti-Roman sentiment and actions gained an unwieldy momentum between 1522 and 1525, it was unclear what the outcome of the movement would be, and which version(s) of 'the Gospel' would take hold. An unprecedented efflorescence of popular pamphlets, exhortatory and critical preaching, and word-of-mouth communication contributed to the spread of the movement in the towns and villages of central and south-western Germany and Switzerland. By the spring of 1525, the Reformation movement had swamped the ideas of any individual reformer, as the 'common man' idealized in so many early evangelical pamphlets and sermons made his presence felt in the form of proactive alliances among hundreds of thousands of energized peasants and sympathetic burghers. Those involved in the Peasants' War rejected Luther's claim that the gospel had nothing to do with altering concrete social, economic, or political realities. They rejected Zwingli's commitment to the role of established authorities in overseeing religious changes— changes that stopped well short of any fundamental reordering of society's hierarchical socio-economic or political relationships. From the Black Forest, where the uprisings began in the summer of 1524, to the Tyrol in Austria where they were finally suppressed two years later, many participants seem to have regarded the redress of socio-economic injustices and political oppression as an expression of a fraternal egalitarianism and Christian brotherly love at the heart of the gospel as they understood it.

The multiple sets of petitions and demands formulated during the Peasants' War reflect different emphases, but many concerns recur frequently: the control over the appointment of pastors by the local community, worship according to the Word of God, the use of tithes to support local worship and pastoral care, an end (where applicable) to feudal obligations and oppressive taxation, and the restoration of traditional access to common woods, meadows, and streams. The Reformation emphasis on 'the Gospel' and the 'pure Word of God' lent new force and meaning to the traditional recourse to godly law and divine justice which had appeared in the peasant rebellions of preceding decades. The *Twelve Articles of the Upper Swabian Peasants*, which very quickly became the most widespread of the peasant demands, stated that 'if one or more of the articles we have composed here is not in accordance with the word of God, we will retract these articles, if they can be shown to be improper according to the word of God...We will renounce them if they are explained to be false on the basis of Scripture.' This is precisely what Luther had said about his own controversial theological assertions in the presence of Charles V at

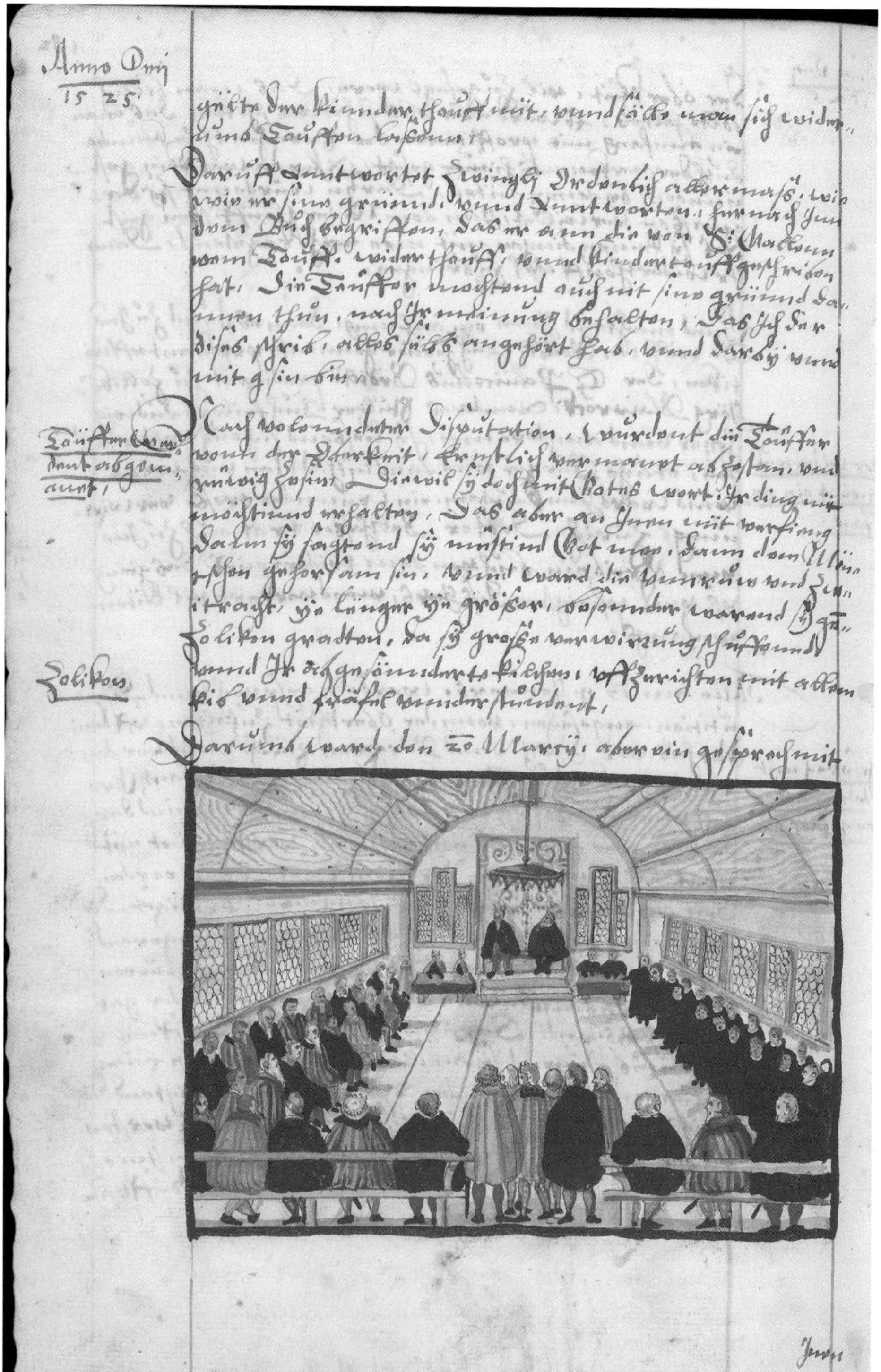

DISPUTATION OVER BAPTISM between Anabaptist leaders and Zwingli with his associates before Zurich city magistrates, 17 March 1525. The first adult baptisms were performed in Zurich two months before the event depicted in this later watercolour. Huldrych Zwingli defended infant baptism, which was rejected by Swiss and other Anabaptist groups as unbiblical and a key to understanding why attempts to reform Christendom had failed.

From Heinrich Thomann (1544–1618), *Die Thomann-Abschrift von Bullingers Reformationsgeschichte* (1605).

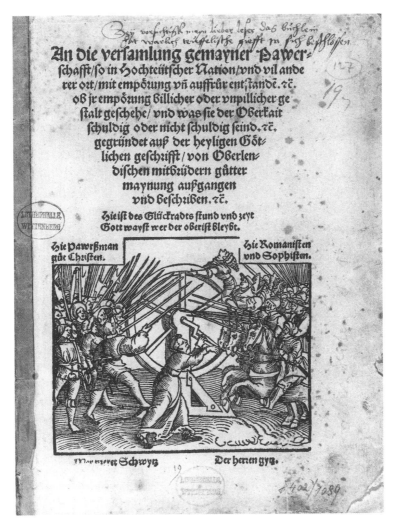

TITLE PAGE OF THE PAMPHLET *To the Assembly of the Common Peasantry* (1525). The German Peasants' War of 1524–6 was the most politically earnest, subversive expression of the early Reformation in central Europe. Dozens of lists of grievances articulated demands for the redress of social, political, and economic injustices, some of which were printed. In this published list from 1525, the 'good Christian peasants' on one side are arraigned over against the 'Romanists and sophists'—Catholic authorities as well as reformers such as Luther and Zwingli—on the other. The defeat of the attempted 'Revolution of 1525' marked the beginning of a sharp separation between the politically supported magisterial Reformation and the politically marginalized and persecuted Radical Reformation.

the Diet of Worms in 1521. Considerable scholarly debate has long surrounded the extent to which the uprisings of 1524–6 were 'religious' in character, and thus critically indebted to the Reformation, or rather essentially 'economic' and 'political' in character, and therefore better understood as an expression of material concerns continuous with central European peasant grievances and rebellions in preceding decades. But in a culture in which human beings were regarded as embodied souls, in which eternal salvation depended on one's actions in the here and now, in which no events transpired outside the reach of divine providence, and in which human justice was never independent of divine justice, this scholarly distinction seems dubious. Neither economic issues nor the exercise of power were any more independent of Christianity in the early sixteenth century than they had been in the Middle Ages.

Some of the most prominent leaders in the Peasants' War certainly did not think so. Thomas Müntzer (*c.*1489–1525), an apocalyptic preacher influenced by late medieval mysticism, referred to the oppressive alliance of secular and ecclesiastical elites over against ordinary Christians as 'the abomination'. Already by late 1521, in the shortest (and probably first) draft of his unpublished 'Prague Manifesto', Müntzer juxtaposed 'mere scripture' to a genuine understanding of the Bible, the prattling of scholars and scribes to the testimony of the Holy Spirit given to God's elect, 'which then gives our spirit ample testimony that we are children of God. For anyone who does not feel the spirit of Christ within him, or is not quite sure of having it, is not a member of Christ, but of the devil.' Increasingly, Müntzer fused this either-or vision of God's elect and the damned with his socio-political distinction between the 'common man' and his privileged oppressors. In early 1525 he became the leader of a Thuringian peasant band, several thousand strong, that in May suffered a cataclysmic defeat at the Battle of Frankenhausen; shortly afterwards Müntzer himself was executed. Müntzer's ardent apocalypticism had rendered superfluous any need to conceive concretely the character and institutions of a restructured Christian society. By contrast, the former secretary to the Prince-Bishop of Salzburg, Michael Gaismair, who became an important leader in the Peasants' War in the Tyrol, envisioned for the future an anti-hierarchical Christian order of peasants, miners, and artisans, one anchored in the political self-determination of local institutions that included a declericalized church. But short of total revolution, such forms of the gospel had no chance of gaining acceptance among established political authorities, predicated as they were on the overthrow of those authorities.

Instead the common man was violently suppressed. The defeat of the attempted 'Revolution of 1525' marks the beginning of an enduring differentiation between the magisterial and Radical Reformations—not only in Germany and Switzerland, but also throughout Europe during the remainder of the era. The early evangelical movement demonstrated that, depending on how one read scripture, understood the Word of God, and sought to apply the gospel, the Bible could pose a serious threat to secular as well as ecclesiastical authorities. Scriptural interpretation and implementation would have to be monitored and controlled, as had happened in Wittenberg as early as January 1522, and in Zurich beginning in 1523. After 1525, those anti-Roman Christians who refused to accept the forms of the gospel sanctioned by political authorities working with cooperative reformers were no longer part of an expanding popular movement; instead, they were precariously exposed as proscribed radical Protestants. Anabaptists were the most numerous and clearly identifiable among them in the decade after the defeat of the 'common man'.

Historians once regarded the first Anabaptists as principled non-resistant separatists who stood at the opposite end of the spectrum from the violent rebels involved in

THOMAS MÜNCER PREDIGER TOT ALSTAT.

TOMAS MVNCER PREDIGER ZV ALSTET IN DVRINGEN.

THOMAS MÜNTZER (*c*.1489–1525). Although he was initially sympathetic to Luther, beginning in 1521 Müntzer started to repudiate the idea that the gospel had no bearing on concrete social, political, and economic realities. A significant leader in the German Peasants' War, Müntzer was captured at the Battle of Frankenhausen and executed in May 1525.

From Christoph van Sichem Arnhemius, *Historische Beschrijvinge ende offbeeldinge der voorneemste Hooft Ketteren* (1608).

the Peasants' War. It has since been demonstrated that the early Anabaptists held many different positions with respect to political authority, and that numerous Anabaptists and future Anabaptists participated in the Peasants' War and shared its protagonists' biblically influenced socio-economic and political concerns. In this light, Anabaptist separatism of the sort paradigmatically expressed, for example, in the Schleitheim Articles (1527) drawn up by the former Benedictine monk Michael Sattler is best seen as a reaction to the defeat of the peasants in 1525–6. Essentially, if the world rejected Christianity, then Christianity had to reject the world. Society as a whole apparently was not to be transformed, at least not in the 1520s. But, this side of the apocalypse, self-conscious Christians might seek to create communities in which their understanding of the gospel could flourish in miniature. Not all early Anabaptist leaders opposed the legitimate exercise of political power, as the example of Balthasar Hubmaier (*c*.1480–1528) makes clear. The most theologically learned among the early Anabaptist leaders—he had earned a doctorate in theology at Ingolstadt under Luther's theological adversary, Johannes Eck—Hubmaier theorized the acceptable use of temporal authority and oversaw the creation of civic Anabaptism: first in the village of Waldshut north-west of Zurich between April and December 1525, then again in Moravian Nikolsburg between mid-1526 and mid-1527.

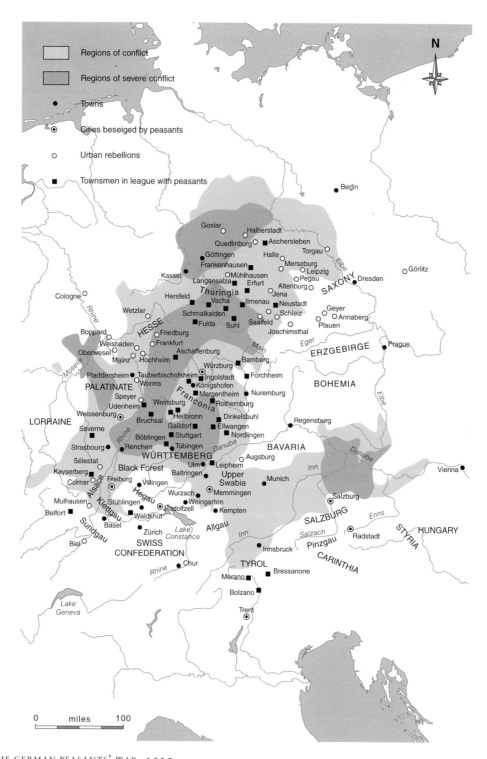

Regions of conflict

Regions of severe conflict

● Towns

⊙ Cities beseiged by peasants

○ Urban rebellions

■ Townsmen in league with peasants

N

Berlin

Goslar
Halberstadt
Quedlinburg
Aschersleben
Göttingen
Halle
Torgau
Frankenhausen
Merseburg
Leipzig
Kassel
Mühlhausen
Pegau
Altenburg
Dresden
Langensalza
Erfurt
SAXONY
Görlitz
Hersfeld
Thuringia
Vacha
Jena
Cologne
Ilmenau
Neustadt
Wetzlar
Schmalkalden
Schleiz
Geyer
Annaberg
HESSE
Fulda
Suhl
Saalfeld
Plauen
Boppard
Friedburg
Joachimsthal
Weisbaden
Frankfurt
ERZGEBIRGE
Prague
Oberwesel
Aschaffenburg
Eger
Mainz
Hochheim
Bamberg
BOHEMIA
Würzburg
Pladdersheim
Tauberbischofsheim
Ingolstadt
Forchheim
PALATINATE
Worms
Königshofen
Speyer
Mergentheim
Nuremburg
Udenheim
Franconia
Rothernburg
Weinsberg
Heilbronn
Dinkelsbuhl
Weissenburg
Bruchsal
Gaildorf
Ellwangen
Regensburg
Saverne
Böblingen
Stuttgart
Nordlingen
LORRAINE
Strasbourg
Renchen
Tübingen
BAVARIA
Danube
Sélestat
WÜRTTEMBERG
Augsburg
Danube
Kayserberg
Ulm
Leipheim
Vienna
Colmar
Freiburg
Baltringen
Upper
Munich
Inn
Black Forest
Villingen
Swabia
Mulhausen
Wurzach
Memmingen
Salzburg
Alsace
Stühlingen
Weingarten
Belfort
Klettgau
Waldshut
Radolfzell
Kempten
SALZBURG
Basel
Zürich
Lake
Allgau
Enns
Biel
Constance
Inn
STYRIA
SWISS
Innsbruck
Salzach
Radstadt
HUNGARY
CONFEDERATION
Pinzgau
CARINTHIA
Chur
TYROL
Rhine
Merano
Bressanone
Lake
Bolzano
Geneva
Trent

Rhine
Moselle
Main

0   miles   100

THE GERMAN PEASANTS' WAR, 1525
Source: Internet: http://germanhistorydocs.ghi-dc.org/map.cfm?map_id=3667. Where credited to Peter Blickle,
The Revolution of 1525, trans. Thomas A. Brady, Jr., and H. C. Erik Midelfort. Baltimore and London: The
Johns Hopkins University Press, 1981, map 1.

1. PATRONAGE, DEVOTION, AND INTERCESSION: Painted in 1484 by Hans Memling for the prominent Bruges family Moreel, this triptych is an image of late medieval salvation, uniting those in this world with the next. The donors and their children kneel in the wings with the saints Christopher, Maurus, and Giles in the centre. The husband Willem, a leading politician in Bruges, is protected by St William of Maleval, while his wife Barbara, from a prominent family, prays under the protection of her namesake, St Barbara. The triptych belonged to the family's altar in the St James church.

2. CHURCH AT PRAYER: In this page from the Sherbourne Missal (early fifteenth-century service book with the texts and music for the mass through the year) the mass for the first Sunday of Lent is decorated with the three temptations of Christ. Christ stands above a medieval church that is the Benedictine abbey at Sherbourne depicted as the Temple in Jerusalem. In the bottom left the Devil tempts Jesus to make bread from stones, while on the right he is taken to a high mountain to view the kingdoms of the world. The Sherbourne Missal with almost 700 beautifully illustrated parchment pages weighs nearly fifty pounds.

TEMPLE DE LYON, NOMME PARADIS.

3. THE CIRCLE OF FAITH. Interior of the Temple de Paradis, Lyon 1564 attributed to Jacques Perrisin. French Calvinists (Huguenots) preferred to call their houses of worship 'temples' rather than 'churches', and they built many of them throughout France, since they could not always take over existing Catholic churches. This circular temple in Lyon reifies the Calvinist attitude toward sacred space as a theater of the Word, devoid of images and altars, where preaching is absolutely central. In this interior view, men and women are segregated, and everyone listens attentively to the preacher, even the children and the dog near the pulpit.

4. WAR AGAINST THE ELECT. Franz Hogenberg, *The Spanish Fury at Antwerp*, 1576; M. Eytzinger, *De Leone Belgico*, Cologne, 1588. Spanish troops capture the city of Antwerp in November 1576 and slaughter its Calvinists. The continuous occupation of this city by the Spanish would restore its Catholic identity, but religious violence would continue to plague the Netherlands for decades to come. Engravings such as this served to memorialize atrocities and forestall reconciliation.

5. ESCAPE OF SWISS ANABAPTISTS FROM THE ZURICH *Hexenturm,* 21 March 1526, from Heinrich Thomann (1544–1618), *Die Thomann-Abschrift von Bullingers Reformationsgeschichte* (1605). Anabaptists were severely persecuted from the beginning of their movement in the early 1520s. The Zurich city council made Anabaptism a capital offence in early 1526, but occasionally those imprisoned were able to escape.

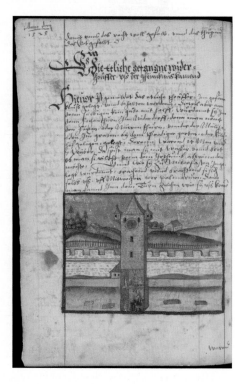

6. EXECUTION BY DROWNING OF HUTTERITE missionaries Heinrich Sommer and Jakob Mandel in Baden, 9 October 1582, from Johann Jakob Wick, *Nachrichtensammlung.* Hutterite missionaries from Bohemia and Moravia sought potential converts in other territories of the Holy Roman Empire, much to the chagrin of local Protestant or Catholic authorities. The story of Sommer and Mandel and their deaths was also taken up in the Dutch Mennonite martyrological tradition and depicted in one of Jan Luyken's engravings in the second edition of Thieleman Jans van Braght's *Martyrs' Mirror* (1685).

7. PORTRAIT OF ST URSULA. This locally painted image of St Ursula, in an exquisitely carved hardwood frame, is dated to the sixteenth/seventeenth century. It shows clear evidence of having been based on a western print even though the saint displays a distinctively non-western physiognomy. It used to hang in the Cathedral, Old Goa. Wood, polychrome and gilt, 97.5 × 53 cm.

8. ST IGNATIUS OF ANTIOCH MAULED BY A LION. Visitors to the church of Santa María de Mediavilla in the small town of Medina de Rioseco (Valladolid) in Northern Spain can still admire today the collection of Hispano-Philippine ivories given by a native of the town, Antonio Paiño (1602–69), Archbishop of Seville. Perhaps the most striking item is this mid-seventeenth-century statue of St Ignatius of Antioch (d. c.107), killed by lions in the Colosseum during the persecution under Emperor Trajan (r. 98–117). So convinced was the saint of the presence within him of the spirit of Christ that he referred to himself in his famous letters as 'bearer of God' (theophoros). Accordingly, the saint is shown standing with the lion, here in the form of an oriental dragon, clawing at his chest and tearing his flesh from behind to reveal the initials 'IHS'—the insignia of the Society of Jesus, which almost certainly commissioned the statue from its Chinese maker.

9. TITLE PAGE OF THE 'GREAT BIBLE', 1539. This is the Reformation as Henry VIII imagined and wanted it to be. An enthroned Supreme Head reinforces order and obedience by distributing the Word of God through the proper hierarchical channels. But as Henry was soon forced to recognize, access to vernacular scripture might encourage people to question the dictates of secular and ecclesiastical authority.

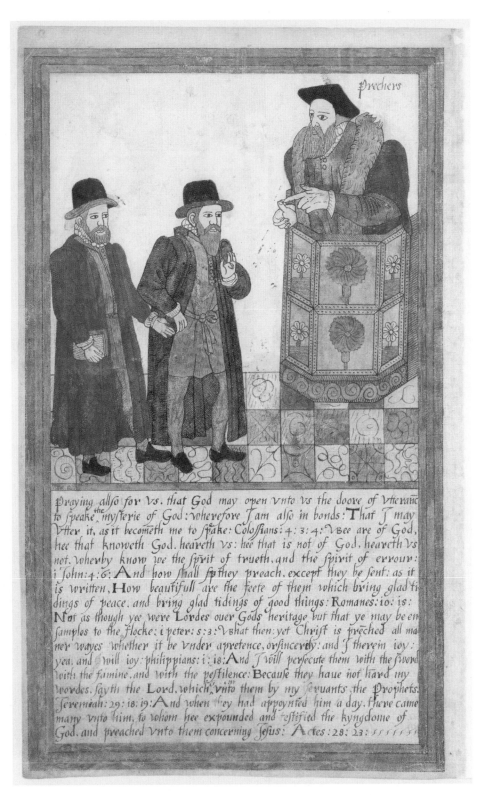

Prechers

Praying allso for vs. that God may open vnto vs the doore of vtteravnc
to speake the mysterie of God: wherefore I am also in bonds: That I may
Vtter it, as it becometh me to speake: Colossians: 4: 3: 4: VBee are of God,
hee that knoweth God. heareth vs: hee that is not of God, heareth vs
not. wherby know we the spirit of trueth, and the spirit of errour:
i John: 4: 6: And how shall fathey preach, except they be sent: as it
is written, How beautifull are the feete of them which bring glad ti
dings of peace, and bring glad tidings of good things: Romanes: 10: 15:
Not as though yee were Lordes ouer Gods heritage but that ye may be en
samples to the flocke: i peter: 5: 3: Vshat then: yet Christ is preched all ma
ner wayes whether it be vnder apretence, orsincerely: and I therein ioy:
yea. and I will ioy: philippians: i: 18: And I will persecute them with the sword
with the famine, and with the pestilence: Because they haue not hard my
wordes. sayth the Lord, which vnto them by my seruants the Prophets.
Ieremiah: 29: 18: 19: And when they had appoynted him a day, there came
many vnto him, to whom hee expounded and testified the kyngdome of
God, and preached vnto them concerning Iesus: Actes: 28: 23: ſſſſſſſ

10. A PREACHER IN THE PULPIT, from the Commonplace Book of Thomas Trevilian, 1608. For most British Protestants, especially of a godly or Puritan bent, the Word of God in scripture was something which had to be, not merely read, but publicly preached, if it was to awaken in people a recognition of faith.

11. PIETER JANSSENS ELINGA, *Room in a Dutch House.* Cleanliness increasingly came to be regarded as a marker of godliness in post-Reformation society. The value placed upon it in the Protestant Netherlands is encapsulated in many Dutch paintings of domestic interiors, which served a didactic rather than merely decorative purpose.

12. GRANT DE VOLSON WOOD, *American Gothic* (1930). The idea that Protestantism fostered an ethic of work, which led its adherents to adopt frugal lifestyles and despise leisure as a frivolity, is now acknowledged to be a myth, but the stereotype persists and has left a wide cultural footprint.

BALTHASAR HUBMAIER (*c*.1480–1528). Hubmaier was the most theologically learned early Anabaptist leader, having received a doctorate in theology under the tutelage of Johannes Eck at the University of Ingolstadt. He briefly established Anabaptism as the civic religion of the small towns of Waldshut and later Nikolsburg, and approved the use of temporal power by magistrates.

From Christoph van Sichem Arnhemius, *Historische Beschrijvinge ende offbeeldinge der voorneemste Hooft Ketteren* (1608).

In the late 1520s severe persecution drove Hubmaier and other early Anabaptists from Zurich and its environs, plus many more from southern Germany and Austria, to seek refuge in Moravia. There political circumstances were less onerous, and the impulse toward separatism was enhanced. Anabaptist identity was profoundly shaped by the expectation of suffering, and the widespread experience of martyrdom, brought about by the actions of hostile political authorities sensitized to the dangers of religious dissent in the wake of the Peasants' War. Nearly 500 executions—almost 60 per cent of the total number of German-speaking Anabaptists put to death between 1525 and 1618—occurred between 1527 and 1530. Subsequent generations of germanophone Anabaptists would be deeply marked by a martyrological mentality, and an identity strengthened by the sacrifices made for the faith by men and women who had died as 'sheep for the slaughter', as Grebel had put it. Those put to death included many of the most important early Anabaptist leaders: Mantz and Sattler in 1527, Hubmaier in 1528, Blaurock in 1529.

Despite their shared experience of suffering, rejection of infant baptism, and commitment to the practice of following Christ as the necessary, exterior complement to interior spiritual regeneration, early Anabaptists disagreed among themselves in ways that divided them as concrete communities of faith. Not only did the Swiss

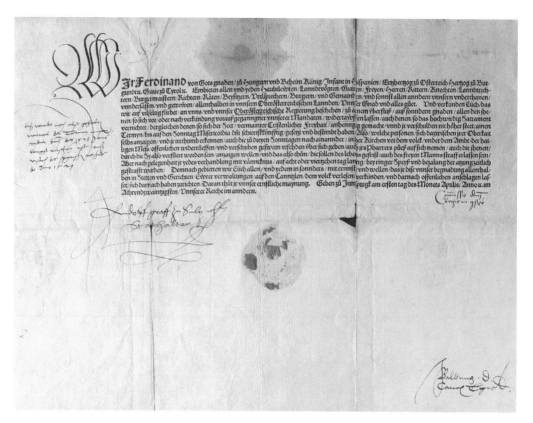

IMPERIAL MANDATE OF ARCHDUKE FERDINAND I defending Catholicism against heresy, 1 April 1528. Early Anabaptists were most severely persecuted in Habsburg lands under direct imperial jurisdiction. Ferdinand I issued eleven mandates against heresy from August 1527 to April 1534. The intensity of the persecution, which claimed the lives of nearly 500 Anabaptists between 1527 and 1530, contributed to the migration of many Anabaptists to safer political circumstances in Bohemia and Moravia.

Brethren include leaders with dramatically different views on the exercise of temporal authority (Hubmaier, Grebel, Sattler), but they also rejected the Moravian groups marked by the practice of community ownership of goods. Yet these groups—the Gabrielites, Austerlitz Brethren, Hutterites, and Philipites—were also distinct from one another. The South German and Austrian Anabaptists indebted to the apocalypticism of Thomas Müntzer, including Hans Denck and Hans Hut, diverged in multiple directions already in the late 1520s. Denck's views, for example, like those of Christian Entfelder and Hans Bünderlin, emphasized much more than those of some other Anabaptists the distinction between the mere letter of scripture and the Word of God—the determination of the latter, in their estimate, turning critically on the inspiration of the Holy Spirit. Moving away from the biblical literalism of many of the Swiss Brethren, such spiritualizing Anabaptists tended also to de-emphasize the importance of external religious practices. As was already mentioned, this emphasis on the necessity of some sort of role of the Holy Spirit in the correct understanding of scripture was an idea shared with all of the magisterial reformers; one cannot on this point draw a neat distinction between radical and magisterial Protestants. Exactly what it meant, how it was to be exercised, and how one recognized it in action remained contested issues throughout the Reformation era. Erasmus had asked the key question already in 1524: 'What am I to do when many persons allege different interpretations, each one of whom swears to have the Spirit?' Nothing close to a common answer appeared regarding criteria for adjudication among rivals, whether in the 1520s or at any time thereafter, a fact that would become especially visible once again during the English Revolution.

This did not prevent certain radical Protestants in the 1520s from pressing the emphasis on the Spirit still further. Advocates such as the Silesian nobleman Caspar Schwenckfeld (1489–1561) and Sebastian Franck (1499–1542) had a point: how was one to sort through all these pullulating evangelical claims about the meaning of the Bible? 'Scripture alone' had manifestly led not to clarity and consensus but to contestation and confusion. As they saw it—and this was a point shared with Catholic critics of the Reformation—the problem lay in the principle itself. Instead of entering the fray of what already looked like (and would indeed prove to be) ongoing, endless disputes about many significant Christian doctrines, with all the contending claims purporting to be derived from scripture, radical spiritualists such as Franck and Schwenckfeld came to champion a direct openness to the Spirit per se as the way to break the impasse. But it did not. In disagreeing sharply with each other they simultaneously established a pattern that would also characterize spiritualist Protestants throughout the era. Schwenckfeld called for a suspension of the Lord's Supper, given the reformers' bitter eucharistic controversies, but he remained more conventional in his theological preoccupations and ecclesiological concerns than was Franck. The latter essentially came to espouse a sceptical and non-cognitive view of Christianity that rejected more thoroughly all religious 'externals', including the home-based prayer gatherings commended by Schwenckfeld. Women, particularly widows and those who were unmarried, were especially prominent in the Schwenckfelders' conventicles: Helena Streicher and her three daughters, for example, were for decades the leaders of a Schwenckfelder network centred in Ulm that stretched across southern Germany. Among spiritualist radicals, as the contrasts between Schwenckfelder and Franck made clear already in the early Reformation, it turned out to be much easier to criticize others' interpretations of the sacraments or views of the Church than it was to convince them that one had divined rightly the direct promptings of the Holy Spirit.

The same sort of difficulty greeted those Christians who in a related manner claimed latter-day prophetic inspiration, beginning with Müntzer and the Zwickau prophets as early as 1521. If God had revealed himself through his prophets in ancient Israel, why could he not do so also in contemporary Germany? Those versed in scripture knew that God, speaking through the prophet Joel, had said: 'I will pour out my spirit on all flesh; your sons and your daughters shall prophesy, your old men shall dream dreams and your young men shall see visions' (Joel 2: 28), a verse that Peter had repeated among those gathered in Jerusalem at Pentecost (Acts 2: 17). This,

CASPAR VON SCHWENCKFELD (1489–1561). A Silesian nobleman, Schwenckfeld was a spiritualist who interpreted the bitter conflict among Protestants over the interpretation of the Eucharist in the 1520s to mean that administration of this sacrament was to be suspended altogether. Women seem disproportionately to have been drawn to his version of Christianity.

Peter said, would happen 'in the last days', the era in which so many Christians of the early Reformation thought they were living. There were plenty of biblical precedents and models, multiple streams of medieval prophetic literature on which to draw, and no shortage in the sixteenth century of those who claimed latter-day prophetic revelations as a direct gift from God. But, among all those that competed for attention and adherents in the early Reformation, whose prophecies, and whose visions, were trustworthy?

Among the most influential, as it turned out, were those of Melchior Hoffman (c.1495–1543), a peripatetic furrier and lay preacher who had spent time in various Baltic cities, as well as Stockholm, Lübeck, Kiel, Wittenberg, and Flensburg, before he arrived in 1529 in Strasbourg, a crossroads for Anabaptists and spiritualist Protestants in the later 1520s and early 1530s. Influenced there by the prophetic visionaries Lienhard and Ursula Jost and Barbara Rebstock, as well as by Hans Denck and Caspar Schwenckfeld, Hoffman became an Anabaptist and prophesied that God would establish Strasbourg as the New Jerusalem, after exterminating the godless at the behest of the city's political authorities. He brought his ideas with him north to Emden and baptized others, including those who from 1531 onwards would carry his distinctive brand of Anabaptism into the Low Countries. By 1533 Hoffman was back in Strasbourg, and Melchiorite Anabaptism began quickly to gain adherents in Holland and in the Westphalian city of Münster.

There was nothing very unusual about the city Reformation that was implemented in Münster in 1531. But tension between a Lutheran city council and the Zwinglian proclivities of the city's leading reformer, Bernhard Rothmann, destabilized conditions and made Münster the site for the single most notorious episode in the history of Anabaptism, and indeed of the Reformation as a whole. Jan Matthijs, a Dutch convert to Melchiorite Anabaptism, prophesied that not Strasbourg but Münster would be the site of the New Jerusalem and that God would effect the city's apocalyptic transformation at Easter 1534. Rothmann and many others in the city joined the Melchiorites; Dutch converts poured into Münster as well, leading to the city council's adoption of Anabaptism in February 1534. Almost immediately, the new regime found itself militarily surrounded and besieged. Matthijs became the town's most important figure and instituted the first of the two mandated practices for which it became notorious, namely community of goods (a practice also of several Moravian Anabaptist groups, as we have seen). After the apocalypse failed to materialize as prophesied, and Matthijs was killed in a skirmish with the besieging army of the Bishop of Münster and his allies, Jan Beukels van Leiden became the regime's new leader. He instituted a second practice for which the city became even more notorious—polygamy—and ruled the city with an iron hand as King of the New Jerusalem. Conditions in the city deteriorated steadily through the end of 1534 and into the following year, until in late June 1535 the besieging forces took the city and slaughtered those inhabitants who had not already perished from starvation. Jan van Leiden and two other civic leaders, Bernhard Knipperdolling and Bernd Krechting, were imprisoned, and in January 1536 tortured before being executed. Their remains were hung in iron cages, suspended from a tower of the city's St Lambert Church, as a reminder of civic justice against a regime that would cast a long shadow throughout the remainder of the sixteenth century and indeed into the seventeenth.

If, after the Peasants' War, authorities needed any confirmation that 'the Gospel' harboured the potential for socio-political subversion, the Anabaptist episode in Münster provided it in dramatic fashion. Control over the interpretation and application of God's Word, especially when understood prophetically or with a strong emphasis on the power of the Spirit, was patently a political necessity. In a parallel to the prosecution of German-speaking Anabaptists following the Peasants' War in the late 1520s, hundreds of Dutch Anabaptists were executed in the later 1530s following the fall of Münster. The executions reinforced the distinction between the politically supported magisterial Reformation and politically proscribed radical Protestants. Any whiff of religious dissent would be regarded with suspicion in subsequent decades throughout Europe, a fact that would colour the experience of radical Protestants throughout the rest of the century and beyond—irrespective of whether they were persecuted, found means of accommodation with political regimes, or dissembled their convictions in public in order to pursue the Christian life as they respectively understood it.

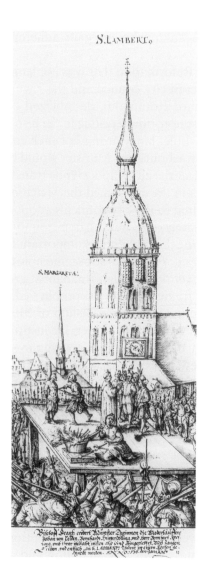

S. LAMBERT.

S. MARGARETA.

Bischoff Frantz erobert Münster Darinnen die Wiederhäuffery
Johan von Leiden, Bernhard Knipperdolling, und Herr Bern Krechting, und ihrer mitlauf, in den die einig Finger riestet, Und Leuten
frissen, rad entlich, An 6. LABRAPP: Thürm im eigen Kercker ge-
ßneckt werden. — (1536.) MDXXXVI.

EXECUTION OF ANABAPTIST LEADERS IN
MÜNSTER, 22 January 1536. The abolition of private property and practice of polygamy in the city of
Münster under the leadership of Jan van Leiden in
1534–5 shocked Europeans, reinforcing the association of religious radicalism with social and political
subversion a decade after the German Peasants' War.
Three leaders of the Anabaptist regime—Jan van
Leiden, Bernhard Knipperdolling, and Bernd
Krechting—were executed in January 1536 and
their corpses left to rot in iron cages suspended from
the tower of the St Lambert Church, cages that
remain in place to this day.
From Georg Berger, *Contrafactur der Osnabrückschen Bischofe* (1607).

Containment and Control: Persecution, Proliferation, and Accommodation

Between the demise of the Münster regime and outbreak of the English Revolution,
the Radical Reformation was politically contained and remained numerically small,
even as its expressions continued to proliferate in open-ended ways. Radical Protestants did not go away, but neither did they cause serious political disruption. As in the
early German Reformation, there remained many more versions of Christian truth
among them than there were among politically protected Lutherans and Reformed
Protestants. Radical Protestants also became much more widespread geographically
than they had been in the 1520s and 1530s, when they were concentrated mostly in

the central European cradle of the Reformation and adjacent lands. Anti-Trinitarian Protestants, for example, of whom there had been only a few, such as Michael Servetus, in the early 1530s, grew significantly in numbers in the second half of the century, partly through the influence of the Italian Fausto Sozzini. They developed a substantial communal existence in relatively favourable political circumstances in Poland and Transylvania. In the seventeenth century they would make their presence felt in the Dutch Republic and England. Just as there were many different sorts of radical Protestants across Europe, so their experiences varied dramatically depending upon the policies and practices of the polities in which they found themselves, and contingent upon their own attitudes toward the character of Christian faith and how it ought to be publicly expressed. Nowhere in Europe were they politically privileged in the manner of Catholics, Lutherans, or Reformed Protestants under their own confessional regimes. At best they were tolerated to some extent in ways that allowed them to live relatively unmolested lives. This treatment was more likely to be experienced by those willing to dissemble their beliefs, or who regarded Christianity purely as a matter of interior experience and conviction, in ways that essentially eliminated the problem of behavioural conformity to politically coercive confessional demands.

In the century or so after Münster, Anabaptists remained divided and frequently inclined to further divisions among themselves on a range of doctrinal and disciplinary matters. This is perhaps unsurprising, given their concern with the visible Christian community as the concrete expression of men and women self-consciously committed to the following of Christ: defining and policing the community's boundaries was important and therefore contested, expressed most consequentially in disagreements over the practice of banning and shunning ('the ban' was the Anabaptist version of excommunication, implying complete ostracism from the community). Their experiences also diverged dramatically, from intense persecution to unexpected prosperity, depending on the political circumstances in which they found themselves and how they reacted to their varied circumstances. We can see this diversity of experience in the two strands of Anabaptism with the most adherents in the later sixteenth century: the Dutch Mennonites and the Moravian Hutterites.

Melchiorite Anabaptism splintered in the later 1530s in the immediate aftermath of Münster. Least numerous, but closest to the Münsterites in their militant opposition to the godless, were the Batenburgers, who have been called 'Anabaptist terrorists'. They sought revenge against the regime's destroyers by plundering property, burning buildings, stealing, and killing while keeping alive Münster's apocalyptic expectations. Although their leader, Jan van Batenburg, was executed in 1538 and the Batenburgers quickly declined in numbers and influence, their existence is attested as late as 1580. The most influential Dutch Anabaptist leader in the later 1530s was the apocalyptically loquacious and prophetic David Joris, a glass painter by training. He adopted increasingly spiritualist views in the early 1540s and in flight from persecution relocated to Basel in 1544, where he lived under the assumed name

Johann van Brugge until his death in 1556. His followers (variously referred to by scholars as Davidites, Jorists, or Davidjorists) maintained a significant presence in the Low Countries into the second half of the century. They clashed with adherents of what became the most numerous and influential of the post-Münsterite Anabaptists in the Low Countries, those who were initially the followers of Obbe and Dirk Philips. Obbe left Anabaptism around 1539, but his brother Dirk became the close collaborator of Menno Simons (c.1496–1561), the leading figure in Dutch Anabaptism for two decades beginning in the early 1540s, and the man who gave this branch of the Anabaptist tradition a name that has endured to the present.

Like many early Protestant reformers, Menno had originally been a Catholic priest. He moved successively from doubts about transubstantiation to enthusiasm for

MENNO SIMONS (*c.*1496–1561). Beginning in the early 1540s, the former parish priest Menno Simons became the most influential Anabaptist leader in the Low Countries until his death in 1561. A series of schisms divided Dutch Mennonites among themselves beginning in the mid-1550s, centred especially around issues of the disciplinary enforcement of banning and shunning that was related to group identity.

From Christoph van Sichem Arnhemius, *Historische Beschrijvinge ende offbeeldinge der voorneemste Hooft Ketteren* (1608).

Luther's writings, and then to recognition that there was no explicit biblical basis for the practice of infant baptism. He thus came to espouse believers' baptism as the external sign of a life of interiorly renewed Christian discipleship, leaving the Catholic Church and the priesthood. An opponent of the Münster regime from the beginning, Menno advocated a non-resistant biblicist literalism similar to that of some of the Swiss Brethren, which for him included the maintenance of morally upright behaviour among members of a congregation 'without spot or wrinkle'. Those who had been reborn in Christ through the Spirit were to live accordingly, sharply rejecting the persecutory godlessness of the sinful world. Not only are Menno's writings filled with biblically based admonitions about the willingness to suffer persecution, but he himself was forced to flee the Low Countries for East Friesland in 1543, even as he continued to minister to and correspond with his Netherlandish followers. They were most severely persecuted in Flanders, close to the seat of the Habsburg government in Brussels, in the 1550s and 1560s. As a response to this persecution, and to Adriaen van Haemstede's Dutch Calvinist martyrology of 1559, there appeared in 1562–3 the first published Anabaptist martyrological collection, *Het Offer des Heeren* (The Sacrifice unto the Lord). Dozens of lesser pamphlets containing prison letters and songs by and about Mennonite martyrs, plus ten further editions of *Het Offer des Heeren* before 1600, attest to the popularity of the genre. A martyrological mentality became part of Dutch Mennonite identity by the middle decades of the sixteenth century, just as it had quickly become constitutive for German-speaking Anabaptists beginning in the later 1520s.

In the second half of the sixteenth century, Dutch Mennonites endured schism from within as well as persecution from without. The first split unfolded between 1555 and 1557. Disagreements about the proper relationship between duties to one's spouse and to the faith community engendered a rift between Mennonites and those known as Waterlanders (who were named after a region in North Holland). Was the innocent party in a marriage obliged to shun a spouse banned for disciplinary reasons, and thus to have no social contact with him or her, before the offender was reconciled with the community? Dirk Philips and another important Mennonite leader, Lenaert Bouwens, insisted on the practice of shunning a banned spouse in order to uphold community purity and identity, and they convinced the ageing Menno of the same. The Waterlanders regarded this practice as unduly harsh, and in 1557 the irreconcilable groups went their separate ways. In addition, the schism precipitated a mutual ban of the Mennonites and the Swiss Brethren, who had followed the feud and also regarded the stricter practice as too severe. The Waterlanders (known in Dutch as *doopsgezinden*, or 'baptism-minded') self-consciously distinguished themselves from Mennonites and flourished in subsequent decades under the leadership of Hans de Ries (1553–1638), a convert from Reformed Protestantism. Under the protective aegis of the new Dutch Republic, some Waterlanders had become wealthy, fashionable urban participants in Golden Age Dutch prosperity by the early decades of the seventeenth century.

The importance of governmental policies and practices for the experience of radical Protestants was no less evident when Mennonites were being treated with relative

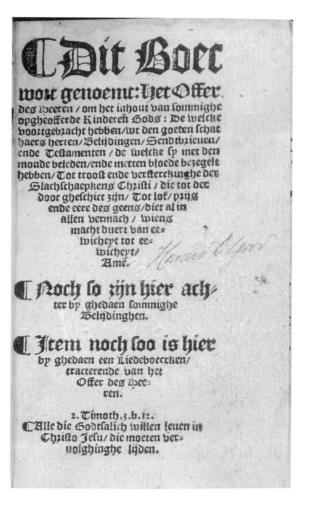

TITLE PAGE OF *HET OFFER DES HEEREN* (1562–3). The first published martyrological collection of any Anabaptist group in the sixteenth century, *The Sacrifice unto the Lord* appeared in eleven editions by the end of the sixteenth century. Its second half consisted entirely of songs, which along with the large number of published Mennonite song collections signals the importance of song-singing to this Anabaptist tradition as indeed it was to others as well.

leniency than when they were being persecuted. In 1566, the unrest of the Dutch Revolt drove large numbers of Mennonites as refugees from Flanders north to Friesland, where Menno had originally ministered. Cultural differences and disputes about congregational autonomy caused first friction and then faction: in 1566, the two groups pronounced a collective ban on each other. After the conflict between the Dutch and the Spanish led to the formation of the Dutch Republic, the commercially rather than confessionally minded urban regents of Holland's cities supported Reformed Protestantism as the 'public church'. But they did not compel membership or mandatory attendance at worship in the way confessionalizing regimes did elsewhere in Europe. With persecutory pressures relaxed, Flemish and Frisian Mennonites could concentrate on disagreeing with one another. A separatism within separatism continued, as the issues over banning and shunning that had led to the Waterlander–Mennonite schism in 1557 precipitated new divisions between 'Old' and 'Mild' Flemish by 1586, and between 'Old' and 'Young' Frisians by 1589. Nor was this the end of the fissiparity. For many decades, debates about and efforts for or against reunion among these and other branches of the Dutch Mennonites remained an abiding feature of their existence, and in fact have done so into the modern era, with Waterlanders at one end of the spectrum tending to press for reconciliation, and the Old Frisians at the other end resisting it the most adamantly. In the seventeenth century, the published martyrologies that swelled far beyond the size of *Het Offer des Heeren* became an important site of contestation about Mennonite and indeed broader Anabaptist self-definition. Was martyrology to function as a cultural tool of identity-reinforcing exclusivity, by emphasizing the issues that had engendered the schisms, or should divisive differences be downplayed so that the genre might serve efforts of reconciliatory bridge-building, not only among Dutch Mennonites but in relationship to other (non-violent) Anabaptist groups as well? By the time the Flemish minister Thieleman Jans van Braght edited the *Martyrs' Mirror of the Defenseless or Baptism-Minded Christians* (1660), the inclusive and conciliatory vision championed by Hans de Ries in previous decades had carried the day. It was the lavish, two-volume second edition of this work, published in 1685, that included a series of more than 100 copperplate engravings by Jan Luyken—a dramatic typographical and artistic indication of the socio-economic and cultural assimilation of most Dutch Mennonites during the preceding century.

The experience of the Hutterites, the communitarian Anabaptist group in Moravia that endured beyond the 1530s, also illustrates the extent to which radical Protestant experience was profoundly dependent on political realities. A severe Habsburg persecution in the mid-1530s claimed the life of Jakob Hutter (from whom the group's name is derived). But from the early 1540s onwards the Hutterites settled into several prosperous decades of a cooperative relationship with a number of Moravian noble families that offered them political protection. In what was by far the most successful manifestation of the practice of community of goods among any Christian group in the Reformation era, the Hutterites lived in multi-family dwellings within disciplined enclave communities, each with several hundred persons. They attracted converts, were economically successful in practising a variety of crafts and agriculture, and, under the leadership of Leonhard Lanzenstil, Pieter Riedemann, Leonhard Dax, and Peter Walpot, supported vigorous missionary efforts to other German-speaking Anabaptists, which lasted from the 1550s until Walpot's death in 1578 and beyond. In contrast to the extensive printed literature found among the Dutch Mennonites, the Hutterites preserved and transmitted chronicles, apologetic texts, songbooks, and martyrs' writings through an extensive network of manuscript copying. By the end of the century, at least 20,000 Hutterites were living in about seventy of their communities on aristocratic lands in southern Moravia and Slovakia. Yet political protection was a highly vulnerable sine qua non of their communal life, as became clear in the early seventeenth century. Turkish troops harmed some Moravian Hutterite communities in 1605, but the opening years of the Thirty Years War marked the abrupt end of their shared existence. The non-Catholic nobility lost their property and influence after the Battle of the White Mountain (1620), and in 1622 the Hutterites

Maria van Beckum, en Urſel, haers Broeders Wijf. 1544.

EXECUTION OF MARIA AND URSULA VAN BECKUM, 1544. Anabaptist women as well as men risked execution for their commitments if they refused to recant them. The well-known Dutch artist Jan van Luyken was commissioned to produce more than 100 engravings for the deluxe second edition of van Braght's *Martyrs' Mirror*, published more than eighty years after the last execution of an Anabaptist for heresy in the Low Countries.

had their property confiscated before being expelled from Moravia. The very lands to which, for nearly a century, persecuted Anabaptists from other regions had fled now became the source of thousands of Hutterite refugees. Many of them went to Slovakia, which saw a modest Hutterite revival from the 1630s into the 1650s. Partly due to the pressures of politically enforced re-Catholicization, however, their numbers declined appreciably in the second half of the seventeenth century.

The Reformation's emphasis on scripture and on the inspiration of the Holy Spirit, shared and divergently manifest among both magisterial and radical Protestants, meant that Anabaptists and spiritualist radicals comprised a spectrum. One of the basic differences between less spiritualizing Anabaptists and spiritualist radical Protestants was the emphasis the former laid on the importance of congruence between

TITLE PAGE OF *HISTORIE DER WARACHTIGHE GETUYGEN JESU CHRISTI*... (1617). The Dutch Mennonite martyrological tradition that began with *The Sacrifice unto the Lord* continued and was expanded considerably in the seventeenth century, becoming a site for the contestation of group identity among divided Mennonite groups. In material terms, the seventeenth-century martyrologies were much larger and longer—and more expensive—than their tiny sixteenth-century ancestor, reflecting the increased prosperity of many Mennonites in the Dutch Golden Age. Note the multiple engravings of martyrdom scenes on the title page of the *True History of the Witnesses of Jesus Christ* (1617), the publication of which was overseen by the Old Frisian Mennonite leader Peter Jans Twisck.

PAGE FROM HUTTERITE MANU-SCRIPT, 1795. In contrast to the extensive use of print made by the Dutch Mennonites, the Hutterites conveyed their religious texts through an extensive network of organized manuscript copying that lasted long past the Reformation era. This annotated copy of a text by the apocalyptic father of Melchiorite Anabaptism, Melchior Hoffman, dates from the last decade of the eighteenth century, more than 250 years after Hoffman wrote it.

one's publicly manifest behaviour and one's beliefs. This was a premise of believers' baptism and Anabaptist ecclesiology, and was related to one of the reproaches Anabaptists had also brought against politically compliant Protestants as early as the 1520s: namely, that commitment to the doctrines of justification by faith alone and salvation by grace alone so often failed to produce lives lived in manifestly Christian ways. It was also a key point at issue in the back-and-forth dispute of the 1530s and early 1540s between Schwenckfeld and Pilgram Marpeck, who spent time among the Austerlitz Brethren in Moravia. To dissemble one's beliefs for the sake of avoiding persecution was branded as 'Nicodemism' by John Calvin, after the figure of Nicodemus who according to John's Gospel came to see Jesus by night (John 3). Such dissimulation was a behaviour condemned by magisterial Protestant, Roman Catholic, and Anabaptist leaders alike. But if dissembling was not viewed as a problem—that is, if one distinguished sharply between interior experience and external behaviours in the manner of many spiritualist radical Protestants—then persecution might more easily be avoided. One could then simply conform to the demands of public worship as mandated by a given confessional regime. To be sure, surviving records make clear that many Anabaptists did abjure their beliefs when faced with the prospect of execution. Others dissembled their convictions in the second half of the sixteenth century, if they found themselves in territories such as Bern or Württemberg whose political leaders remained hostile to Anabaptists, in contrast to those territories whose leaders came to accommodate them once they were persuaded that their Anabaptists posed no politically subversive threat. But spiritualist radical Protestants took a different approach, accepting such behaviour as a matter of principle. Because, in their view, rituals, worship, and external practices had nothing to do with the essence of Christianity, then conformity to the demands of confessional authorities was a thing of indifference.

By the time David Joris had taken up residence with his family in Basel in 1544, for example, he had moved away from his earlier embrace of Melchiorite Anabaptism and become a spiritualist. For more than a decade, his external conformity to the city's prescribed worship led Basel's Reformed Protestants mistakenly to think he was one of them—when they learned otherwise after his death, they exhumed and burned his bones. Very different were the views of Dirck Coornhert (1522–90), an advocate for religious freedom against the strictures of Reformed Protestants in the Dutch Republic. He emphasized reason no less than the Spirit in sharply rejecting the Catholic Church as hopelessly corrupt, and Reformed Protestantism as gravely mistaken in its doctrines of predestination, justification by faith alone, and denial of free will in matters pertaining to salvation. If religious freedom for individuals had been effectively enforced, as Coornhert had desired, it would have made dissembling unnecessary. But that was far from the contemporary reality everywhere in late sixteenth-century Europe. Hence, dissimulation of a quite spectacular sort was eminently necessary for Valentin Weigel (1533–88) in Lutheran Saxony: for decades he served as a university-trained, ordained Lutheran minister, all the while concealing heterodox cosmological and Christological views that were deeply indebted to Platonism and to the intellectually eclectic ideas of the apocalyptic, alchemical physician Paracelsus.

More ambitious as a radical Protestant leader was the founder of the Family of Love, Hendrik Niclaes (1502–80). His followers regarded him as he regarded himself: as an inspired, messiah-like prophet who would lead them to become 'Christed with Christ and Godded with God', an exalted state that he had supposedly achieved, in an invisible Church free from all externals. The Family of Love gained some adherents in England in the reign of Elizabeth I, and although their English conventicles apparently petered out in the early seventeenth century, Familist writings continued to exert an influence in England in subsequent decades. An important circle of Familists in late sixteenth-century Antwerp included the printer Christophe Plantin, who like Niclaes continued outwardly to practise Catholicism, just as Weigel kept ministering as a Lutheran pastor in Saxony. In 1573, Niclaes's efforts to organize the Family of Love hierarchically as a visible Church precipitated a schism with those known as Hielists, who followed one of Familism's earliest converts, the Anabaptist weaver Hendrik

Jansen van Barrefelt. The schism between Hielists and Familists makes clear that the Anabaptists had no monopoly on internal divisions among radical Protestants in the later sixteenth century.

Direct access to the Spirit was quite plainly no more stable a basis for persuasively establishing reformed Christian truth than was insistence on the perspicuity of scripture. The same proved to be the case among those radical Protestants who revisited and rejected as mistaken the Trinitarian Christian notion of God. From inauspicious beginnings around 1530, this became one of the defining doctrines among a significant strand of radical Protestantism that would eventually feed into modern Unitarianism. In Poland and Lithuania during the 1560s and 1570s, for example, those who rejected the traditional Nicene understanding of the Trinity were riven by disagreements about the conceptualization of God's nature, Christology, and the practice of baptism: did the rejection of infant baptism, for example, require as a

HENDRIK NICLAES (1502–80). Niclaes was the founder of the Family of Love, a radical spiritualist Christian group that began in the Low Countries and spread to England during the reign of Elizabeth I. Familists' sharp distinction between the importance of interior experience and the insignificance of exterior behaviour meant they could and did conform to the politically mandated expression of Christianity in any given confessional regime.

From *Greuwel der vornahmsten Hauptketzeren, So wohl Wiedertauffer, als auch anderen* (1608).

corollary the embrace of adult baptism in the manner of the Anabaptists? Criticizing the 1553 execution of Michael Servetus for anti-Trinitarianism in Calvin's Geneva, Sebastian Castellio (1515–63) championed the decisive importance of reason in overcoming controverted Christian doctrines. In his posthumously published treatise *On the Art of Doubting and Believing* (1563), he asserted that 'Reason . . . is a certain eternal word of God, far more ancient and certain than writings and ceremonies, according to which God taught his own before there were any ceremonies and writings, and according to which he will teach when ceremonies and writings no longer exist, so that men may truly be taught by God.' But in fact, reason proved no more decisive in arbitrating among contested doctrines than had recourse to the Spirit. Both means sought to transcend the socially divisive, rival readings of scripture that derived from the Reformation's cornerstone emphasis on the Word of God. In fact, they exacerbated the pluralism they sought to overcome, as would also be clear among various rationalizing Protestants in the seventeenth century, and indeed into the modern era.

But after the wild and anarchic early years of the evangelical movement, for a century the Reformation's socially and politically threatening manifestations were

MICHAEL SERVETUS (1511–53). On the basis of his interpretation of scripture and theological reflection, Servetus denied the Christian doctrine of the Trinity and as such contributed to a strand of radical Protestantism that eventually influenced modern Unitarianism. With the zealous approval of John Calvin and his successor, Theodore Beza, Servetus was burned alive by order of the Genevan city council on 27 October 1553.

From Christoph van Sichem Arnhemius, *Historische Beschrijvinge ende offbeeldinge der voorneemste Hooft Ketteren* (1608)

contained and controlled. Radical Protestantism persisted and proliferated, but all told its adherents remained small in number compared to those men and women who were part of the large-scale efforts of socially transformative, gradual confessionalization in magisterial Protestant and Catholic lands. Nor did radical Protestants during this century threaten basic societal structures or assumptions. The only thing keeping scripture's revolutionary potential in check, however, was the largely effective exercise of political control, and the social stability it made possible. Without these things, the Reformation as such would again cease to look so set in its institutionalized magisterial exceptions and resume its more unsettled and unpredictable character.

Reformation Radicalism Renewed: England in the 1640s and 1650s

What distinguished radical from magisterial Protestants was sustained political support for a legally approved form of anti-Roman Christianity, and the proscription (extending in many cases to the prosecution) of the other forms of Christianity generated by the Reformation. In the century after the Anabaptist Kingdom of Münster, confessional alliances between secular and ecclesiastical authorities proved largely effective in curbing socially or politically subversive expressions of radical Protestantism of the sort that had culminated in the German Peasants' War. Yet, as we have seen, radical Protestants did not go away. They continued to offer divergent interpretations of Christian truth throughout the remainder of the sixteenth century, at odds not only with Roman Catholics but also with Lutherans and Reformed Protestants, just as they also disagreed and thus remained socially divided among themselves. Whatever particular form their religious commitments assumed, however, by and large they sought in the later sixteenth and seventeenth centuries to reach some *modus vivendi* with established authorities, from the dissimulation sanctioned by Flemish Familists, to the relative toleration enjoyed by Dutch Mennonites, to the nobility's protection afforded to Moravian Hutterites. A serious disruption in the political support for an established Church, however, would create the conditions for a reappearance of the open-ended fecundity of the Reformation's appeal to God's Word. The only place this happened in the seventeenth century was England in the 1640s and 1650s, where religio-political opposition to Charles I precipitated a civil war, socio-political unrest, and extraordinary institutional changes—thus creating the circumstances in which the Reformation's character became visible in a manner analogous to that it displayed in Germany in the 1520s. England's revolutionary years would once again manifest some expressions of the gospel that were socially and politically subversive.

The complicated sequence of events that precipitated and constituted the English Revolution, from Charles I's provocative political and religious proactivity in the later 1630s, to his execution and the establishment of the Republic and Cromwellian Protectorate, are important with respect to the Radical Reformation for at least two reasons. First, they demonstrate through the radicalization and fragmentation of English Puritanism the inherent absence of interpretative stability in Reformed

Protestantism itself. Given the shared emphasis on the importance of the Holy Spirit for understanding the Word of God, the fissiparity of Puritanism shows the lack of any clearly sustainable distinction between magisterial and radical Protestantism with respect to the interpretation of scripture. The most committed, zealous members of the doctrinally Reformed Protestant Church of England, in other words, were inherently potential radical Protestants. And insofar as conformist 'Prayer Book Protestants' (those satisfied with the official formularies of the Church of England) might become ardent Puritans for any number of reasons, they too inherently were potential radical Protestants. Second, the destabilizing events of the 1640s and 1650s are important for the Radical Reformation because they created the conditions for the public emergence of a wide variety of divergent, rival Protestant groups in a manner unseen since the early German Reformation. Given the interpretation offered here, these groups should be seen *both* as an efflorescence of the Radical Reformation in the mid-seventeenth century, *and* as simply a manifestation of the Reformation *itself* in the absence of enforced political control of officially approved religious ideas and practices.

As was true elsewhere in Europe, England had its share of radical Protestants in the century between Henry VIII's Reformation and the English Revolution, from Dutch Anabaptist refugees in the later 1530s, to the Marian 'Freewillers', to Elizabethan members of the Family of Love, and contemporary separatists such as Robert Browne and Henry Barrow (who was hanged for sedition in 1593). John Smyth (*c*.1570–*c*.1612) led a small separatist congregation from England to Holland in 1608 and baptized himself early the following year, inaugurating what is usually regarded as the first congregation of English Baptists. This small emigrant community merged with Dutch Waterlanders in 1615, but others from the group returned to England and became part of a growing number of separatist Baptists who were Arminian (that is, critical of Calvinist predestination) in their soteriology. They were in turn socially distinct from another group of English Baptists that emerged in the 1630s and adopted Calvinist views on predestination, grace, and free will. Smyth himself had been an ardent Puritan within the Church of England before leaving it, and thus illustrates the lack of any stable boundary between radical and Reformed Protestantism. Importantly for understanding the profusion of groups that emerged in the 1640s, recent research has established the existence in early seventeenth-century England of a radical Puritan underground, a fractious world of zealous Protestants who took up different doctrinal positions in dealing with various tensions within Reformed Protestant theology. For example, if the Puritan insistence on the relationship between concretely expressed moral order and the animating role of the Holy Spirit in personal experience were pressed toward the first of these poles, it became legalistic, inspiring carefully parsed lists of regulations for the guidance of Christian life; if pressed in the other direction, it became antinomian, eliminating any role for the Mosaic law in the life of the Spirit-filled Christian. How one's views might be translated into attitudes and actions toward the status quo depended on the specific position one adopted on any number of controverted issues, from the relationship between the Word and the Spirit to the Catholic-looking liturgical innovations of

Archbishop William Laud's 'Beauty of Holiness'. Especially when influenced by Familist, (Ana)baptist, or other currents of Protestant thought, the results might lead in any number of unpredictable directions. Already in the decades prior to the English Revolution, by far the most important source of radical Protestants was the hotter sort of Protestants who belonged to the Church of England.

However one interprets the opposition to Charles I, and the weight one assigns to politically activist Puritanism in 1640–1—an issue that has vexed generations of historians since the nineteenth century—the English Revolution *was* in important respects a politically efficacious expression of radical Protestantism that toppled an objectionably establishment Laudianism. Without question, though, the 1640s created circumstances in which the early Stuart Puritan underground could come into the open: the royalist/parliamentarian political division that led to civil war, the breakdown of censorship, the abolition of episcopacy and establishment of an ineffectual Presbyterian Church, the execution of Charles I and creation of a Republic, and then the Protectorate under Oliver Cromwell. In the wake of these dramatic upheavals, radical Protestants appeared, in ways unseen for more than a century, under the penumbra of parliamentarian 'Independency'. In another parallel to the early German Reformation, nearly all of them were marked by apocalyptic sensibilities. Already in 1646, the Presbyterian minister Thomas Edwards viewed their profusion as a socially subversive disease in his famous heresiographical work, *Gangraena*. A defender of episcopacy imprisoned for his convictions, Daniel Featley, published an extensive denunciation of Anabaptists in *The Dippers Dipt* (1645), a work that originated in a disputation with the Baptist leader William Kiffin in 1642.

Once monarchy was abolished and the Republic declared, radical Protestants emerged with particular vigour. In *The New Law of Righteousness* (1649), Gerrard Winstanley espoused an agrarian and communitarian Christian commonwealth without private property. After the execution of the king, in the spring of 1649, a number of Winstanley's Digger communities sought to put their re-Edenizing vision into practice. George Fox, James Nayler, and other early Quakers were radical spiritualists who claimed illumination by the same 'inner light' that had animated Jesus' Apostles. Their refusal to acknowledge social superiors in the manner to which the latter were accustomed (for example, by the doffing of hats) struck at the heart of the deference critical to the ordinary functioning of England's hierarchically ordered society and marked the Quakers as social subversives. Seventh-Day Baptists set themselves apart from General (Arminian) and Particular (Calvinist) Baptists by their insistence, like some other radical Christians in the Reformation era, that the Sabbath be celebrated on Saturday rather than Sunday. Antinomian extremism was manifest among the Ranters, who allegedly dispensed with conventional norms regarding sexual restraint. They included among their number Abiezer Coppe, who like many other radicals of the revolutionary period had spent time at university (in Coppe's case, at Oxford). Fifth Monarchists not only shared in the more general apocalyptic expectations characteristic of their radical contemporaries, but also claimed the duty to take up arms against Cromwell's regime to usher in the millennium they anticipated would

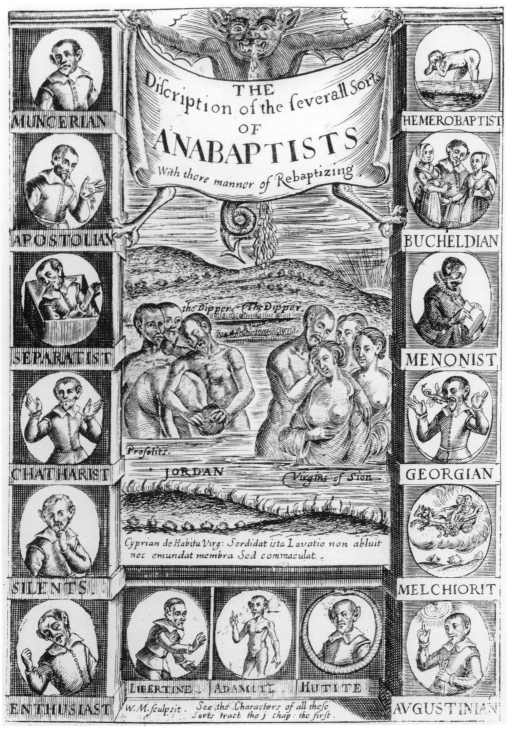

WILLIAM MARSHALL, *The discription of the severall Sorts of Anabaptists* in Daniel Featley, *The Dippers Dipt* (1646). Polemical denunciations of Anabaptists and other radical Protestants were common throughout the Reformation era, but acquired renewed urgency with the proliferation of radical Protestantism during the 1640s and 1650s in England. Daniel Featley (rather fancifully) categorized different types of Anabaptists based on the ways in which they administered the sacrament in *The Dippers Dipt*, which saw six editions 1645–51.

precede the imminent Second Coming of Christ. Without political authorities standing behind the interpretative authorities that stipulated what Christianity was in an established church, what prevented individual men and women from defining it in whatever way they pleased?

Nothing. Nor was this a characteristic only of the early German Reformation or the English Revolution. The Golden Age Dutch Republic, too, including Holland above all, demonstrated that the deliberate uncoupling of religious preference from political obedience led in a direction similar to the one manifest across the English Channel. Whereas in England it was the destructive disruptions of the 1640s that created the political breakdown facilitating the profusion of rival Protestantisms, in the cities of Holland it was the result of ruling regents' self-consciously commercial rather than confessional priorities. Without mandatory membership in a state church, Protestant preferentiality prospered. The Reformation as such was visible, unconstrained by the shackles imposed by Lutheran or Reformed Protestant political authorities. Hence the Mennonites, for example, were free to pursue their various schisms and efforts at reconciliation, which continued into the second half of the century with the divide between Lamists and Zonists. Quakers, too, in 1655 began missions to Holland, where they made contact with rationalizing spiritualists known as Collegiants, some of whom were friends with the philosopher Baruch Spinoza. Socinians were officially prohibited in the Dutch Republic, but arrived from Poland nonetheless. Despite the objections of Reformed Protestant ministers in the state-supported public Church, radical Protestants found a place alongside Catholics and Jews in early modern Europe's most religiously diverse and intellectually open regime. The Dutch Republic therefore encompassed, in a less fitful and less threatening way, the indeterminate open-endedness of the Reformation itself that was also manifest in England's mid-seventeenth-century convulsions.

The Radical Reformation does not deserve marginal treatment in our understanding of the Reformation era. On the contrary, its reintegration with the magisterial Reformation yields a different understanding of the Reformation as a whole. Numerically, radical Protestants indeed remained at the margins of society in countries across Europe during the Reformation era, save for the early German Reformation and the English Revolution. But seen from the perspective of the commitment to God's Word that they shared with magisterial Protestants, theirs were by far the more numerous expressions of anti-Roman Christianity in the sixteenth and seventeenth centuries. Not until much later, with the eventual institutionalization of an idea for which radical Protestants such as Sebastian Castellio, Dirk Coornhert, John Milton, and Roger Williams were pioneers—that of individual religious freedom—would the character of the Reformation itself become clear. Early modern political support for two particular Protestant traditions—Lutheranism and Reformed Protestantism—has led to a long-standing conflation between them and theologically normative Protestantism, and thus obscured the nature of the Reformation itself.

Ironically, only long after the Reformation era would the Reformation's character become permanently visible, beginning across the Atlantic in a new nation that by self-conscious deliberation was never a confessional country: the United States of America. Only in the modern era would there be institutions that offered political protection to the animating commitment of the Reformation as such, and this at the level of the individuals who read and reflected on God's Word. Given the empirical social effects of *sola scriptura* and its related concepts, it could hardly have been otherwise. As had been clear at every point from the early 1520s onwards, it was at the level of individuals that men and women disagreed about what God's Word meant, and thus about what Christians were to believe and how they should live. So eventually everyone, and not only Luther, gained the political protection necessary to say, in uncoerced ways, 'Here I stand.' So long, that is, as those who were thus protected agreed to abide by the laws of the State, obedience to which became the price of modern religious freedom, and the way in which unintended Christian pluralism was eventually politically managed. Paradoxically, it is in the extraordinary heterogeneity and conflicting claims of the history of American Protestantism that we can finally see in a sustained fashion what we can only glimpse at the beginning and end of the Reformation era itself: the social product of 'scripture alone' and the triumph of the Reformation in its true essence.

5 Catholic Reformation and Renewal

SIMON DITCHFIELD

Introduction: The Global Circulation of the Sacred

THIS story of Catholic reformation and renewal will be told from a global perspective. It thus begins not in Luther's Wittenberg but in the Indian port of Goa, which in 1534 had become the first bishopric of the Portuguese Indies. Seven years later, the College of St Paul was founded, initially for the training of local indigenous clergy (though here, as elsewhere, such a policy was soon abandoned), by members of the reformed Franciscan order of the Piedosos, who had reached India in 1517. With the arrival of the Jesuit Francis Xavier in 1542, the running of the college was taken over by the Society of Jesus. In 1548, the chapel received a very special boost to its status: the head of S. Gerasima, one of the 11,000 companions of the British early Christian princess St Ursula. A locally-painted image of this saint from about this time, with a distinctly non-Western physiognomy and in an exquisitely-carved Indian hardwood frame, still hangs on the walls of the Museum of Christian Art in the Old City. Owing to a series of alleged miracles, the saint's relic immediately became the focus of a vigorous cult and the following year the Confraternity of St Ursula was founded in her honour. This relic had been brought to Goa from the Rhineland city of Cologne by the Dutch Jesuit Jasper Berze (1515–53). During the following three decades relics of other companions of St Ursula migrated as far east as Melaka (Malacca) on the Malaysian peninsula. So by the time, in the early seventeenth century, that a suitably large chapel—the so-called Golden Chamber—had been made ready in the Cologne church of St Ursula to redisplay the 120 reliquary busts (and no fewer than 670 additional skulls), their cult enjoyed global reach.

This Rhenish 'mine of sanctity' was but the first of several significant sources of relics whose contents came 'on stream' and circulated the length and breadth of the Roman Catholic world during this period, making Catholicism the globe's most kinetic religion. Undoubtedly, the most famous 'mine' of all was the network of early Christian catacombs which lay beneath the immediate environs of Rome itself. Although several of them had been visited continuously throughout the Middle Ages, and over fifty had been listed in the written account by the Dominican scholar Onofrio Panvinio (1530–68) published in 1568, the accidental discovery of what were believed to be the catacombs of St Priscilla in 1578 ushered in a new age of rediscovery and martyrmania.

A CATACOMB SAINT: GRATIAN. From the 1580s onwards, catacomb relics were exported throughout Roman Catholic Europe, particularly to frontier zones, such as the Upper Rhine Palatinate, where the Wittelsbach dukes of Bavaria replaced holy bodies destroyed during the Thirty Years War (1618–48). In the area covered by present-day Bavaria it is reckoned that over 1,000 catacomb saints were translated from Rome during the long seventeenth century (*c.*1580–*c.*1750). This example comes from the Stiftsbasilika Waldsassen, Bavaria, and shows the saint dressed as a Roman centurion, resplendent in lace armour made by the Cistercian nuns of the connected convent.

On the other side of the world, in the year 1590, the Spanish Dominican Bishop of Manila, Domingo de Salazar, wrote a letter home containing the following passage:

The *sangleyes* [Chinese craftsmen in the Philippines] make marvellous things. They are so skilful and clever that as soon as they see any object made by a Spanish workman, they reproduce it accurately, and they have executed marvellous pieces . . . I think that nothing more perfect could be produced than some of their ivory statues of the Child Jesus which I have seen. Churches are beginning to be furnished with the images which the *sangleyes* made, and which we lacked before; and considering their ability to copy images which come from Spain, I think soon we will no longer need those made in Flanders.

Just eight days' sailing from the Chinese coast, Manila was by 1639 home to a community of some 30,000 Chinese, many of whom were craftsmen and traders. The Hispano-Filipino ivories the bishop referred to combined the attraction of the valuable and exotic material they were carved out of (itself imported from Africa on

Portuguese ships) with a modest size, which made them extremely portable. There is evidence from the very earliest colonial period—the Philippines had only been colonized by the Spanish from 1565—of such ivories being exported across the Pacific Ocean by means of the annual Spanish galleon fleet which made its way from Manila to Acapulco to the New World—particularly Mexico and Peru. They were also sent on to the Old World itself, where, such was the excellence of their workmanship, that they were considered equal even to the greatly prized ivories of Flanders. A fine collection of Hispano–Philippine ivories can still be viewed in the church of Santa María de Mediavilla in the small town of Median de Rioseco in northern Spain, gifted by Archbishop of Seville Antonio Paiño (1602–69), a native of the place. These include a statue of St Ignatius of Antioch, killed by lions in the Colosseum during the persecution of Emperor Trajan. The saint was convinced of the presence within him of the spirit of Christ, referring to himself in his letters as 'bearer of God' (theophoros), and the lion tears at his flesh to reveal the initials 'IHS' (Jesus) beneath the skin.

Perhaps the most widespread example of the translation or diffusion and appropriation of a Western Christian image of the Old World by the New was that of the Madonna of the Snows. This was sometimes referred to as the Saviour of the Roman people (*Salus Populi Romani*), and the original icon, kept in the Roman basilica of S. Maria Maggiore, was considered not to have been made by human hands. The Jesuits should perhaps be even more closely linked to this image than they are to the device 'IHS' (*Iesus hominum salvator*—Jesus saviour of mankind), which appeared on the façade of all their churches, and on the frontispieces of books written by members of the Society. The third Father General of the order, Francisco Borgia (1510–72), successfully petitioned Pope Pius V (1566–72) to make and distribute copies of this wonder-working image. Indigenous artists from Mexico to Ming China and Mughal India made it their own, in strikingly individual ways. In the case of Mexico, we know that, following the arrival of the Jesuits in 1576, officially sanctioned copies were venerated in the chapels of the four provincial houses of the Society. In China, Matteo Ricci made the gift of a large copy of the Madonna of the Snows to the Wan-li emperor in 1601, as part of the Jesuit missionary's campaign to ingratiate himself at the imperial court. Although this copy has not survived, we do have evidence from the same period (1573–1620) of what a Chinese artist made of this image, in the form of a full-length Madonna of St Luke, drawn using indigenous watercolours and mounted on a silk scroll (now in the Field Museum, Chicago). The delicately arched pose of this figure, combined with her slender frame, closely resembles contemporary depictions of Guanyin, the Bodhisattva (enlightened being) associated with compassion and venerated by Chinese Buddhists. Quite possibly copied from Ricci's original image, the Virgin's facial features—in particular her eyes and nose—clearly indicate her European origins, while the Christ child is shown with his head entirely shaved, save for a Chinese-style topknot. In a similar fashion, a Japanese depiction of the same subject, rediscovered in the 1960s and now held at the Twenty-six Martyrs' Museum, Nagasaki, in Japan, was painted using indigenous inks and mounted on silk, only this time preserving the half-length bust format of the original icon. It likewise reveals the clear contours of the original composition but, once again, the

THE MADONNA GOES GLOBAL. These two images and the following one represent a succession of recreations of the 'Salus popoli romani' icon from the Roman basilica of S. Maria Maggiore, which is now spectacularly framed in the Borghese chapel. In each case they have been translated into a local idiom but without sacrificing the essential features of the original European prototype.

Madonna of St Luke, Chinese, late sixteenth to early seventeenth century, ink and colours on silk.

NICCOLÒ [JESUIT] SCHOOL, Japan. *Madonna of the Snows*, oil and Japanese colours on paper, mounted on a hanging scroll, *c.*1600–14.

oriental touches are to be found in the details: in this case the high, arched eyebrows, narrow eyes, and 'bee-stung' lips reflect specifically Japanese notions of beauty.

Copies of the *Salus populi Romani* icon were also sent to Goa in India. They arrived here in 1578, about the same time as they did in Mexico. A further copy was painted by the Jesuit artist Manuel Godinho, and was hung in the Jesuit church of the first mission to the Mughal court in Agra (1580–3). The Emperor Akbar (1542–1605) was so impressed with what he saw that he returned and brought with him his court painters, who then went on to make their own copies of the icon. One of these, painted by the so-called School of Manohar (c.1590–5) is now in the Victoria and Albert Museum in London. In it, as with the Japanese and Chinese versions, the Virgin is shown as an indigenous beauty, with highly arched eyebrows and almond eyes.

However, perhaps the most important vector which made possible the global circulation of saints' cults in this period was engravings. If the frontier city of Cologne was a prominent source of saints' relics in our period, then the nearby city of Antwerp was, in the sixteenth and early seventeenth centuries, the most important European distribution hub for books and prints going to the New World. It was home to the Plantin printing house, which enjoyed extensive royal privileges granted to it by Philip II (1556–98) as exclusive supplier of breviaries and related liturgical books throughout the Spanish Empire. One of the press's most important publications for purposes of our story was the posthumously published *Evangelicae Historiae Imagines* (Images of the Gospel Story) of 1593. It was reissued in several volumes in 1594–5 as the *Adnotationes et Meditationes in Evangelia* (Notes and Meditations on the Gospels) by the Majorca-born Jesuit Jerónimo Nadal (1507–80). This handsome work presented the life of Christ using no fewer than 153 folio-sized engravings, each of which had been carefully labelled alphabetically and annotated so that, notwithstanding the work's origins as a prompt for meditation for the specific use of Latinate Jesuit scholastics, the text could also function as a very effective teaching tool in the overseas missions. Paul Hoffaeus, German assistant to the Jesuit Father General, Everard Mercurian (1514–80), wrote in a letter addressed to the work's eventual dedicatee, Clement VIII (1592–1605), that although it was

useful and profitable to all classes of persons who know Latin, especially to candidates for the priesthood...[the book] is not only much desired by contemplatives in Europe, but also coveted in both the Indies by the Society's workers who, using the images, could more easily imprint new Christians with all the mysteries of human redemption, which they retain with difficulty through preaching and catechism.

Such was its perceived usefulness that the Jesuit missionaries Marco Ferrero in Japan, Matteo Ricci (1552–1610) and Niccolò Longobardo (1565–1655) in China, and Jerónimo Xavier (1549–1617), superior of the Mughal mission in India, all wrote to Rome asking for copies of Nadal's magnificently illustrated work—the earliest series of the whole of the New Testament of any size or importance ever produced. In China, for example, Giovanni da Rocha used images from Nadal's book as models for Chinese artists to copy when representing the fifteen mysteries of the rosary in a locally produced woodblock printing of 1608. Nadal, who was inspired to become a

THE VIRGIN MARY, school of Manohar *c*.1590–5. Ink, colours, and gold on paper.

Jesuit by reading Francis Xavier's letters from India, would have been supremely gratified to know just how important his work was for the making of Roman Catholicism as the first world religion. However, notwithstanding such new technologies of instruction, certain (overwhelmingly politico-economic) preconditions needed to be met for successful conversion to take place.

Since Emperor Constantine's conversion to Christianity in the fourth century AD, and on to the decision of the rulers of Poland–Lithuania to become Christian in 1386, top-down conversion had been the principal means by which Christendom had extended its geographical boundaries. Indeed, notwithstanding the Protestant emphasis on individual conversion, this enduring reality was enshrined as the core principle underlying the Peace of Augsburg (1555): *cuius regio, eius religio* (whose kingdom, his religion). It was to be no different outside of Europe, even allowing for the degree to which the indigenous peoples of Africa, India, East Asia, and the Americas appropriated the rituals of Christianity to create their own particular Christendoms. Accordingly, in the period covered by this book, Christianity flourished outside Europe only where political conditions made it possible for the Europeans to make advantageous political and economic alliances. This happened first in the case of the Kingdom of the Kongo,

'ANNUNCIATION'. Jerónimo Nadal, *Adnotationeset meditationes in Evangelia* (Antwerp, 1607). Engraving by Hieronymus Wiericx after Bernardino Passeri. This image shows the importance of the gospel story to the pedagogic purpose of the Jesuits and was used both in the preparation of their own priests as well as for catechetical instruction of non-Christians outside Europe.

A. *Conuentus Angelorum, vbi declarat Deus Incarnationem Christi, & designatur Gabriel legatus.*
B. *Veniens Nazareth Gabriel, sibi ex aëre corpus accommodat.*
C. *Nubes è cælo, vnde radij ad Mariam Virginem pertinent.*
D. *Cubiculum, quod visitur Laureti in agro Piceno, vbi est Maria.*
E. *Ingreditur Angelus ad Mariam Virginem; eam salutat; assentitur Maria: fit Deus homo, & ipsa Mater Dei.*
F. *Creatio hominis, quo die Deus factus est homo.*
G. *Eadem die Christus moritur, vt homo perditus recreetur.*
H. *Piè credi potest, Angelum missum in Limbum, ad Christi incarnationem Patribus nunciandam.*

whose ruler Nzinga a Nkuwu requested baptism in 1491. Although the king soon tired of his new religion, his son, who took the name Afonso I, seems to have been more sincere in his adherence to the Christian faith, and sent his own son to train as a priest in Rome. By the time Afonso died in 1543, it is estimated that some two million people, half the population of his kingdom, had been baptized.

In the case of Mesoamerica, the favourable political climate was brilliantly engineered by Hernan Cortés (1485–1547). The conquistador was able to exploit Tlaxcallan determination not to accept Aztec hegemony in Mesoamerica to the extent that Tlaxcallans supplied 90 per cent of the army which successfully besieged the Aztec capital, Technochtitlán. Only then were first Franciscan (1523) and then Dominican (1528) and Augustinian (1533) friars able to commence their millenarian-inspired 'Spiritual Conquest'. In fact, Giovanni Botero (*c.*1544–1617), in his 1589 treatise

'ANNUNCIATION' FROM JUAN DE ROCHA SJ, Metodo de Rosario (Song nian zhu gui cheng). This is an example of local appropriation and adaptation of the corresponding image from Nadal's illustrated version of the gospels. Here the annunciation is depicted by a Chinese artist as the first of the five joyful mysteries of the Rosary

Della ragion di stato (Concerning Reason of State), singled out Cortéz for his astute use of religion to strengthen colonial rule. Similarly, Francisco Pizarro was able to secure a favourable political context for the spread of Christianity in South America. He made his entrance in the immediate aftermath of the death in 1527—most probably from 'Western' smallpox—of the Inca ruler Huayna Capac, an event which had precipitated his empire collapsing into a civil war fought between his two sons. A process of gradual Christianization followed, with the Jesuits taking a prominent role in the late 1570s, though even in the mid-seventeenth century it was felt necessary to launch a vigorous campaign against pagan idolatry.

By contrast, in Asia the European incomers were only able to insert themselves where the local powers were divided—as in India and, initially, in Japan—or where they were fitfully tolerant-cum-indifferent, as in China. In all of East Asia, it was only in the Spanish Philippines, where the Jesuits' mission was much less significant than those from the Augustinian, Dominican, and Franciscan orders, that Roman Catholicism was able to make a territorial as well as spiritual conquest. This success was due to the region's geographical and social fragmentation, but even here the low number of missionaries—by 1655 there were still only 60 secular clergy and 254 regulars to minister to a population of 500,000—meant that Christianity was unable to put down proper roots, except in the larger islands such as Luzón.

The Catholic mission in New France (Canada) has hitherto tended to be viewed apart from other evangelizing campaigns, but the latest research has attempted to integrate it into a truly global and comparative perspective. Perhaps the most interesting finding shows how reliant the Canadian missionaries were on their Iberian and Italian colleagues' reports from the mission in Japan in helping them formulate their own tactics. The famous settlements of indigenous Christians established by members of the Society of Jesus, known as reductions (*reducciónes*), are traditionally associated with the Jesuit province of Paraguay, an area which encompassed also northern parts of modern-day Argentina. But it is now argued, not only that they were also used in New France, with the Innu and Algonquin peoples in the St Lawrence Valley, but that the strategy also owed a direct debt to a Japanese prototype: the Christian villages of Hizen province.

The Jesuits have enjoyed the attentions of historians not only because they were active in so many parts of the globe, but also because they have left behind a fantastically rich archival paper trail. Furthermore, their policy of cultural 'accommodation' to local customs and practices has bestowed on them an enduring topicality. In fact, accommodation was not a Jesuit invention. The willingness to tailor missionary strategies to local traditions goes back at least to the famous letter from Gregory the Great (590–604) to Abbot Mellitus, who was about to join Augustine of Canterbury on a mission to the pagan Anglo-Saxons. Here the pontiff advocated that temples should not be destroyed, but merely cleansed of their idols and re-equipped with Christian relics. Nor was the policy restricted to Jesuits. For example, the Carmelite Juan Tadeo de San Eliseo (1574–1633), missionary to the court of Shah Abbas the Great of Persia (1557–1624), and from 1604 first Bishop of Isfahan, engaged extensively with local cultural traditions. So did the Mission étrangère (secular) priest, Louis Laneau (1636–96), who was head of the mission to Indochina. He became Bishop of Ayutthaya in 1674, and composed a dialogue between a Christian and a Buddhist sage written in Siamese.

It has become a truism that priests and missionaries found it necessary to adapt themselves to the people's capabilities. However, they also had to adapt themselves to *their own* capabilities. These were circumscribed, above all, by their low numbers, in both relative and absolute terms. Between 1493 and 1819, some 15,000 missionaries travelled to the New World on Spanish ships, with a peak of 130 per annum during the decade 1570–79. This was followed by a steep decline that only picked up from the mid-seventeenth century, after which the annual number fluctuated between thirty and seventy. In China, at its peak (1699–1702) the Jesuit mission numbered just thirty-six priests, who had to divide their attentions between thirty-three residences, though not all of them were staffed at the same time. Next, there was the issue of whether or not missionaries were operating in areas which were effectively controlled by one of the European powers. Such was the degree of identification in the minds of indigenous peoples between Christianity and the European settlers and traders that, for example, Christianity was known in Cochinchina as 'the Portuguese law', while the version of Portuguese spoken in Melaka is to this day simply called 'Kristang'.

Another major issue was one of language: how were the missionaries to communicate the substance of Roman Catholic doctrine to their non-European converts? In the short term, the answer is that, more often than not, they didn't. Or rather, they largely limited themselves to instilling ortho*praxy* rather than ortho*doxy*: right action rather than right belief. That said, if we limit discussion to Spanish Central and South America, there were no fewer than sixty-six religious works printed in Nahuatl between 1524 and 1572. Mostly composed by Franciscans, these ranged from catechisms and collections of prayers to sermons and scenes of sacred theatre. Further south, the Inca language, Quechua, which like Nahuatl had not been written down using alphabet characters before the arrival of the Spaniards, became the vehicle of a completely new and rich pastoral literature. Although recent research has drawn attention to the fact that there were some Jesuits who regarded language learning as little more than manual work, the Society's members contributed disproportionately to the flood of dictionaries and grammars of non-European languages. In the process, they laid the foundations of what would become, in due course, comparative linguistics.

It is perfectly valid to draw up a provisional balance sheet of the successes and failures of the missions to the New World, the East Indies, and Asia. Yet, arguably, it is still more interesting to consider the ways in which the experience of evangelization outside Europe affected the practice within it. The connection was freely acknowledged at the time. Numerous missionaries, reflecting on their experiences of evangelizing the backwoods of Europe, thought of the wider world beyond. Early evidence for this state of mind may be found in a letter of 7 February 1553, from the Jesuit missionary Silvestro Landini (1503–54) to Ignatius Loyola. Relating his experience of evangelizing Corsica, Landini wrote: 'I have never experienced lands which have more need of the Lord than this one . . . This island will be my India, just as worthy as that of Prester John.' Before long, the term 'other Indies' (*otras indias*) began to circulate widely, and to be applied to various geographically marginal areas, from the Basilicata in southern Italy to Brittany in north-western France.

A key work here is the widely disseminated missionary manual *De procuranda Indorum salute* (On Gaining the Salvation of the Indians), published in 1590 by the Jesuit missionary José de Acosta (1540–1600). Acosta spent sixteen years in the New World, mostly in Peru where he was Jesuit Provincial from 1576 to 1581. He wrote an accompanying, widely translated treatise, *Historia natural y moral de las Indias* (On the Natural and Moral History of the Indies) (1588), as well as the important *Tercero catecismo y esposición de la doctrina cristiana por sermones* (Third Catechism and Exposition of Christian Doctrine through Sermons) (1585). The latter was issued throughout Spanish South America under the authority of the third Provincial

Council of Lima (1583), whose importance for the New World has led to its being called 'the Trent of the Americas'.

Acosta is perhaps best known for his three-tier model of development to guide conversion strategy, which he outlined in the preface to *De procuranda*. There he divided the 'barbarians' (even the best of whom were necessarily inferior to any Christian society) into distinct categories. There were those who possessed sophisticated, urban-based social structures and full rates of literacy, something he believed might be found in China and Japan. These societies required the method of peaceful persuasion used by Christ and his Apostles. Next came those who lived in cities, who were able to impose taxes and raise armies, but who did not possess literacy in the sense that they used only pictogram or other non-alphabet or character symbols. For Acosta, this described the Aztec and Inca empires. Here, the imposition of rule by Christian princes, though preferably accompanied without too much military violence, was more appropriate. Finally came those who were neither city dwellers nor literate in any sense, a group which included what remained of the indigenous peoples of the Caribbean, such as the Tainos. Acosta observed that this third class of barbarian should, according to Aristotle, be hunted like wild beasts and dominated by force.

Equally germane to the purposes of my argument in this chapter is the following quotation from *De procuranda*. After citing Bede's *Ecclesiastical History*, Acosta wrote: 'Let anyone read about the customs of the ancient English. They will find they were much wilder than our Indians.' Behind this remark is the recognition that what they (Indians) now are, we (sixteenth-century Europeans) once were! This 'discovery of the indigenous' in the Old World was an insight which profoundly affected the way missionaries in the 'Other Indies' went about their business. In Columbus' *Book of Prophecies*, or the writings of the first Franciscan chroniclers of the missions in the Americas, it is clear that the authors believed that they were witnessing, not the dawn of a New World, but the fulfilment and end of time itself. In the oft-quoted words of Matthew 24: 14, 'And the gospel of the Kingdom shall be preached in all the world as a witness unto all nations; and then shall the end come.' By contrast, Acosta's lesson from the early history of the Christian missions provided him and his contemporaries with a historically informed perspective, one which would reanimate and revolutionize the way the Old Word was to be (re-)Christianized. New times required new methods.

The global spread of Roman Catholicism sketched here was thus far from inevitable. Indeed, from the perspective of 1500, it seemed highly unlikely. Columbus had, after all, failed to find what he was looking for—a short cut to the East, both for trading advantage and for launching a crusade with non-European Christians against the infidel occupiers of Jerusalem. The promise and potential of the New World as either a fertile field for conversion, or for economic exploitation, had yet to make an impact. Save for such relatively isolated communities as the Syriac 'Thomas' Christians of south-western India, the Syriac Maronite Church of Antioch, the minority Coptic Church of Egypt, and the Coptic Kingdom of Ethiopia, Christendom was boxed into the western extremity of the Eurasian landmass by considerable Islamic powers, notably the Ottoman Empire to the east and the Mamluk sultanate of Egypt to the south-east. In North Africa, from Morroco to Tunis, Portuguese and Spanish influence was precarious and restricted to the coastline.

In East Asia, Islam had been enjoying a wave of continuous expansion for over a century. Its pace was to accelerate from *c.*1500, in parallel with, and not unrelated to, the arrival of Christianity. In the Americas, the Aztec and Inca kingdoms had reached their pagan apogee. In China, the Confucian Middle Kingdom of the Ming dynasty had admittedly abandoned its early fifteenth-century practice of sending gargantuan armadas on flag-waving voyages as far as East Africa. But this was not in response to hostile reception, but because of perceived irrelevance to China's continental concerns as Asia's most considerable power. In the territory represented by modern-day Afghanistan, Zahir ud-din Babur (1483–1530), the great-grandson of Tamerlane, was poised to invade the Indian subcontinent. He would establish what came to be known as the Mughal Empire, in which a Muslim minority ruled successfully for more than two centuries over a Hindu majority. If the early modern period, as has been argued recently, was in global terms an 'age of empire', then the West had but a single contestant: the Habsburgs, who managed to unite their various Burgundian, Austrian, and Spanish patrimonies with the title of Holy Roman Emperor for just a little under four decades (1519–56). The 'triumph of the West over the Rest' would have to wait until the late nineteenth and early twentieth centuries. Even then, it was a 'victory' expressed in terms of economic and political rather than religious dominance. The Scottish explorer and missionary to Africa David Livingstone (1813–73) famously converted just two Africans to Christianity, one of whom subsequently reconverted.

Thus the period *c.*1500–1700 did not see the realization of the vision of Roman Catholicism as the first world religion embracing all four of the known inhabited continents—a vision celebrated in unashamedly propagandistic fashion by the Jesuit artist Andrea Pozzo in his dizzyingly illusionistic nave ceiling fresco in the church of S. Ignazio in Rome. Rather, it saw the triumph of the *idea* of the global reach of Rome, and that of its universal pastor—the pope. This was a different kind of victory, to be sure, but it was one which ensured that the European Counter-Reformation, initially prompted by Martin Luther, would become the global Catholic Reformation. It also ensured that the laity in both the Old and New Worlds was engaged to an unprecedented degree, and by means of unprecedentedly various methods, with orthodox devotional practice and doctrine. The triumph of this idea laid the foundations for the eventual realization of a global Roman Catholicism in the twentieth century.

Taking the Christian Message from the New to the Old Worlds

It has been suggested that, chronologically speaking, the Christianization of the New and Old Worlds roughly coincided. However, I would argue that it was only thanks to the expanded missionary imagination, and set of practical skills, developed in response to the challenge of evangelizing the New World that the Old World came to be (re-)Christianized in the way that it was. Put simply, the New World converted the Old, a process which is still unfolding today. It is rare, but not unknown, to find the

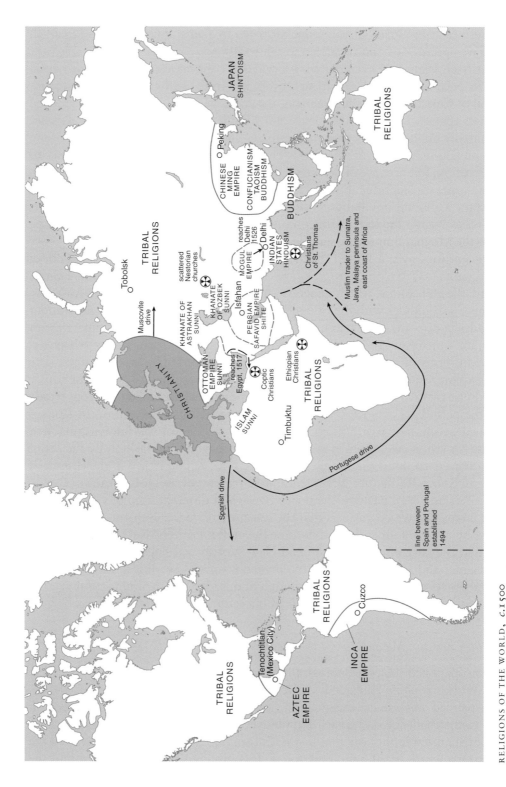

RELIGIONS OF THE WORLD, *c.*1500
Source: John McManners (ed.), *The Oxford History of Christianity* (OUP, 1993).

same people involved in missions to both the New and the Old Worlds, but it is less uncommon to find missionaries who moved from one overseas mission to another: notably from Europe to Mexico, and then on to the Philippines and China. However, of massive importance to the process whereby the Old World recalibrated its understanding of mission and conversion were the reports about the experience and findings of the missions to Asia and the Americas. Such reports, many of which came to be printed, flooded western Europe in the early modern period. From publication of one of the very first New World descriptions, the *Paesi Novamente Ritrovati* (Countries recently discovered) of 1507, down to the thirty-four volumes of *Lettres édifiants et curieuses* (1702–76), culled from Jesuit reports about their global missionary enterprise, information poured from Europe's printing presses in an uninterrupted flow. Such reports took myriad Latinate and vernacular forms: carefully edited missionary letters; copiously illustrated volumes of sacred geography and topography; histories of missionary religious orders; collective and individual saints' lives; theatre and epic poetry. Tales of missionary derring-do reinvented chivalric romance for a confessional age. Indeed, sacred romance became a recognized literary genre in the seventeenth century. One of its most successful Italian examples was the evocatively entitled *Il Cappuccino scozzese* (The Scots Capuchin) of 1644 by Giovanni Battista Rinuccini (1592–1653), later to be much less successful as a papal nuncio to Ireland (1645–9). This was loosely based on the story of George Leslie, who became a Capuchin friar and a successful missionary, before returning to Scotland to convert and console many of his countrymen and women, including his heretic Calvinist mother, won over by the avowedly rational arguments he proposed in debate with her Protestant chaplain. Such stories provided entertaining yet uplifting listening matter for the religious in refectory (both male and female); consolation for those Roman Catholics who were living under oppressive regimes; and encouragement for those on the confessional frontier.

Amidst this veritable tsunami of print there is one title that deserves special mention. This was the *Rhetorica Christiana*, published in 1579. The title alone does not single it out, since the genre of treatises on Christian eloquence was already well established, and this title resembled, in important ways, the almost contemporary (1582) *Rhetoricae Ecclesiasticae* by the Dominican Luis de Granada (1505–88), whose collected works represent for the literature of spiritual guidance much the same as Thomas Aquinas's do for Scholasticism. What makes the *Rhetorica Christiana* special, however, is that its author, Diego de Valadés (1533–82?), was a *mestizo*. His father was a conquistador and his mother an Indian from Tlaxcala. He was educated with members of the Indian elite at the school run by Peter of Ghent, and entered the Franciscan order in *c.*1550, just five years before the Provincial Synod of Mexico decided that only pure blooded white settlers known as *creoles* could become priests. For two decades, Valadés worked as 'a missionary in his own land', preaching and hearing confessions in the Nahua, Tarascan, and Otomi languages.

He commented proudly that the conversion of the New World Indians had been more successful than that of the former Muslims (*moriscos*) in Spain. First, this was

GLORY OF ST IGNATIUS LOYOLA AND THE MISSIONARY WORK OF THE JESUIT ORDER, sometimes just called *The Apotheosis of St Ignatius*, Andrea Pozzo, St Ignazio, Rome (1688–94). This has become the emblematic representation of the idea of global Roman Catholicism even if the reality was decidedly more complicated and less triumphant.

because the missionaries were themselves better prepared and, secondly, the Indians were more disposed to conversion than the stubborn *moriscos*. A vital part of the missionaries' preparation—apart from knowledge of the relevant languages—was their knowledge about distinctive features of the culture of those being proselytized. In the case of the Mexica Indians, it was their aptitude for, and extensive reliance upon, images. This made artificial memory a matter of particular importance, thus explaining its prominence in Valadés' text, where it assumed the job usually given to *inventio* (the means of finding material for argument). It also explained what was undoubtedly the most striking feature of the *Rhetorica Christiana* to anyone consulting it today: its extensive use of illustrations. One of these showed a missionary teaching a congregation of Indians with images—known as *lienzos* (literally,

DIEGO DE VALADÉS, *Rétorica cristiana* (1579), illustration of preacher teaching indigenous indians using images painted onto canvas (*lienzos*). The prominently seated figure indicated with a 'C', who has his right hand pressing his chest, is supposedly the chief (cacique) of the indigenous congregation expressing how he has been touched by the preacher's words.

linens)—and included the detail of a chief sitting in the front row with his hand on his heart to indicate that he has been moved by the preacher's message.

The century *c.*1648–*c.*1750 became a 'golden age' of European missions, and of superstar revivalist preachers. The Jesuit Paolo Segneri the Elder (1624–94)—the Billy Graham of the baroque—conducted no fewer than 540 missions, usually lasting between a week and nine days and involving up to three priests, between 1665 and 1692 in central and southern Italy, an average of twenty a year. These involved theatrical, hellfire sermons and (if secular authorities' fears for public order could be overruled) dramatic, torch-lit processions of wailing penitents, which were interspersed with catechism classes, public recitations of the rosary, Adoration of the Sacrament and individual confession. Each mission, although differing in particulars, always ended in the same fashion, with the erection of a large mission-cross and the administering of general communion. Further north, in the Upper Palatinate—a region reclaimed for Roman Catholicism by the Wittelsbach dukes of Bavaria during the Thirty Years War (1618–48)—the Jesuits conducted three missions between 1716 and 1722. Several of these Jesuit missioners had been apprenticed to members of the 'Segneri school', and they adapted themselves to the ubiquitous, unquenched demand for miraculous healing in the Old World by deploying a powerful relic from the non-European missions: 'Xavier-Water'. This was water which had been made holy by coming into contact with relics belonging to St Francis Xavier, or with medals which had been blessed in his memory. This Jesuit strategy of promoting such sacramentals—holy objects or practices not instituted by Christ but nevertheless regarded as spiritually efficacious—has been seen as a form of 'reverse assimilation', whereby the missionaries ended up being 'converted', or at least changed, by the popular culture of the missionized. But the deployment of such techniques cannot be viewed in isolation from lessons learned on the missions to Asia and the Americas. This missionary strategy climaxed, in a milder and 'sweeter' form, with Alphonsus de Liguori (1696–1787), founder of the Redemptorists, for whom the boundary between the work of secular parish priests and that of his missionaries in southern Italy became blurred and indistinct: parish religion *was* missionary religion. The New World had become teacher of the Old.

'Re-placing' Trent: The Limits of Tridentine Catholicism

To any reader possessing more than a passing acquaintance with the traditional story of the Catholic Reformation, perhaps the most striking absence from the narrative up to this point has been the Council of Trent (1545–63). Such has been its iconic status—as symbol of everything that is to be valued or abhorred about official religion—that one has to make a conscious effort to see the Council in its 'local' specificity, as a response to immediate, pressing concerns. Above all, it is important to remember that the Council was not a single event, but an unfolding and discontinuous process, which took place over the reigns of five popes, four kings of France, and two Holy Roman Emperors. The choice of location is revealing. Trent was a small town which, although geographically in Italy, was jurisdictionally speaking part of the Holy Roman Empire. Its selection as venue was determined by this hybrid status, and reflected the tensions between the pope and the emperor. For the former, the reassertion of traditional doctrine against Lutheran heresy was of paramount concern. For the latter, who counted the Lutherans amongst his imperial subjects, reform of clerical abuses was a necessary precondition for the healing of his divided realm.

There were four main periods in which the Council met: December 1545–March 1547 (at Trent); April 1547–January 1548 (in Bologna); May 1551–April 1552 (back in Trent); January 1562–December 1563 (Trent again). The opening session was attended by just four cardinals, twenty-one bishops, and five generals of the religious orders. Revealingly, in view of the pope's overriding concern with doctrine, these prelates and senior clerics were, until the final period of the Council, outnumbered by attendant theologians. By the closing session, however, attendance had increased to 247 bishops: 187 'Italian', which included many from Spanish-controlled territories in the peninsula, 31 Spanish, 26 French, and 2 German. Some important decrees were drafted, debated, and decided upon in both the first and second periods—most notably the decree on Justification (September 1546–January 1547) and also those on the Real Presence (transubstantiation) in October 1551 and Penance (the following month). But the lion's share of business was conducted during the final period of the Council, particularly the last six months, July to December 1563. During these final few months decrees were issued on a panoply of topics: the establishment of diocesan seminaries; the desirability (whenever possible) of church weddings; the need for annual episcopal visitations (and triannual provincial meetings); the bishop's duty of preaching and the source of his authority; the efficacy of the veneration of saints and images; the reform of the regular or monastic clergy, as well as a reassertion of the enclosure of nuns. In addition, the papacy was mandated by the Council with the reform of the liturgical books of the Roman rite, beginning with the breviary in 1568, as well as the issuing of a new catechism and the new edition of the Index of Prohibited books. Papal responsibility here is an important distinction that has been obscured by the misleading adoption of the adjective 'Tridentine' to describe all these texts.

That so much was covered in such a short space of time is only partly to be explained by fears for the health of the then pope, Pius IV (1559–65). A more immediate cause was the arrival of the French delegation of bishops, led by the charismatic and politically astute Charles of Guise, Cardinal of Lorraine (1524–74). It was Lorraine who forced such issues as the veneration of saints and images onto the agenda, since for the French, on the verge of religious civil war, such a topic was of, literally, burning significance. For the numerically dominant Spanish and Italian bishops, from the Mediterranean heartlands of Roman Catholicism, attention was focused more on such jurisdictional matters as the origins of episcopal authority. Were they divine or papal? If the former, then not even the pope could dispense bishops from their duty of residence. Above all other issues, this was the one which almost derailed the Council, and things were only saved by a skilful fudge achieved by that incomparable curial diplomat, Cardinal Giovanni Morone (1509–90).

However, the Council of Trent was arguably more important for what it left out than for what it defined. It has been observed that several of the key issues which really

GENERAL CONGREGATION OF THE COUNCIL OF TRENT in S. Maria Maggiore in the year 1563, by Claudio Duchetti. The serried ranks of the delegates seated hierarchically in a (specially constructed) wooden amphitheatre has communicated to posterity a misleading image of the Council as a harmonious monolith. Its seated participants are neatly bounded by a wooden wall whose sole point of access is guarded by two custodians standing bottom left who supervised the comings and goings of the endless stream of couriers that kept Rome and Trent in touch with each other. The open end of the amphitheatre is completed by a row of cardinal legates (representing the pope, who was careful to remain absent so as not to be seen to be in any way subject to the Council) and who sit on a raised platform flanked by lay representatives of princes. The inscription tells us that the engraving represents a general congregation in session at the church of S. Maria Maggiore, rather than the cathedral, which hosted only the more formal ceremonies at which the decrees, which had been previously debated at the general congregations, were read out.

mattered to Catholics fighting on the front line of a confessionally divided Europe—communion in both kinds, a vernacular liturgy, clerical celibacy, and the veneration of saints—were adroitly sidestepped at Trent. In the case of the last of these, a decree was rushed through in the closing days of the Council—as we have seen, largely owing to French pressure—that did little more than restate the teaching of the Second Council of Nicea (787). Moreover, in its entire omission of the subject of missions, Trent betrayed its essentially Old World preoccupations. One might even say that missions did not fit 'the Trent template' of the Church, one conceived in terms of pope, bishop, and pastor. Viewed from this perspective, 'the Church' as such had no interest in missions, which were the responsibility of the religious orders, backed by their secular rulers. This was not to change until the foundation of the Roman Congregation of *Propaganda Fide* (for the Propagation of the Faith) in 1622.

What importance, then, does Trent still have for our new, global narrative of Catholic Reformation and Renewal? The answer is twofold. First, by keeping reform of the papacy off the agenda, the cardinal legates at Trent paved the way for the eventual triumph of *Roman* Catholicism: a papally led Church, whose clergy owed their authority to the universal pastor and successor of St Peter. Secondly, by directing so much attention to the reform of the episcopate, the Council made bishops the key building blocks of the Church. Not only in the Old World but also in the New, reforming bishops were to provide pastoral leadership for their flocks, notwithstanding the fact that the missionary religious orders were excluded from their jurisdiction.

Papal Prince and Pastor: The Dynamics of Roman Catholicism

Like the Council of Trent, the papacy and Rome itself have come late to this chapter. The fifteenth-century papacy's experience of Conciliarism, which had attempted to subject the pope to the authority of regular church councils, was recent enough for Julius II (1503–13) to insist on having the Fifth Lateran Council (1512–17) meet in Rome where he could keep a beady eye on proceedings. The delays over the calling of the Council of Trent are to be understood not only by reference to the Habsburg–Valois rivalry between the Holy Roman Emperor Charles V and King Francis I of France; they also owed much to the papacy's fear of Conciliarism.

Indeed, the currently dominant view of the early modern papacy considers its priorities almost exclusively in terms of how it got over the trauma of Conciliarism by creating a papal monarchy with its own consolidated territorial state. In the short term, the papal prince was able to exercise both temporal and spiritual authority in order to pioneer various innovations in the fields of taxation and administration, only to find himself, in the longer term, the victim of his own relative success. The sclerotic, bloated bureaucracy that fed off the carcass of a non-productive Roman economy would prove unable to reverse the increasing marginalization of the papacy in international politics after the Treaty of Westphalia (1648). This narrative is seriously problematic, however, since it largely ignores the pope's identity as supreme pastor, and the symbolic importance of Rome as the capital of a universal Church with global reach. In this context, Rome's brief appearance at the start of this chapter was a revealing one, since the city functioned as the source of what was the richest and oldest of several 'mines of sanctity': the catacombs, whose relics circulated widely within northern Europe, and whose counterparts circulated much farther afield. Here the Eternal City enjoyed a unique status, not only as home of the papacy, but also for having witnessed the sufferings, and been the place of burial, of an unrivalled number of early Christians martyred at the hands of the Roman emperors.

To borrow the words of Pius V (1566–72): 'this earth [of St Peter's Square] is drenched (*inzuppata*—literally soaked like bread in soup) with the blood of the martyrs'. Rome was itself a most precious reliquary. This was the ultimate follow-up to the Roman Catholic taunt to Protestants, where was your Church before Luther? Rome was not only a place but also a state of mind. Moreover, it enjoyed the prestige conferred by 'double apostolicity', since it had witnessed the life and death of both St Peter and St Paul.

Historians of papal Rome have traditionally privileged Venetian ambassadorial reports as a source of evidence. But a more reliable guide to the city's significance as headquarters of a religion with global pretentions is provided by the English cleric, and translator of the Douai Bible, Gregory Martin (1542–82), who spent some eighteen months (December 1576–June 1578) criss-crossing Rome as a pilgrim. *Roma Sancta*—the extraordinary portrait of Roman Catholic 'best practice' which he left in manuscript at his death—was divided into two parts: 'Of devotion' and 'Of charitie'. Gregory's text provided his readers with a gazetteer-cum-meditation on the Eternal City, one that not only enumerated its churches and their relics but also testified to the overwhelming *praesentia* of the saints buried there:

And if anywhere a man stand nigh to these tombs, he perceiveth his sense by and by ravished with this said force, for the sight of the coffin entering into the heart, pearceth it, stirreth it up, and moveth it in such a manner, as if he that lieth there dead, did pray with us, and were visibly present to be seen. Besides it cometh to pass, that he which feeleth himself so sweetly moved, is marvelous jocund, and gladsome, and being clean altered after a sort into another man, in such heavenly plight departeth he out of the place.

Here, Rome was itself an agent of conversion by means of its material relics, which functioned as portals that transported a person with the right interior disposition to early Christian Rome. Place had become the most fundamental form of embodied experience, where self, space, and time coincided.

Rome's unique status was also foregrounded in the new sacred history that was currently being made fashionable by members of the Congregation of the Oratory, an order which had been founded by that Christian Socrates, Filippo Neri (1515–95), and whose rule had been approved in 1575. The leading figure here, after Neri himself, was undoubtedly Cesare Baronio, who is best known for his reply to the Protestant 'Magdeburg Centuriators', whose history of the first 1,300 years of church history (written in 1559–74) was portrayed in terms of a progressive decline from apostolic purity from *c*.600 onwards. At the root of Baronio's enterprise lay his work on the historical notes to the list of saints, mostly but not exclusively martyrs, arranged by calendar month to be read out at the daily office of Prime, and known as the Roman Martyrology. Baronio's scholarly edition of these came out in 1586, was frequently reprinted, and became the basis of the standard version used throughout the Roman Catholic world until 2001. His erudite notes invited readers to dig down with their mind's eye beneath Rome's topsoil to the early Christian layer of the city's past.

The Roman Calendar only included the names of those saints who had been martyred in the Eternal City or whose bones had been buried there. But it also contained the names of those non-martyr (confessor) saints who enjoyed an officially recognized, universal cult. Indeed, for a saint to enjoy universal cult status, his or her inclusion in the Roman Martyrology was mandatory. In other words, Rome stood also for the Universal, Catholic Church. Rome's importance was further underlined by the numerous colleges established there in the later sixteenth century which trained priests for missionary work. Most of these institutions were entrusted to the Jesuits, who assumed oversight of the Collegium Germanicum-Hungaricum, the Maronite seminary, the House of (former Jewish) Neophytes, the English College, and the Greek College. Other colleges for the training of seminarists were established at frontier posts in Brandenburg, Fulda, Augsburg, Vienna, Rheims, Lithuania, and Moravia, and there were no fewer than four such foundations in Japan. Indeed, it should not be forgotten that, until the foundation of these institutions, even Rome lacked the infrastructure for training priests in adequate numbers for its increasingly global responsibilities. Here the Jesuits deserve full credit for having made Rome *the* centre for the training of priests which it remains to this day. The foundation in 1622 of the curial department (congregation) with direct responsibility for the papal supervision of missionary training and policy—that of the Propagation of the Faith (*Propaganda Fide*)—was thus preceded and prepared for by several decades of papal interest and enterprise.

Rome's universal significance was enhanced, not only because it was the home of martyrs' bones from the early Christian period, but also because, from the twelfth century onwards, the papacy had asserted a monopoly over the making of saints. (Until the tenth century, people generally became saints as a result of popular acclamation, achieved with the support of the local bishop.) This monopoly was reasserted after Trent, when the practice of papal canonization resumed after a period of nervous neglect during the central Reformation decades: although some non-universal cults were approved, no saint for the whole Church was declared between 1528 and 1588. In 1588, however, Sixtus V (1585–90) canonized the Spanish Franciscan Diego of Alcalà (d. 1463). The first period of revival continued down to a particularly triumphant ceremony of 1622, at which no fewer than five saints were proclaimed: Ignatius Loyola, Francis Xavier, Philip Neri, Teresa of Avila, and Isidor the Farmer. This was not only a cause for papal display of its universal authority in matters of worship and devotion, it was also an occasion for the Jesuits to celebrate the global reach of their apostolate, with theatrical performances based on the lives of their holy heroes. However, it was only from 1624–5, with the intervention of the Roman Inquisition or Congregation of the Holy Office, that canonization procedure took the form it was to exhibit down to 1983. The extent of the involvement in saint-making of this new curial department or congregation, founded in 1542, in conjunction with the Congregation of Sacred Rites (founded in 1588), has only recently been recognized. This is perhaps surprising in view of the overlap in personnel between the two curial departments. For example, Francisco Peña (1540–1612), who assembled the documentation for the canonization trial of Diego of Alcalà, including writing his printed life, was

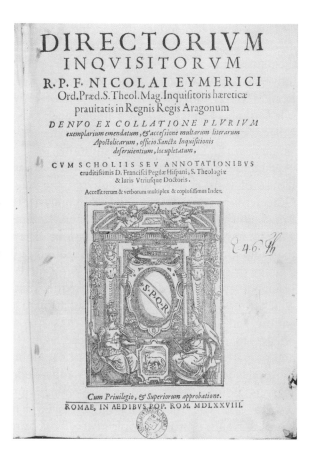

FRANCISCO PEÑA, *Directorium Inquisitorum*, ed. Nicolaus Eymerich (Rome, 1578), frontispiece. The author responsible for the update to this classic medieval inquisition manual from the fourteenth century, Francisco Peña, was also the key player in the first canonization since the Reformation—that of Diego of Alcalá in 1588. This serves to remind us that saint- and heretic-making should be seen as part of the same process of boundary marking which particularly characterized this period of confessional conflict.

also responsible for an important new edition (1578) of the standard medieval inquisitorial manual by Nicolaus Eymerich, the *Directorium Inquisitorum* (1376). This serves to remind us that heretic-making and saint-making should be considered as two aspects of a single, educative purpose: the creation of models for good Catholics to emulate or avoid.

The Catholic Prince: Confessionalization and the Struggle over Patronage Rights

One of the most influential approaches to the Reformation over the last generation has sought to identify structural similarities between the various 'reformations' of the sixteenth and seventeenth centuries. According to this view, Lutheranism, Calvinism, and Reformed Catholicism should be seen not as opposites but as parallel movements, which, by raising the bar on what was expected of their church members, imposed an unprecedented degree of social discipline on western Europeans. Put another way, Europe in this period experienced a profound shift, from being a single community of believers to becoming a patchwork of rival confessions of belief. This process of 'confessionalization' manifested itself particularly in the unprecedented deployment by both religious and secular authorities of propaganda in all print media, from engravings to sermons, catechisms to books of spiritual guidance. It was also accompanied by a wholesale reformation of ritual, which reflected an internalization of behaviour via education and training. A key role here was played by secular rulers who, as equally enthusiastic generators of printed orders and decrees, were only too delighted to use religion to reinforce social obedience. In the words of the sometime Jesuit Giovanni Botero (*c.*1544–1617):

Of all laws there is none more favourable to princes than the Christian law, for it makes not only the bodies and goods of those they rule subject to them...but also their souls and consciences, and binds not only hands but also thoughts and feelings.

It is in this overall context that one needs to place the three Inquisitions: of Spain (1478–1834), Portugal (1536–1821), and Rome itself (1542–the present; renamed in 1965 The Congregation for the Doctrine of the Faith). Their capacity to prosecute and to punish was heavily dependent on the secular powers. In theory, all three inquisitions were formally unified under the single jurisdiction of the papacy, and so could (and did) share information, as well as a common legal culture and procedures. But despite this, the Iberian inquisitions were directly subject on a day-to-day basis to the Spanish and Portuguese crowns.

Any 'global history' of the Inquisition thus needs to take account of the local circumstances surrounding the foundation of each of its three branches. At its height, the Spanish Inquisition comprised twenty tribunals, including those in its overseas territories where only *creoles* and *mestizos* (i.e. those of European, or mixed European–indigenous, ancestry) were subject to its jurisdiction. Its initial targets, however, were the Jews (*conversos*) and Moors (*moriscos*) who had been forcibly converted as a consequence of the successful conclusion of the Iberian reconquest. Between 1478 and 1530 the Spanish Inquisition prosecuted 2,350 people, 90 per cent of whom were *conversos*, and 750 of whom were put to death. Between 1530 and 1609, 4,250 persons were brought to trial, almost 70 per cent of whom were *moriscos*, and of whom 24 received capital punishment. Thereafter, Inquisition activity declined, from an average of 507 cases per annum in 1560–1607 to 168 per annum in 1615–1700. *Conversos* once again became targets in the later period, but within the context of a shift of focus from heresy or apostasy to one on morals and 'superstition'.

From its foundation in 1536, the Portuguese Inquisition—with just four tribunals to cover Portugal and its overseas territories, where both settlers and indigenous Christians were subject to its jurisdiction—was similarly concerned with *conversos*. Some 84 per cent of all defendants prosecuted at Evora down to 1668, and 68 per cent of those proceeded against at Lisbon down to 1629, were accused of being 'Judaizers'. As with its Spanish cousin, the range of jurisdiction broadened over time, to encompass sodomy in 1562, solicitation of female parishioners by priests in 1599, and bigamy in 1612. Between 1536 and 1605, 256 of 3,376 persons tried were put to death, though in contrast to the Spanish pattern of greater severity at home, no fewer than 1,821 were tried and 103 condemned to death by the overseas tribunal at Goa. Between 1606 and 1674, more than twice as many people were brought before the tribunal there as before that of Lisbon (7,691 versus 3,210).

The Roman Inquisition was founded as the curial congregation of the Holy Office in 1542, specifically to target Lutheran heretics. There were forty-three tribunals in the Italian peninsula, though this excluded Sicily and Lucca, and nor could the Inquisition operate openly in Naples, where the archiepiscopal court retained parallel jurisdiction in this area. In Venice, there were three locally appointed lay observers at the tribunal. The Roman Inquisition also had jurisdiction in Avignon, the Franche-Comté, Carcassonne, Toulouse, and Cologne; but elsewhere in France and Germany it was absent. The medieval Inquisition, which had operated with notorious effectiveness in the thirteenth century against the Cathars in southern France, had consisted of a network of individual tribunals organized by bishops but not linked vertically to Rome. In our period, by contrast, Rome claimed the right to nominate all 'Judges of the Faith', and the Roman Inquisition sought to scrutinize all sentences made by its local tribunals. Nonetheless, death by burning—carried out by the secular arm—was restricted to the obstinate and unrepentant and the relapsed. There was a low death rate, with, for example, only a single person being put to death in Modena during a period of over 200 years of activity. No more than 1,250 death sentences were carried out throughout the Roman Inquisition's whole jurisdiction over more than two centuries, though this was doubtless of little comfort to the victims. Moreover, all defendants were entitled to defence counsel, trial transcriptions were made available to them, appeals were possible, and 'life imprisonment' usually meant two to three years' custody. As with its sister Inquisitions, after a relatively short-lived sixteenth-century burst of anti-heretical activity, the Roman Holy Office became concerned overwhelmingly with superstition and priestly misdemeanours such as solicitation (that is, the seduction of penitents in the confessional). Overall, viewed in comparison with contemporary secular legal institutions, the tribunals of the Spanish, Portuguese, and Roman Inquisitions offered defendants better provision of legal, if not moral, justice. In particular, the tribunals were sceptical about accusations for witchcraft, and it is striking how incidents of the witch-craze which affected both northern Europe and English North America in this period, and led to some 60,000 executions, were conspicuous by their absence in territories subject to the jurisdiction of the three Inquisitions.

Notwithstanding the common interests that the Roman Catholic Church and Roman Catholic states shared in their desire to exercise control over their subjects' bodies and souls, there was no guaranteed recipe for harmony between papacy and princes. Philip II of Spain, though king of the Roman Catholic superpower of the age, was not the secular arm of the Counter-Reformation. Indeed, his prompt ratification of the decrees of the Council of Trent throughout Spanish territories was accompanied by the significant proviso that exceptions would be made whenever their implementation might threaten royal privileges. This was followed, in October 1572, by a royal decree which declared null and void papal briefs which cited Spaniards before foreign courts in ecclesiastical causes. This ensured that a Catholic Spaniard had almost as little chance of appealing a case to Rome as did a Protestant Englishman.

At the root of the tensions between the papacy and the King of Spain was the issue of royal ecclesiastical patronage—known as the *patronato real*. This term—together with its cousin the Portuguese *padroado real*—refers to the privilege, first granted in 1486 by Innocent VIII (1484–92) to Ferdinand and Isabella, for rulers to nominate to all benefices in newly conquered territories in order that the conversion and spiritual welfare of indigenous peoples be catered for. It was accompanied by the regular granting of crusade indulgences, to be administered by their Most Catholic Majesties in support of, first, the reconquest of the Iberian Peninsula, and then the expansion and defence of their Christian territories. In actual fact, such papal privileges became an integral means for the ever cash-strapped early modern Spanish administration to raise tax revenue. Given that an agreed proportion of this income made its way back to Rome, it also became a vital supplement to the papacy's own fragile fiscal foundations, doing so in a highly visible fashion. It has recently been calculated that revenue from this indulgence, and related papal privileges raised from Spanish imperial territories, directly accounted for no less than 65 per cent of the costs of building the new St Peter's in Rome between 1529 and 1620.

These *politique* arrangements between the papacy and the monarchies of Spain and Portugal made possible a near-global campaign of evangelization to be undertaken in the name of *Roman* Catholicism, a campaign which the papacy lacked the resources to carry out on its own. But popes have struggled ever since to reclaim the jurisdictional initiative and actually realize their pretensions as universal pastors. This was despite the combined efforts of the papal Congregations of the Holy Office and, particularly, the *Propaganda Fide* (from its foundation in 1622), which made extensive use of *faculties* or special privileges, issued to secular clergy. These enabled them to administer the sacraments in lands dominated by the missionary orders, and where the ordinary canon law (*ius comune*) was supplanted by that which obtained in the missions (*ius missionum*). In this context, one might justifiably question whether it makes sense to label, even for convenience's sake, the Catholic Churches which were established under the aegis of Portugal and Spain as specifically *Roman* Catholic in identity. Arguably, this is so even for Latin America, where there existed a developed diocesan structure staffed, at least by the end of our period, by a significant proportion of secular clergy. Instead, perhaps we should employ the prefixes *Lusitanian-* and *Hispanic-* to the plural noun 'Catholicisms'. This would appear to be supported by the fact that not only were the overwhelming majority of cases (98 per cent) considered in the representative year of 1664 by one of the key curial congregations of the Counter-Reformation papacy—that of bishops and regulars—of Italian origin, but of these cases 80 per cent related just to the Papal States and southern Italy. In light of this, it makes more sense to view the institution presided over by the early modern papacy less as a monarchy and more as a commonwealth of national churches.

This is confirmed if we recall that one of the most important ways in which Roman Catholic towns, regions, nations, and empires refashioned and renegotiated their religious identities during our period was through the cult of saints. This was particularly so when communities were not only faced with the Protestant challenge but also had to respond to attempts by Rome to tighten up procedures for the making of new saints and to exercise control over the ways in which existing cults were presented in visual and textual forms. The manner in which this was invariably resolved—by means of a prefatory note by the author that he was using the term 'saint' merely in the colloquial rather than formal sense—is typical of *ancien régime* government in general, where blanket prohibition was invariably accompanied by tacit, if unofficial, acknowledgement of the existence of local exceptions.

The early modern period was therefore the Golden Age of Sacred History and saw the publication of such universal treatments as Baronio's history of the first twelve centuries of the Church (the *Annales ecclesiastici*, 1588–1607) and the greatest collection of saints' lives ever assembled, the *Acta sanctorum* begun in 1643. Moreover, as one might expect, this period also saw an unprecedented number of histories of missionary religious orders, which in the case of the multi-volume history of the Jesuits (*Istoria della compagnia di Gesù*, 1650–73) by the 'Dante of Baroque prose', Daniello Bartoli, was also effectively global in range. An age of resurgent national churches was also reflected in such works as Ambrogio de Morales' history of the Spanish Church (*La coronica general de España*, 1574), Rodrigo da Cuhna's ecclesiastical history of the Lisbon Church (*Historia ecclesiastica da igreja de Lisboa*, 1642), Scévole de Sainte-Marthe's collective history of French bishoprics (*Gallia cristiana*, 1656), Ferdinando Ughelli's Italian counterpart (*Italia sacra*, 1644–62), and Bohuslav Balbìn's history of the Bohemian Church (*Epitome historica rerum Bohemicarum*, 1677). A similar sentiment was also behind such collective hagiographies as John Colgan's collection of Irish saints' lives (*Acta sanctorum hiberniae*, 1645) and Matthäus Rader's account of the deeds of Bavaria's saints: *Bavaria sancta*, 1615–27. The latter was even prefaced by the unambiguous epithet (worthy of Giovanni Botero for whom religion was *the* essential cement of nation-building): 'There can be no kingdom without religion' (*Tota regio nil nisi religio*).

The Diocese in Global Perspective

The canons and decrees of the Council of Trent might be seen as having provided the 'theory' of Tridentine Catholicism—in particular, its focus on the bishop as the building block of the reformed Church. Undoubtedly, though, the practical 'how to' manual for the conscientious prelate was to be found in the *Acta ecclesiae Mediolanensis* (1582) by the Archbishop of Milan, Carlo Borromeo (1538–84). This volume consisted not only of the acts of the six provincial and eight diocesan synods held by Borromeo in his capacity as archbishop (1563–84), but also of his detailed instructions on how to build and arrange the interior space of churches in order to provide a dignified setting for the Eucharist. In addition, he included advice on how to deliver effective sermons and hear confessions, two central elements to Borromeo's pastoral vision. Finally, the last third of the 708-page text was given over to the archbishop's pastoral letters, which together constitute a history of the application of Trent-inspired measures in his archdiocese. Although there were to be only five editions of the *Acta* published during the sixteenth and seventeenth centuries, the diffusion of the work was astonishing: from Milan to Mexico, Poland to Peru. Toribio de Mogrovejo (*c*.1538–1606), Archbishop of Lima, drew extensively on Borromeo's advice on outfitting churches in the legislation for the Third Council of Lima (1582–3), a body which in view of its significance for later diocesan synods in the New World has come to be known as the 'Trent of the Americas'. The following century, in his *Direcciones pastorales* (1646), Juan de Palafox y Mendoza (1600–59), Bishop of Puebla and for six months also acting Viceroy of Mexico (1642), made clear the extent of his debt to Borromeo, referring to the prelate of Milan as 'the finest example for prelates of these times'.

Borromeo was also an influential champion of sacred history, to the extent that an injunction of his Third Provincial synod (1573) laid down a charge on every bishop:

[as holder of] an office instituted at the very beginning of the history of the Church, [he] should diligently collect together the names, pastoral character and pastoral actions of his predecessors, and he should make certain that all these things are written down, arranged in order and put into a certain book so that the memory be conserved of those things which have been done or instituted by those bishops and so that they [the books] may be of perpetual use and assistance to the good governance of that Church.

Here, Borromeo was recognizing the crucial role played by such carefully archived information in the daily battle against those who sought to challenge episcopal jurisdiction. Limits to the bishop's right to appoint clergy within his diocese were undoubtedly one of the greatest obstacles to reform both before and after Trent. Guillaume Briçonnet, reforming Bishop of Meaux (1516–34), was in a stronger position than many when he could boast to possessing patronage rights to 89 out of his 209 parishes. More typical was the Bishop of Paris, who in 1533 was able to present candidates to only six parishes in his entire diocese.

Jurisdictional conflict between bishops and regular clergy, even after Trent, was so endemic as to be structural. With this in mind, the tendency in traditional accounts of the Catholic Reformation to chart its progress at least partly in terms of the successive foundation of new or reformed religious orders is somewhat misleading. This is because religious orders could, and did, stand in the way of attempts by bishops to reform their dioceses. Moreover, the prowess of Capuchins (founded in 1528), Lazarists (1625), Redemptorists (1732), and of course Jesuits as preachers and spiritual directors reduced the demand for a better-educated secular clergy. Spiritually needy or neurotic parishioners could invariably find a more professional alternative to their overworked and undertrained parish priest, or more likely, his underpaid vicar, from amongst the regular clergy.

All this said, those who travel today through Latin America—or even Asia—in search of Tridentine-Borromean influence on local Roman Catholicisms do not need to access ecclesiastical archives or even visit research libraries to find confirmation of

AFTER THE COUNCIL OF TRENT (1545–63) the emphasis on the Real Presence of Christ in the Eucharist led to the development of elaborate altar tabernacles. These two examples, one commissioned in the sixteenth century by the reforming bishop of one of the wealthiest sees in Roman Catholic Europe and the other, undated but quite possibly twentieth century, made in a rustic style for a small parish church in the Andean highlands, illustrate the enduring and truly global influence of Old World Counter-Reformation prototypes.

Top: High altar of the Church of Santiago Apostol, Corporacque, Peru, date unknown.

Bottom: Tabernacle in the presbytery *of Milan Cathedral* (detail), executed according to the design of Pellegrino Tibaldi by Giovanni Andrea Pellizzone (1581–90) at the behest of St Carlo Borromeo. The tabernacle is underneath the tempietto made by Aurelio and Ludovico Solari in 1561 and was the gift of Pope Pius IV to his nephew Borromeo.

the phenomenon. They should simply enter any Roman Catholic church and note two prominent visual details: the high altar (which is often supporting a ciborium for the display of the consecrated Eucharist) and at least one confessional, frequently lavished with colour and decoration rarely found in its Old World prototypes. Both of these elements were central to Borromeo's pastoral vision, and testify to a 'Tridentine' reality of pastoral practice, even where the Church was run by missionaries from regular orders exempt from oversight by Rome via the *Propaganda Fide*, or, as in Latin America, where many of the bishops were themselves members of religious orders rather than secular clergy.

A more accurate thermometer of the spiritual health of the 'average soul' in the century and more after Trent, however, is perhaps provided by attention to confraternities, associations of pious laity. Also sometimes called sodalities, brotherhoods, fraternities, or religious guilds, these organizations originated at the time of the urban economic expansion of the twelfth century, and were at first little more than burial clubs or mutual support associations. However, encouraged by the theology of good works, which after the Reformation became a distinguishing characteristic of Roman Catholicism, they evolved into charitable institutions frequently dedicated to particular devotions, such as the Blessed Sacrament or the Virgin Mary. Their range of good works was extensive: providing dowries for poor girls, sometimes specifically former prostitutes, to marry honestly or to enter a nunnery, supporting battered wives, caring for foundlings, giving alms to 'deserving poor' (particularly the female elderly), teaching the catechism, comforting condemned prisoners, even providing a Christian burial for suicides who drowned themselves in the river Tiber. To this day, the so-called *Sacconi rossi* hold a memorial service at the church of S. Bartolomeo on the Tiber Island in Rome on 2 November.

During the post-Reformation period, the devotional aspect of confraternity life received added impetus owing to its promotion by religious orders. The Marian sodalities championed by the Jesuits are an excellent example of the 'new style' confraternities. Founded in 1563 at the Jesuit Roman College by the Liégeois Jean Leunis, membership demanded weekly confession and at least monthly communion, as well as daily mass, weekly meetings, ascetical practices, and active charity. At first they were socially inclusive, but soon different social groups had their own confraternities. One such, the 'Congregation of Gentlemen' (*Messieurs*), was founded in 1630 in Paris by the superior of the Jesuit college, Louis de la Salle. Its model was the great congregations of Roman and Neapolitan nobles. Louis XIII's Jesuit confessor, Nicolas Caussin, summed up the thinking behind such elite associations when he wrote in *La Cour sainte* (The Holy Court, 1655): 'Do you see, O Nobles, what influence example can exercise over the hearts of men? It is up to you to create here and now a new world.'

A very different Jesuit-inspired confraternity was that dedicated to the Blessed Virgin in China (known as *Shengmu hui*), a development which illustrates well the responsiveness of this promethean form of Roman Catholic life to the varied circumstances encountered by priests and their flocks across the globe. The women gathered

IT NEEDS TO BE REMEMBERED THAT THE CONFESSIONAL, like any other piece of ecclesiastical furniture, has a history. It was introduced by St Carlo Borromeo in his archdiocese of Milan from the 1560s and appears to have been disseminated with surprising speed throughout the Roman Catholic world. It reflects the growing emphasis on privacy needed for the confessor to conduct the investigation of his penitents with unprecedented thoroughness. Such were its demands on the skills and training of priests that for much of the early modern period members of religious orders, particularly the Jesuits, were preferred over ordinary parish clergy in the role of confessor.

Top: Confessional in Sucre, Bolivia, undated but possibly twentieth century.

Bottom: Confessional in S. Fedele, Milan, carved by Giovanni, Giacomo, and Gianpaolo Taurini, 1596–1603. The scenes depicted on the six confessionals which were designed and built as an integral part of the church interior were taken from Jerónimo Nadal's *Evangelicae historiae imagines* (1593).

in Chapels of the Holy Mother (*Shengmu tang*) and there were also associated Confraternities of Angels (*Tianshen hui*) for the teaching of children. Here, the confraternity mode of organization was ideal for dispersed pockets of converts in rural areas, where priests were few and their visits infrequent. In particular, the role of *huizhang* (confraternity president) was very important for the growth of Christianity in China. It enabled a single priest, the Jesuit Francesco Brancati, to manage forty such confraternities in 1647, each with its own leader to coordinate prayers and act as intermediary with Brancati, who invited each one once or twice a year to Shanghai for confession and the Eucharist. Between 1643 and 1658, the number of confraternities in China increased from 30 to 120. Church membership meanwhile doubled, from *c.*105,000 in 1663 to *c.*200,000 in 1695. In South America, the silver-mining boom town of Potosí (Bolivia) was recorded as hosting no fewer than 112 indigenous confraternities in 14 native parishes by 1690—though the precipitous decline in the population of this Latin American Johannesburg from an early seventeenth-century peak of 160,000 to only 60,000 a century later leads one to wonder precisely how many of these organizations were still functional.

What position did female religious hold in Borromeo's pastoral vision? All too predictably, perhaps, he was determined to ensure that the Ursulines—a teaching order of young girls founded by the Brescian Angela Merici in 1535—obeyed the requirement of Trent that strict enclosure be enforced; in doing so he was merely reasserting the papal decree *Periculoso* of 1298. This runs counter to the current revisionist view which sees convents as places where women found relative autonomy and agency, rather than having to submit to the patriarchal demands of the marriage market. In Roman Catholic cities, provision of social welfare, mechanisms for the cult of remembrance, civic marital strategies, property regimes, and even Church–State relations all depended to a considerable extent upon female monasticism. Moreover, the economics of the marriage market, in which the cost of marriage dowries increased massively more than nuns' dowries, ensured that there was an explosion in the number of nuns. In Florence, for example, in 1338 the proportion of nuns to women as a whole was just 1:220; by 1515 it had increased to 1:26, and in 1552 to 1:19. By the seventeenth century, around half of Florentine patrician daughters were becoming nuns.

In this context, the careers of such extraordinary female religious as Mary Ward (1585–1645) and Marie de l'Incarnation (1599–1672) were the exceptions that proved the rule. The former was born near Ripon, North Yorkshire, and from the age of 5 was looked after mainly by female relatives and educated at home, where she learned Latin. Two of her uncles were involved in the Gunpowder Plot, and were killed while resisting arrest. Aged just 20, she left England for Saint-Omer in the Spanish Low Countries, and joined a community of Poor Clare nuns. She subsequently founded her own Poor Clare convent, specifically for English girls, before a series of visions led her to spend the rest of her life attempting to set up a female counterpart to the Society of Jesus, free to catechize and engage in missionary work outside the cloister. Her Institute of English Ladies found favour in several European cities: Liège

(1616), Cologne and Trier (1620–1), Rome (1622), Naples (1623), Perugia (1624), Munich and Vienna (1627), and Pressburg (1628). But Ward's attempt to gain papal approval failed, and ended up provoking the suppression of the Institute with the papal bull *Pastoralis Romani Pontificis* of 1631. The community in Munich survived, however, thanks to the support of the Wittelsbach dukes, and Ward herself established a branch in her native York. It was only in 2004, almost four centuries after her original petition, that John Paul II granted Jesuit constitutions to the Mary Ward sisters. For long known as the Institute of the Blessed Virgin Mary, they have now changed their name to the Congregation of Jesus.

Marie Guyart Martin was born in Tours in France, and only joined the Ursulines aged 32 as a widow with a 12-year-old son (he was old enough to be looked after by the Benedictines, whose order he subsequently joined). In 1639, she sailed to Quebec where she founded a convent and spent the remainder of her life teaching the children of local indigenous tribes. She composed a catechism in Huron, and dictionaries in both Huron and Algonquin. Her 273 surviving letters, many of them addressed to her son, who disobeyed his mother's order to destroy them, constitute an important testimony to the early years of the mission to New France and to her own indefatigable energy, though they represent less than 10 per cent of the 3,000 letters which she actually wrote. They also testify to the degree to which—far from the beady eyes of Rome—female religious were able to take personal initiative, and undertake a missionary apostolate that was in no respect inferior to that of their male counterparts.

However, closer to Rome, innovations could still take place. In 1633, the Franciscan-educated Gascon peasant Vincent de Paul (1581–1660) succeeded where even his mentor Francis de Sales failed, by founding, with the aristocratic widow Louise de Marillac (1591–1660), the Daughters of Charity. This was the first congregation of unenclosed women to be entirely devoted to the poor and the sick. Mostly drawn from peasant and artisan families, since they could better cope with the challenges of ministering to the poor and sick in their own homes, these women did not take any vows at all until 1642. Since then—and to this day—they have taken their vows on an annual basis, renewable until death.

Conclusion

This chapter has sought to present a new view of Roman Catholicism during this period, one that fully incorporates the global dimension. Rather than depicting non-European and local features of Roman Catholicism as syncretic, bastardized hybrids, we should afford equal 'authenticity' to the many, varied, local manifestations of the Church. Although Roman Catholicism might have reached the four continents, it had relatively little impact in two of them (Asia and Africa), and was creatively reinterpreted in a third (the Americas). Moreover, the fiercely defended royal monopoly over ecclesiastical appointments in the Portuguese and Spanish overseas empires—the so-called *padroado real*—meant that until well into the twentieth century the papacy was in no position to assert its jurisdiction over the missions. The realization of the vision of a truly global Roman Catholic Church, led from Rome, came in the pontificate of St Pius X (1903–14) *not* that of St Pius V (1566–72). The subsequent publication of the revised Corpus of Canon Law of 1917, not that of the canons and decrees of the Council of Trent in 1564, may thus be considered the true watershed. Nonetheless, it remains the case that the impact on European Catholicism in 1500–1700 of the missionary encounters outside Europe has been seriously underestimated. This unprecedented enterprise produced a tsunami of print, which changed how European Catholics thought about their own 'indigenous' religious practices, and the methods used in missions in Asia and the Americas influenced those used on missions in Italy and France. Moreover, Rome today relies heavily on missionaries from the 'peripheries' to minister to the faithful of western Europe. At the start of the third millenium of the Christian era, the conversion of the Old World by the New is still very much a work-in-progress.

6 Britain's Reformations

PETER MARSHALL

IN 1498, Don Pedro de Ayala, Spanish ambassador to the court of Henry VII of England, reported to Queen Isabella and King Ferdinand on the diplomatic visit he had recently made to Scotland. He began with some basic geography. 'Your Highnesses know that these kingdoms form an island. Judging by what I have read in books and seen on maps, and also by my own experience, I should think that both kingdoms are of equal extent. In the same proportion that England is longer than Scotland, Scotland is wider than England.' He went on to praise the surprising magnificence of some Scottish abbeys, and the qualities of the young king, James IV, in trying to master a people who wanted to spend all their time fighting one another. But the enduring impression was a more visceral and sensory one: 'it is impossible to describe the immense quantity of fish.' A few years later, the great European scholar Erasmus, who was unusual in having himself visited England several times, complained that 'the salt fish to which the common people are so surprisingly addicted' was one reason why the country was beset with continual pestilence—that, along with the ubiquity of marshes and brackish rivers, and the annoying inability of the English to situate a room for a through draft.

For most educated Europeans in the early sixteenth century, the British Isles were distant, little known, and unenticing places, inhabited by peoples speaking barbarous languages no one else could understand. Their claim to special and detailed treatment in a history of the Reformation is far from self-evident. None of the first Reformation movements of the sixteenth century originated in the British Isles. Neither did Britain or Ireland in this period produce any theologian of truly European stature—no Luther, Calvin, Zwingli, or even a Bullinger or Oecolampadius.

But the story of the Reformation in these islands is more than just an interesting case study in how religious change percolated to the European periphery. After Spain (decisively) and France (hesitantly and painfully) rejected the alternatives to Catholicism, England was to become the only truly front-rank power to opt for the Reformation, the pre-eminent Protestant nation of sixteenth- and seventeenth-century Europe. And the distinctive ways in which reform was planted there were to lead, through some complex patterns of growth, to the flowering of remarkably diverse forms of Protestant expression. One of these would in due course become known as Anglicanism, and, exported by missionaries and colonialists, would make a major and lasting contribution to the complexion of world Christianity.

In Europe's north-western island archipelago, the Reformation ran in parallel with a process of state-building and political convergence. The government of Wales was remodelled along English lines in 1536, and Ireland was incorporated as a kingdom into the Tudor state in 1541. In 1603 England and Scotland—old enemies—were united under a single monarchy. Yet bucking a pattern found elsewhere in western Europe, the growing consolidation of secular authority was not accompanied by any homogenization of religion. Scotland—which had already in the sixteenth century largely adopted Protestantism in defiance of a Catholic queen—showed no desire to conform itself to the styles of worship and church government practised in its larger southern neighbour. Most of the Irish proved stubbornly impervious to the attractions of Protestantism of all kinds. Significant religious minorities remained everywhere— Catholic in England, Wales, and Scotland; Protestant in Ireland. The supposed golden rule of the European Reformation—*cuius regio, eius religio* (your ruler's religion is your religion)—was thus rejected in two out of three of the 'British' kingdoms, and only patchily adopted in the third. Serious rebellions with a distinctly religious flavour took place in all three states in the sixteenth century, and were replayed as full-scale civil wars in the seventeenth. The common idea that Reformation in the British Isles was a process simply imposed from above, and largely peaceful in character, is scarcely borne out by the facts. It was at every stage contested, and paid for in tears, sweat, and blood. In the event, its very first martyrs were victims of the salt fish about which Erasmus complained. In 1528, a dozen scholars suspected of Lutheran heresy in Oxford were imprisoned in the cellar under Cardinal College where the salt fish was stored. In these unpleasant surroundings, three of them perished over the course of a sweltering summer.

Catholic Kings, Catholic People

Nowhere in Britain or Ireland was a Reformation predicted, or eagerly anticipated, at the start of the sixteenth century, even though the constituent parts of the island world differed greatly from each other in character. England was the dominant regional power. A unified kingdom for more than five centuries, it emerged from the dynastic disorders of the fifteenth-century 'Wars of the Roses' with the authority of its monarchy significantly enhanced. After his 1485 victory over the usurping Richard III at the Battle of Bosworth, Henry VII strove to keep over-mighty nobles in their place through a combination of low politics and high claims to divinely sanctioned authority. He also asserted the place of his family at the top table of European royalty. The two preceding monarchs had wed English ladies, as Henry did himself. But he arranged glittering international marriages for his own children: his daughter Margaret to James IV of Scotland, and daughter Mary to Louis XII of France. His son and heir Prince Arthur was married in 1502 to Catherine, daughter of the Spanish 'Catholic Monarchs' Isabella and Ferdinand, who, thanks to the dispatches of Ambassador de Ayala, were now rather better informed about the misty island kingdoms.

Henry VII's practical authority was heavily centred in the south-east of his kingdom, and decreased the further one moved from what was, in European terms, Britain's only real city: London. Powerful nobles like the Percy earls of Northumberland were still needed to govern the lawless borderlands of the far north, and everywhere the crown relied on the cooperation of local landowners for its authority to be recognized and enforced. There was a growing 'English' sense of nationhood, fed by still recent memories of a hundred years, and more, of war against the French. But local identities generally trumped national ones, and regional dialects were often mutually incomprehensible. Northerners travelling in the south sometimes carried special written certificates to prove they were not Scotsmen. And in 1497 the people of Cornwall rose in bloody rebellion rather than pay taxes for a Scottish war which did not seem to concern them. Long before the creation of 'Great Britain', the Tudor kingdom was a multi-ethnic one. Many of the 1497 rebels conversed in Cornish, not English, and the people of Wales also spoke their own language. Henry VII had Welsh ancestry, but Wales was a conquered land, governed in peculiar ways. A large western principality was directly subject to the English crown, but the descendants of Norman conquerors enjoyed much jurisdictional independence in a swathe of 'marcher' lordships.

Ireland both was and was not a conquered nation. Henry II launched an invasion in the twelfth century, with his claims to lordship over the island recognized by the pope. But the descendants of the Norman lords who sailed with him and stayed, such as the Fitzgerald earls of Kildare and the Butler earls of Ormond—the 'Old English'—were largely a law unto themselves. Direct control was effectively restricted to the English-speaking lowland 'Pale' of land around Dublin. Beyond this, English laws and customs meant proverbially little, especially in those large parts of the island, chiefly in the north and west, still under the sway of traditional Gaelic lordship.

The linguistic and ethnic division running through Ireland was paralleled in Scotland, divided between the feudal Scots-speaking society of the lowlands, and the ancient clan structures of the Gaelic highlands (not to mention the Old Norse culture of Orkney and Shetland, recently acquired as part of a marriage settlement from the Danish crown). The Stewart rulers were known as King of Scots, not King of Scotland—a significant distinction. More so than English kings, their authority was personal and moral rather than institutional, reflecting their position as first-among-equals in a querulous aristocratic world. James IV went further than his predecessors in imposing his authority on the barons, destroying several castles with state-of-the-art artillery pieces. But his taste for new military technology proved his undoing in 1513, when a Scots army, untrained in the use of French-style fifteen-foot pikes, was cut to pieces at Flodden by an English force equipped with old-fashioned billhooks. James, along with the flower of Scots nobility, was left dead on the field.

What united all these disparate territories was the Christian and Catholic faith of their peoples. It too displayed some profoundly indigenous characteristics—for example, in the rootedness in the landscape of localized shrines, and the worship of particular saints. Thomas Becket and (somewhat incongruously) St George were widely honoured in the south of England; St Cuthbert in the north. The Welsh

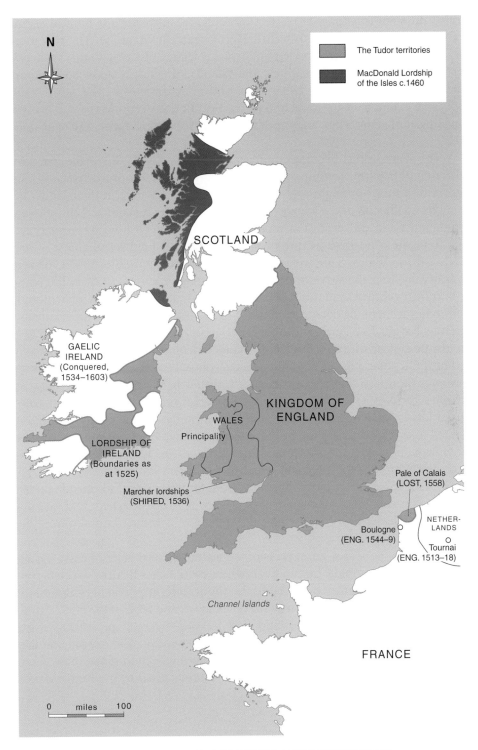

N

The Tudor territories

MacDonald Lordship
of the Isles c.1460

SCOTLAND

GAELIC
IRELAND
(Conquered,
1534–1603)

KINGDOM OF
ENGLAND

WALES
Principality

LORDSHIP OF
IRELAND
(Boundaries as
at 1525)

Marcher lordships
(SHIRED, 1536)

Pale of Calais
(LOST, 1558)

NETHER-
LANDS

Boulogne
(ENG. 1544–9)

Tournai
(ENG. 1513–18)

Channel Islands

FRANCE

0   miles   100

POLITICAL BOUNDARIES IN THE BRITISH ISLES ON THE EVE OF THE REFORMATION
Source: Patrick Collinson (ed.), *The Sixteenth Century*, Short Oxford History of the British Isles (OUP, 2002),
p. 281.

venerated the semi-legendary St Derfel; the Scots, the authentically biblical St Andrew (and Orcadians, their martyred twelfth-century earl, St Magnus). The rich monastic history of early medieval Ireland left an inspiring legacy of Celtic saints, such as Colm Cille (St Columba). But throughout the islands, the Latin mass and sacraments supplied the core of religious experience, and even the cult of the saints was to a considerable extent transnational and transcultural: the Virgin Mary was everywhere a prime object of veneration, and other saints, like John the Baptist, had near-universal appeal.

In recent years, it has become common to contrast England's orthodox devotion and thriving parish life, accompanied by generally good relations between priests and people, with a more stagnant and dissatisfied scene elsewhere in the islands. In fact, this may be an illusion of the sources: the many surviving sets of local churchwardens' accounts and episcopal visitation reports which have been used by 'revisionist' historians to create a positive picture of pre-Reformation English religion are virtually non-existent for Wales, Scotland, and Ireland. Surviving architectural evidence suggests, however, that the wave of church-building and church-repair in fifteenth- and early sixteenth-century England was paralleled in Wales and Ireland. In Scotland, too, new churches were being constructed in the early sixteenth century, especially in more prosperous burghs like Perth and Aberdeen.

An attitude of hostility to the clergy—anticlericalism—has arguably been underplayed in the scholarship on England and overplayed for elsewhere. Once thought to have been profoundly subversive of devout Catholic belief, anticlericalism may in fact have been a form of its expression, present wherever priests failed to live up to widely espoused ideals; that is, everywhere. The shortcomings of the clergy aroused disappointment and resentment, though there seems to have been a more relaxed attitude towards 'concubinage' (de facto clerical marriage) in Wales and Ireland than in England. In Scotland, the problem was not too much local clerical power but too little. The vast majority of parish incomes were 'appropriated' to outside bodies like monasteries, cathedrals, and universities, leaving impoverished and ill-educated priests to serve the livings. Meanwhile, high-born lay 'commendators' were siphoning off the income of abbeys.

Anticlericalism was also an expression of jealousies and resentments, not against but within the institutional Church. Everywhere there was a healthy satirical tradition of 'antifraternalism'—criticism of the friars, the wandering preachers and confessors who competed with the secular clergy for the respect, and fees, of the laity. An irony is that the friars—especially in Scotland and Ireland—were experiencing a marked revival of activity and fervour, in contrast to the generally more torpid and complacent monastic orders, such as the Benedictines. No fewer than ninety new communities of friars were established in Ireland in the century prior to the Reformation, and

ST JAMES'S CHURCH, LOUTH, LINCOLNSHIRE. The magnificent spire of this imposing parish church was completed in 1515, after a fifteen-year fundraising campaign by the parishioners. The usually dry churchwardens' accounts recount the festive atmosphere as the weathercock was blessed by the priests and raised into position: the bells were rung, organs played, bread and ale was given to everyone present, 'and all to the loving of God, Our Lady, and all saints'.

A PRIEST HEARING CONFESSIONS, FROM A WOODCUT OF 1503. Despite occasional tensions over fees and slack performance of duties, the parish clergy were woven deeply into the fabric of late medieval British communities, baptizing babies, presiding at weddings, anointing and taking communion to the dying, and hearing confessions as a prelude to Easter communion. One Berkshire Lollard admitted in 1491 that his neighbours often expressed incredulity at his violently anticlerical views, asking, 'what were a man at his first beginning and his later ending without the help of a priest?'.

two-thirds of the Franciscan friaries there transferred their allegiance to the stricter 'Observant' branch of the order.

There were fewer Observant Franciscan houses in England (six) and Scotland (nine), but most were royal foundations. The priory at Greenwich lay cheek by jowl with Henry VII's palace there. 'Religion' and 'politics' are modern abstractions, scarcely separable from each other in the late medieval world. Kingship was sacral, part of the divinely ordained fabric of the universe; kings were anointed with oil at their coronation, like priests at an ordination. There were benefits in posing as a loyal son of the Church: Henry VII was careful to secure papal blessing for his usurpation in 1485, and for the marriage of his son Henry to his other son Arthur's widow in 1502.

James IV acquired diplomatic leverage by ostentatiously throwing himself behind the outdated papal aspiration for a crusade against the Turks, while Henry VIII received the kudos of a papally awarded title—Defender of the Faith—for his literary efforts against Martin Luther in 1521. Calculation of advantage was quite compatible with genuine piety. In 1507 James IV went on pilgrimage to the tomb of St Ninian at Whithorn in Galloway to give thanks for the birth of a son; in 1511 Henry VIII did likewise at the shrine of Our Lady of Walsingham. But in a world of terrifying infant mortality, God did not play favourites: both babies died within a few months of birth.

Pious kings sought rather than shirked control over the Church in their lands. In particular, it was vital to ensure that bishops—major landowners, as well as wielders of moral and spiritual authority—were in tune with royal priorities. The relative political weakness of the Renaissance papacy, locked in the cockpit of Italian politics, meant popes were willing to make concessions in return for political support, allowing rulers influence over church appointments, and the opportunity to tax the clergy in their lands. English kings acquired the de facto right to nominate bishops to all English dioceses, and to bishoprics in at least the English-speaking parts of Ireland; by the end of the fifteenth century, the kings of Scots had caught up. The income from bishoprics was a useful way of getting Church rather than State to pay the salary of royal administrators: the career of Thomas Wolsey, successively Bishop of Lincoln, Durham, and Winchester, and (simultaneously) Archbishop of York, is a case in point. Scotland followed a common European habit in giving plum bishoprics to younger sons of the aristocracy, a pattern much less common in England. But in neither kingdom did royal influence produce a spiritually inert cohort of episcopal politicians. Many were imbued with the spirit of Renaissance humanism, and proved notable patrons of education. These included John Fisher of Rochester (and indeed, Wolsey) in England, as well as William Elphinstone of Aberdeen, who in 1495 founded a brand new university in his cathedral city.

Nor did loyalty to their king make bishops craven when it came to the perceived rights of the Church. The pre-Reformation English bishops were robust in defence of the jurisdiction of ecclesiastical courts against the encroachment of secular common law courts, and in upholding the freedom of churchmen from judgement in lay tribunals—this was known as 'benefit of clergy', the principle for which Thomas Becket had been martyred. Henry VII and Henry VIII were periodically willing to slap the bishops down over this, encouraging subjects to appeal to the law of *praemunire*, a loosely formulated fourteenth-century statute designed to prevent undue papal interference with the exercise of royal administration and justice. But there was no endemic 'Church–State conflict' in any part of the British Isles. Medieval society was a mishmash of overlapping 'corporations', all with claims to rights, privileges, jurisdictions, and exemptions. This produced ever-present potential for conflict, but also practical and well-rehearsed mechanisms for conflict resolution. Disputes—whether between an abbey and local townspeople over fishing rights, or between king and pope over foreign policy—came and usually went again.

The Rejection of Rome

Disagreements involving the Church invariably rose in temperature whenever allegations of heresy were thrown into the mix. There was a furore in London over the death in episcopal custody in 1514 of the merchant Richard Hunne, partly because of a suspicion that his arrest for heresy was really due to his refusal to pay a priest's fee. Hunne was accused of being a Lollard, one of the amorphous set of religious dissidents who rejected orthodox teaching on the presence of Christ in the mass, and the legitimacy of venerating saints, and whose origins lay in the teachings of the fourteenth-century heterodox theologian John Wyclif. Much modern scholarship—in reaction against an old tradition of Protestant triumphalism—has minimized to virtual insignificance the part played by Lollardy in the story of the English Reformation. The pendulum here may have swung too far—Lollardy's persistence, in spite of periodically serious episcopal attempts to eradicate it, points to a stubborn substratum of popular scepticism and religious individualism in some southern and Midland counties, and in a few towns like Coventry and Bristol. It is tempting to draw inferences from the apparent absence of popular heresy anywhere in later medieval Ireland. But even within Britain, let alone Europe as a whole, a tradition of medieval heresy was no necessary precondition for a popular Reformation movement. Scotland—with the exception of a small cluster of alleged Lollards in Ayrshire—also seems to have been a heresy-free zone, as indeed was much of England and virtually all of Wales.

In fact, most of the people expressing interest in Luther's ideas in the early 1520s came not from the heretical and anticlerical fringes of society but from the heart of orthodox religion. It was the pious, not the impious, who were most interested in hearing what this radical German friar had to say about holiness and salvation. His insistent focus on the person of Christ resonated with much that was precious and familiar in late medieval religious culture. The first English 'evangelicals' tended to be Oxford and Cambridge students, and preaching clergy, especially friars. The apparent imperviousness of the Irish friars to Luther's ideas is somewhat mysterious, though the lack of a university in Ireland may explain the limited traction of his ideas there.

There was perhaps an indirect connection with Lollardy. Wyclif had taught that scripture alone—not scripture mediated through the traditions and interpretations of the Church—was the source of religious authority, and at the end of the fourteenth century his disciples translated the Latin Vulgate Bible into English. The authorities took fright, and banned all translations of the Bible into the vernacular without episcopal permission—permission which was never subsequently forthcoming. Ironically, most 'Wycliffite' Bible texts seem to have been in the hands not of Lollards but of perfectly respectable layfolk and devout clergy (including the super-orthodox Carthusian monks of the London Charterhouse). But this in itself suggests there was a demand for vernacular scripture which could not be satisfied through official channels. The patron saint of the English Reformation Bible, however, was not Wyclif, but Erasmus. The Dutch humanist's vision of ordinary working folk singing the words of scripture at the plough or the loom inspired a young English priest, William Tyndale, to produce a fresh translation of the

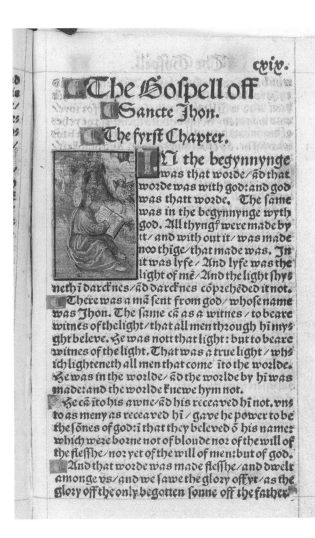

WILLIAM TYNDALE'S NEW TESTAMENT (1526): the opening of St John's Gospel. Tyndale's English translation of the core texts of Christianity fed a demand among pious and literate Catholics, but was at the same time an explosive and revolutionary document. In the opening words of St John's Gospel—'in the beginning was that Word'—Tyndale saw a confirmation of his belief that the authority of scripture was logically and chronologically prior to that of the institutional Church.

New Testament into English from the original Greek text, of which Erasmus in 1516 had supplied a widely available printed text. Tyndale initially sought the patronage and permission of Erasmus' friend, the humanist Bishop of London, Cuthbert Tunstall. But after being rebuffed, Tyndale became increasingly radicalized and fled into exile. He issued his New Testament from presses in Cologne and Worms in 1525–6, with explicitly Lutheran commentary, and some translation choices that had philological merit, but also a clearly subversive intent. These included 'repent', rather than 'do penance', for the Greek *metanoeite*—a notice of redundancy for the priestly sacrament of confession.

Prior to 1526, Lutheranism seemed a distant danger to the Catholic establishment. Continental heretical books were burned and banned—in England from 1521 and in Scotland from 1525—and a few wayward scholars were made to do public penance for what seemed to many of the bishops little more than youthful indiscretion. But the influx of printed New Testaments, into both England and anglophone Scotland, and the formation of organized cells to facilitate the smuggling, changed the nature of the response. The first burning of a new evangelical (as opposed to old Lollard) took place in St Andrews in 1528, when a young scholar, and returned exile, Patrick Hamilton, refused the recantation Archbishop James Beaton fully expected him to make. A clutch of English heretics were burned in 1530–2 as the result of a concerted campaign of repression led by Chancellor Thomas More and Tunstall's replacement as Bishop of London—another humanist—John Stokesley. Erasmus may or may not have laid the egg which Luther hatched, but some of his closest friends and supporters in England wanted to club the fledgling to death before it could fly the nest.

Whether they could have succeeded is probably an unanswerable question. Luther's seductive theology of justification by faith was garnering converts among clergy, artisans, merchants, and lower gentry in both Scotland and England, bolstered by a raft of arguments—many of them diverging from Luther's own views—against pilgrimage, Purgatory, saints, and the Real Presence in the mass. But the movement's activities were severely constrained by police action, and, crucially, it had not yet managed to capture the support of any powerful nobles, the people who alone could give it meaningful military and political protection.

What changed all this was the stricken conscience of Henry VIII. Popular understanding of this familiar story is not entirely wrong. It is true that Henry's failure to conceive a son by Catherine of Aragon, and his falling hopelessly in love in 1525–6 with her lady-in-waiting, Anne Boleyn, led him to question whether his marriage to Catherine—his brother Arthur's widow—was valid in the eyes of God. It is also true that the refusal of the current pope, Clement VII, to grant Henry a 'divorce' (actually an annulment) led ultimately to Henry throwing off the authority of the pope and declaring himself Supreme Head of the Church in England. And it is true that Clement's non-cooperation was largely contingent and political—Catherine was the aunt of the Emperor Charles V, and Charles had his foot firmly on the pope's neck in Italy.

But it is not true that none of this had anything to do with the larger questions of faith and authority convulsing Europe at this time; that Henry's divorce was a purely 'jurisdictional' matter, designed to leave in place a neatly amputated 'Catholicism without the pope'; or that in the space of only a few years an almost pathetically loyal son of the papacy was turned into one of its fiercest critics. Henry had in fact for many years been interested in the 'imperial' character of his kingship, and at the time of the Hunne case in 1515 he was moved to declare 'that kings of England in time past have never had any superior but God alone'. A posse of intellectuals, including Thomas Cranmer, were set the task of combing scripture, chronicles, and the writings of the early church fathers to find arguments in favour of the divorce. These men were pushing at an open door when they reported back in 1530 that English kings had historically exercised complete authority over the clergy in their lands, and that the Catholic Church was really a kind of federation, one in which all important disputes should be decided at the national level. There were various legal loopholes and technicalities through which, conceivably, the divorce might have been 'fixed'. But from the outset Henry never wavered from staking his case on the moral high ground: a passage in the book of Leviticus allegedly taught that marriage to a brother's wife was wrong in all circumstances. The authority of 'the Word of God' was thus foundational for the political revolution that decoupled Canterbury from Rome.

It is also significant that sympathizers with evangelical reform were from the start among the strongest advocates of the divorce, and instrumental in bringing it to fruition. Henry's annulment was finally declared in 1533 by Thomas Cranmer, the surprise choice (for those who didn't know he was a protégé of the Boleyns) to replace the aged William Warham as Archbishop of Canterbury. Cranmer was a slow but steady convert to evangelical ideas, who in the summer of 1532 had taken the radical step for an English Catholic priest of secretly acquiring a wife. The architect of religious revolution in parliament was another evangelical supporter, the lawyer Thomas Cromwell, who oversaw the severing of ties with Rome through a series of statutes which culminated in the unambiguous declaration of the 1533 Act of Appeals that 'this realm of England is an Empire'—a fully independent and self-contained sovereign state. But more important, at first, than either of these men was a powerful patroness of reform, the new queen, Anne Boleyn. She introduced Henry to the writings of William Tyndale. Henry had no time for Tyndale's heretic opinions on sacraments or salvation, but he warmly endorsed his view of the unquestioning obedience due to kings, as well as his radical reinterpretation of English history. This was a story in which a corrupt and power-crazy papacy had schemed and plotted to control the kingdom, and to bring down those—like good King John—who stood in their way. It was also through Anne's influence that a clutch of zealous reformers, such as the preacher Hugh Latimer, were elevated to the ranks of a hitherto solidly orthodox episcopate.

Henry's Reformation began with a declaration (in the 1534 Dispensations Act) that there was no intention 'to decline or vary from the congregation of Christ's Church in any things concerning the very articles of the Catholic faith of Christendom'. He retained the Latin mass, and all the domestic institutional structures of the medieval Church. But in many ways 'Henricianism' was more like Lutheranism without justification by faith than it was like Catholicism without the pope. Official formularies cast doubt on the existence of Purgatory, severely attacked 'abuses' in the cult of the saints, and cut the number of holy days. Most dramatically, the entire edifice of medieval monasticism, and a world of associated shrines and pilgrimage sites, was swept away between 1536 and 1540. This was a demonstration of royal power that had as much to do with Henry's anxieties about the loyalties of the religious orders (and the evangelical prejudices of his advisers) as it did with a desire for monastic estates. In 1538, Henry ordered the placing in all parish churches of an officially sanctioned translation of the Bible (largely—unacknowledged—the work of Tyndale). But in 1543, alarmed by the social consequences of unfettered Bible-reading, he placed tight restrictions on who might have access to it. Such coherence as there was in any of this was supplied by Henry's unshakeable conviction that his own

position as Supreme Head, under Christ, of the Church of England was God-given and non-negotiable.

The question is often posed of why opposition to Henry's Reformation was so patchy and ineffective. The answers generally stress deep popular loyalty to the crown, or limited emotional attachment to the papacy and aspects of traditional religious practice. But some underlying assumptions here are questionable. Opposition—broadly defined—was in fact remarkably widespread, and was contained only through a combination of coercion and relentless propaganda from press and pulpit. A few dozen conscientious objectors, including the Bishop of Rochester, John Fisher, the former Chancellor, Thomas More, and the priors of several Carthusian monasteries, were put to death. A few hundred more fled to the safety of papally loyal territories, including, at this stage, Scotland. Most dangerous of these was the king's cousin Reginald Pole, whom the pope created a cardinal, with a commission to galvanize European support for a 'crusade' against schismatic England. But at home, and from across the country, reports continued to accumulate of priests and laypeople discontented with the direction of policy and hoping for its reversal. Some urged patience and caution. One priest in Kent used the opportunity of confession to advise parishioners, 'suffer awhile and ye shall see the pope in as great authority as ever he was'. But in the north of England discontent erupted in the autumn of 1536 into a massive popular revolt against the Dissolution and other changes, christened by its leaders a 'Pilgrimage of Grace for the Commonweal'. Only good fortune, and some wise counsel from his level-headed commander on the ground, the Duke of Norfolk, enabled Henry to surmount the crisis with his authority intact.

The Pilgrims obeyed the rules of late medieval protest by insisting on their basic loyalty to the king, focusing their anger on 'wicked counsellors' such as Cromwell. It was a different story in Ireland in the summer of 1534, when rebellion was raised by 'Silken Thomas' Fitzgerald, son of the Earl of Kildare, and Henry's own vice-deputy. Fitzgerald's motives were mixed, but he denounced Henry as a heretic, and required his followers to take an oath of allegiance to the pope and the emperor. In a pattern that was many times to repeat itself, the traditional unruliness of Ireland was acquiring an explicitly ideological edge.

The oath was a back-handed tribute to Henry's own policy. Earlier that year he had ordered all male subjects to swear to recognize the Boleyn succession and repudiate any 'foreign authority or potentate'. On one level, the policy was a master-stroke, securing the public consent of the nation to the king's actions—only a handful of clergy and a single layman (Thomas More) refused to swear. But it is clear that many who assented did so with agonies of remorse: 'O that I had holden with my brother, Fisher, and not left him, when time was,' Bishop Stokesley is reported to have lamented on his deathbed in 1539. Or they swore casuistically, with mental reservations and insertions. From the outset, the official Reformation was creating spaces for the very thing it wanted to obliterate: the exercise of private conscience in matters of religion. Henry, who throughout his reign continued sporadically to execute both evangelical 'heretics' and papist 'traitors', was never quite sure whom he could trust. Even the most assertively loyal servants, like Cranmer's great rival, the mercurial Bishop of Winchester, Stephen Gardiner, might be suspected of secret hankerings to return the nation to Rome. Henry's own religious philosophy—an idiosyncratic blend of good-works Catholicism, aggressive anticlericalism, and messianic royalism—was unlikely ever to create convinced believers as opposed to dutiful subscribers. Increasingly, English people made their own religious choices. In a speech to parliament in 1545, Henry bemoaned the lack of unity and charity evident among his subjects: 'the one calleth the other heretic and anabaptist, and he calleth him again, papist, hypocrite and pharisee.' He did not ask himself who was principally to blame for this lamentable state of affairs.

North of the border, Henry's nephew James V posed as defender of the faith the English had seemingly abandoned. A crackdown on heresy, relaxed in England after 1532, continued in Scotland through the 1530s, with nine dissidents burned in 1538–9. James wore his orthodoxy on his sleeve, to coax financial and jurisdictional concessions from the papacy, and to re-forge the old alliance with France. This was symbolized in his 1538 marriage to Mary of Lorraine, a daughter of the powerful noble house of Guise. But at the same time he played a subtle and risky hand, seeking to intimidate bishops by dropping hints that he might emulate the reforms of his 'uncle of England', and by sponsoring anticlerical authors such as Sir David Lindsay, and Protestant sympathizers like George Buchanan, who was made tutor to one of James's (many) illegitimate sons. James's slipperiness finally got the better of him when in 1541 he failed to turn up for a planned summit with Henry VIII at York. His exasperated uncle responded by preparing for war. A counterattacking Scots army was ignominiously defeated at Solway Moss in Cumbria in November 1542. Whether or not James greeted the news, as romantic legend maintains, by dying of a broken heart, he was dead within a month—another of those dynastic mishaps that so often determined the pattern of Reformation in the British Isles.

For Ireland, following the crushing of Kildare's rebellion, the 1540s were a period of relative stability. In 1541, the island was reconstituted as a kingdom in its own right, partly because of anxieties that English 'lordship' depended historically on papal grant. The Gaelic chieftains were to some extent brought into the fold through an imaginative policy of 'surrender and regrant': in return for recognizing Henry's authority they were confirmed in their lordships and flattered with English-sounding noble titles. A reformation, of sorts, proceeded fitfully. A reforming archbishop, George Browne, was appointed to Dublin, and, in the Pale at least, monasteries and shrines were dissolved. But the English Lord Deputies, Lord Grey and then Anthony St Leger, were more interested in political acquiescence than in doctrinal reform: Grey thought Browne 'a poll-shorn knave friar'. It was in fact in Ireland that Catholicism without the pope probably came closest to being a reality. Traditional ways were little disturbed, but most secular and ecclesiastical leaders seemed content to accept Royal Supremacy. Two Jesuits were dispatched to Ireland in February 1542, but concluded that prospects for a restoration of the Catholic Church were gloomy, and soon withdrew.

Minorities

By the end of the 1540s, the future of the Reformation in all parts of the British Isles was in the care of minorities, in various senses of the term. James V's death in 1542 had left the crown in the tiny hands of an infant daughter, Mary. The governorship belonged to James Hamilton, Earl of Arran, who as a grand-nephew of James III was heir presumptive to the throne. Arran sought peace and stability through the prospect of a marriage between Mary, Queen of Scots and the English heir, Edward, progeny of Henry VIII's (third) marriage to Jane Seymour. Within Scotland, the plan had considerable support, but was strongly opposed by pro-French elements, including the powerful Cardinal Archbishop of St Andrews, David Beaton, and Matthew Stewart, Earl of Lennox. Arran was forced to reverse his policy and renege on the 1543 Treaty of Greenwich. A furious Henry was soon encouraging destructive cross-border incursions to compel a further reversal, a policy which became known, with bitter irony, as the 'rough wooing'.

In furtherance of his pro-English agenda, Arran—a thorough *politique* in religious matters—had allowed vernacular Bible reading and encouraged anti-papal preaching. But evangelical fervour was not a tap the government could turn on and off at its pleasure. Heresy was soon spreading in Scotland at an alarming rate, winning converts both in towns like Dundee (where both friaries were destroyed by rioters in September 1543) and in the countryside, where increasing numbers of lairds were lending social and political weight to the movement. In the teaching of charismatic preachers like George Wishart, Scots Protestantism exhibited a distinctly Zwinglian rather than Lutheran tendency, energized by its hatred of the 'idolatry' of the mass and image-veneration. It was capable of violent political action. When Wishart was arrested and burned on Beaton's orders in 1546, a group of lairds retaliated by murdering the cardinal in his castle at St Andrews, and holding it for several months until a French fleet forced the rebels to surrender.

These were pivotal times for the Reformation across Europe. Luther died in February 1546, a few months after a general council had belatedly convened at Trent to orchestrate a coordinated Catholic response to the challenge he had issued almost thirty years earlier. In England, another colossus was removed from the scene in January 1547, when spirit departed from the bloated body of Henry VIII, leaving regality and supremacy to the 9-year-old Edward VI. A minority dominated the Minority. Political manoeuvring in the final months of Henry's reign had marginalized the conservative councillors Norfolk and Gardiner, and in consequence the regency council was dominated by a clique of evangelical supporters, headed by the young king's uncle Edward Seymour, who adopted the title of Lord Protector and rewarded himself with the dukedom of Somerset.

What followed was a religious revolution. It was driven partly by the zealous conviction of evangelicals like Archbishop Cranmer—a survivor (unlike Thomas Cromwell) of the deadly factional politics of the late Henrician court, and now freed from the restraining hand of his late royal master—and partly by the cynical desire of politicians to extort still more revenue from the Church under the guise of its godly Reformation. These councillors understood the importance of retaining the favour of an increasingly assertive boy-king, himself an ardent adherent of 'the gospel'. Against widespread expectations, there was an intensification rather than reversal of Protestant reform when Somerset was overthrown in October 1549 in a coup orchestrated by his rival John Dudley, Duke of Northumberland. The sequence of reforms was rapid, and for countless lay people and clergy in English and Welsh parishes, disorienting and upsetting. A royal visitation in 1547 renewed the attack on 'abused' images, and resultant confusion about what was permissible was soon

ST ANDREW'S CASTLE, FIFE. Protestant zealots seized the castle in May 1546, murdering its principal resident, Cardinal David Beaton. The cardinal's naked body was hung from the castle walls, and a sympathizer with the plotters urinated into his open mouth. Henry VIII, whose ambassador was involved in planning the assassination, was delighted. But the English were not able to offer effective help to the garrison, which was overwhelmed by a French bombardment in July 1547. One of the chaplains to the 'Castilians' was the fiery preacher John Knox, who spent the next eighteen months as a French galley-slave before England's Protector Somerset negotiated his release.

resolved in an order for all religious imagery to be removed from churches. Purgatory was declared a delusion, and over the course of 1548 the endowments of chantries were seized and religious guilds wound up. Priests were allowed to marry, and lay people were no longer required to confess their sins to them. Traditional ceremonies of numerous kinds were simplified, or abrogated. Most significantly of all, the mass was abolished and replaced by a vernacular communion service, the liturgical centrepiece of Thomas Cranmer's Book of Common Prayer. This happened in two stages: a new liturgy in 1549 retained points of connection with the mass and seemed to permit some form of belief in the Real Presence, but a revision in 1552 unambiguously asserted the purely memorial character of 'the Lord's Supper'. To the churchwardens keeping the accounts of Stanford in the Vale, Berkshire, all this, and not the self-exaltation of Henry VIII in the 1530s, represented 'the time of schism when this realm was divided from the Catholic Church'.

For a short time, England was both the laboratory and the engine room of the wider Protestant movement. Its political and military weight was far greater than that of any of the German Lutheran principalities, or of the Scandinavian kingdoms which had either declared for the Reformation (Denmark) or were cautiously edging towards it (Sweden). Charles V's victories over the Lutheran Schmalkaldic League in Germany, and his severe crackdown on heresy in his Netherlandish territories, led to a wave of exiles washing up in London and other coastal cities. The emigrants included such leading Protestant theologians as Martin Bucer and Peter Martyr Vermigli, who received regius chairs of divinity at Cambridge and Oxford, respectively. They

PORTRAIT OF EDWARD VI BY AN UNKNOWN ENG-LISH ARTIST, *c.*1547. Reformers identified the young Edward VI with Josiah, the godly boy-king of Israel in the Old Testament. He did not live to exercise real authority on his own account, but had he done so reform might have taken a still more fervent and ideological turn. Edward, educated by Protestant tutors, loathed 'idolatry' and wanted to prevent his sister Mary, even privately, from hearing mass.

urged Archbishop Cranmer towards further Reformation, while he dreamed of a Protestant international council in England to confute the papal assembly at Trent. From Geneva, Calvin sent letters full of solidarity and exhortation, as did Zwingli's successor at Zurich, Heinrich Bullinger.

These were whirlwind years of change. But what was retained was ultimately as important as what was rejected. Almost everywhere the Reformation took hold in Europe, the parish structure remained in place. But Edward's Church—mindful of the needs of monarchical control—also kept the entire institutional apparatus of episcopal and diocesan government, along with the cathedrals and their large bodies of clergy, originally designed to maintain an elaborate round of Catholic services, but of uncertain use or ornament in a Reformed Church. One continuity was accidental and regretted. Cranmer, encouraged by Bucer, planned a complete over-haul of English canon law, and the setting forth of that distinctive pattern of right 'discipline' which many Protestant reformers believed to be a mark of the true Church. But the scheme was vetoed by Northumberland, who feared it would put too much power in the hands of clerics, and it was never successfully revived. One result was that the Church of England—uniquely among Protestant churches—had no provision for divorce, something which, until the nineteenth century, required a private Act of parliament.

The Edwardian Reformation was unfinished, a work-in-progress at the moment the premature death of its teenaged royal patron brought it to an end in the summer of 1553. What was achieved had the support of a vocal and growing minority, concentrated in London and the south-east, but represented in most parts of the country and all the major urban centres. It is safe to say that the greater part of the population disliked what was taking place, sometimes to the extent of armed rebellion against it. A protest against the new liturgy breaking out in Devon and Cornwall in 1549 was bloodily suppressed, as was a parallel rising in Oxfordshire and Buckinghamshire. Twenty-three rebels were executed in the wake of a little-studied revolt against the dissolution of chantries in East Yorkshire. The widespread agrarian protest of that summer had in some places a popular Protestant character, but even Ket's Rebellion in Norfolk, which appropriated the socio-religious rhetoric of the 1525 German peasant rebels, drew on a religiously mixed base of support, with some rebels marching to the camps behind their (prohibited) parish saints' banners.

The Catholic majority was bruised and battered in Edward's reign, and suffered from a lack of articulate leadership. The south-western rebels recognized this in demanding the recall from exile of Cardinal Pole to be 'first or second of the king's counsel'. Deprived of their bishoprics, the old conservative leaders like Gardiner and Tunstall could do little more than weakly protest that there should be no substantial changes till the king came of age. But in the meantime an awareness of the religious disunity of which Henry VIII had complained was reaching all levels of society, and all parts of the realm. At Bodmin in Edwardian Cornwall, the boys at the free school formed two playground gangs, 'the one whereof they called the old religion, the other the new'. This little episode (which came to the authorities' attention after it led to the accidental death of a cow) points to significant changes taking place in society: not a normalizing of division, and still less a growing attitude of toleration, but a situation in which religious dissidents were no longer a tiny minority to be eradicated or simply ignored. Twenty years earlier, Thomas More had described a nightmare vision of the future:

I pray God, that some of us, as high as we seem to sit upon the mountains, treading heretics under our feet like ants, live not in the day, that we gladly would wish to be at league and composition with them, to let them have their churches quietly to themselves; so that they would be content to let us have ours quietly to ourselves.

It was a nightmare because nearly all thinking people believed, like More, that there could only be one truth, one form of worship acceptable to God. Yet the seeds of this once barely imaginable scenario were starting to germinate in the troubled mid-Tudor years.

And even, perhaps, in Ireland. The English reformer John Bale's autobiographical account of his brief tenure (1552–3) of the bishopric of Ossory in the south-east of the country is a rueful catalogue of insults and indignities heaped upon the hapless bishop by vindictive conservative opponents. But at the same time it makes clear that Bale had built up a significant support base in the town of Kilkenny, where 'people in great number' came out to greet him after an unsuccessful attempt on his life, 'the young men singing psalms and other godly songs'. Had there been more preachers like him on the ground, then a substantial Protestant movement might have developed, at least in anglophone areas. The failure of the Reformation in Ireland was not a foregone conclusion. But preachers were pitifully few, and the English Prayer Book and Bible were literally incomprehensible to the great majority of clergy and lay people. In all parts of the British Isles, Protestant minorities were critical of the mass, but they needed to achieve their own critical mass, if they were to stand any chance of achieving their goals.

The Monstrous Regiment of Women

For much of the 1550s God seemed to have turned his face against the cause of the gospel in Britain. Somerset had continued Henry VIII's rough wooing: he won the only major battle, a slaughter of Scots greater even than Flodden at Pinkie near Musselburgh in September 1547, but he lost the war. Scotland was driven firmly into the French camp, and in 1548 the young Queen of Scots was sent to France to be betrothed to the dauphin, Francis. Northumberland recognized a lost and hideously expensive cause and made peace in 1550. The following year, French ascendancy was symbolized by the return to Scotland of James V's widow, Mary of Guise, a formidable politician in her own right. Mary proceeded to wrest power from Governor Arran, and when the absentee queen's minority formally ended in 1554, her mother was installed as regent and, in effect, French governor of Scotland.

In the meantime, Scottish Catholicism had begun to recover its nerve and its sense of purpose. In 1549, inspired by the first sessions of Trent, Archbishop Hamilton of St Andrews (a half-brother of the Earl of Arran) began a series of reforming provincial councils, which made provisions for preaching and clerical education, and issued a detailed vernacular catechism for the edification of the laity. The council of 1552 declared that the 'frightful heresies' which had lately run riot in the kingdom were now 'almost extinguished'. That was premature and optimistic. Mary of Guise was more interested in political consensus-building than in doctrinal purity, and there was no serious effort to crack open the network of Protestant 'privy kirks' which had established themselves across much of the country. Even the firebrand John Knox was able to return from Geneva for a year in 1555–6, and minister in relative safety.

Reform without coercion was not the strategy adopted by the leaders of English Catholicism. Here too female rule established itself in 1553, in the person of Mary I, daughter of Catherine of Aragon, and elder half-sister of the boy-king Edward VI. In an indication of how the new confessional certainties were asserting themselves in the generation following Henrician ambiguities, Edward had been desperate to prevent Mary's accession. On his instructions, Northumberland sought to place on the throne Lady Jane Grey, a great-granddaughter of Henry VII and a convinced Protestant. The scheme's rapid collapse in the face of a wave of popular support for Mary is usually portrayed as a triumph of dynastic legitimism over sectarian loyalties. But Mary's core supporters were convinced (Roman) Catholics, and no one should have been in any doubt as to what her accession portended. Mary had resisted intense pressure to give up hearing mass in her brother's reign, and in May 1551 she had ridden defiantly into London with 130 attendants. Each ostentatiously wore a set of rosary beads at his or her belt, thus transforming a private devotional object into a militant symbol of confessional identity.

The idea that Mary's reign was somehow a bizarre aberration (reflected in the curious historical habit of referring to her as 'Mary Tudor', rather than Mary I), or that the progress of Protestant Reformation in England by 1553 was effectively unstoppable, is an inherited myth, slow in the dying. Across much of central and eastern Europe, Catholic (Counter-)Reformation would later succeed in halting, and permanently reversing, the advances of Protestantism. And Mary's religious policy *was* a Catholic Reformation, not a dewy-eyed attempt to wish back into existence a vanished medieval past. Cardinal Pole returned from exile in 1554 to replace Cranmer as Archbishop of Canterbury. Pole had played a pivotal role in the early sessions of the Council of Trent, and the synod he convened at Westminster in 1555 anticipated reforms that Trent would later make normative for the wider Catholic world: an official catechism, insistence on episcopal residence, provision for seminaries to train parish clergy. Mary's reign proved too short for all these measures (including a belated decision to produce a Catholic translation of the Bible) to be implemented, but there was real progress at the parish level. Across the country, altars and images were restored, with apparently impressive degrees of popular support. 'All her loving subjects was very well contended with her godly proceedings,' claimed the Yorkshire priest and chronicler Robert Parkyn, though he admitted that 'such as was of heretical opinions spoke evil thereof'.

What most people were thinking is of course impossible to say. Under Mary, as under Henry and Edward, obedience to the dictates of authority—conformity—was the most common outward response. But that people were totally confused by the shifts and reversals of official policy is perhaps less likely than that they were educated by them, and encouraged to think about the meanings and importance of rites and objects which were alternately removed and restored, to an accompaniment of explanatory preaching. For English Protestants, Mary's reign was traumatic but deeply formative. The burning for heresy of almost 300 Protestants, including Cranmer and four other bishops, between 1555 and 1558 was an unprecedented episode in England, and a ferocious religious repression by any contemporary European standards. Whether—had it been allowed to continue—it might have succeeded in irreparably destroying the Protestant movement is much debated, though there is no real reason to think it could not have done. Persecution is not always counter-productive.

What is not in doubt is that it served to widen and deepen the religious divide. Dying—and killing—for principles of faith is a powerful bond of ideological commitment, even for faint-hearts and temporizers among the onlookers. There were of course those (more than the later Protestant propaganda of John Foxe's *Book of*

PORTRAIT OF CARDINAL REGINALD POLE, *c*.1550, anonymous, after Sebastiano del Piombo. The last Roman Catholic Archbishop of Canterbury was a brilliant, if complex, scholar and churchman. Formed in the humanist world of Thomas More and Erasmus, he was driven by a forward-looking vision of Catholic reform. While wholeheartedly committed to church unity and hierarchical authority, his understanding of justification resembled Luther's, and some in Rome—including the irascible Pope Paul IV—considered him a heretic.

Martyrs would admit) who broke under the pressure or threat of persecution. But the accused in Marian heresy trials were considerably less likely than early Lollards or Henrician evangelicals to dissemble their true opinions and recant their beliefs. This was part of a wider European reaction against 'Nicodemism', the habit of seeking safety in outward compliance (named for the Pharisee Nicodemus, who visited Jesus secretly at night). English clergy among the roughly 1,000 Protestants who fled to continental exile after 1553 echoed Calvin's anti-Nicodemite arguments, particularly regarding attendance at the 'idolatrous' mass. Knox delivered the same message to his Scottish co-religionists. In places like Geneva, English exiles mixed with Scots and others to discover themselves part of a godly Protestant fellowship that transcended national allegiances. For some at least, it also transcended the demands of political obedience. John Ponet, the deposed Bishop of Winchester, and Christopher Goodman, former Lady Margaret Professor of Divinity in Cambridge, argued in print that rulers who enforced idolatry could be actively opposed, or even overthrown and killed.

THE BURNING OF THOMAS CRANMER, from John Foxe's *Acts and Monuments*. The stirring accounts—and even more, the action-filled woodcuts—of Foxe's Elizabethan *Book of Martyrs* fixed the image of Mary's reign as a time of bloody persecution. Not all burnings were likely as detested as Foxe claimed, but Cranmer's execution in 1556 was a notable 'own-goal' for the regime. His admission of error in prison was a potential propaganda disaster for the reformers, but he recanted his recantation and died bravely when it became clear there was to be no reprieve.

The rulers in question—Mary I, Mary Queen of Scots, Mary of Guise—were a suspiciously female trio, and the sinful unnaturalness of feminine lordship was the predominant theme of a third British resistance theorist. John Knox's *First Blast of the Trumpet Against the Monstrous Regiment* [i.e. Rule] *of Women* was published in Geneva in 1558. It was an unintended masterpiece of tactlessness and political bad-timing. For in November of that year, the death of Mary I, childless and unmourned by her absent royal husband, Philip of Spain, opened the path to the throne for yet another woman: Anne Boleyn's daughter Elizabeth.

Settlement and Revolution

Elizabeth had survived the reign of Mary by doing the opposite of what the clerical moralists advised: she kept her head down, attended mass, and ensured her contact with Protestant opposition was so discreet that accusations of disloyalty could not be made to stick. In this, she was temperamentally more in tune with the mass of her subjects than with the Protestant exiles retuning from Zurich and Geneva. The former exiles' black-and-white view of the world was one Elizabeth never found appealing. In particular, it was made clear to Knox there would be no welcome for him in England. Elizabeth's first Archbishop of Canterbury, Matthew Parker (Pole had conveniently died on the same day as Mary), was, like her, a stay-at-home Protestant who had managed to resist the siren-call of martyrdom.

Nonetheless, the idea that Elizabeth and her advisers were intent on creating a *via media* or middle way in religion, a mélange of Catholic and Protestant elements equidistant from Geneva and Rome, is another myth. This is a back-projection from much later self-understandings found among Anglican theologians and historians, and the word 'Anglican' was in fact never used in this period. More plausible is the idea that Elizabeth might have been content with something not unlike her father's religious settlement. But this was never really on the cards. In the first place, the existing bishops (bar one) all refused to recognize Elizabeth's renewed authority over the Church, even when it was reframed as a Supreme 'Governorship' rather than Headship. This episcopal refusal to remain in office was an unprecedented development, and indicative of how religious alternatives were becoming clearer and more compelling, at least for members of the elite. To fill the empty dioceses, Elizabeth was forced to turn to zealous returnees from the Continent. At the same time, not only former exiles but also Elizabeth's own most trusted advisers, such as William Cecil, were pressing for a clear 'alteration' in religion. What was achieved in parliament in the spring of 1559 was in fact largely a reactivation of the Edwardian Reformation as it had been put on hold in the summer of 1553. In addition to the severance of links with Rome in the Act of Supremacy, an Act of Uniformity restored a slightly revised version of the 1552 Book of Common Prayer, and a couple of years later the Forty-Two Edwardian Articles of Religion were reconstituted as Thirty-Nine Elizabethan ones. The idea that any of this was likely, or intended, to conciliate traditionalist Catholics is fairly laughable.

But some peculiarities undoubtedly attended the birth of the Elizabethan Reformation. The words accompanying the reception of communion in the 1559 Prayer Book yoked together formulae from 1549 and 1552 in such a way as to create ambiguity over the presence or non-presence of Christ in the sacrament. The Uniformity Act was vague about the vestments to be worn by officiating clergy—a source of controversy in Edward's reign because of the association of vestments with a mass-saying priesthood. Elizabeth subsequently insisted on the wearing of white surplices, and instructed Archbishop Parker to suspend ministers for whom this dress code was simply too 'popish'. The Prayer Book and Royal Injunctions contradicted each other, meanwhile, on whether communion tables should stand in the traditional position of altars when not in use for services, and on whether plain bread, or Catholic-style wafers, were to be used for the celebration. The queen's own communion table, in the chapel royal, was distinctly altar-like, and to the scandal of Protestant clergy, it housed a cross and candlesticks.

The 'Elizabethan Settlement' is in fact a spectacular misnomer. The potential for serious dispute lurked in such anomalies. Yet most Protestants expected that ruffles of this sort would be ironed out, as the Church, like its Edwardian predecessor, continued the work of reform. Perhaps the single most crucial factor in the development of the British Reformations was that the queen herself did not see it this way. Almost uniquely, Elizabeth considered that the Reformation of the Church of England was not a process, but a done-deal: she would countenance no deviation or advance from the positions arrived at, almost by accident, at the very start of her reign. If the English Reformation was to go anywhere after 1559—and large numbers of clergy and laity were sure that it should and must—the dynamism and leadership was not going to come from the very top.

Yet the accession of this most cautious and conservative of queens would prove the decisive factor for revolutionary change in England's neighbour to the north. Mary of Guise's tolerant policy had emboldened rather than conciliated Protestant leaders, and at the end of 1557, five noblemen subscribed the 'Band of the Lords of the Congregation', a document promising mutual support and demanding further reform. The signing of bands or bonds—a common feature of Scottish social life—was here conflated with the Calvinist notion of a religious covenant. The Lords provided protection for radical preachers, including Knox, who had returned to Scotland in May 1559. The death of Mary I, and the prospect of Scottish rebels allying themselves with a re-Protestantized England, belatedly nudged Mary of Guise towards repressive action. Open rebellion ensued, along with fresh rounds of iconoclasm and attacks on friaries. Still, Mary could draw on substantial amounts of French military support to sustain the conflict, exclaiming after one victory (or so at least Knox claimed), 'Where is now John Knox's God? My God is stronger than his, yea, even in Fife.'

The deadlock was broken by English intervention. The Lords of the Congregation had for months been begging for aid, but Elizabeth was extremely reluctant to commit herself, and did so only after her chief minister Cecil threatened to resign. A small

A PROTESTANT COMMUNION SERVICE, from Richard Day, *A book of Christian Prayers*, 1578. In contrast to the 'sacrificial' character of the mass, English Protestant eucharistic practice was designed to enhance the symbolism of a shared meal of thanksgiving. The communicants gather around what is clearly a table rather than a stone altar, and receive the sacrament in the form of ordinary bread.

English army and naval force laid siege to the port of Leith in March 1560. By the summer, the French had agreed with the English to cut their losses and withdraw, Mary of Guise having died in the meantime. The 'Reformation Parliament' which convened in Edinburgh in August 1560 was an impromptu assembly of largely Protestant lairds. It endorsed a full-blooded 'Confession of Faith', drafted by Knox, and passed Acts abolishing the mass and papal jurisdiction. It also commissioned the drawing up of a 'Book of Discipline'. This proposed a thorough Genevan-style overhaul of the Church's structure, with congregational election of ministers, and oversight of parish discipline by kirk sessions staffed by elders and deacons. But the Book's proposal for transferring the funds of the Church into ministerial hands led to its rejection by lay parliamentarians with a vested interest in the old financial arrangements. The new Scottish Kirk began life with an ambiguous and autonomous relationship to secular authority. More fundamentally, the entire basis of the Scottish Reformation settlement was rejected by the crown. Mary, Queen of Scots refused to ratify the Acts of the Reformation Parliament, both before and after her return to Scotland in 1561, following the death of her husband Francis II.

To govern successfully, as a Catholic, a nation so deeply divided, though now largely Protestant in its political class, demanded greater political skills than Mary possessed. Matters were not helped by the noisy off-stage zealotry of John Knox, endlessly denouncing the concession by more pragmatic Protestant leaders that Mary be permitted to hear mass in private. Mary's missteps culminated in a disastrous marriage to her cousin, the feckless Henry Stewart, Lord Darnley. Mary may or may not have been complicit in Darnley's murder in February 1567; the evidence on balance suggests she was not. But her subsequent remarriage to the man widely suspected of carrying out the deed, the Earl of Bothwell, caused predictable howls of protest. After surrendering to a rebel army in June 1567, Mary was forced to abdicate in favour of her (and Darnley's) infant son, James VI, who in the coming years was to be raised a Protestant under the tutelage of the Calvinist intellectual George Buchanan, an advocate of resistance theory and the legitimacy of 'tyranni-cide', as well as an enthusiastic beater of his young royal pupil. James never again saw his mother. She escaped from captivity in May 1568, and raised considerable forces against the regent, the Earl of Moray. But after her army suffered defeat at the Battle of Langside, Mary made the momentous—and personally catastrophic—decision to flee to England and seek the mercy of the English queen.

Counter-Reformation

Mary's flight into England precipitated a twenty-year political crisis in the host nation, and ensured that the fates of the Reformations in Scotland and England would remain intimately bound up with each other. It also underlined what contemporaries well understood, but later generations have been apt to forget: that the permanence of Protestant ascendancy was by no means assured, and that unforeseen dynastic even-tualities would continue to be a principal determinant of religious change, as they had been ever since Henry VIII's failure to conceive a surviving son with Catherine of Aragon. The crucial dynastic factors of Elizabeth I's reign were a series of non-events: the queen's refusal to marry; her consequent inability to produce an heir of her body; and her unwillingness to die until she had reached the age of 69 and political stability of a sort had been achieved (her paternal grandfather died at 52, her father at 56, her regal siblings at 15 and 42). But none of this was predictable in the 1560s.

Elizabeth's ministers and parliaments expected, and occasionally demanded, that she fulfil the expectations on her gender and take a husband. Her disinclination to do so was eventually glossed in a positive way as the dedication to her country of the 'Virgin Queen'. But at the time this was in fact a persistent source of anxiety and instability, to the extent that most of her reign assumed the character of an extended 'succession crisis'. Had Elizabeth succumbed to illness, accident, or, as some feared, assassination, the strongest claim in blood was that of the erstwhile Queen of Scots, great-granddaughter to Henry VII. But Mary's Catholic candidacy was unacceptable on any terms to a considerable section of English opinion. In the early 1560s William Cecil was planning the extraordinary step of keeping her from the throne by turning England into a kind of short-term republic if Elizabeth were to die. In the mid-1580s, a time of Catholic plots against Elizabeth's life, he and other councillors drafted 'the Bond of Association'—a vigilante oath, requiring its many signatories to hunt down and kill Elizabeth's murderers, as well as anyone who benefited from the act (i.e. Mary). Religious ideology had become a potent political motivation, trumping any unquestioning loyalty to royal bloodlines. That England avoided the kind of blood-letting that afflicted France in the later sixteenth century had more to do with good luck than with any intrinsic instinct of moderation.

Elizabeth might have defused some of the tension by marrying and reproducing. But that too was fraught with difficulties. A home-grown husband (as Mary, Queen of Scots had discovered) was a recipe for jealousies and factionalism, but the potential foreign ones of any respectable stature were nearly all Catholics. Elizabeth seemed to consider seriously the candidature of the French Duke of Anjou, arousing both hopes and fears among her subjects. During the last round of these negotiations, in the early 1580s, one curate in Warwickshire pre-emptively shaved off his beard, the distinguishing mark of a Protestant minister, 'upon rumour of a change in religion'.

Catholics, then, did not know that they had 'lost' the contest over the religious future. In England, early Elizabethan Catholicism manifested in two principal forms: the deeply conservative predilections of a large mass of the population, especially in the north and west, and the more articulate doctrinal Catholicism of the former clerical leaders of Mary's Church. Many of these went into exile in the Low Countries in the years after 1559 to begin a printed propaganda war with the former Protestant exiles moving in the opposite direction. The two strands of Catholicism came together with a vengeance in 1569, catalysed by the arrival of Mary, Queen of Scots. With the aim of freeing her from captivity, a serious popular rebellion broke out in the north, headed by two Catholic earls and cheered on by pro-papal priests. The rising was crushed, but before this news reached Rome, Pius V weighed in with a bull excommunicating and deposing Elizabeth, and releasing her subjects from any obligation to obey her. The bull was in practice a dead letter, but it lent credence to arguments that Catholics were, by definition, traitors, and it encouraged the passing of more punitive legislation against 'recusants' (Latin: *recusare*, to refuse) who declined to attend Protestant church services. The stakes were raised further when the English clerical exiles made the decision to send missionary priests, trained in continental seminaries, back to their homeland to bolster the faith of their co-religionists. These were joined after 1580 by members of the Society of Jesus. The resolute dedication and unconventional ways of working of the Jesuits made them a particular object of fear and hatred among Protestants, as well as among some fellow Catholics.

To the government, these missionary priests, coming from Douai in the Spanish Netherlands, from Valladolid, or from Rome, were traitors and foreign agents. Before the end of the reign, 124 of them had been put to death, along with 59 lay helpers. The tally does not include Mary, Queen of Scots, beheaded in 1587 when a reluctant Elizabeth was finally pushed by her councillors into taking action against her, after conclusive evidence was produced of Mary's complicity in a plot against the queen. But the Armada that Philip of Spain launched in partial revenge for this execution increased dangers for missionary priests. English Catholic identity, like that of its Protestant counterpart, was now sealed with the blood of martyrs. Others suffered a martyrdom of the pocket, as swingeing fines were exacted for non-attendance at church. But the full weight of government policy was never quite behind what many godly Protestants would have favoured: a thorough drive to eradicate Catholicism and systematically convert its benighted adherents. Elizabeth, as Sir Francis Bacon observed, had no desire 'to make windows into men's hearts and secret thoughts': she was content with the outward conformity of mere church attendance, and she vetoed attempts to make reception of the Protestant communion (a much more spiritual matter) into a requirement of statute law. In consequence, another space was created for the separation of inner belief and outward compliance. Catholic Nicodemism— known disparagingly as 'church papistry'—was widely practised through the six-teenth century and beyond, despite the condemnations of Protestant preachers and Jesuit writers alike. The number of strict recusants was always relatively small, but how many actual 'Catholics' there were, or might be if the wind changed, was any-body's guess and some people's nightmare.

It was a source of particular apprehension with respect to Ireland, always seen as a potential bridgehead for Spanish invasion. The prospects for Protestant advance, and Catholic decline, in mid-century Ireland were not, as we have seen, entirely negligible. But such limited promise as there was increasingly faded over the course of Elizabeth's reign. This was not, as is often supposed, entirely due to cultural and linguistic factors. Doubtless, it did not help that there was no Irish translation of the New Testament till 1602, or of the Book of Common Prayer till 1608. But Calvinist preachers managed to make considerable progress in the Gaelic-speaking Western Highlands of Scotland despite similar obstacles. A shortage of Protestant preachers of any sort continued to be the main problem. This left the field to the friars, with their deep roots in Irish society, later reinforced by Jesuits. With no university in Ireland (Trinity College Dublin was belatedly founded in 1592), sons of the elite went overseas to Catholic ones, and at home were educated by priests in a network of Catholic schools. Recusancy was virtually the norm, and the Protestant Archbishop of Dublin com-plained wearily that 'this miserable realm is overwhelmed with idolatry'. There were few material incentives for the 'Old English', let alone the native Irish, to abandon the faith of their fathers. An instructive contrast can be made with the other Celtic nation of Wales, where incorporation into the English county structure supplied the crown with a welter of attractively remunerated administrative posts to offer to willing gentry. Wales was by no means entirely conformable and quiescent, but there were in the end no Catholic rebellions there. Ireland, however, was persistently troubled with revolts led by indigenous nobles whose political disaffection was energized by religious resolve. The last and most serious of these, the Nine Years War (1594–1603), was instigated by the defiance of Hugh O'Neill, Earl of Tyrone. With some Old English support, and military backing from Spain, Tyrone rallied the native Irish. His eventual defeat and flight into exile signalled a military subjugation of the

Viri plurimi in Anglia pro fide Catholica retinenda hoc qui expressus
est modo eousq; cruciantur donec universi corporis artus singulatim
luxentur. Sic Edmundus Campianus Societatis Iesu religiosus,
Rodulphus Sheruinus, Alexander Briantus, alijq; Sacerdotes summi
Pontificis Alumni acerbissimè torti fuere. Anno Dñi 1581.1582.et.1583.

31

THE RACKING OF EDMUND CAMPION, from Giovanni Battista de Cavalleriis, *Ecclesiae Anglicanae Trophea*, 1584. Edmund Campion, a brilliant scholar and convert from Protestant conformity, returned to England on the first Jesuit mission of 1580, and was executed in December 1581. The authorities tortured Campion for information about the Catholic mission, and sought to discredit him in a series of 'disputations' staged at the Tower. But his impressive performance in these debates, disavowal of any 'political' motives, and demeanour on the scaffold strengthened the Catholic cause.

island, but also the extent to which the battle for hearts and minds there had been lost. The future of Protestantism in Ireland would not be secured by conversion, but by 'plantation' of English and Scots immigrants, particularly into the Gaelic heartland of Ulster.

ENGLAND'S 'DOUBLE DELIVERANCE', from Samuel Ward, *Deo trinuni Britanniae bis ultori In Memoriam classis invincibilis subversae submersae*, 1621. Protestant anxieties about Catholic threats, and a hopeful belief that God would providentially preserve England, are displayed in this Jacobean print. On the left, the Spanish Armada is scattered by a heavenly wind, and on the right Guy Fawkes's Gunpowder Treason is exposed by the all-seeing eye of God, while in the centre, the pope, Jesuits, and a Spanish king plot with the devil. But its publication landed the author in trouble at a time when James I was seeking to negotiate a Spanish marriage for his son.

AN IRISH CHIEFTAIN AT DINNER, from John Derricke, *The Image of Irelande*, 1581. This image of the chieftain of the MacSweeney clan of County Donegal, feasting with his followers, is an invaluable source for Gaelic culinary customs and costume. But it also displays a sneering English attitude towards the native Irish. These are depicted as 'wild' and unmannerly, and their leaders as under the thrall of sinister priests and friars.

Godly Cultures

Catholicism remained a worry for the leaders of Scotland's adolescent Kirk, yet conservative sentiment, though strong in some areas, such as the Aberdeenshire fiefdom of the Gordon earls of Huntly, was after the early 1570s never quite organized enough on a national level to offer a coherent challenge to the new religious regime. Anxieties were ratcheted up during the brief regency, 1580–2, of the suspiciously French-born Duke of Lennox, a favourite of the young James VI. But for much of the time Catholic belief seemed less a pressing political danger than part of the challenge to sweep away superstition and build a truly godly society in Scotland. The campaign was pursued along a twin-track: right structures and right belief. The Reformed Kirk of Scotland is generally called a 'Presbyterian' Church, though that was an aspiration more than an immediate reality. Presbyteries were assemblies of presbyters, or elected ministers, exercising oversight over the congregations in a particular geographical region—a crucial link between the parishes and the General Assembly that formulated

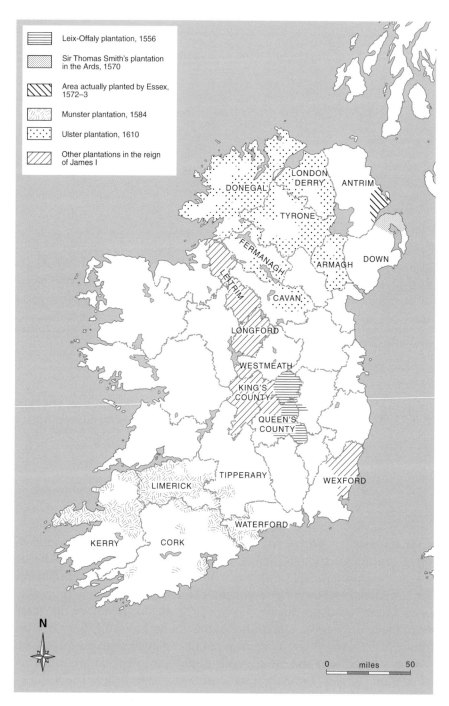

PLANTATIONS IN IRELAND, 1556–1622
Source: Nicholas Canny, *Making Ireland British* (OUP, 2001), p. 186.

policy for the Kirk as a whole. They obviated the need for bishops, and indeed the fundamental equality of all ministers was a principle insisted on in the 1578 Second Book of Discipline, drafted by the presbyterian leader Andrew Melville. The Book was explicitly designed to assert the Kirk's independence and to oppose the 'conformity with England' preferred by royal ministers, for whom bishops were an attractive instrument of state control. Presbyteries and bishops were alternately instituted and suppressed, in the course of some hard-fought factional battles through the 1570s, 1580s, and 1590s. James VI, as he grew to adulthood, favoured retaining vestiges of the episcopal model, with bishops represented in parliament. The result was a messy amalgam of both systems, and a distinctly uneasy relationship between Calvinist king and Presbyterian leadership. In 1596, Melville told James to his face that he needed to remember he was but 'God's silly [weak] vassal', and that in the kingdom of Christ, he was 'not a king nor a lord, nor a head, but a member'.

In England, Thomas Cranmer had failed to institute a uniform system of godly discipline, in which all members of Christ's kingdom could be held to standards of moral and spiritual rectitude. Scots Protestants prided themselves that they, like the Genevans on whose consistories their system was modelled, had achieved this mark of a true church. Kirk sessions took some time to set up, but were eventually to be found in every parish. The elders who staffed them were charged with seeking out and rebuking sin of all kinds. If suspects proved recalcitrant, they would be required to undergo humiliating public penance, or face the ultimate penalty of excommunication. The sins under inspection were not just the usual human failings around charity and sexuality, but spiritual offences such as unlawful recreation on the Sabbath, or continued resort to ancient places of healing and pilgrimage. More than almost anywhere else in Europe, the Kirk sought to write its message on a clean slate, wiping out the traces of the old devotional world and banning celebration of all traditional religious festivals, including Easter and Christmas (only in 1958 did Christmas finally become a public holiday in Scotland). Yet the standards of purity aimed at almost guaranteed they would not be fulfilled. Some recent scholarship has set itself to overturn the image of a dour, doctrinaire, and dictatorial system of social control, arguing that kirk sessions could be flexible and even forgiving, and that campaigns against pre-marital sex—which might burden the parish with bastard children to feed—could enjoy wide social support. But if the local kirk—through its office of deacons—increasingly took on responsibility for sustenance of the poor, its social discipline was also increasingly directed at the poor, reflecting the values of a dominant middling group in local society. The aged poet Richard Maitland of Lethington (d. 1586) was probably not alone in wondering, 'where is the blitheness that hath been... dancing, singing, game and play?'

Similar nostalgia for a lost world of good fellowship could be found among English writers—nominally Protestant—in the later sixteenth century. But others looked north with admiration and envy. Those who felt most strongly that the Elizabethan 'settlement' was an unnaturally arrested development of reform had by the later 1560s acquired the derisive nickname of 'Puritan'. They spoke about themselves, without

SEVENTEENTH-CENTURY PENITENTS' SEAT, Holy Trinity Church, St Andrews. Scottish churches contained a variety of seats, stools, or pillars (high stools) of repentance, where those found guilty of moral offences by the kirk session were obliged to sit during services for specified periods, sometimes as long as a year. This form of public humiliation was intended as both deterrence and punishment for sin, but reception back into 'the bosom of the kirk' on completion of penance was an important part of the ritual.

irony, as 'the godly', and they considered their opponents to be ungodly. Puritans were, as their leading modern chronicler Patrick Collinson observed, the 'hotter sort' of Protestants. They were devoted to preaching, and took with intense seriousness the Ten Commandments' injunctions about 'idolatry', and strict observance of the Sabbath. But they also had specific objections to forms of worship mandated by the Church: the wearing of clerical vestments, an insistence on using the sign of the cross in baptism, kneeling to receive communion, or exchanging rings in the wedding service. Some were convinced that such abuses would be removed only when forms of church government conformed to the model of the New Testament, and they agitated in parliament for the introduction of presbyterianism. Others looked to build the system from the ground up, organizing regular meetings of like-minded ministers, such as the 'classis' based at Dedham in Essex in the 1580s.

To the queen and a number of her ministers, Puritan activism looked like political subversion. In 1577, Elizabeth suspended her Archbishop of Canterbury, Edmund Grindal, for refusing to ban the 'Prophesyings'—local gatherings of godly clergy for the purpose of critiquing each other's preaching. Grindal's successor, John Whitgift, was a new broom and a new breed, a disciplinarian willing to enforce subscription to the Prayer Book. By the early 1590s, Whitgift and his allies had broken presbyterianism as a political movement. The godly seemed then to turn inwards, from reform of the Church to reform of themselves, in many places practising a type of 'semi-separatism' to insulate themselves socially from the ungodly 'multitude'—people apparently addicted to the alehouse and Sunday afternoon football, and who attended church without any real understanding of the doctrines of justification by faith or predestination.

Like recusant Catholicism, 'godly' Protestantism was a minority religious culture, brought into being through a critical relationship with official church requirements. The long-standing notion that Puritanism and Catholicism were mirror-images of each other, rival oppositions in respect of a moderate 'Anglican' establishment, is, however, wide of the mark. Puritanism and mainstream, or conformist, Elizabethan Protestantism had much in common with each other, not least a profound reverence for the teaching of John Calvin, and a deep-seated anti-Catholicism. But godly hopes for further reform of the Church did not simply evaporate in the heat of an intensified personal piety. When Elizabeth, having outlived so many of her rivals, finally died in 1603, James VI of Scotland was the only plausible Protestant candidate to succeed her. As he travelled south, he was presented with a 'Millenary Petition', claiming to have the support of a thousand ministers and rehearsing old grievances about the Prayer Book. James agreed to a meeting with the leading Puritan spokesmen at the Hampton Court Conference of 1604, where he accepted measures to encourage preaching and prepare a new translation of the Bible (the 1611 Authorized or King James Version). But any suggestion of replacing episcopacy with the presbyterian model of Scotland was kicked firmly into touch: 'no bishop, no king' was the lesson James had learned from his dealings with the truculent clerical leaders of the northern Kirk.

Wars of Religion

James was proved right: episcopacy and monarchy were both to be—temporarily—extinguished in the years to come. Starting in the 1640s, political conflicts with a markedly religious colouring erupted in all parts of the Stuart state: the English Civil War was part of a wider pattern of interconnected British Civil Wars, which consumed the better part of two decades. Prime responsibility for these calamities is often laid at the door of one man. The political ineptitude of Charles I, it is suggested, knocked over the edifice of religious and political stability bequeathed by Elizabeth I, and maintained, in somewhat eccentric fashion, by James. There is some justification for this view, but in truth what Charles inherited was not so much stability as a set of ambiguous and contested interpretations of what the Reformation was, or ought to be, and a precarious balance of increasingly hostile forces. The willingness of large numbers of Charles's subjects to defy him over matters of religious conscience, up to and beyond the point of armed resistance, was unprecedented. But it was not

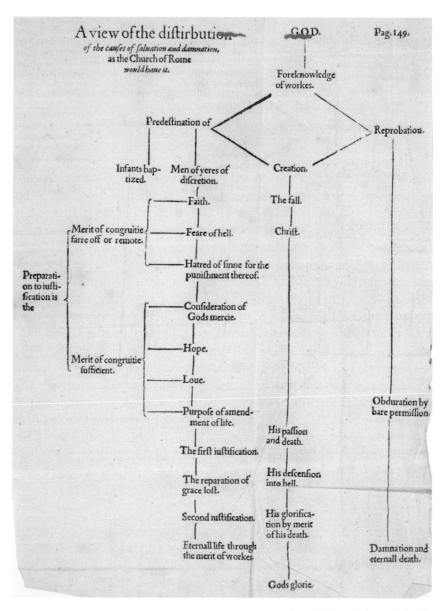

A view of the diftirbution
of the caufes of faluation and damnation,
as the Church of Rome
would haue it.

GOD.

Pag. 149.

Foreknowledge of workes.

Predeftination of

Reprobation.

Infants baptized.

Men of yeres of difcretion.

Creation.

The fall.

Faith.

Chrift.

Merit of congruitie farre off or remote.

Feare of hell.

Hatred of finne for the punifhment thereof.

Preparation to iuftification is the

Confideration of Gods mercie.

Hope.

Merit of congruitie fufficient.

Loue.

Obduration by bare permiffion.

Purpofe of amendment of life.

His paffion and death.

The firft iuftification.

His defcenfion into hell.

The reparation of grace loft.

His glorification by merit of his death.

Second iuftification.

Eternall life through the merit of workes.

Damnation and eternall death.

Gods glorie.

A TABLE SHOWING THE ORDER OF SALVATION AND DAMNATION, from William Perkins, *A Golden Chaine*, 1600. The outlook of English Puritans received its most respectable expression in the 'practical divinity' of the best-selling theologian William Perkins. His famous charts illustrate the subtleties of spiritual introspection Puritans might undergo, and also graphically illustrate the rigour of Calvinist teaching on predestination. This example illustrates the false Catholic understanding of the doctrine, based on God's foreknowledge of people's good works.

previously unimaginable. The remarkable thread of continuity running through the British Reformations is the surprising inability of the crown to direct or control the processes of religious identity-formation, or to make a reality of the uniformity in religion it officially required from its subjects.

It is often said that what Charles so disastrously dismantled was the 'Calvinist Consensus' that had for decades underpinned English, and indeed British, Protestantism. Elizabethan Puritans and conformists disagreed over matters of ceremony, and sometimes church governance. But they were united by a fundamental acceptance of Calvin's doctrine of salvation—the idea that human destinies in the next life were predestined by God, irrespective of individual merit. At least in the early part of his reign, James silenced preachers who dared to question the doctrine of predestination. He agreed to a very Calvinist statement of doctrine for the Church of Ireland—the Irish Articles of 1615. And he threw England's weight behind the pronouncements of the Dutch Synod of Dort, a meeting convoked in 1618 to condemn the challenge to predestination issued by the renegade Reformed theologian Jacob Arminius (1560–1609).

Arminius and his followers taught that people could resist God's offer of salvation, and fall from his grace after it had been offered them. This increased emphasis on human capacity appealed to clergymen who saw a greater role for the institutional Church as an instrument of salvation, rather than just a guardian of order and discipline. The hitherto almost accidental survivals of the English Reformation—the bishops, cathedrals, church courts, the feasts and ceremonies of the Prayer Book—began in some quarters to be regarded in a newly positive light. They were not embarrassing, or at best neutral, leftovers from the papistical past, but proud tokens of continuity with a medieval Church of England which had not been entirely bad after all. Neither the theologian Richard Hooker (1554–1600)—perhaps the inventor of 'Anglicanism'—nor the celebrated bishop and preacher Lancelot Andrewes (1555–1626) openly attacked predestination, but they inspired those who did. Andrewes was one of a number of 'ceremonialist' senior clergymen promoted by James to counterbalance the more orthodox Calvinists in the ranks of the episcopate.

This policy of perilous equilibrium was abandoned when James was succeeded by his son Charles in 1625. Charles had a dangerously telescoped view of religious positions: all Calvinists were Puritans, and all Puritans were subversives. He consistently advanced Arminian sympathizers, culminating in the appointment of William Laud to Canterbury in 1633. For the rest of the decade, Laud spearheaded a national campaign for 'the beauty of holiness', emphasizing ceremony at the expense of preaching, restoring imagery to churches, and insisting that communion tables be reverently positioned, and railed, in the traditional 'altar' position. To its critics—and there were many at all levels of society—this looked alarmingly like popery. Conspiracy theorists who believed Charles was being manipulated by a clique of well-positioned papists noted that the king, like his predecessor, had a Catholic wife. James's consort Anne of Denmark was discreet about the practice of her faith, but Charles's French bride Henrietta Maria was flamboyantly and provocatively devout.

LAUDIAN COMMUNION RAIL (1637), ST ANDREW WROXETER, SHROPSHIRE. The railing-off of the 'sacred space' around the altar was a central component of Archbishop Laud's campaign to elevate the importance of sacraments (at the expense of preaching) and restore dignity and reverence in worship. Puritans, and indeed many other Protestants, thought this looked like a return to popish ways.

Yet what were ultimately to test and prove the limitations on the State's power to compel consciences were royal attempts to harmonize the fractious and disparate Reformations of the British Isles. James, proud of his status as first sovereign of 'Great Britain', made some moves in this direction. In 1612 he persuaded the Scottish parliament to pass an Act acknowledging him as 'supreme governor' of the Kirk, and he tried (not very successfully) to get Scots churchgoers to kneel when receiving communion, and mark the festivals of Easter and Christmas. Charles completely lacked his father's political craftiness, and his willingness to strike a deal. For him, the disorderly variety of religious practice in his kingdoms was simply intolerable. In 1637, his attempt to impose an English-style Prayer Book on the Scottish Kirk provoked open rebellion, and widespread subscription to a National Covenant. Signatories swore to resist religious innovations and to settle a long-standing tension in Scottish ecclesiastical life by abolishing episcopacy. The resultant Bishops' Wars (1637–40) were militarily and politically disastrous for Charles, obliging him to summon a parliament in London for the first time in eleven years. The 'Long Parliament' (it sat from November 1640 to 1653) impeached Archbishop Laud and Charles's minister the Earl of Strafford; it reversed ceremonial innovations and the Laudian altar policy in parish churches; and it encouraged popular demands for the abolition of episcopacy and the Prayer Book. Meanwhile, a violent outbreak of rebellion in November 1641 by the oppressed Catholic majority in Ireland seemed to vindicate fears that the malign forces of popery—and therefore, of the Antichrist—lay behind the arbitrary government of Charles I.

SOLDIERS BREAKING ALTAR RAILS, from John Vicars, *A sight of ye trans-actions of these latter yeares*, 1646. The British civil wars were the occasion for fresh rounds of iconoclasm, as Laudian 'innovations' were reversed in countless parish churches. Here, soldiers enact some practical eucharistic theology by converting the 'popish' altar into an emphatically Protestant communion table.

The issues at stake when civil war broke out in England in the summer of 1642 were financial, political, and constitutional, rather than narrowly theological. But in the end only religion had the motivating power to turn anguished argument into armed conflict. Charles's mistakes had left him isolated in 1640. But the growing radicalism of his parliamentary opponents over the succeeding two years recruited a party for the king among conformist Protestants with no desire to see bishops abolished or the venerable Prayer Book of the martyred Archbishop Cranmer swept out of the churches.

The explosion of sectarian religious energies unleashed by the wars, and an eventual legacy of pluralism and grudging toleration, are described elsewhere in this volume (Chapters 4 and 7). There was never any probability, let alone certainty, that things would work out in the way they did. Yet, over a century and more, the failure of monarchical policy to provide much of a beacon for religious identification handed agency and creativity to individuals and groups who made their own Reformations, in parallel, or in opposition, to the religious requirements of the State. Various causes can be identified for this: the theological incoherence of Henry VIII, the timed-out regimes of Edward VI and Mary I, the waverings of James V and Mary, Queen of Scots, the mulish conservatism of Elizabeth I, and the inability of James I, and especially Charles I, to rise to the challenges of their multi-ethnic, multi-confessional dominions.

Over the longer term, the distinctive forms of Reformation evolved in the British Isles would arguably prove more significant than those of any other European nation for the development of Protestantism as global variant of Christian belief. The process began as early as 1620: the 'Pilgrim Fathers' were refugees to colonial and unconstrained America from hated episcopal policies demanding conformity to practices like kneeling to receive communion. Such policies were to encourage still more Puritan departures to New England in the succeeding reign. Later emigrations had a more kaleidoscopic character, transporting English Episcopalians to Virginia, Quakers to Pennsylvania, and Baptists to Rhode Island and elsewhere. The expansion of the western frontier in both the infant United States and Canada drew waves of hardy Scots-Irish Presbyterian farmers across the Atlantic to set their seal on the political and social structures of their adopted homelands. Britain's empire at its zenith in the nineteenth century sprinkled its variant home-grown Christianities—Anglican, Protestant Nonconformist, and Irish Catholic too—across Australasia, Africa, and Asia. Here they made their mark through settlement, missionary endeavour, and the transformative effects of eventual indigenization. British Reformations, then, are a study in unintended consequences. The aspiration for reformed religious uniformity in one small group of islands was a well-spring of the plural and diverse character of subsequent world faith.

7 Reformation Legacies

THE notion that the Reformation was a critical turning point in the history of Christianity and of the Western world is now so deeply embedded in popular consciousness that we rarely pause to ask when and why it came be to be regarded as a transformative, landmark event. Although it might be assumed that Protestantism's bold challenge to the hegemony of the medieval Church only gradually entered into memory and legend, there is much to suggest that the process of myth-making began within the lifetime of Martin Luther himself. Convinced of his status as a prophet and apocalyptic witness, the monk and his publicists readily embraced the medium of print and the woodblock image to depict him as a figure, foreshadowed in the pages of scripture, who was charged with a divine and historical mission to liberate the true religion from the obscurity and thraldom in which it had been kept by the Antichristian papacy for nearly a millennium. They themselves were in large part responsible for inventing the tradition that the Reformation marked the triumph of light over darkness, truth over falsehood, and set European civilization on a path towards modernity.

And this powerful myth gathered momentum as the years passed. The 100th anniversary of Luther's provocative protest against indulgences in 1517 was marked by celebrations across Protestant Germany and engendered commemorative broadsides and books. The precise circumstances surrounding the famous posting of the Ninety-Five Theses on the church door at Wittenberg are now difficult to unravel from the weight of fictitious embellishment that has subsequently accumulated around this episode, which became an instantly recognizable symbol of the birth of the Reformation. The circulation of images depicting the event reflected and fostered the elevation of Luther and his fellow reformers into a gallery or pantheon of heroes. Absorbing commonplaces that had their roots in early Protestant polemic and apologetic, people began to believe that their predecessors had witnessed a decisive juncture in history. The historical writings about these momentous developments that became the staple reading of subsequent generations, together with biographies and martyrologies of the illustrious men and women who had participated in them, laid the foundations of lasting historiographical myths about the significance and impact of the Reformation that still persist today.

Uniting Protestant piety with national pride, these myths helped to create a celebratory narrative of a swift and warmly welcomed Reformation that efficiently swept away the spiritual apathy, superstition, and credulity into which the papacy and

GÖTTLICHER SCHRIFFTMESSIGER, WOLDENCKWÜRDIGER TRAUM... (1617): broadside published on the centenary of the German Reformation. The notion that the posting of the Ninety-Five Theses had been foreseen in a supernatural dream by Frederick the Wise of Saxony became an integral part of the evolving legend of the birth of Protestantism. Dozens of centenary woodcuts depicted Martin Luther wielding a huge quill pin, which pokes through the ears of a lion and dislodges the triple tiara of Pope Leo X.

THE PROTESTANT REFORMERS (1654). Anonymous painting in the Society of Antiquaries of London. Group portraits of the Protestant reformers seated around the lighted candle of the Gospel, which the pope, devil, and a cardinal desperately endeavour to blow out, proliferated across Europe in the later sixteenth and seventeenth centuries. Adapted to incorporate local religious celebrities, they gave visual expression to the widespread belief that the Reformation had been a watershed.

priesthood had allowed the European populace to sink. They sowed the seeds of the empowering idea that Protestantism was an instrument and agent of progress—a movement which converged with the invention of the printing press to bring about a revolution in communications and to foster the spread of mass literacy; helped to banish the religious bigotry of the Middle Ages, usher in the liberal creed of toleration, and pave the way for the Enlightenment; instilled an ethic of work and habits of discipline that explain the economic prosperity of the capitalist West; and played a key part in the decline of magic, the rise of 'rational' science, and the disenchantment of the world. In other words, it brought about change for the better. Such assumptions flourished alongside their uglier sister and twin: the belief that Catholicism was essentially a negative and reactionary force in all these processes, an opponent of the grand enterprise of modernization. This too was a residue of the confessional struggles of the sixteenth and seventeenth centuries and a measure of the insidious and tenacious influence of the anti-popish prejudices that animated Protestantism from the beginning. Unsurprisingly, these ideas have less purchase in the heartlands of the Counter-Reformation, Italy, Spain, and Latin America, where Catholicism remains a key element of social identity. In recent years, however, many of the settled common-places underpinning these models of historical interpretation have been fruitfully reassessed and critically cast into question.

Drawing on a wide body of research, the purpose of this concluding chapter is to explore the disputed legacies of the parallel and intertwined impulses for religious renewal that we now crown with a capital 'R' and call the Reformation. It seeks to assess their long-term implications and ramifications, to investigate the claims made about their direct consequences, and to probe their often inadvertent side-effects.

Toleration, Pluralism, and Patriotism

The Catholic and Protestant Reformations were both movements predicated on religious intolerance. Committed to the recovery of Christianity in its primitive purity, their leaders and adherents believed that there was only one institutional route to salvation and a single and indivisible version of the truth. They repudiated each other as false churches invented by the Devil and they regarded the repression, not to say extermination, of those who wilfully persisted in soul-destroying doctrinal error as a divinely imposed duty. Mimicking their medieval forebears, they put considerable numbers of heretics to death and utilized the machinery of ecclesiastical and civil justice to coax and discipline others. Notoriously, despite the iron curtain that they were busy erecting between them, Rome and Geneva shared the conviction that anti-Trinitarians like Michael Servetus deserved to be burned without mercy for the blasphemies that they committed against God.

Furthermore, the convergence of Church and State, which was one of the charac-teristic by-products of the magisterial Reformation, had the effect of politicizing spiritual deviance and transforming it into a species of disloyalty and treason. Stimu-lating assassination plots and desperate efforts to effect regime change, it turned some religious dissidents into actual fugitives and terrorists. All this served to fuel the fires of persecution, to encourage large waves of religiously inspired exile and migration, and to create conditions conducive to the eruption of conflict within and between the nations of Europe. The sixteenth and seventeenth centuries constituted an age of religious wars *par excellence*. This was an era marked by prolonged and vicious military confrontations, from the Schmalkaldic Wars (1546–55) and Thirty Years War (1618–48) in the Holy Roman Empire to the French Wars of Religion (1562–98), the Dutch Revolt (1568–1648), and the British Civil Wars (1638–60). And if the passions unleashed by the advent of Protestantism and the belligerent Catholic reaction to it catalysed and fused with other sources of tension to bring about armed hostility between Christians, they also heightened antagonism towards Jews and Muslims. The former were expelled en masse from the Iberian Peninsula in the late fifteenth century and compelled to seek refuge in other regions, where they were the subject of discrimination. In the guise of the Ottoman Turks, the latter represented a significant threat to their western European neighbours, who feared them as another horn of the Beast foretold in the book of Revelation. Suspected of superficial conversion to Christianity to save their skins, the *conversos* and *moriscos* in Spain and Portugal were regular victims of scrutiny by the Inquisition. The same religious impulses stimulated and complicated the activities of European powers engaged in territorial expansion overseas. They provided an incentive and a mandate for colonial violence, coercion, and acculturation. In the Americas and Asia, evangelical Christian mission was often accompanied by the attempted subjugation of indigenous peoples, and this involved force as well as persuasion.

Yet the period between 1500 and 1700 also witnessed the gradual unravelling of at least some of the assumptions that underpinned the intolerant pursuit of religious uniformity. The concept of a united Christendom came to be recognized, regretfully, as an unattainable ideal. The notion that ideological diversity was a certain recipe for political chaos and social anarchy began to wither in the face of tangible evidence that toleration could work as a strategy for bringing peace to bitterly divided cities, regions, and nations. Reluctant steps started to be taken towards a society in which the formal coexistence of men and women who held different beliefs was enshrined in law. This is not to say that the theory and practice of tolerance was entirely absent from the medieval world. However, it cannot be denied that the early modern age saw a significant reconfiguration of arrangements and attitudes.

These were processes in which the Reformations played an important part. They brought into being an unprecedented level of pluralism to which it became necessary to find both temporary and more enduring solutions. They stimulated the search for mechanisms to defuse the destructive spasms of intolerance which Reformation had simultaneously served to intensify. And even as these movements reinforced the older conviction that harsh discipline was the best remedy for heresy they also stirred into life alternative ideas embedded in the Bible and born of practical experience.

We may begin by observing that the outcome of the mid-sixteenth-century battles between the Holy Roman Emperor Charles V and the alliance of rebel Lutheran princes was not a clear victory for one side but rather a moratorium and truce. Its end-product was a precarious and unstable agreement to differ. The Peace of Augsburg of 1555 established the principle of *cuius regio, eius religio*, by which individual rulers were permitted to choose whether Catholicism or Protestantism should be professed in their states. It secured their rights to religious independence but did not recognize those of their subjects, though those who did not wish to conform to their sovereign's decision were given a short period in which to emigrate elsewhere. Nor did it give legal recognition to the full spectrum of confessions that existed within the Empire: by ignoring the Anabaptists, and more particularly the Calvinists, it fostered resentments and outbreaks of aggression that culminated in the Thirty Years War. Three decades of fighting did little to settle the difficult territorial questions that precipitated this conflict and the result was a new treaty, the Peace of Westphalia of 1648, which gave Calvinism parity with the Lutheran and Catholic churches and granted more concessions to the members of minority denominations. Across the patchwork of principalities to which it applied, a range of intriguing compromises and ecumenical experiments emerged. Some were extensions of medieval civic strategies for preserving concord between Christians and Jews; others were newer, including the phenomenon of *Simultankirchen* or shared churches. From 1548 onwards, for instance, the parish church of the Upper Swabian town of Biberach was a bi-confessional building, employed for worship alternately by Catholics and Lutherans, who must have passed each other as they went to and from their respective services. The sharing of liturgical space was never without tension. Nor did it resolve or suppress religious conflict; on the contrary, it helped to perpetuate it. But it was one of the forms of *modus vivendi* which allowed Christians from competing traditions to live alongside each other in relative, if still uneasy, peace. Another strategy was the widespread practice of crossing borders to attend church in a neighbouring territory. Known as *Auslauf* (literally 'walking out'), it similarly required the cooperation and collusion of the authorities.

In France too, the internecine wars waged between Catholics and Huguenots led to attempts to bring an end to these terrible conflicts and bred a growing sense that the only way to save the French state from complete collapse might be to concede some form of toleration. This was the argument put forward by *politiques* like Jean Bodin and Michel de L'Hopital. Various colloquies and interim treaties of pacification failed, but their spirit was preserved in the more lasting Edict of Nantes of 1598 issued by the convert King of Navarre, Henry IV, who presented it as a means of quelling the 'storm' stirred up by 'innumerable factions and sects' in his realm and of bringing the nation to a new 'port of safety'. It gave Protestants permission to practise their faith openly, albeit within strict limits and as second-class citizens. Always envisaged as a temporary measure until religious reunification became possible once more, its revocation by Louis XIV in 1685 is an index of the vulnerability of tolerance as a political ideology in the final decades of the seventeenth century. In other parts of Catholic Europe, including Poland, long a haven for religious minorities, there was a similar drift back towards to policies of harsher repression as the Counter-Reformation gathered momentum.

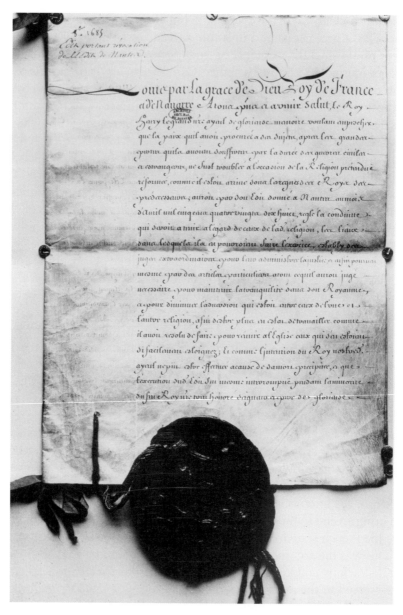

THE EDICT OF FONTAINEBLEAU of 22 October 1685 revoked the Edict of Nantes, which had permitted the coexistence of Protestants and Catholics in France. Thousands of Huguenots fled in its wake, to Britain, the Netherlands, Sweden, Denmark, Switzerland, and to new settlements in North America and southern Africa, where they have left an enduring cultural imprint.

The Low Countries were another crucible from which a variety of sanctioned coexistence somewhat unexpectedly emerged. The rebellion against Spanish Habsburg rule that gave birth to the Dutch Republic was accompanied by eighty years of intermittent violence but it also served to cement the religious diversity of the loose federation of states that comprised the new nation. Technically, Calvinism enjoyed a privileged and monopolistic position, but membership of the Church remained voluntary and other denominations had considerable room for manoeuvre, sometimes bribing officials to ignore their illegal activities. In Amsterdam and other cities, the presence of clandestine churches (*schuilkerken*) was an open secret. The Dutch reputation for tolerance has its roots in the struggles which the Reformation sparked off in this region, but we should recognize the degree to which this was a de facto response to social and political turmoil, remaining intertwined with a powerful undercurrent of confessional enmity. Retrospectively created and repeatedly articulated by patriots in later centuries, it was also a component of a potent national myth.

The post-Reformation history of the British Isles is no less paradoxical. The Civil Wars of the 1640s and 1650s may be seen as a belated consequence of the efforts of monarchs, politicians, and ministers to implant Protestantism in the diverse kingdoms that comprised it. In England, the policy of seeking merely outward conformity had contradictory effects: on the one hand, it created the conditions in which some conservatives and moderate dissenters felt able to remain under the expansive umbrella of the Church; on the other, it entrenched pluralism within it and stored up grievances and troubles that came to a head a century later. Fear that the Reformation for which their ancestors had sacrificed their lives in the martyrs' fires was being subverted led some Puritans to abandon this British Babylon and settle in Massachusetts, Connecticut, and other New England colonies. The same anxieties, combined with resentment at high-handed attempts to bring the Scottish liturgy into line with the ceremonial priorities of Archbishop Laud, led to the start of the Bishops' Wars in 1639. The outbreak of war between parliament and Charles I three years later likewise occurred in a climate of intense concern about Catholic conspiracy in the wake of anti-Protestant atrocities perpetrated during the Irish rebellion of 1641. Neither side set out with the objective of establishing freedom of conscience for anyone other than themselves: this was a clash between two groups who shared the view that toleration was an abomination in the eyes of God as well as a route to earthly confusion. The explosion of radical sects such as the Quakers, Ranters, and Muggletonians that accompanied the collapse of order, and which followed the revolutionary act of beheading the king in 1649, horrified the majority and fostered renewed demands for fierce persecution. The intemperate three-volume polemic against the sectarian menace entitled *Gangraena* which the Presbyterian Thomas Edwards wrote in 1646 is indicative of the resilience of such convictions: it doubled as an extended manifesto against the evils of the spiritual liberty for which some of these new religious groups openly and eloquently called. In the guise of the Instrument of Government of 1653, the Interregnum regime of Oliver Cromwell effectively abandoned the policy of enforcing uniformity, though its professed tolerance of anyone who believed in Jesus Christ in practice applied only to a small spectrum of fervent Protestants, and excluded Anglicans and Catholics.

Even before the Restoration of the Stuart monarchy in 1660, there was a discernible retreat from this high-water mark, and thereafter parliament sought to turn back the

OUR LORD IN THE ATTIC, AMSTERDAM. Hidden behind the thin façade of a fashionable townhouse was an elaborate Catholic chapel in which the sacrament of the holy Eucharist was regularly celebrated. Anabaptist places of worship and Jewish synagogues were similarly disguised. Their architectural claddings as domestic residences maintained a fiction of privacy that allowed Protestants to reconcile their sense of superiority with their more pragmatic instinct to find a way of living with neighbours who espoused other faiths.

clock and harass religious Dissent out of existence. The sense of crisis to which the alleged Popish Plot (1678–9) and public pope-burning processions through the streets of the capital gave graphic expression was the intolerant prelude to the Glorious Revolution of 1688, the constitutional coup that toppled the Catholic James II from the throne and purchased the support of Protestant nonconformists with the bait of toleration. The famous Act of 1689 was a form of indulgence akin to that which the ejected king had so controversially bestowed upon his co-religionists, though it did not extend either to them or to Arians (who denied the doctrine of the Holy Trinity). It also treated its beneficiaries with suspicion, prohibiting them from locking their meeting houses while service was in session, and merely exempting them from the penal legislation rather than repealing it. Reversal of the Act of 1689 remained a real possibility, for which some petitioned vociferously in the ensuing decades. Only later, after Enlightenment values entered the intellectual mainstream, did it become celebrated as a triumphant achievement, part of what the eighteenth-century Bishop of Gloucester William Warburton called 'our matchless constitution in Church and state'.

The raft of legislative measures that developed in the two centuries after the Reformation in many respects represented an overdue recognition of forms of confessional coexistence that had already evolved on the ground. In France, for example, detailed local studies reveal considerable evidence of amicable relations between members of the two faiths responsible for tearing France apart in the later sixteenth century: they served as godparents to each other's children, and as apprentices and servants in households that espoused the opposite creed. Catholics and Protestants extended hospitality to each other and shared financial transactions and leisure activities. In Besse, in Dauphiné, in 1672, the parish curé was found to be playing boules and sharing meals with the Huguenots. In France and elsewhere, people with different doctrinal commitments also frequently intermarried—a striking demonstration of the porosity of social barriers in these religiously divided societies. In England too there is plenty of evidence to suggest that both dissenters and recusants were often respected and well-integrated members of their communities, trusted as business partners, appointed as executors of wills, elected to positions of local responsibility such as churchwarden and parish constable, and treasured as friends. Sometimes Anglicans even intervened to protect their nonconformist neighbours from persecution: a Quaker labourer imprisoned in 1658 for his conscientious refusal to pay tithes was freed when fellow inhabitants of the Lincolnshire town of Leverton paid his debt. Sources from Germany, Switzerland, and the Netherlands yield many similar instances of interconfessional cooperation and conviviality. Bonds of emotion and obligation were capable of transcending the boundaries erected by theology. We should not be sentimental about these episodes and see them as evidence that ordinary people were more foresighted than their rulers and that local impulses for social harmony overrode the bigotry exhibited by contemporary bureaucrats. Nevertheless, these reciprocal gestures of good will at the grass roots must have contributed to eroding the ingrained belief that the inevitable offspring of diversity was appalling disorder. They helped, in their own way, to create an atmosphere in which toleration ceased to be regarded as an anathema. Reacting against the fragmentation of society that they saw happening around them, some began to contemplate the possibility that truth itself was plural. The Utrecht lawyer Arnoldus Buchelius was a committed Calvinist, but he also yearned for concord and meditated in his diary in the 1590s: 'Since we all gaze at the same stars, and all aim for the same goal of eternity, what does it matter . . . by which road he has reached the end of his course?' The long experience of *convivencia* (the coexistence of Christians, Jews, and Muslims) in medieval Iberia helped to plant the seed of a similar idea in the soil of that peninsula. Hundreds of people were hauled before the Inquisition in Spain, Portugal, and Latin America for articulating the heterodox view that people of all faiths could be saved.

Yet the virus of intolerance that the Reformation had released into the European body politic proved extremely resilient and, like the epidemics of plague that periodically devastated cities, towns, and villages across the Continent, it flared up at regular intervals. Confessional relations remained tense in France, and the memory of the ghastly massacre on St Bartholomew's Day 1572 proved hard to lay to rest: in 1645 a rumour swept through the Parisian congregation at Charenton that Catholics were gathering in the local woods to slaughter everyone present, while in 1690 talk that the Huguenots were planning to burn their way across regions of the Midi led to the militia being placed on full alert. The Gordon Riots in London in 1780, a reaction to tentative moves to alleviate discrimination against Catholics, revealed that the slogan 'No Popery' continued to be capable of rousing crowds of tens of thousands to violent action. In Ireland, meanwhile, the ill-fated efforts of the English crown to utilize religious reform as a tool of political subordination left livid scars and engendered a tradition of sectarian violence that has persisted into our own time.

A further prejudice that the advent of Protestantism and Tridentine Catholicism served to re-inflame was medieval Christian animosity towards the Jewish people. As Luther's initial expectation that the Jews would embrace the faith he had rescued from popish corruption gave way to disillusionment, the tenor of Reformation discourse turned in the direction of anti-Semitism, albeit without the explicitly racial dimension it acquired, with such tragic consequences, in later centuries. In the early modern period, animosity towards these traditional enemies of God continued to jostle with millenarian sentiments that predicted their mass conversion as a precursor of the Second Coming: this was the atmosphere in which discussions took place in the 1650s for their formal readmission to England. Part of a much longer cycle of waxing and waning hostility, the reconstruction of Judaism as a religious 'other' in the sixteenth and seventeenth centuries also owed something to the growth of strategies of segregation. The establishment of the Roman Ghetto by Pope Paul IV in 1555 may stand as an emblem of this development in the context of Italy. The physical distancing of Judaism assisted in fostering increased suspicion. In Spain and Portugal, crypto-Jews and Muslims became the new targets of anxiety. Worries that the Christianity of converts might be skin-deep engendered another sinister development in the Iberian peninsula: the so-called blood purity laws (*limpieza de sangre*), behind which lay the view that religious deviance was a kind of hereditary disease that could not be cured. Meanwhile, European fear of Islam was also complicated and exacerbated by the religious turbulence within Christianity: the Turk became polemically conflated with the menace of idolatry and heresy, and the struggle against the might of the Ottoman Empire assumed the appearance of a new crusade. At the same time, certain points of contact within Protestant and Muslim thinking about the evils of popish superstition facilitated the forging of some unexpected political alliances, such as between Elizabeth I and the Sultan Murad III.

The ambiguities of the Reformation as an agent and engine of toleration in practice are matched in the area of theory. Modern readers' ears are instinctively tuned to hear voices that anticipate the values which they hold dear. There has been a long-standing tendency to identify the advent of Protestantism with the origins of advanced ideas about freedom of conscience and to elevate prominent advocates of religious liberty, such as Roger Williams and John Locke, onto a pedestal as enlightened thinkers. The latter's famous *Letter concerning Toleration* (1689) is widely regarded as a prelude to the yet more emphatic defences of freedom of conscience articulated by Voltaire and other Enlightenment heroes. Most of the arguments late seventeenth-century writers advanced for toleration had their foundation in scripture, which Protestants acknowledged as the fount of all truth and knowledge. And the insistence that human rulers have no jurisdiction over the souls of their subjects was most clearly articulated in the circles of radical reformers like the Anabaptists. But the severance of Church and state for which they called was at odds with the principles that underpinned the political reformations overseen by Luther, Calvin, and the monarchs and princes of northern Europe. The idea, articulated by the Italian refugee Jacopo Acontius in 1565, that persecution was a 'satanic stratagem' competed with the equally powerful conviction that toleration was a diabolical device. One English Protestant minister of the Restoration era described it as 'the last and most desperate design of Antichrist', another as 'the whore of Babylon's backdoor'. Catholic writers also participated in the development of a body of political and religious thought that defended coexistence, just as they helped to crystallize discourses that vindicated resistance to tyrannical rule. Notable here is the Dominican Bartholome de las Casas' *In defence of the Indians* (c.1550), which denounced the atrocities perpetrated against the indigenous peoples of America by settlers and conquistadors and defended Indian rights on the grounds that indigenous peoples possessed an inherent potential for salvation. On both sides of the divide, toleration was often a losers' creed, a position adopted by religious minorities who would not have hesitated to become persecutors had the tables been turned. Only gradually did this come to be regarded as hypocritical.

The forging of a closer link between religious and political power that was both a cause and effect of the magisterial Reformation ensured that patriotism acquired a confessional flavour and imbued monarchy with a sacred aura. It fostered the creation of competing Catholic and Protestant myths of nationhood and helped to turn kingship into a subsidiary form of divinity. Sixteenth- and seventeenth-century England celebrated its providential deliverances from the malign machinations of the pope, Spain, and homebred conspirators. The defeat of Philip II's Armada in 1588 and the

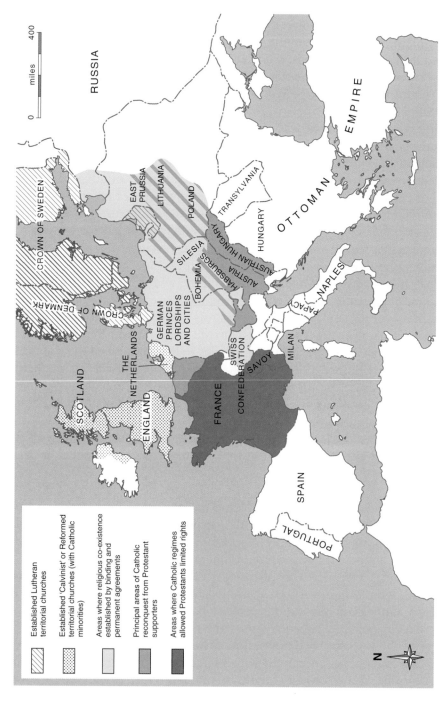

RELIGIOUS COEXISTENCE AND CONFLICT IN EUROPE, c.1600
Source: Euan Cameron, *The European Reformation* (OUP, 2nd edn, 2012), p. 371.

Legend:

- Established Lutheran territorial churches
- Established 'Calvinist' or Reformed territorial churches (with Catholic minorities)
- Areas where religious co-existence established by binding and permanent agreements
- Principal areas of Catholic reconquest from Protestant supporters
- Areas where Catholic regimes allowed Protestants limited rights

RUSSIA

CROWN OF SWEDEN

CROWN OF DENMARK

SCOTLAND

THE NETHERLANDS

ENGLAND

GERMAN PRINCES LORDSHIPS AND CITIES

EAST PRUSSIA

LITHUANIA

POLAND

SILESIA

BOHEMIA

HABSBURGS

AUSTRIA

AUSTRIAN HUNGARY

TRANSYLVANIA

HUNGARY

OTTOMAN EMPIRE

SWISS CONFEDERATION

SAVOY

MILAN

PAPACY

NAPLES

FRANCE

SPAIN

PORTUGAL

N

0   miles   400

Gunpowder Plot of 1605 proved that God was on England's side. Calvinism likewise inserted itself firmly into the stories which the Dutch told about their successful revolt against Habsburg rule. On the other side of the divide, Catholicism became integral to the national identity of the Spanish: from as early as the 1570s, the word 'luterano' (Lutheran) was synonymous with foreigner. Catholicism was also central to the public piety and the absolutist pretensions of the French monarchy. The Counter-Reformation in seventeenth-century Bavaria and the Upper Palatinate saw a similar sacralization of their histories which enhanced the authority of the Wittlesbach dynasty. The resurrection of a glorious Christian past and the embellishment of the cults of native saints became key elements in the militant resurgence of the Church of Rome in these regions.

The intolerance which Catholics and Protestants meted out to each other also became embedded in social memory. A black legend of Romanist cruelty developed. Central components of this were the burnings of Marian evangelicals in the reign of

La SALE de L'INQUISITION.

Diverses Manieres dont le S.t OFICE fait donner la QUESTION.

BENARD PICART, INQUISITION TORTURE CHAMBER, 1722. The Inquisition was the centrepiece of a Protestant black legend of Catholic cruelty. The hideous tortures it allegedly inflicted upon its victims continued to be the subject of visual depiction well into the eighteenth century, when they became the target of the critique of Enlightenment writers.

'bloody' Mary I, the evil and Machiavellian Jesuits who practised equivocation and killed kings, and perhaps above all the hideous institution that was the Inquisition. The reputation of the latter as a chamber of torture etched itself on the Protestant imagination early on and has proved hard to shift despite more recent work stressing its pastoral and therapeutic objectives: severe discipline was the tool it used in order to save souls from eternal damnation. In counterpoint, there emerged myths about the tyranny of the Genevan consistory and the excessive rigour of Scots kirk discipline. In fact, the real legacy of the Reformations was not persecution or toleration, but an unstable and schizophrenic mixture of both attitudes and instincts.

Paradoxically, alongside the gradual acceptance of denominational diversity as a fact of everyday life was the growth of an impulse within religious communities to differentiate themselves from their rivals. In order to live together it became necessary, both metaphorically and literally, to live apart. This heightened awareness of doctrinal and liturgical difference manifested itself in external ways. It led some groups and sects to turn away from promiscuously intermingling with the members of other churches in secular affairs, to the decline of mixed marriage, and to the rise of other ritual markers of difference. It fostered the development of the distinctive cultures and codes of behaviour which are the subject of discussion in the next two sections of this chapter, and which continue to shape the world we inhabit today.

Work and Play: The Reformations, Economic Relations, and the Rhythm of Everyday Life

Protestantism has long been credited with playing a critical role in a development of immense consequence for the making of modern society: the emergence of capitalism as the dominant model of economic organization in western Europe. The thesis that the Reformation, especially in the guise of Calvinism, Lutheran Pietism, and subsequently Methodism, promoted instincts of industriousness, self-discipline, and thrift conducive to the accumulation of wealth and the pursuit of business success has a long history. Its roots lie in the scholarship of the early twentieth-century German sociologist Max Weber, whose arguments were refined but also reinforced by the English Christian socialist R. H. Tawney, writing in the 1920s. Their influence has significantly declined in academic circles, but the theories that have helped to make Weber and Tawney household names continue to percolate more widely. They find expression in a phrase still in everyday use, 'the Protestant work ethic'. Carrying with it connotations of frugality, self-denial, and a dogged commitment to labour above leisure and pleasure, it remains part of a popular stereotype of the puritanical lifestyle that began to be formulated in the sixteenth century itself.

At the heart of this idea lies the psychological anxiety engendered by the Calvinist doctrine of predestination: the forbidding notion that only a tiny remnant of humanity chosen by God would be saved and that nothing an individual did could make any difference to his or her fate in the afterlife. The good works by which medieval Catholics had been taught they could earn merit in the eyes of the Almighty and secure themselves a safe berth in Heaven were rendered completely irrelevant in this regard. Nevertheless, as reformed Protestantism progressed into its second generation, its disciples increasingly sought assurance that they numbered among the elect. According to Weber, they found this external proof of divine approbation in their worldly prosperity. The search for signs that one was in a state of grace transformed monetary and material gain into a measure of spiritual health and made hard work the mechanism by which this connection was cemented. The emphasis placed upon the duty of following one's allotted calling or vocation in sermons and devotional literature was another important component. By contrast with medieval Catholicism, which privileged monastic retreat from this world as the best method of attaining everlasting happiness in the next, the Protestant faith promoted active engagement in earthly affairs. Diligent devotion to one's occupational duties was conceptualized as a demonstration of religious dedication. In some sense, the Reformation sanctified the conscientious labour of the laity as a type of worship itself.

Claims of this kind have helped to supply an explanation for why the Protestant nonconformists and dissenters of seventeenth- and eighteenth-century England acquired a reputation as sober and industrious sorts of people and enjoyed such success in the various commercial and manufacturing enterprises in which they engaged. Famous chocolate-making Quaker families such as the Rowntrees and Cadburys and the Huguenot clothworkers who congregated in Spitalfields have been seen as emblems of this entrepreneurial spirit. It has also been reinforced by anecdotes about godly artisans who read their bibles while they sat over their looms and arose early to attend sermons before they set to work, like the London turner Nehemiah Wallington, who recorded his daily routines in a series of voluminous notebooks. The same assumptions have been invoked to account for the contrasting economic fortunes of early modern European countries: the prosperity of England and the Netherlands, and their increasing prominence in finance and trade, is pitted against the steady stagnation and decline of Italy during the same period. They are a strand in the not entirely positive image of long, lazy afternoon siestas that continues to cling to Mediterranean cultures. And they continue to underpin commentary about the origins of the United States as a bastion of wealth and capitalist values.

The causal links between Protestantism and economic success upon which such observations and interpretations rest are difficult to substantiate and have been much contested. There are many other reasons for these patterns of development, which have little direct connection with the religious movements of the sixteenth and seventeenth centuries, let alone clear theological origins. The shift of the focus of mercantile activity and entrepreneurial innovation from the Mediterranean to the north-west of the European continent is probably more a consequence of the disruptive wars that engulfed the Italian peninsula and the challenge presented by the rise of the Ottoman Turks as a major political power in the region. If dissenters poured their energies into business, this was less a subconscious effect of their doctrinal convictions than a direct consequence of their marginalization from public life and civic office. Meanwhile, the religiosity of the many merchants and skilled tradesmen who migrated to escape persecution in the sixteenth and seventeenth centuries may have been a product rather than a cause of their decision to flee: the experience of exile fostered a sense of affinity with the exodus of the Old Testament Israelites that intensified their commitment to the Protestant faith.

Nor is it legitimate to regard the Reformation as one of the founts of the aggressive and selfish individualism which Karl Marx regarded as integral to the capitalist ethos. Early modern Calvinism in particular was communal in orientation and character: it placed great emphasis on the relationship between God and the corporate body of true believers. Theologically speaking, it enjoined individuals to subordinate their own interests to the collective welfare of the Church and commonwealth. It also reinforced an older undercurrent of criticism of the immorality of those who grew rich at the expense of their poorer neighbours: rack-renting landlords, rogue traders, and usurers. Covetousness was a sin which Protestant preachers and pamphleteers continued to denounce with vehemence in sermons and treatises, a measure of the discomfort they felt at changes that had deeper sources and broader structural causes. This was one of the ways in which the Reformations helped to shape the economic culture of early modern society, a society in which the exchange of money and goods was never a purely secular affair. They were one of the elements that helped to ensure that economic relations in the sixteenth and seventeenth centuries retained a strongly ethical dimension.

They also contributed to a reorientation of attitudes towards poverty and its relief. The notion that poverty was a consequence of idleness and a moral blight had ancient roots and was reinforced by humanism, but the Reformations crystallized sharper distinctions between the deserving and undeserving poor, between those unwilling to work and those who were incapacitated from doing so by illness or other circumstances beyond their control. Protestantism dispelled the aura of holiness that surrounded the voluntary asceticism of the mendicant friars and redefined it as a form of vagabondage. There was also a bifurcation of the ways in which the indigent were treated. In Catholic Europe the Church and its associated agencies remained the chief agent for dispensing charity and medical care; in Protestant Europe social welfare was more emphatically secularized and civic authorities took greater control of its provision and distribution. Alms-giving and philanthropy lost their instrumentality as a virtuous work through which one could win divine favour and became instead an external manifestation of the saving grace God had freely bestowed upon the truly faithful. Theological and ecclesiastical change reconfigured the circumstances in which people displayed human compassion and the institutional forms which it took.

It also left a mark on consumer behaviour. Renaissance Europe's burgeoning market for material possessions cannot be abstracted from the religious events that were occurring at the same time. The acquisitiveness of the Dutch at every social level coexisted with a certain embarrassment at their riches which owed more than a little to the moral strictures of Calvinist ministers. Their homes were filled with furniture, pictures, and other decorative objects; they invested in speculative schemes and participated in state lotteries; and some lavished large sums on tulip bulbs, driving their prices to inordinate heights. No more than Catholicism did Protestantism reject the purchase and display of luxury goods, but it did stress the importance of utilizing them with moderation and with the edification of one's neighbours in mind. Wealth brought with it the capacity to exercise choice and with choice came certain moral dilemmas. We cannot understand what historians now describe as the 'industrious revolution'—the increasing desire of households to acquire non-essential items—without reference to the religious environments in which it developed and by which it was coloured. Protestant and Catholic piety alike fuelled the growth of consumerism in this period and shaped the way in which these impulses found expression in everyday life.

One aspect of this is the process by which clothing became not merely a badge of social status but also a marker of moral rectitude and confessional identity. The restrained and 'plain' style of dress of the English Puritans and Quakers reflected the conviction that their outward apparel should match the simplicity for which they strove in spirit. Sartorial ostentation was a manifestation of pride. It scandalized observers, could be a source of sexual temptation, and turned people themselves into idols. These were the arguments raised in the flurry of tracts that flowed from the pens of fervent Protestants denouncing the monstrous neck ruffs donned by so many of their contemporaries. In turn, the black coats and gowns in which they attired themselves became the subject of mockery. Shakespeare encapsulated the resentment generated by these preferences in the figure of Malvolio in *Twelfth Night*, whose yellow stockings exposed him as a hypocrite and made him a laughing stock. By the mid-seventeenth century, the long curly locks fashionable at court became an identifying feature of the cavaliers, while the pudding basin haircuts of parliamentarians earned them the epithet 'Roundheads'. When Sir William Temple, ambassador to The Hague, wrote his observations on the Netherlands in the 1660s, he favourably compared the sober dress of the Calvinist elite of Amsterdam with the extravagant fashions of the French aristocracy in Paris.

Catholics too, quite literally wore their confessional colours on their sleeves. The crucifixes and rosary beads they carried about their persons were symbols of their commitment to a religion that their enemies denounced as a system of superstition. In contexts where the Church of Rome was prohibited, wearing jewellery of this kind amounted to a gesture of overt defiance and a deliberate flirtation with danger. And if belief and piety were woven into the very fabric in which people wrapped their bodies, it also helped to inculcate characteristic modes of conduct. The assiduous tidiness for which Dutch housewives became renowned was one expression of the precept that cleanliness accompanied godliness. Keeping one's house swept free of dust was akin to keeping one's heart free of the detritus of sin. While other factors independently fostered these tendencies, post-Reformation religion converged with fresh emphasis on good manners and civility to cultivate habits of this kind. Even that most basic of human activities, sleep, was no longer confessionally neutral: the manner in which people retired to and arose from bed, the prayers they said, and the devotions they practised there also became self-conscious markers of their religious and denominational identity.

THE QUAKERS' MEETING, English print of c.1640–80. The sober and plain style dress adopted by the Society of Friends soon became the subject of the satire of hostile and bemused observers. Dress was a badge of spiritual and confessional identity.

There were other ways in which the advent of the Reformations altered the routine and rhythm of people's everyday lives. One was the radical pruning of the liturgical calendar of saints' days which was a feature of Protestant reform everywhere it took root. Henry VIII and his political advisers axed no fewer than forty-nine in one fell swoop in 1536, while a synod of the Reformed Church in the Netherlands got rid of all traditional Catholic holidays, including Christmas, in 1574, though this met with such resistance that it was forced to reinstate six. The anniversary of the Saviour's nativity was a victim of Puritan rule in England in 1644, but once again its abolition proved short-lived and it was officially restored, to much popular rejoicing, at the Restoration in 1660. The reduction in the number of days for which people were

SABBATH-BREAKERS,

In their unlavvful Sports, Collected out of several Divine Subjects,
VIZ

Mr. H. B. Mr. Beard, and the Practice of Piety: A fit Monument for our present Times, &c.

Remember that thou keep holy Sabbath day.

A Woman and her two Daughters, pull and dry flax on the Lord's day, are all Burnt.

A Miller's House, and Mill Burnt, &c.

London, Printed for T. C. and sold by William Miller, at the Sign of the Gilded Acorn in St. Paul's Church-Yard, near the Little North Door, 1671.

DIVINE EXAMPLES OF GOD'S SEVERE JUDGEMENTS UPON SABBATH BREAKERS (1671). Protestantism powerfully reinforced the biblical precept that the sabbath day should be kept holy. Gory stories of the terrible punishments that befell those who worked or played on Sunday circulated widely, and in the late seventeenth century were encapsulated in graphic images. Here, the penalties meted out to modern sabbath breakers are combined with an image of the stoning of sabbath breakers in the Old Testament.

dispensed from labour was also a feature of Catholic reform in Europe: in 1642 Pope Urban VIII issued a bull which trimmed the list of holy days to thirty-two. These developments not only expanded the scope of the working year, they also focused more attention on Sunday as a weekly day of rest. For Protestants, the profanation of the Sabbath by the obligations of one's ordinary employment was insupportable, a contravention of the fourth commandment and the Mosaic law, which they insisted remained firmly in force. The lingering influence of sabbatarianism prevented shops from opening in some countries until the late twentieth century. It also affected attitudes towards the playing of sport, which certain reformed communities regarded as an equally heinous crime against the Decalogue. The film *Chariots of Fire* tells the story of one Scottish Presbyterian who refused to compromise his conscientious convictions and run a race at the 1924 Paris Olympics on a Sunday.

More generally, both Reformations sought to regulate more closely the ways in which people spent the hours in which they were not engaged in work or attending liturgical services. These movements converged with wider concerns about social disorder to promote measures to restrain recreational pursuits and seasonal festivities which posed a threat to the stability of communities and were regarded as residues of pagan superstition. Rowdy games were the target of complaint when they led to unseemly scuffles and physical injury. Protestant moralists deplored the hours which the poorer sort spent in taverns, alehouses, and bowling alleys wasting money that they should have used to support their families. Tirades against these 'nests of vice' and the culture of idleness and drunkenness that clustered around them were commonplace, and preachers joined forces with civil officials in efforts to correct such abuses. Traditional drama and the commercialized theatre also came under the attack of English Puritans, who called for the prohibition of play-acting as a type of idolatrous duplicity. Traditional pastimes such as May games, which preachers condemned as remnants of pre-Christian fertility rites, were another focal point of godly hostility: in Banbury, Oxfordshire, for instance, the chopping down of the town's maypole in the 1580s was a source of acrimonious controversy, while others were casualties of the Puritan revolution of the 1640s. A few years earlier, in 1579, a council in Milan forbade similar ceremonies as heathen, and the fires conventionally lit on the feast of the nativity of St John the Baptist were the subject of denunciation by the French Catholic bishop Jacques-Bénigne Bossuet in 1665. Especially in Protestant regions, the language employed to announce and justify many such reforming initiatives was often providential and scriptural: they were seen as a necessary mechanism for appeasing the wrath of a God who would not tolerate transgressions of his commandments and who would send down punishments in the guise of natural disasters like plagues and fires.

These efforts to reform the contemporary culture of leisure reflected a growth of concern about morality that was a further by-product of the sixteenth- and seventeenth-century movements for religious renewal. As they progressed into their second and later generations, both Protestantism and Tridentine Catholicism became increasingly preoccupied with stamping out individual sin and especially forms of sexual deviance. They competed with each other in the realm of moral rigour. Intimate activities that had hitherto been popularly regarded as legitimate after espousal but prior to marriage were re-branded as fornication, their perpetrators subjected to humiliating penances by Calvinist consistories, Anglican church courts, and the Spanish and Roman Inquisitions. Over time, shame and re-education helped to persuade many people that pre-marital sex was a serious offence; in some places rates of illegitimacy fell in response, though other factors also contributed to this dip. Adultery and sodomy were likewise the targets of greater interference and legal activity, including efforts to revive the Mosaic code of law and introduce the death penalty for having intercourse with someone other than one's spouse. Pope Sixtus V endeavoured to push this through in Rome in 1586 unsuccessfully; a small but not insignificant number were executed in Geneva and Scotland for this offence; and in 1650 a statute to this effect was passed by the English Interregnum parliament, though it was more symbolic than functional. Prostitution was another obvious target for prosecution and the post-Reformation period coincided with fresh efforts to repress, or at least more tightly regulate, brothels in cities such as Augsburg and Venice. Contemporaries termed these initiatives and measures the 'Reformation of Manners'. While it is intractably difficult to measure their cultural effects, they did represent a major attempt to narrow the boundaries of acceptable behaviour in the sphere of love. They helped to make the family and household a space into which the Church and state claimed the right to intrude, and they contributed to altering the climate in which people gave expression to their deepest and most private desires.

Material Cultures and Environments

The processes of cultural differentiation and confessional identity formation catalysed by the Protestant and Catholic Reformations also left a lasting and visible imprint on the physical landscape and built environment of Europe and those parts of the world to which they spread their influence in the course of the sixteenth and seventeenth centuries.

The objective of the waves of iconoclasm that accompanied both the earliest and some later phases of Protestant reform was to destroy potent symbols of Catholic error and to efface the memory of popery forever. Churches that were the target of such onslaughts bore enduring scars in the form of defaced images, woodwork screens, and bench-ends, empty niches, and damaged statues and tombs. Figures from which hands and limbs have been lopped off and eyes scratched out bear compelling witness to the anger and zeal of those who carried out these rites of violence and the passionate abhorrence of idolatry that underpinned their actions. The bare whitewashed walls of public places for Calvinist worship in the Netherlands, Switzerland, and Scotland, sometimes adorned with texts from scripture, contrast with the iconographical schemes of Lutheran churches in Germany and Scandinavia, where much traditional imagery was allowed to remain *in situ*—their interiors were a palpable reminder to passing travellers of the differences of opinion on the critical issue of idolatry that fomented friction and division at the heart of the Reformation itself. In turn, the very design of the new churches that reformed communities constructed to serve their needs testified to doctrinal priorities that differed decisively from those of the Church of Rome. Houses for services centring around the sermon rather than the miracle of transubstantiation, some French and Dutch churches employed an octagonal shape with rows of galleries facing the pulpit to reflect the primacy accorded to preaching. Beyond ecclesiastical precincts, Protestant landscapes were distinctive in other ways: they were often littered with the shells of abandoned and half-demolished monasteries, the stumps of standing and wayside crosses, and the crumbling vestiges of derelict shrines. As the centuries passed, many of these were eroded by weather, overgrown with foliage, or looted for re-use as building material.

The sight of structures that had suffered at the hands of iconoclasts evoked a variety of different emotions in the centuries following the Reformation. For some they were memorials and monuments to the triumph of the gospel over superstition and idolatry which prompted feelings of pride. For Catholics, they were evidence of heretical excess, victims of a kind of architectural martyrdom, and sites that became a rallying point for resistance. In Ireland, the complex of caves and stations on the holy island known as St Patrick's Purgatory in Lough Derg in County Donegal was repeatedly destroyed by the authorities and repeatedly rebuilt by the faithful in defiance. In south-western Germany, statues and shrines attacked by Swedish soldiers during the Thirty Years War became the object of fresh veneration: the life-sized crucifix with a bullet hole in Jesus' head at Geisingen was a major regional shrine by the 1730s. 'Popish' people in the Netherlands and Britain persisted in visiting, praying, and performing time-honoured rituals at former pilgrimage chapels for many decades, provoking further Protestant irritation. Over time, however, a different set of attitudes evolved in some reformed circles: regret and embarrassment about the fanaticism of their forebears, one consequence of which was a surge of concern about sacrilege—the sacrilege committed by those who had purchased lands and buildings once conse-crated to religious purposes and turned them to profane and secular uses. The lurid stories of ghostly hauntings and of the grim misfortunes that befell the current possessors of monastic estates which circulated in later seventeenth-century England attest to escalating anxiety that acts of purification carried out by previous generations had drawn the curse of God down upon their heirs. The nostalgia for the lost medieval past that often accompanied this found expression in vigorous historical activity. Antiquaries such as William Dugdale laboured to preserve records of the country's architectural heritage for posterity: the finely engraved plates of abbeys, priories, and collegiate churches in his three-volume *Monasticon Anglicanum* (1655–73) are emblematic of a gradual reorientation of attitudes towards the pre-Reformation Church. Ecclesiastical buildings erected before the break with Rome ceased to be regarded as terrible eyesores and became a source of aesthetic and sentimental pleasure. Incorporated by the gentry and nobility into their private parks as garden features, their ivy-clad ruins were seen as romantic and picturesque.

JOSEPH MALLORD WILLIAM TURNER, *Tintern Abbey, west front*, *c.*1794. Captured in atmospheric prints and paintings, by the eighteenth century the ruins of medieval monasteries dissolved in the 1530s, such as Tintern Abbey, were the subject of a kind of cult. The modern British tourist industry continues to benefit from lingering fascination with the melancholy sight of these 'bare ruined choirs'.

Protestantism also engendered a landscape of memory of its own: one centred on locations associated with its founders and martyrs. In Germany, places associated with Martin Luther, such as the Augustinian monastery in Wittenberg and the house in Eisleben where he was born, became the destination of a form of pilgrimage within a century of the great reformer's death. In England, memorials were erected to the men and women who were victims of the fires of the 1550s, a project revived and continued by the Victorians, whose monument to the bishops Latimer, Ridley, and Cranmer burned there remains a feature of central Oxford.

As Protestant visitors observed in their travel journals and diaries, the landscapes created by the Catholic Church and Counter-Reformation were conspicuously different. They were embellished with visible symbols of this resurgent faith—the grand Gothic cathedrals and churches constructed in the late Middle Ages which towered above the skylines of European towns and cities were complemented by the products of an ebullient baroque piety. Over the course of the sixteenth century, Rome was lavishly remodelled as a Renaissance capital, with St Peter's basilica and the Capitoline hill as its centrepiece. Elsewhere, the renewed confidence of the Church of Rome manifested itself in new building and refurbishment projects, which encapsulated its religious values in fabric and stone. The more than thirty churches erected and renovated by the Jesuits in Germany between 1570 and 1648 were the settings of sensuous worship: their artistic schemes sought to stimulate the emotions and senses of their congregations and facilitate their spiritual development to a higher state of intellectual comprehension. Early modern Catholicism also left a powerful mark on the topography of France and Spain. Mont Valerian, the spectacular array of tableaux and chapels constructed on a hillside just west of Paris, was a kind of religious theme park for the pious: a place where they could vicariously experience the Passion of Christ at Calvary in a series of stages. Three-dimensional replica Jerusalems were particularly fashionable in the Iberian peninsula and sprang up in significant numbers in the sixteenth century. Reflecting and projecting the perception that Spain was a kind of second Palestine, inhabited by a chosen people, they were a vehicle for a powerful narrative of national exceptionalism. Across Catholic Europe, the revival of pilgrimage after a short interval of humanist caution further contributed to the saturation of the landscape with loci of holiness. Famous shrines like Altötting and the Holy House of Loreto were only one element in a burgeoning sacred geography that included large wayside crosses and images of the Madonna and child built into street corners and on the walls of houses. Prompts to instinctive devotional gestures like genuflection, their continuing presence is a measure of how far Catholicism has managed to engrave itself upon the material world.

This is also true of its mission fields overseas, particularly Latin America, where the Christianity imported by priests and conquistadors has made a significant mark on the physical environment in the guise of churches, open air crucifixes, and pilgrimage sites such as Our Lady of Guadalupe. Incorporating motifs and themes from indigenous systems of belief, these epitomize the processes of mutual acculturation and syncretism that characterized early modern Catholicism as a global religion. Even urban planning

IN LATE SEVENTEENTH-CENTURY PRAGUE, the Charles Bridge was transformed from a commercial thoroughfare into a devotional route: lined with statues of Counter-Reformation saints and heroes such as St John Nepomuk and adorned with iconography that slighted Catholicism's triad of enemies, Muslims, Jews, and Protestants, it conveyed an aggressive confessional message to those who used it to cross the river.

reflects the convictions that underpinned colonial activities: the ground plans of the new settlements (or *reducciónes*) were modelled on St Augustine's City of God and embodied an attempt to create order and civilization out of the diabolical chaos that prevailed in this dark continent. In a comparable way, the Puritan settlers of New England set out to create a new Jerusalem quite literally, devising and constructing towns like New Haven in Connecticut in accordance with the blueprint for a holy city laid down in the Bible. The evangelical movements of the sixteenth and seventeenth century have thus helped to shape the surroundings in which, to this day, people live their lives.

This is also true of the domestic spaces they owned or occupied, where they slept, ate, worked, and ultimately died. Catholic homes were characterized by an

SHRINE TO THE VIRGIN MARY ON A
WALL IN MONTEPULCIANO, Tuscany.
The distinctive character of Catholic
devotion has left a conspicuous mark
on the streetscapes of Italy. The local
shrines to the Virgin and saints erected
in the early modern period in urban and
rural locations evoked pious gestures
from those who passed them. They also
prompted derogatory comments from
Protestant visitors, who saw them as
relics of popish superstition and
idolatry.

accumulation of religious objects—statues and images of the Crucifixion, Holy Family, and other scenes from the life of Christ, miniature triptychs, and portable items like rosaries and medallions of the *agnus dei* (lamb of God) that supported private devotion and supplied a form of sacred protection. Another index of how piety fuelled the emergent culture of conspicuous consumption, they proliferated in late Renaissance and Tridentine Italy, filling the chambers not merely of wealthy villas, but also those in more humble artisan dwellings. The same was true of Habsburg-ruled lands of the Southern Netherlands, where high levels of disposable income generated a similar thirst for devotional accessories, together with a mass market for art—as inventories of the furniture and possessions of the citizens of Antwerp and other cities reflect. In post-Reformation England, the discovery of such religious paraphernalia in the houses of recusants was incriminating evidence of their adherence to a false and prohibited religion. The authorities repeatedly confiscated this imported merchandise as popish 'trumpery' and 'trash', and sometimes burnt it on public bonfires of vanities.

It has often been supposed that Protestant homes, by contrast, were bereft not merely of religious icons, but of any kind of imagery at all. The stern warnings of the reformers about the dangers of idolatry and the intolerable sin of depicting God in human form have fed the impression that societies that embraced the Reformation were starved of pictorial stimulation and suffered from a severe form of 'visual anorexia'. It is increasingly clear that this is a distorting fallacy. Lutheranism was by no means hostile to artistic representation in either ecclesiastical or secular settings. Nor did Calvin and his disciples ban iconography in and of itself: they certainly regarded traditional images in churches as unacceptable, but they admitted that they could legitimately be set up in other places and spaces for the sake of memory and moral instruction. The themes of the art of the Dutch Golden Age reflect the influence of this theological climate. Avoiding subjects tainted by association with popery, printmakers and painters turned to the genres of landscape and still life, to depictions of mundane activities within domestic interiors, and to favourite episodes from the Old Testament such as Jonah and the whale and Abraham and the sacrifice of Isaac. In the British Isles, biblical imagery was also an omnipresent feature of the decorative schemes of godly households in the late sixteenth and seventeenth centuries. Mantelpieces, firebacks, wood panels, tapestries, and cushion covers all became the canvases upon which scriptural stories, together with exhortatory verses, were represented for the edification of their members. Others echoed and mimicked the emblematic title pages of popular works of practical divinity. Where Catholic piety required sustained meditation on devotional images, Protestant 'art' was designed to resist prolonged viewing, since this might lead one down the slippery slope to idolatry. One of the more subtle legacies of the Reformation may have been a divergence in ways of seeing and habits of vision.

Vessels, platters, jugs, and pots also became badges of Protestant identity and media for conveying moralistic messages. Decorated with familiar biblical and historic images, or with admonitory verses such as 'FEARE GOD HONOR GOD' and 'WHEN YOU SEE THIS REMEMBER ME. OBEAY GODS WOURD', these too were props for reformed piety and mnemonic devices. The very crockery from which people ate and drank gave expression to their religious allegiance. So too did their books. The commonplace that Protestantism forged an exclusive alliance with the printing press has now been exposed as yet another myth rooted in confessional polemic, together with the notion that it was overwhelmingly reliant upon reading. Nevertheless, it did stimulate literacy and engender a distinctive culture of the book, which revolved, above all, around the written Word of God. Together with prayer books, sermons, and tracts, bibles could be found in the halls, libraries, kitchens, and

CEILING PLASTERWORK, THE BUTTERWALK, DARTMOUTH, DEVON, c.1635. The presence of pictures such as the Tree of Jesse upon plaster ceilings was intended to remind people that they were constantly being watched by the all-seeing eye of an exacting but also benevolent deity and to reinforce the values of Protestant patriarchy.

closets of committed Protestants. The enemies of English Puritans mocked as show-offs those who left them in open windows and self-consciously turned their pages as they sat in church, but there can be little doubt that books played a critical part in post-Reformation piety. Women and girls lovingly stitched embroidered bindings to cover them and they were given as gifts and passed down to younger family members as precious heirlooms. Containing the autographs of Luther and Melanchthon, and covered with leather tooled with their portraits, others became in some sense relics of the reformers themselves. Like the portraits of Luther that miraculously survived devastating fires, some of these objects displayed incombustible and prophylactic qualities. Laid by the bedsides of the sick, they were sometimes credited with cures; carried by soldiers into battle, they were said to have repelled showers of bullets.

Despite the claims of its Protestant adversaries to their contrary, early modern Catholicism was not inherently hostile to the new technology of print, and it readily embraced the opportunities created by its invention to assist its programme of religious renewal. Jesuits and the members of other new and reinvigorated religious orders were

ENGLISH EMBROIDERED BOOK-BINDING WORKED BY ELIZABETH ILLINGWORTH, 1613, showing Jonah and the whale and Abraham and the sacrifice of Isaac. The material culture of the Protestant home reflected the deep diffusion of biblical knowledge across reformed societies. Bound in covers embroidered by women and girls, books were transformed from aids to devotion into precious personal objects and artefacts.

in the vanguard here and the many devotional texts that flowed from their pens in the sixteenth, seventeenth, and eighteenth centuries made some Protestants worry that they were in danger of being outdone by their enemies in the sphere of spiritual instruction. These books too could acquire a reputation for working thaumaturgic wonders: reports of miracles worked by copies of the Spiritual Exercises of Ignatius Loyola, as well as by specimens of his signature, for instance, were a regular feature of the Annual Letters compiled for circulation within the Society of Jesus. And where the Church of Rome was proscribed and persecuted, Catholics quickly recognized that books could function as surrogate and silent preachers. They could travel into regions where harsh penal laws made missionary priests fear to tread and provide laypeople with religious sustenance that compensated for restricted access to the sacraments.

The Reformations thus created a series of parallel textual communities, just as they engendered competing visual and material cultures. These reflected the ways in which faith and belief became a self-conscious component of individual and collective identity and decisively shaped how people lived their day-to-day lives.

Disenchantment, Science, and Enlightenment

Finally, we must consider the disputed connections between the Reformations and the processes historians have called the Scientific Revolution, the Enlightenment, and the 'disenchantment of the world'. To what extent and in what respects were these religious movements implicated in long-term transformations in our understanding of the workings of the universe and the role of God and the Devil in earthly affairs?

We may begin by registering the fact that Protestantism has conventionally been accorded a starring role in these processes, which are themselves integrally linked with theories about the origins of modernity. It has been credited with playing a notable part in eliminating 'magic' from belief and practice, with catalysing a more 'rational' analysis of nature, and with laying the foundations for key transformations in science. Once again, these claims have been challenged by research undertaken over the last few decades. The picture that now appears before us is very much more complex than previous scholarship implied.

The theology of the Protestant reformers, especially Zwingli and Calvin, was certainly powerfully corrosive of some fundamental assumptions about the nexus between the divine and temporal realms. It challenged a number of ingrained ideas about how the sacred functioned and manifested itself in the human and natural world. Developing and strengthening intellectual and philosophical tendencies that pre-dated the Reformation, it denied that material objects could be conduits and receptacles of holy power and that liturgical rituals could bring about mysterious or metabolic alterations of either spirit or substance. Reformed Protestantism's insistence that images were merely representations, and its repudiation of transubstantiation and redefinition of the Eucharist as a memorial or sign, struck at the heart of Catholic piety. It curtailed the cult of saints and relics and declared emphatically that miracles had ceased after the Church had cast off its infant swaddling bands. The wonders allegedly performed by famous statues and crucifixes were either diabolical illusions or evidence of human fakery and fraud. Purgatory was dismissed as another clerical fiction and invented tradition, designed to pull the wool over the eyes of the unwary laity and fill ecclesiastical coffers. Accusing the papacy and priesthood of deceiving the populace and encouraging credulity, Protestants presented themselves as the agents of a vigorous assault upon 'superstition' and embraced the language of liberation and enlightenment to describe the effects of their endeavours. Their own self-congratulatory rhetoric has intensified the impression that the Reformation marked a decisive juncture in the desacralization and secularization of European society.

It would be quite wrong to deny that the religious upheavals of the sixteenth and seventeenth centuries unsettled and destabilized the foundations upon which the medieval economy of the sacred rested. Those who witnessed ceremonies in which hallowed images were exposed as mere blocks of wood and stone, or relics of the blood of Christ were revealed to be milk coloured by red dye or saffron, had first-hand experience of the demystification of objects that they had hitherto revered. Allegations of pious forgery were not new in themselves; the difference was that in the wake of the Reformation they became entangled with claims about the authenticity and integrity of opposing churches and the political regimes with which they were affiliated. The result, in some circles, was probably a greater propensity for scepticism about all manifestations of celestial intervention.

Yet in other ways, the advent of Protestantism served to buttress existing beliefs about the supernatural. Some recent commentators have even suggested that it led to a 'super-enchantment' of the world, which lasted until 1650. First, it rode upon the back of eschatological anxiety about the end of the world, which in turn it served to heighten, at least in the short term. The mood of Luther and the early reformers was fraught with a mixture of fear about the impending Apocalypse and hope for the long awaited Millennium, when Jesus would return and oversee a thousand years of harmony and peace. This was intimately linked with a vision of history that saw the truth engaged in a cosmic struggle with falsehood, into which the Reformation became firmly integrated. Reformers identified the Church of Rome with the beast of Babylon described in the book of Revelation and found a template in scripture for their own daring challenge to the evil machinations of Antichrist. This fostered increased sensitivity to the tell-tale signs in nature that the last days were nigh and a growing preoccupation with enumerating portents and unravelling their religious significance and meaning. In mid- and late sixteenth-century Germany, learned writers like Conrad Lycosthenes, Job Fincelius, and others obsessively collected and recorded prodigies such as monstrous births, comets, peculiar optical illusions, beached whales, strange fish, and aberrant vegetables and fruit, which were also the subject of ephemeral broadsheets which still survive in large numbers. This was a pan-Protestant phenomenon: in France the same enterprise was taken up by the Huguenot minister Simon Goulart, while in England and the Netherlands ballads, pamphlets, and tracts likewise gathered evidence that doomsday was imminent.

This was an atmosphere in which Catholics themselves were caught up, and which their escalating clashes with Protestantism played their own part in exacerbating. Early sixteenth-century Italy was awash with prophecies of the end time and reports of apparitions and deformed births, and these were readily harnessed to the cause of attacking Lutheranism in the 1520s. The production of monsters in nature was seen as a microcosm of the human disorder wrought by the re-emergence of heresy. Similar sentiments and strategies flourished in the context of the French Wars of Religion, when the Catholic league and its propagandists tapped into the deep vein of apocalyptic feeling that ran through this society and derived from it inspiration for radical acts of violence against the monarch and his Reformed subjects. In Spain, they underpinned the messianic pretensions of Philip II, who regarded himself as an instrument of God to avenge the damage to Christendom caused by Protestantism.

Ein tröstliches vnd wunderbarliches Gewechs das warhafftig vor augen ist / das vns Gott Der Allmechtig inn disem geferlichen zeyten hat sehen lassen damit das wir sollen getröst sein vnd seyner güte warten / der die seynen nit will verlassen die zu im ruffen tag vnd nacht mit glaubigen Hertzen.

IN disem 1 5 5 3. Jar / Jitzu nechst bey Nürnberg inn einen Dorff hayst zu dem Thon / eynen Bawern hayst der Höfler / inn seinem Acker / auff einem stengel / 16. Heupteley Weyß Kraut gewachssen / vn yedes sonderbar fein zusam geschlossen / vnd das alles inn der gröss vnd form / wie dise Figur auffweyst / Das haben etlich hundert menschen warhafftig wachsent vn abgeschnitten gesehen / ob Got will / ein gut fruchtbar Jar anzeygent.

Gedruckt zu Nürnberg / durch Steffan Hamer Brieffmaler.

The struggles of his deputies to repress the Dutch rebels in the Netherlands and his ill-fated attempt to launch a naval invasion of England in 1588 must be seen in this context.

The theology of the reformers also placed renewed emphasis on the omnipotence and providence of God, whose busy interference in the world became an article of Protestant belief. Calvinists saw his hand in the smallest of incidents—in the chance fall of a branch from a tree, in the spider that crawled into a porridge bowl, and in the

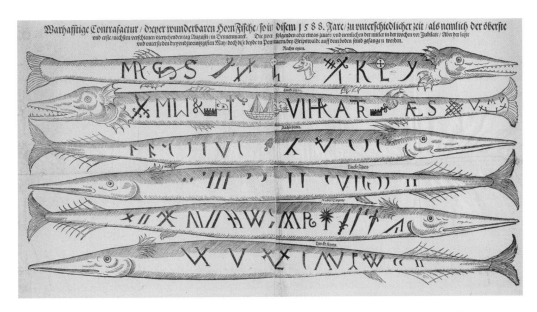

BROADSHEETS REPORTING a curious cabbage found near Nuremberg in 1553 and wondrous fish caught off the coast of Denmark and found on land in Pomerania in 1588. Protestant ministers and scholars across Europe were fascinated by prodigies of nature, which they carefully scrutinized as evidence of the impending apocalypse and read as a series of divine messages sent from heaven. Similar sentiments circulated in Catholic countries and stories of celestial, vegetable, and medical portents spread widely across national and confessional borders.

minor ailments that afflicted their children and themselves. They read them as a kind of Morse code, through which they could decipher clues about their spiritual status in relation to predestination, and by which they were alternately chastized, schooled, and comforted. Calamities and catastrophes on a grander scale were likewise interpreted as the 'extraordinary preachers' and 'visible sermons' sent by the deity when people failed to heed ordained ministers. Worry abounded in many Protestant communities that these were presages of much greater judgements to come.

The unprecedented wave of accusations of and trials for witchcraft had multiple causes, yet religious division and conflict was the backdrop against which perhaps as many as 100,000 people across the Continent (the majority of them women) were put to death in the period between 1500 and 1750. The Reformations served in various respects to catalyse the campaign to eradicate practitioners of black magic and servants of Satan. They helped to attune contemporaries to the hyperactivity of the Devil and his agents as the end drew nigh and the preoccupation with idolatry and heresy they fostered assisted in redefining witchcraft as a crime of spiritual apostasy rather than just physical assault or sorcery—in short, as a kind of Devil worship. Some Protestants equated Catholicism directly with witchcraft. The biblical fundamentalism which became a keynote of the age invested the text of Exodus 22: 18, 'Thou shall not suffer a witch to live', with enhanced importance and provided a mandate for decisive action. This influenced the context in which allegations about acts of malicious magic were made and in which magistrates and clergymen investigated and prosecuted their perpetrators, whether individually or, during epidemics of panic, collectively. Religious zeal was an ingredient in the so-called witch-craze on both sides of the Reformation divide, and contributed to its regional variations and patterns. It also helps to account for the proliferation of cases of diabolical possession that occurred in the wake of the religious upheavals of the period. Both confessions developed distinctive rites of exorcism to eject unclean spirits from the victims of bodily assault by Satan and his minions. Disturbed children and teenagers brought up in pious Protestant households were released from their torments by marathon sessions of fasting and prayer, while Catholics made use of the spiritual power associated with relics and the sacraments. The phenomenon flourished particularly in enclosed convents: the ecstasies of nuns were often suspected by their confessors to derive from the Devil rather than from divine revelation.

At the same time, the turn inwards to scrutinize one's conscience which was a hallmark of Protestant and Catholic piety alike undercut the impulse to seek external scapegoats for the domestic troubles that were blamed on witches. People were encouraged to find the real source of divine wrath in their sins, to regard sorcerers simply as the Lord's instruments to punish them, and to repent rather than initiate legal proceedings. The pastoral thrust of reformed demonological treatises counteracted the forces that pulled in the direction of witch-hunting. It was not just Protestants like the English gentleman Reginald Scot, author of *The Discovery of Witchcraft* (1584), and the Dutch physician Johann Weyer who wrote against the prosecution of witches and declared that most of those tried and executed were merely misguided (if not mentally deluded) old crones. Jesuits such as Friedrich Spee were also strong opponents of a process that had a destructive momentum of its own. Based on his own experiences in Westphalia, his *Cautio Criminalis* (1631) stressed that the torture used to extract confessions from the accused often produced lies rather than truth. Why the heat behind the drive to punish and exterminate witches diminished in the late seventeenth and eighteenth centuries remains a source of puzzlement, but one element in the equation was overuse of witchcraft as a category of deviance. In mid-seventeenth-century England, for example, Quakers were often conflated with witches: their leader George Foxe was 'vehemently suspected to be a sorcerer' by mainstream Protestant ministers, and the tendency of the early Friends to meet in lonely isolated places raised the spectre of nocturnal gatherings to perform the sabbat. The utilization of demonological language to castigate other enemies and its entanglement in sectarian dispute helped to discredit it as an arbiter of truth and rendered it a weapon of party and faction. In respect of witchcraft, then, the Reformation was double-edged: it both fomented and fragmented the body of beliefs that led men and women to allege that their neighbours were disciples of the Devil and enemies of God and carried a substantial number of those convicted to death at the stake or on the gallows.

There are other reasons to question the suggestion that the Reformation was a landmark in the evacuation of supernatural forces and creatures from the world.

Despite the fact that the Protestant doctrine of death rendered the return of souls from the afterlife untenable, ghosts continued to appear, their presence accounted for by redefining them as demons in disguise. Fairies were similarly assimilated into a reformed theological framework and tolerated as a relatively harmless aspect of folk belief in Calvinist Scotland. Sightings of angels also persisted: in Lutheran Germany and Scandinavia hundreds of cases of humble individuals to whom celestial messengers appeared and charged them with conveying warnings of divine punishment to their communities have been excavated from archives and books. The merciful assistance rendered by invisible helpers was also the subject of many narratives incorporated into anthologies and catalogues of providences in seventeenth-century England and Holland, a reflection of the Calvinist precept that angels no longer took human form. Such stories and experiences attest to the conviction that God still sent heavenly intermediaries to guide, instruct, and govern his people. He also intervened more directly in the guise of miracles. Across Protestant Europe, the proclivity of people to perceive miracles—conventionally defined as events above, beyond, or against the forces of nature—seems to have increased the further the Reformation progressed into its later phases. The wariness of the first-generation reformers about the miraculous waned and their successors celebrated the Lord's intercessions to assist godly people and nations. Even the idea that English kings had the capacity to heal scrofula through the royal touch survived the theological turmoil of the mid-sixteenth century and became a critical component of the Stuart monarchy's attempt to augment its absolutist pretensions.

It is therefore hard to concur with the view that Protestantism was unable to rival the appeal of Catholicism in the sphere of the supernatural. Instead, it created an outlook and a culture that overlapped in many respects with that of the latter, but which also diverged from it in various ways. For its part, after the scandal and embarrassment caused by humanist and early Protestant polemic faded, the Church of Rome reasserted its credentials as a repository of divine power. Miracles associated with pilgrimage shrines flourished afresh; others were at the centre of the cults of new saints like Teresa of Avila and Francis Xavier, whose remains at Mechelen in modern-day Belgium were regularly visited by those hoping that he would intercede to aid them and eager to benefit from the associated indulgences. Recognizing the appetite of the laity for the sacred, in their missions in the Upper Palatinate in the 1720s the Jesuits distributed new sacramentals, including water consecrated by contact with the relics of Xavier and Ignatius. The Augustinians competed by handing out *tolentinobrot*—loaves blessed in the name of St Nicholas of Tolentino, which gave protection against a range of accidents and illnesses.

But, like Protestants, Catholics harboured doubts about the validity of cures and the rash of mystical visions that was a by-product of intense baroque piety. Hundreds of aspiring saints and self-styled holy women were hauled before the Inquisition and other tribunals after they claimed to have received revelations from Heaven, and many of them were denounced and publicly humiliated as charlatans and tricksters. The ecclesiastical authorities invoked the expertise of doctors to help them decide whether the revelations of these visionaries were real or just hallucinations, and they deployed techniques like autopsy to assist in the verification of the relics of those under consideration for canonization. The case of the thirteenth-century Augustinian nun Clare of Montefalco, whose heart was dissected and discovered to bear symbols of Christ's passion—a crucifix and scourge—is symptomatic of a tendency that became more widespread after the Council of Trent. It was not until 1737, some four centuries after her death, that she finally secured the crown of beatification. The search for signs of sanctity compelled the Church to embrace the insights and experimental practices of medical science, and necessitated an attitude of healthy and selective scepticism.

It is increasingly apparent that to situate religion and science as polar opposites is to subscribe to a conventional dichotomy that postdates the early modern period. We have unconsciously absorbed the post-Enlightenment assumption that the Scientific Revolution of the seventeenth century reflected the triumph of secular reasoning over religious devotion and dogma. But this obscures the more creative and intricate relationship that evolved between the theological and institutional revolutions of the period and the transformation of natural philosophy. In fact, religious conviction was an important stimulus to the investigation of nature, which contemporaries regarded as a second book of revelation complementary to scripture. The Lutheran reformer Philip Melanchthon was at the forefront of efforts to produce a new Christian synthesis of Aristotelian ideas about the universe, and he actively defended astrology as a tool for investigating God's mysterious purposes. Tracing the movements of planets and stars was a legitimate method of uncovering his intentions for mankind, as well as revealing the glory of his creation. By exploring secondary causes one could come to know more fully the first cause of all things, the world's Creator and Lord. Astronomy was, in short, a form of piety. It is not surprising that Wittenberg proved an environment in which critical interest in the Polish canon Nicholas Copernicus' radical theory of a heliocentric (sun-centred) universe took root, despite the tremendous challenge it presented to the story told in the Bible. Another Lutheran, the Dane Tycho Brahe, made important discoveries through his observations of celestial phenomena including the supernova of 1572. Trained in Tübingen, his assistant Johannes Kepler also had deeply religious motivations for seeking to unravel the mathematical laws that underlay planetary motion, and his devout Protestantism prompted him to try to find the logic of the Trinity in triadic features of the heavens. Theophrastus Paracelsus, a native of Württemberg, was another figure whose personal faith was a critical factor in his scientific activity, most particularly in relation to pharmaceutical medicine. He eclectically combined insights from the Bible with those derived from cabbalistic and gnostic literature to challenge the dominant medical orthodoxy of Galenism. Paracelsianism fostered a quasi-religious conception of the office of the physician which earned it the nickname 'chemical divinity'.

The trial and condemnation of Galileo Galilei in 1633 for advocating Copernican ideas has made it easy to caricature Catholicism as a reactionary force and a fierce enemy of new scientific developments. So too has the burning in Rome in 1600 of the maverick Italian Dominican friar and hermetical scholar Giordano Bruno, whose heterodox opinions included the now universally held view that the universe comprised many solar systems—an infinite number of earths revolving around an equally infinite number of suns. These cast a lasting shadow over the kind of cosmology that Catholic scholars could teach and defend, and it was not until 1833 that Copernicus was finally removed from the Index. In the case of another natural philosopher of note, Ulisse Aldrovandi, first professor of natural sciences at the University of Bologna, who was also accused of anti-Trinitarian heresies in 1549, a period of imprisonment provided him with leisure to augment his growing interest in the fields of zoology, botany, and ornithology, upon which he wrote prolifically. But these episodes should be set against the very considerable contribution made by the Jesuits to the physical and mathematical sciences in the seventeenth century.

THE GERMAN JESUIT POLYMATH ATHANASIUS KIRCHNER combined important work on geology, notably volcanoes and fossils, with a fascination with Egyptology and oriental culture and some strikingly advanced biological ideas regarding infectious disease, which he developed by inspecting the blood of plague victims through a microscope. This image from his *Mundus Subterraneus* shows the interior of the earth, while the Latin text describes his theory that underground water channels, heated by its internal fires, emerged in the sea, causing tides, and in mountains, causing volcanic eruptions.

Turning to other branches of natural science, it may be observed that the fervent providentialism and apocalypticism of the era provided a fillip to the activities of their practitioners. The anxious fascination that preachers and ministers displayed with anomalies like seven-headed cabbages and conjoined human and animal twins cannot easily be disentangled from philosophical curiosity: these were inextricably linked and fused to cultivate close empirical and clinical scrutiny and to prioritize the quality of verisimilitude in scientific illustration. This was also one of the factors responsible for encouraging an outpouring of erudite demonology—the science of understanding the ingenious methods by which the Devil and his minions manipulated nature to effect their malicious ends. In the eyes of the divines and scholars who produced these

JOSEPH GLANVILL's *Sadducismus Triumphatus*, edited and posthumously published in 1681, is one of the more famous products of the impulse to combat the scepticism of seventeenth-century Saduccees using the techniques of experimental science. The tract is emblematic of the extent to which belief in the supernatural was an integral part of natural philosophy in the seventeenth century.

voluminous texts, Satan was nothing less than a master scientist. Witchcraft now seems to many the epitome of silly 'superstition'; in the sixteenth and seventeenth centuries its study was an intellectual pursuit of the utmost seriousness and respectability. And from the 1650s, the methods of scientific observation promoted by Francis Bacon and institutionalized in England's Royal Society were being harnessed as a weapon against the apparently rising tide of indifference and atheism. They were being utilized to vindicate the existence of an invisible world populated by God, angels, demons, ghosts, and spirits. The chief targets of these efforts were those who had begun to embrace a mechanistic view of the universe as a system that could function, as it were by clockwork, without the interference of the deity. These ideas were synonymous with the Frenchman René Descartes and they proved increasingly influential. Yet, for all the feverish concern they stimulated, the trends of which they were representative were not necessarily incompatible with piety or corrosive of the doctrine of providence. Isaac Newton's findings about gravity were part of his wider attempt to demonstrate the sovereignty of God, who was increasingly reconceptualized less as a vengeful Jehovah and more as a benevolent dispenser of mercy.

In the Netherlands, however, one of Descartes's disciples, the Reformed pastor Balthasar Bekker, published in 1691 *Die Betooverde Wereld* (*The Enchanted World*), a powerful critique of belief in witchcraft and the supernatural that was rapidly translated from Dutch into several other languages. The publicity it garnered was more negative than positive and it aroused strong opposition among those who saw it as a threat to orthodox Calvinism, not to say Christianity itself. But by the middle of the eighteenth century, these views had begun to enter the intellectual mainstream. A sea change was taking place in public taste, but this should not be mistaken for the complete evaporation of ideas about the occult from the realm of private belief. All of the religious cultures engendered by the Reformations contained elements that foreshadowed these developments, even as, ironically, they were also the source of countervailing tendencies. Protestant (and Catholic) zeal was itself part of the problem tackled by the advocates of Enlightenment, rather than a clear solution or stepping stone to it.

Other currents of dissent and doubt which had always flowed through the veins of European society came to the surface in the later phases of the long Reformation. Some of these sprang from the well of religious radicalism, especially the anti-Trinitarianism (or Unitarianism) of the Socinians, whose denial of the tripartite nature of the deity represented a serious affront to orthodoxy. More idiosyncratic and cynical was the Englishman Thomas Hobbes, who ridiculed the doctrine of the Trinity, questioned whether a God without material substance could exist, and implied that Christian truth was not to be assumed as a given. Changing the metaphor, other seeds germinated in the soil of crypto-Judaism, notably that of the Portuguese-Jewish merchant Benedict Spinoza, who repudiated the idea of human immortality and providential intervention, rejected the tenet of God's essential goodness, and called for the Bible to be analysed with the same critical philological rigour as other texts. These iconoclastic views outraged his contemporaries and made him a byword for

CREDULITY, SUPERSTITION, and FANATICISM.
A MEDLEY.

Believe not every Spirit but try the Spirits whether they are of God: because many false Prophets are gone out into the World.

1 John. C.4. V.1.

Design'd and Engrav'd by Wm Hogarth.

Publish'd as the Act directs March 5.th 15.th 1762.

WILLIAM HOGARTH'S celebrated satirical print of 1761 entitled 'Credulity, Superstition and Fanaticism' may be regarded as an index of a sea change in opinion in the eighteenth century, which marginalized the miraculous and supernatural from public discourse and from the religion practised by polite society.

unbelief. His *Tractatus Theologico-Politicus* (1670) had the distinction of being banned both by the authorities in Protestant Holland and by the Roman Inquisition, while he himself was expelled from the Amsterdam synagogue in 1656. His extreme views made him the bugbear of all the Semitic religions. The intellectual tendency known as deism also provoked concern as it won more adherents among the learned: deists accepted the existence of an intelligent and supreme creator of the universe, but saw religion as a matter of natural law and reason rather than blind faith, and were dismissive of the institutional structures within which it was practised. A key intervention, which sparked heated debate, was the Irishman John Toland's provocative manifesto against 'priestcraft', *Christianity not Mysterious* (1696), which led to his prosecution by a London grand jury.

Alongside these streams of thought and scholarship ran another tradition of rationalism more rooted in practical experience, visible only in the utterances captured by hostile witnesses and recorded by the scribes of tribunals. This centred around questions such as how could the Almighty God be present in a piece of bread and why he permitted terrible suffering in the world when he had the power to prevent it: some found it hard to swallow the complex explanations provided by theologians and reached the conclusion that the deity was simply cruel, tyrannical, and sadistic, and not to be honoured or trusted. The threat presented by 'atheism' in the late seventeenth and early eighteenth centuries was exaggerated by contemporaries, who feared the collapse of the social and political order if Christianity lost its monopoly, and who used the term to deride a bundle of tendencies better described as impiety than outright irreligion. But it was neither intellectually nor culturally an impossibility. Outspoken expressions of atheistical convictions still placed one beyond the pale, as the execution for blasphemy of the young medical student Thomas Aikenhead in Edinburgh in 1697 revealed, though this was to be one of the last great public show trials for this crime. European society still conceived of itself as a Christian one, but the contours of the religious landscape were gradually changing. The path from the ecclesiastical and ideological upheavals in the early sixteenth century to the so-called 'Enlightenment' is therefore a broken and meandering one: here too the Reformation's role as an agent of change was indirect and equivocal. Each of these movements provoked innovative thinking, but each also constituted an effort to reassess and resolve the fundamental tensions and questions at the heart of Christian life. The alter ego of this spirit of scrutiny and speculation was religious enthusiasm. The eighteenth century was the age of Voltaire, but it was also the age of charismatic revivalists like John Wesley and Jonathan Edwards, and of Pietism, Methodism, and the American 'Great Awakening'. Both were the progeny of impulses released or reignited in the heady decades surrounding the 1520s.

This chapter has charted a careful course through the choppy waters of scholarship about the long-term legacies and repercussions of the Reformations. It has engaged with the bold claims made by earlier commentators about the role played by Protestantism in the making of modernity and with the corresponding myths about the 'backwardness' of Catholicism that linger on in modern Western (and especially Anglo-American) historiography and popular consciousness. It has contended that these legends and paradigms of interpretation are themselves among the most lasting effects of the polemical conflicts of the sixteenth and seventeenth centuries and of the efforts of the reformers to project the movement which they inaugurated as an historical watershed. The essence of the argument presented here is that the consequences of the Reformation were contradictory. The spiritual and political passions they unleashed had wide ramifications: they entrenched, and eventually accommodated, the confessional and denominational pluralism which they initially opposed; they converged with social and economic pressures to alter the ways in which people behaved and the material surroundings in which they conducted their daily lives; they both fostered and complicated intellectual and cultural trends that were changing how people conceived of God and the natural and supernatural worlds; and they critically shaped how individuals, communities, and nations identified and defined themselves. These developments must be seen less as a consequence of intrinsic features of these religions than of the energy generated by the clashes, confrontations, and dialogues to which they gave rise. The ripples created by these interactions are still being felt in the twenty-first century.

FURTHER READING

1. LATE MEDIEVAL CHRISTIANITY

THEOLOGY, SACRAMENTS, AND LITURGY

Robert J. Bast (ed.), *The Reformation of Faith in the Context of Late Medieval Theology and Piety: Essays by Berndt Hamm* (Leiden, 2004)

D. Catherine Brown, *Pastor and Laity in the Theology of Jean Gerson* (Cambridge, 1987)

Dallas G. Denery II, *Seeing and Being Seen in the Later Medieval World: Optics, Theology, and Religious Life* (Cambridge, 2005)

Aden Kumler, *Translating Truth: Ambitious Images and Religious Knowledge in Late Medieval France and England* (New Haven, 2011)

Ulrich G. Leinsle, *Introduction to Scholastic Theology* (Washington, 2010)

Ian Levy, Gary Macy, and Kristen Van Ausdall (eds), *A Companion to the Eucharist in the Middle Ages* (Leiden, 2011)

Brian Patrick McGuire, *Jean Gerson and the Last Medieval Reformation* (Philadelphia, 2005)

Donald Mowbray, *Pain and Suffering in Medieval Theology: Academic Debates at the University of Paris in the Thirteenth Century* (Woodbridge, 2009)

Richard G. Newhauser and Susan J. Ridyard (eds), *Sin in Medieval and Early Modern Culture: The Tradition of the Seven Deadly Sins* (Woodbridge, 2012)

Miri Rubin, *Corpus Christi: The Eucharist in Late Medieval Culture* (Cambridge, 1991)

David Steinmetz, *Misericordia Dei: The Theology of Johannes Von Staupitz in its Late Medieval Setting* (Leiden, 1968)

Rik van Nieuwenhove, *An Introduction to Medieval Theology* (Cambridge, 2012)

Morimichi Watanabe, *Nicholas of Cusa: A Companion to his Life and his Times* (Aldershot, 2011)

Katherine Zieman, *Singing the New Song: Literacy and Liturgy in Late Medieval England* (Philadelphia, 2011)

DEVOTION AND POPULAR RELIGION

Margaret Aston, *Lollards and Reformers: Images and Literacy in Late Medieval Religion* (London, 1984)

Margaret Aston, *Faith and Fire: Popular and Unpopular Religion, 1350–1600* (London, 1993)

Jessica Brantley, *Reading in the Wilderness: Private Devotion and Public Performance in Late Medieval England* (Chicago, 2008)

Andrew D. Brown, *Popular Piety in Late Medieval England: The Diocese of Salisbury, 1250–1550* (Oxford, 1995)

Nicole Chareyron, *Pilgrims to Jerusalem in the Middle Ages* (New York, 2013)

Linda Kay Davidson and Maryjane Dunn (eds), *The Pilgrimage to Compostela in the Middle Ages: A Book of Essays* (Abbington, 1996)

Eamon Duffy, *The Stripping of the Altars: Traditional Religion in England, c.1400–c.1580*, 2nd edn (New Haven and London, 2005)

Eamon Duffy, *Marking the Hours: English People and their Prayers 1240–1570* (New Haven, 2006)

Mary C. Erler, *Women, Reading, and Piety in Late Medieval England* (Cambridge, 2002)

John Henderson, *Piety and Charity in Late Medieval Florence* (Oxford, 1994)

Carole Hill, *Women and Religion in Late Medieval Norwich* (Woodbridge, 2010)

John C. Hirsh, *The Boundaries of Faith: The Development and Transmission of Medieval Spirituality* (Leiden, 1996)

Lester K. Little, *Religious Poverty and the Profit Economy in Medieval Europe* (Ithaca, NY, 1978)

Stephen Mossman, *Marquard von Lindau and the Challenges of Religious Life in Late Medieval Germany: The Passion, the Eucharist, the Virgin Mary* (Oxford, 2010)

Ben Nilson, *Cathedral Shrines of Medieval England* (Woodbridge, 2008)

Steven Ozment, *The Age of Reform (1250–1550): An Intellectual and Religious History of Late Medieval and Reformation Europe* (New Haven, 1980)

Virginia Reinburg, *French Books of Hours: Making an Archive of Prayer, c.1400–1600* (Cambridge, 2012)

Derek A. Rivard, *Blessing the World: Ritual and Lay Piety in Medieval Religion* (Washington, 2009)

Miri Rubin (ed.), *Medieval Christianity in Practice* (Princeton, 2009)

R. N. Swanson, *Religion and Devotion in Europe, c.1215–c.1515* (Cambridge, 1995)

R. N. Swanson, *Indulgences in Late Medieval England: Passports to Paradise?* (Cambridge, 2007)

Caroline Walker Bynum, *Holy Feast and Holy Fast: The Religious Significance of Food to Medieval Women* (Berkeley and Los Angeles, 1987)

Caroline Walker Bynum, *Wonderful Blood: Theology and Practice in Late Medieval Northern Germany and Beyond* (Philadelphia, 2007)

Anne Winston-Allen, *Convent Chronicles: Women Writing about Women and Reform in the Late Middle Ages* (University Park, Pa, 2005)

CLERICS AND PREACHING

Katherine Ludwig Jansen, *The Making of the Magdalen: Preaching and Popular Devotion in the Later Middle Ages* (Princeton, 2001)

Daniel R. Lesnick, *Preaching in Medieval Florence* (Atlanta, 2012)

Thom Mertens, Hans-Jochen Schiewer, Maria C. Sherwood-Smith, and Michael Mecklenburg (eds), *The Last Judgement in Medieval Preaching* (Turnhout, 2013)

Franco Mormando, *The Preacher's Demons: Bernardino of Siena and the Social Underworld of Early Renaissance Italy* (Chicago, 1999)

Helen Parish, *Clerical Celibacy in the West, c.1100–1700* (Aldershot, 2010)

Ronald J. Stansbury (ed.), *A Companion to Pastoral Care in the Late Middle Ages* (Leiden, 2010)

Larissa Taylor, *Soldiers of Christ: Preaching in Late Medieval and Reformation France* (Oxford, 1992)

John van Engen, *Sisters and Brothers of the Common Life: The Devotio Moderna and the World of the Later Middle Ages* (Philadelphia, 2008)

Nancy Bradley Warren, *Spiritual Economies: Female Monasticism in Later Medieval England* (Philadelphia, 2001)

POPES, ROME, AND COUNCILS

Silvio A. Bedini, *The Pope's Elephant* (Nashville, 1998)

Debra J. Birch, *Pilgrimage to Rome in the Middle Ages: Continuity and Change* (Woodbridge, 1998)

Joseph Canning, *A History of Medieval Political Thought, 300–1450* (Abington, 1996)

D. S. Chambers, *Renaissance Cardinals and their Worldly Problems* (Aldershot, 1997)

D. S. Chambers, *Popes, Cardinals and War* (London, 2006)

John F. D'Amico, *Renaissance Humanism in Papal Rome: Humanists and Churchmen on the Eve of the Reformation* (Baltimore, 1983)

Jan L. de Jong, *The Power and the Glorification: Papal Pretensions and the Art of Propaganda in the Fifteenth and Sixteenth Centuries* (University Park, Pa, 2013)

Peter Partner, *The Pope's Men: The Papal Civil Service in the Renaissance* (Oxford, 1990)

Loren W. Partridge, *The Renaissance in Rome, 1400–1600* (London, 2012)

Carol M. Richardson, *Reclaiming Rome: Cardinals in the Fifteenth Century* (Leiden, 2009)

Christine Shaw, *Julius II: The Warrior Pope* (Oxford, 1993)

Paul Valliere, *Conciliarism: A History of Decision-Making in the Church* (Cambridge, 2012)

ETERNITY AND INTERCESSION

Martina Bagnoli, *Treasures of Heaven: Saints, Relics and Devotion in Medieval Europe* (London, 2011)

Paul Binski, *Medieval Death: Ritual and Representation* (Ithaca, NY, 1996)

Clive Burgess and Martin Heale (eds), *The Late Medieval English College and its Context* (Woodbridge, 2008)

Christopher Daniell, *Death and Burial in Medieval England 1066–1550* (London, 1997)

Bruce Gordon and Peter Marshall (eds), *The Place of the Dead: Death and Remembrance in Late Medieval and Early Modern Europe* (Cambridge, 2000)

Jacques Le Goff, *The Birth of Purgatory* (Chicago, 1984)

Virginia Nixon, *Mary's Mother: Saint Anne in Late Medieval Europe* (Philadelphia, 2004)

Marjorie Reeves, *The Influence of Prophecy in the Later Middle Ages: A Study in Joachimism* (Oxford, 1969)

Simon Roffey, *The Medieval Chantry Chapel: An Archaeology* (Woodbridge, 2007)

Jean-Claude Schmitt, *Ghosts in the Middle Ages: The Living and the Dead in Medieval Society* (Chicago, 1998)

Larissa Taylor, *The Virgin Warrior: The Life and Death of Joan of Arc* (New Haven, 2009)

André Vauchez, *Sainthood in the Later Middle Ages* (Cambridge, 1997)

Caroline Walker Bynum and Paul Freedman (eds), *Last Things: Death and the Apocalypse in the Middle Ages* (Philadelphia, 2000)

LEARNING

Cornelis Augustijn, *Erasmus: His Life, Works, and Influence* (Toronto, 1995)

Jerry H. Bentley, *Humanists and Holy Writ: New Testament Scholarship in the Renaissance* (Princeton, 2012)

Alan J. Hauser and Duane Frederick Watson (eds), *A History of Biblical Interpretation: The Medieval Through the Reformation Periods* (Grand Rapids, Mich., 2009)

Jozef Ijsewijn and Jaques Paquet (eds), *The Universities in the Late Middle Ages* (Leuven, 1978)

Alastair Minnis, *Medieval Theory of Authorship: Scholastic Literary Attitudes in the Later Middle Ages* (Philadelphia, 2011)

Anders Piltz, *The World of Medieval Learning* (Oxford, 1981)

Eyal Poleg and Laura Light (eds), *Form and Function in the Late Medieval Bible* (Leiden, 2013)

David H. Price, *Johannes Reuchlin and the Campaign to Destroy Jewish Books* (Oxford, 2010)

Albert Rabil, *Erasmus and the New Testament: The Mind of a Christian Humanist* (Lanham, Md, 1993)

Hilde de Ridder-Symoens (ed.), *A History of the University in Europe*, i: *Universities in the Middle Ages* (Cambridge, 2003)

Erika Rummel (ed.), *Biblical Humanism and Scholasticism in the Age of Erasmus* (Leiden, 2008)

THREATS

Craig D. Atwood, *The Theology of the Czech Brethren from Hus to Comenius* (Philadelphia, 2009)

Michael David Bailey, *Battling Demons: Witchcraft, Heresy, and Reform in the Late Middle Ages* (Philadelphia, 2003)

Michael David Bailey, *Fearful Spirits, Reasoned Follies: The Boundaries of Superstition in Late Medieval Europe* (Ithaca, NY, 2013)

Peter Biller and Anne Hudson (eds), *Heresy and Literacy, 1000–1530* (Cambridge, 1996)

Alain Boureau, *Satan the Heretic: The Birth of Demonology in the Medieval West* (Chicago, 2006)

Euan Cameron, *Waldenses: Rejections of Holy Church in Medieval Europe* (Oxford, 2000)

Jennifer Kolpacoff Deane, *A History of Medieval Heresy and Inquisition* (Lanham, Md, 2011)

Thomas A. Fudge, *The Magnificent Ride: The First Reformation in Hussite Bohemia* (Aldershot, 1998)

Joan Young Gregg, *Devils, Women, and Jews: Reflections of the Other in Medieval Sermon Stories* (Albany, NY, 1997)

Sara Lipton, *Images of Intolerance: The Representation of Jews and Judaism in the Bible moralisée* (Berkeley, 1999)

Chris Lowney, *A Vanished World: Muslims, Christians, and Jews in Medieval Spain* (Oxford, 2006)

Vivian B. Mann, Jerrilyn D. Dodds, and Thomas F. Glick (eds), *Convivencia: Jews, Muslims, and Christians in Medieval Spain* (New York, 1992)

R. I. Moore, *The War on Heresy: Faith and Power in Medieval Europe* (London, 2012)

R. Po-Chia Hsia and Hartmut Lehmann (eds), *In and Out of the Ghetto: Jewish–Gentile Relations in Late Medieval and Early Modern Germany* (Cambridge, 1995)

Norman Roth, *Conversos, Inquisition, and the Expulsion of the Jews from Spain* (Madison, 2002)

Karen Sullivan, *The Inner Lives of Medieval Inquisitors* (Chicago, 2011)

Michael Van Dussen, *From England to Bohemia: Heresy and Communication in the Later Middle Ages* (Cambridge, 2009)

2. MARTIN LUTHER

GENERAL AND BIOGRAPHICAL STUDIES

Martin Brecht, *Martin Luther* (3 vols, Minneapolis, 1985–93)

Scott Hendrix, *Martin Luther: A Very Short Introduction* (Oxford, 2010)

Helmar Junghans, *Martin Luther und Wittenberg* (Munich and Berlin, 1996)

Thomas Kaufmann, *Martin Luther* (Munich, 2006)

Thomas Kaufmann, *Der Anfang der Reformation* (Tübingen, 2012)

Rosemarie Knape (ed.), *Martin Luther und Eisleben* (Leipzig, 2007)

Robert Kolb, *Martin Luther as Prophet, Teacher and Hero* (Grand Rapids, Mich., 1999)

Volker Leppin, *Martin Luther* (Darmstadt, 2006)

Donald McKim (ed.), *The Cambridge Companion to Martin Luther* (Cambridge, 2003)

Heiko Oberman, *Luther: Man between God and the Devil* (New Haven and London, 1989)

Lyndal Roper, *Martin Luther: Renegade and Prophet* (London, 2016)

Heinz Schilling, *Martin Luther* (Munich, 2012)

LUTHER'S GERMANY

Thomas A. Brady, *German Histories in the Age of Reformations* (Cambridge, 2009)

Miriam Chrisman, *Lay Culture, Learned Culture. Books and Social Change in Strasbourg 1480–1599* (New Haven and London, 1982)

Susan Karant-Nunn, *The Reformation of Ritual: An Interpretation of Early Modern Germany* (London, 1997)

Susan Karant-Nunn, *The Reformation of Feeling: Shaping the Religious Emotions in Early Modern Germany* (Oxford, 2009)

Rosemarie Knape (ed.), *Martin Luther und der Bergbau im Mansfelder Land* (Leipzig, 2000)

Andrew Pettegree, *The Book in the Renaissance* (New Haven and London, 2010)

Tom Scott, *The Early Reformation in Germany* (Farnham, 2013)

R. W. Scribner, *For the Sake of Simple Folk: Popular Propaganda for the German Reformation* (Cambridge, 1981)

R.W. Scribner, *Popular Culture and Popular Movements in Reformation Germany* (London, 1987)

LUTHER'S THEOLOGY AND POLEMICAL BATTLES

David Bagchi, *Luther's Earliest Opponents: Catholic Controversialists 1518–1525* (Minneapolis, 1991)

Amy Nelson Burnett, *Karlstadt and the Origins of the Eucharistic Controversy: A Study in the Circulation of Ideas* (Oxford, 2011)

Mark U. Edwards, *Luther and the False Brethren* (Stanford, Calif., 1975)

Mark U. Edwards, *Luther's Last Battles: Politics and Polemics 1531–46* (Ithaca, NY, and London, 1983)

Adam Francisco, *Martin Luther and Islam: A Study in Sixteenth-Century Polemics and Apologetics* (Leiden, 2007)

Thomas Kaufmann, *Luther's Jews: A Journey into Anti-Semitism* (Oxford, 2017)

Peter Matheson, *The Rhetoric of the Reformation* (Edinburgh, 1998)

Hans Medick and Peter Schmidt (eds), *Luther zwischen den Kulturen* (Göttingen, 2004)

GENDER, MARRIAGE, AND SEXUALITY

Joel Harrington, *Reordering Marriage and Society in Reformation Germany* (Cambridge, 1995)

Susan Karant-Nunn and Merry E. Wiesner-Hanks (eds), *Luther on Women: A Sourcebook* (Cambridge, 2003)

Peter Matheson (ed.), *Argula von Grumbach: A Woman's Voice in the Reformation* (Edinburgh, 1995)

Steven Ozment, *When Fathers Ruled: Family Life in Reformation Europe* (Cambridge, Mass., 1983)

Lyndal Roper, *The Holy Household: Women and Morals in Reformation Augsburg* (Oxford, 1989)

Lyndal Roper, *Oedipus and the Devil: Witchcraft, Sexuality and Religion in Early Modern Europe* (London, 1994)

ART, IMAGES, AND LEGACY

P. N. Brooks (ed.), *Seven-Headed Luther: Essays in Commemoration of a Quincentenary, 1483–1983* (Oxford, 1983)

Carl Christensen, *Princes and Propaganda: Electoral Saxon Art of the Reformation* (Kirksville, Mo., 1992)

Leo Koerner, *The Reformation of the Image* (Chicago, 2004)

Steven Ozment, *The Serpent and the Lamb: Cranach, Luther and the Making of the Reformation* (New Haven and London, 2012)

Lyndal Roper, 'Martin Luther's Body: The "Stout Doctor" and his Biographers', *American Historical Review*, 115 (2010)

Ulinka Rublack 'Grapho-Relics: Lutheranism and the Materialization of the Word', *Past and Present Supplement* (2010)

R. W. Scribner, 'The Reformer as Prophet and Saint: 16th Century Images of Luther', *History Today*, 33 (1983)

3. CALVINISM AND THE REFORM OF THE REFORMATION

GENERAL

Philip Benedict, *Christ's Churches Purely Reformed: A Social History of Calvinism* (New Haven, 2002)

Carlos M. N. Eire, *War Against the Idols: The Reformation of Worship from Erasmus to Calvin* (Cambridge, 1986)

Bruce Gordon, *The Swiss Reformation* (Manchester, 2002)

John T. McNeill, *The History and Character of Calvinism* (New York, 1967)

Graeme Murdock, *Beyond Calvin: The Intellectual, Political and Cultural World of Europe's Reformed Churches, c.1540–1620* (New York, 2004)

Herman J. Selderhuis (ed.), *The Calvin Handbook*, trans. H. J. Baron et al. (Grand Rapids, Mich., 2009)

Max Weber, *The Protestant Ethic and the Spirit of Capitalism*, trans. Stephen Kalberg (Los Angeles, 2002)

JOHN CALVIN: BIOGRAPHY

William J. Bouwsma, *John Calvin: A Sixteenth-Century Portrait* (New York, 1988)

Bernard Cottret, *Calvin: A Biography*, trans. M. Wallace McDonald (Grand Rapids, Mich., and Edinburgh, 2000)

Bruce Gordon, *Calvin* (New Haven, 2009)

Alister McGrath, *A Life of John Calvin: A Study in the Shaping of Western Culture* (Oxford, 1990)
Willem van't Spijker, *Calvin: A Brief Guide to his Life and Thought* (Louisville, Ky, 2009)

CALVIN AND GENEVA

Robert Kingdon, *Geneva and the Coming of the Wars of Religion in France, 1555–1563* (Geneva, 1956)
Robert Kingdon, *Adultery and Divorce in Calvin's Geneva* (Cambridge, Mass., 1995)
William Monter, *Calvin's Geneva* (New York, 1967)
William Naphy, *Calvin and the Consolidation of the Genevan Reformation* (Louisville, Ky, 2003)
Ronald S. Wallace, *Calvin, Geneva and the Reformation: A Study of Calvin as Social Reformer, Churchman, Pastor and Theologian* (Grand Rapids, Mich., 1988)

CALVINIST THOUGHT

Paul Helm, *John Calvin's Ideas* (Oxford, 2004)
Peter A. Lillback, *The Binding of God: Calvin's Role in the Development of Covenant Theology* (Grand Rapids, Mich., 2001)
Richard A Muller, *The Unaccommodated Calvin: Studies in the Foundation of a Theological Tradition* (Oxford, 2000)
T. H. L. Parker, *Calvin: An Introduction to his Thought* (London, 1995)
Charles Partee, *The Theology of John Calvin* (Louisville, Ky, 2008)
Keith Randell, *John Calvin and the Later Reformation* (London, 1990)
David Steinmetz, *Calvin in Context* (Oxford, 2010)
R. Ward Holder, *John Calvin and the Grounding of Interpretation: Calvin's First Commentaries* (Leiden, 2006)
Randall Zachman, *John Calvin as Teacher, Pastor, and Theologian: The Shape of his Writings and Thought* (Grand Rapids, Mich., 2006)
Randall Zachman, *Image and Word in the Theology of John Calvin* (Notre Dame, Ind., 2007)

INTERNATIONAL CALVINISM

Barbara Diefendorf, *Beneath the Cross: Catholics and Huguenots in Sixteenth-Century Paris* (Oxford, 1991)
Alastair Duke, *Reformation and Revolt in the Low Countries* (London, 1990)
Philip Gorski, *Disciplinary Revolution: Calvinism and the Rise of the State in Early Modern Europe* (Chicago, 2003)
Michael F. Graham, *The Uses of Reform: 'Godly Discipline' and Popular Behaviour in Scotland and Beyond, 1560–1610* (Leiden, 1996)
Ole Peter Grell, *Brethren in Christ: A Calvinist Network in Reformation Europe* (Cambridge, 2011)
Mack Holt, *The French Wars of Religion, 1562–1629* (Cambridge, 2005)
Benjamin Kaplan, *Calvinists and Libertines: Confession and Community in Utrecht, 1578–1620* (Oxford, 1995)
Donald Kelley, *The Beginning of Ideology: Consciousness and Society in the French Reformation* (Cambridge, 1981)
Robert Kingdon, *Geneva and the Consolidation of the French Protestant Movement, 1564–1572* (Geneva, 1967)
R. J. Knecht, *The French Wars of Religion, 1559–1598* (Boston, 2010)
John McCallum, *Reforming the Scottish Parish: The Reformation in Fife, 1560–1640* (Farnham, 2010)
Phyllis Mack Crew, *Calvinist Preaching and Iconoclasm in the Netherlands 1544–1569* (Cambridge, 1978)
Guido Marnef, *Antwerp in the Age of Reformation: Underground Protestantism in a Commercial Metropolis, 1550–1577*, trans. J. C. Grayson (Baltimore, 1996)
Graeme Murdock, *International Calvinism* (Basingstoke, 2003)

Bodo Nischan, *Prince, People, and Confession: The Second Reformation in Brandenburg* (Philadelphia, 1994)

Andrew Pettegree, *Emden and the Dutch Revolt: Exile and the Development of Reformed Protestantism* (Oxford, 1992)

Judy Sproxton, *Violence and Religion: Attitudes Towards Militancy in the French Civil Wars and the English Revolution* (London, 1995)

Allan Tulchin, *That Men Would Praise the Lord: The Triumph of Protestantism in Nîmes, 1530–1570* (Oxford, 2010)

ENGLISH PURITANS

R. J. Acheson, *Radical Puritans in England, 1550–1660* (London, 1990)

Francis Bremer, *Puritanism: A Very Short Introduction* (Oxford, 2009)

Patrick Collinson, *The Elizabethan Puritan Movement* (London, 1982)

Patrick Collinson, *English Puritanism* (London, 1983)

Dan G. Danner, *Pilgrimage to Puritanism: History and Theology of the Marian Exiles at Geneva, 1555 to 1560* (New York, 1998)

Peter Lake, *Moderate Puritans and the Elizabethan Church* (Cambridge, 2004)

Nicholas McDowell, *The English Radical Imagination: Culture, Religion, and Revolution, 1630–1660* (Oxford, 2003)

Michael Walzer, *The Revolution of the Saints: A Study in the Origins of Radical Politics* (Cambridge, Mass., 1965)

Austin Woolrych, *Britain in Revolution, 1625–1660* (Oxford, 2002)

NEW ENGLAND PURITANS

Peter N. Carroll, *Puritanism and the Wilderness: The Intellectual Significance of the New England Frontier, 1629–1700* (New York, 1969)

Stephen Foster, *The Long Argument: English Puritanism and the Shaping of New England Culture, 1570–1700* (Chapel Hill, NC, 1991)

David Hall, *Worlds of Wonder, Days of Judgment: Popular Religious Belief in Early New England* (Cambridge, Mass., 1990)

Charles Hambrick-Stowe, *The Practice of Piety: Puritan Devotional Disciplines in Seventeenth-Century New England* (Chapel Hill, NC, 1982)

Perry Miller, *The New England Mind: From Colony to Province* (Cambridge, Mass., 1953)

Perry Miller, *Errand into the Wilderness* (Cambridge, Mass., 1956)

Samuel Eliot Morison, *Those Misunderstood Puritans* (North Brookfield, Mass., 1992)

Edmund Morgan, *Visible Saint: The History of a Puritan Idea* (New York, 1963)

Robert Pope, *The Half-way Covenant: Church Membership in Puritan New England* (Princeton, 1969)

Harry S. Stout, *The New England Soul: Preaching and Religious Culture in Colonial New England* (Oxford, 1986)

CALVINISM AND THE ARTS

William Dyrness, *Reformed Theology and Visual Culture: The Protestant Imagination from Calvin to Edwards* (Cambridge, 2004)

Paul Corby Finney (ed.), *Seeing Beyond the Word: Visual Arts and the Calvinist Tradition* (Grand Rapids, Mich., 1998)

Charles Garside, *The Origins of Calvin's Theology of Music, 1536–1543* (Philadelphia, 1979)

Mia Mochizuki, *The Netherlandish Image after Iconoclasm, 1566–1672: Material Religion in the Dutch Golden Age* (Burlington, Vt, 2008)

4. THE RADICAL REFORMATION

GENERAL

Michael G. Baylor (ed.), *The Radical Reformation* (Cambridge, 1991)

Hans Jürgen Goertz (ed.), *Profiles of Radical Reformers: Biographical Sketches from Thomas Müntzer to Paracelsus* (Kitchener, Ont., 1982)

Brad S. Gregory, *The Unintended Reformation: How a Religious Revolution Secularized Society* (Cambridge, Mass., and London, 2012)

Walter Klaassen, *Living at the End of the Ages: Apocalyptic Expectation in the Radical Reformation* (Lanham, Md, 1992)

John D. Roth and James M. Stayer (eds), *A Companion to Anabaptism and Spiritualism, 1521–1700* (Leiden, 2007)

George Hunston Williams, *The Radical Reformation*, 3rd edn (Kirksville, Mo., 1992)

ANABAPTISM

C. Arnold Snyder, *The Life and Thought of Michael Sattler* (Scottdale, Pa, 1984)

C. Arnold Snyder, *Anabaptist History and Theology: An Introduction* (Kitchener, Ont., 1995)

C. Arnold Snyder and Linda A. Huebert Hecht (eds), *Profiles of Anabaptist Women: Sixteenth-Century Reforming Pioneers* (Waterloo, Ont., 1996)

Torsten Bergsten, *Balthasar Hubmaier: Anabaptist Theologian and Martyr*, ed. William R. Estep (Valley Forge, Pa, 1978)

Klaus Deppermann, *Melchior Hoffman: Social Unrest and Apocalyptic Visions in the Age of Reformation*, ed. Benjamin Drewery, trans. Malcolm Wren (Edinburgh, 1987)

Michael Driedger, *Obedient Heretics: Mennonite Identities in Lutheran Hamburg and Altona during the Confessional Age* (Aldershot, 2002)

Brad S. Gregory, *Salvation at Stake: Christian Martyrdom in Early Modern Europe* (Cambridge, Mass., and London, 1999)

Leonard Gross, *The Golden Years of the Hutterites: The Witness and Thought of the Communal Moravian Hutterites during the Walpot Era, 1565–1578*, 2nd edn (Scottdale, Pa, 1998)

Sigrun Haude, *In the Shadow of 'Savage Wolves': Anabaptist Münster and the German Reformation during the 1530s* (Boston, 2000)

Werner O. Packull, *Hutterite Beginnings: Communitarian Experiments during the Reformation* (Baltimore and London, 1995)

Claus Peter-Clasen, *Anabaptism: A Social History, 1525–1618. Switzerland, Austria, Moravia, and South and Central Germany* (Ithaca, NY, and London, 1972)

James M. Stayer, *Anabaptists and the Sword*, 2nd edn (Lawrence, Kan., 1976)

Gary K. Waite, *David Joris and Dutch Anabaptism, 1524–1543* (Waterloo, Ont., 1990)

GERMAN PEASANTS' WAR

Peter Blickle, *The Revolution of 1525: The German Peasants' War from a New Perspective* (Baltimore and London, 1981)

Abraham Friesen, *Thomas Muentzer, a Destroyer of the Godless: The Making of a Sixteenth-Century Religious Revolutionary* (Berkeley and Los Angeles, 1990)

Hans Jürgen Goertz, *Thomas Müntzer, Apocalyptic Mystic and Revolutionary* (Edinburgh, 1993)

Tom Scott, *Thomas Müntzer: Theology and Revolution in the German Reformation* (Houndmills and London, 1989)

Tom Scott and Bob Scribner (eds), *The German Peasants' War: A History in Documents* (Atlantic Highland, NJ, and London, 1991)

James M. Stayer, *The German Peasants' War and Anabaptist Community of Goods* (Montreal, 1991)

SPIRITUALISM AND ANTI-TRINITARIANISM

R. Emmet McLaughlin, *Caspar Schwenckfeld, Reluctant Radical: His Life to 1540* (New Haven, 1986)
Andrew C. Fix, *Prophecy and Reason: The Dutch Collegiants in the Early Enlightenment* (Princeton, 1991)
Jerome Friedman, *Michael Servetus: A Case Study in Total Heresy* (Geneva, 1978)
Alastair Hamilton, *The Family of Love* (Cambridge, 1981)
Christopher W. Marsh, *The Family of Love in English Society, 1550–1630* (Cambridge, 1994)
Gerrit Voogt, *Constraint on Trial: Dirck Volckhertsz Coornhert and Religious Freedom* (Kirksville, Mo., 2000)

RELIGIOUS RADICALISM AND THE ENGLISH REVOLUTION

Mark R. Bell, *Apocalypse How? Baptist Movements during the English Revolution* (Macon, Ga, 2000)
David Como, *Blown by the Spirit: The Emergence of an Antinomian Underground in Pre-Civil-War England* (Stanford, Calif., 2004)
Christopher Hill, *The World Turned Upside Down: Radical Ideas during the English Revolution* (New York, 1972)
Ann Hughes, *Gangraena and the Struggle for the English Revolution* (Oxford, 2004)
H. Larry Ingle, *First among Friends: George Fox and the Creation of Quakerism* (New York, 1994)
Nicholas McDowell, *The English Radical Imagination: Culture, Religion, and Revolution, 1630–1660* (Oxford, 2003)
J. F. McGregor and Barry Reay (eds), *Radical Religion in the English Revolution* (London, 1984)

5. CATHOLIC REFORMATION AND RENEWAL

THE GLOBAL CIRCULATION OF THE SACRED

T. Alberts, *Conflict and Conversion: Catholicism in Southeast Asia, c.1500–1700* (Oxford, 2013)
G. A. Bailey, *Art on the Jesuit Missions in Asia and Latin America* (Toronto, 1999)
L. Clossey, *Salvation and Globalisation in the Early Jesuit Missions* (Cambridge, 2008)
J. Darwin, *After Tamerlane: The Rise and Fall of Global Empires, 1400–2000* (London, 2007)
S. Ditchfield, *Liturgy, Sanctity and History in Tridentine Italy* (Cambridge, 1995)
J. O'Malley et al. (eds), *The Jesuits: Cultures, Sciences, and the Arts, 1540–1733* (2 vols, Toronto, 1999–2005)
M. C. Osswald, *Written in Stone: Jesuit Building in Goa and their Artistic and Architectural Features* (Goa, 2013)
D. Pierce and R. Otsuka (eds), *Asia and Spanish America: Trans-Pacific Artistic and Cultural Exchange, 1500–1850* (Denver, 2009)
M. Trusted, *Baroque and Later Ivories* (London, 2013)

TAKING THE CHRISTIAN MESSAGE FROM THE NEW TO THE OLD WORLDS

T. Abé, *The Jesuit Mission to New France: A New Interpretation in the Light of the Earlier Jesuit Experience in Japan* (Leiden, 2011)
C. R. Boxer, *The Christian Century in Japan, 1549–1650* (Berkeley, 1951; repr. Manchester, 1993)
L. Brockey, *Journey to the East: The Jesuit Mission in China, 1579–1724* (Cambridge, Mass., 2007)
C. Burgaleta, *José de Acosta SJ (1540–1600): His Life and Thought* (St Louis, 1999)
L. Châtellier, *Religion of the Poor: Rural Missions in Europe and the Formation of Modern Catholicism, c.1500–c.1800* (Cambridge, 1997)
A. R. Disney, *A History of Portugal and the Portuguese Empire: From Beginnings to 1807* (2 vols, Cambridge, 2009)
A. Durston, *Pastoral Quechua: The History of Christian Translation in Colonial Peru, 1550–1650* (Notre Dame, Ind., 2007)
D. Lach (with E. van Kley), *Asia in the Making of Europe* (3 vols in 9 parts, Chicago, 1965–94)
G. Nadal, *Annotations and Meditations on the Gospels* (3 vols, Philadelphia, 2003–5)

J. Phelan, *The Hispanization of the Philippines: Spanish Aims and Filipino Responses, 1565–1700* (1959; repr. Madison, 2010)

M. Restall, *Seven Myths of the Spanish Conquest* (Oxford, 2003)

B. Sundkler, *A History of the Church in Africa* (Cambridge, 2000)

PAPAL PRINCE AND PASTOR: THE DYNAMICS OF ROMAN CATHOLICISM

R. Finucane, *Contested Canonizations: The Last Medieval Saints, 1482–1523* (Washington, 2011)

I. Fosi, *Papal Justice: Subjects and Courts in the Papal State, 1500–1750* (Washington, 2011)

G. Martin, *Roma Sancta (1581)*, ed. G. B. Parks (Rome, 1969)

P. Prodi, *The Papal Prince: One Body and Two Souls: The Papal Monarchy in Early Modern Europe* (Cambridge, 1987)

P. Prebys (ed.), *Early Modern Rome, 1341–1667* (Ferrara, 2012)

'RE-PLACING' TRENT: THE LIMITS OF TRIDENTINE CATHOLICISM

A. Bamji, G. Janssen, and M. Laven (eds), *The Ashgate Research Companion to the Counter-Reformation* (Farnham, 2013)

J. W. O'Malley, *Trent and All That: Renaming Catholicism in the Early Modern Era* (Cambridge, Mass., 2000)

J. W. O'Malley, *Trent: What Happened at the Council* (Cambridge, Mass., 2013)

THE CATHOLIC PRINCE: CONFESSIONALIZATION AND THE STRUGGLE OVER PATRONAGE RIGHTS

F. Bethencourt, *The Inquisition: A Global History, 1478–1834* (Cambridge, 2009)

R. Bireley, *Religion and Politics in the Age of the Counter-Reformation: Emperor Ferdinand II, William Lamormaini S.J. and the Formation of Imperial Policy* (Chapel Hill, NC, 1981)

C. Black, *The Italian Inquisition* (New Haven and London, 2009)

L. Homza (ed.), *The Spanish Inquisition, 1478–1614: An Anthology of Sources* (Indianapolis, 2006)

H. Kamen, *Spain's Road to Empire: The Making of a World Power, 1492–1763* (London, 2003)

H. Rawlings, *The Spanish Inquisition* (Oxford, 2006)

K. van Liere, S. Ditchfield, and H. Louthan (eds), *Sacred History: Uses of the Christian Past in the Renaissance World* (Oxford, 2012)

THE GLOBAL RELEVANCE OF CARLO BORROMEO'S DIOCESAN VISION

C. Alvarez de Toledo, *Politics and Reform in Viceregal Mexico: The Life and Thought of Juan de Palafox, 1600–1659* (Oxford, 2004)

C. Black and P. Gravestock (eds), *Early Modern Confraternities in Europe and the Americas: International and Interdisciplinary Perspectives* (Farnham, 2005)

L. Châtellier, *The Europe of the Devout: The Catholic Reformation and the Formation of a New Society* (Cambridge, 1989)

S. Evangelisti, *Nuns: A History of Convent Life, 1450–1700* (Oxford, 2007)

C. Kenworthy-Browne (ed.), *Mary Ward (1585–1645): A Briefe Relation with Autobiographical Fragments and a Selection of Letters* (Woodbridge, 2008)

K. Melvin, *Building Colonial Cities of God: Mendicant Orders and Urban Culture in New Spain* (Stanford, Calif., 2012)

S. Strocchia, *Nuns and Nunneries in Renaissance Florence* (Baltimore, 2009)

A. C. Van Oss, *Catholic Colonialism: A Parish History of Guatemala, 1524–1821* (Cambridge, 1986)

6. BRITISH REFORMATIONS

BRITISH PERSPECTIVES

Brendan Bradshaw and Peter Roberts (eds), *British Consciousness and Identity: The Making of Britain, 1533–1707* (Cambridge, 1998)

Susan Brigden, *New Worlds, Lost Worlds: The Rule of the Tudors 1485–1603* (London, 2000)

Steven G. Ellis, *The Making of the British Isles: The State of Britain and Ireland, 1450–1660* (Harlow, 2007)

Ian Hazlett, *The Reformation in Britain and Ireland: An Introduction* (London, 2003)

Felicity Heal, *Reformation in Britain and Ireland* (Oxford, 2003)

Clare Kellar, *Scotland, England, and the Reformation 1534–61* (Oxford, 2003)

Michael Mullett, *Catholics in Britain and Ireland 1558–1829* (Basingstoke, 1998)

Alec Ryrie, *The Age of Reformation: The Tudor and Stewart Realms 1485–1603* (London, 2009)

Alexandra Walsham, *The Reformation of the Landscape: Religion, Identity and Memory in Early Modern Britain and Ireland* (Oxford, 2011)

ENGLAND

Margaret Aston, *England's Iconoclasts: Laws against Images* (Oxford, 1988)

George Bernard, *The King's Reformation: Henry VIII and the Remaking of the English Church* (New Haven and London, 2005)

John Bossy, *The English Catholic Community, 1570–1850* (London, 1975)

Susan Brigden, *London and the Reformation* (Oxford, 1989)

James Clark (ed.), *The Religious Orders in Pre-Reformation England* (Woodbridge, 2002)

Patrick Collinson, *The Religion of Protestants: The Church in English Society 1559–1625* (Oxford, 1982)

Patrick Collinson, *Elizabethan Essays* (London, 1994)

A. G. Dickens, *Reformation Studies* (London, 1982)

A. G. Dickens, *The English Reformation*, 2nd edn (London, 1989)

Eamon Duffy, *The Stripping of the Altars: Traditional Religion in England 1400–1580* (New Haven and London, 1992)

Eamon Duffy, *The Voices of Morebath: Reformation and Rebellion in an English Village* (New Haven and London, 2001)

Eamon Duffy, *Fires of Faith: Catholic England under Mary Tudor* (New Haven and London, 2009)

Kenneth Fincham and Nicholas Tyacke, *Altars Restored: The Changing Face of English Worship, 1547–c.1700* (Oxford, 2007)

Christopher Haigh (ed.), *The English Reformation Revised* (Cambridge, 1987)

Christopher Haigh, *English Reformations: Religion, Politics, and Society under the Tudors* (Oxford, 1993)

Anne Hudson, *The Premature Reformation: Wycliffite Texts and Lollard History* (Oxford, 1988)

Arnold Hunt, *The Art of Hearing: English Preachers and their Audiences 1590–1640* (Cambridge, 2010)

Ronald Hutton, *The Rise and Fall of Merry England: The Ritual Year 1400–1700* (Oxford, 1994)

Eric Ives, *The Life and Death of Anne Boleyn* (Oxford, 2004)

Norman Jones, *The English Reformation: Religion and Cultural Adaption* (Oxford, 2002)

Peter Lake and Michael Questier (eds), *Conformity and Orthodoxy in the English Church, c.1560–1660* (Woodbridge, 2000)

Diarmaid MacCulloch, *Tudor Church Militant: Edward VI and the Protestant Reformation* (London, 1999)

Diarmaid MacCulloch, *The Later Reformation in England, 1547–1603*, 2nd edn (Basingstoke, 2001)

Judith Maltby, *Prayer Book and People in Elizabethan and Early Stuart England* (Cambridge, 1998)

Christopher Marsh, *Popular Religion in Sixteenth-Century England* (Basingstoke, 1998)

Peter Marshall (ed.), *The Impact of the English Reformation 1500–1640* (London, 1997)

Peter Marshall, *Reformation England 1480–1642*, 2nd edn (London, 2012)

Peter Marshall and Alec Ryrie (eds), *The Beginnings of English Protestantism* (Cambridge, 2002)

Andrew Pettegree, *Marian Protestantism: Six Studies* (Aldershot, 1996)

Richard Rex, *Henry VIII and the English Reformation*, 2nd edn (Basingstoke, 2006)

J. J. Scarisbrick, *The Reformation and the English People* (Oxford, 1984)

Ethan Shagan, *Popular Politics and the English Reformation* (Cambridge, 2003)

John Spurr, *English Puritanism 1603–1689* (Basingstoke, 1998)

Keith Thomas, *Religion and the Decline of Magic: Studies in Popular Beliefs in Sixteenth- and Seventeenth-Century England* (London, 1971)

Alexandra Walsham, *Church Papists: Catholicism, Conformity and Confessional Polemic in Early Modern England* (Woodbridge, 1993)

Robert Whiting, *The Blind Devotion of the People: Popular Religion and the English Reformation* (Cambridge, 1989)

SCOTLAND

Jane E. A. Dawson, *Scotland Re-Formed 1488–1587* (Edinburgh, 2007)

Gordon Donaldson, *The Scottish Reformation* (Cambridge, 1960)

Michael F. Graham, *The Uses of Reform: 'Godly Discipline' and Popular Behaviour in Scotland and Beyond, 1560–1610* (Leiden, 1996)

Crawford Gribben and David George Mullan (eds), *Literature and the Scottish Reformation* (Farnham, 2009)

John Guy, *My Heart is my Own: The Life of Mary Queen of Scots* (London, 2004)

John McCallum, *Reforming the Scottish Parish: The Reformation in Fife, 1560–1640* (Farnham, 2010)

Alec Ryrie, *The Origins of the Scottish Reformation* (Manchester, 2006)

Margaret H. B. Sanderson, *Ayrshire and the Reformation* (East Linton, 1997)

Margo Todd, *The Culture of Protestantism in Early Modern Scotland* (New Haven and London, 2002)

Jenny Wormald, *Court, Kirk and Community: Scotland, 1470–1625* (London, 1981)

IRELAND

Brendan Bradshaw, *The Dissolution of the Religious Orders in Ireland in the Reign of Henry VIII* (Cambridge, 1974)

Nicholas Canny, *Making Ireland British, 1580–1650* (Oxford, 2001)

Steven G. Ellis, *Tudor Ireland: Crown, Community and the Conflict of Cultures, 1470–1603* (London, 1985)

Alan Ford, *The Protestant Reformation in Ireland, 1590–1641*, 2nd edn (Dublin, 1997)

Alan Ford and John McCafferty (eds), *The Origins of Sectarianism in Early Modern Ireland* (Cambridge, 2005)

Raymond Gillespie, *Devoted People: Belief and Religion in Early Modern Ireland* (Manchester, 1997)

Henry A. Jefferies, *The Irish Church and the Tudor Reformations* (Dublin, 2010)

Colm Lennon, *Sixteenth-Century Ireland: The Incomplete Conquest*, 2nd edn (Dublin, 2005)

Samantha A. Meigs, *The Reformations in Ireland: Tradition and Confessionalism, 1400–1690* (Basingstoke, 1997)

James Murray, *Enforcing the English Reformation in Ireland: Clerical Resistance and Political Conflict in the Diocese of Dublin, 1534–1590* (Cambridge, 2011)

WALES

J. Gwynfor Jones, *Early Modern Wales, 1525–1640* (Basingstoke, 1994)

Katharine Olson, *Popular Religion, Culture, and Reformation in Wales and the Marches, c.1400–1603* (Oxford, forthcoming)

Glanmor Williams, *Renewal and Reformation: Wales c.1415–1642* (Oxford, 1993)

Glanmor Williams, *Wales and the Reformation* (Cardiff, 1997)

7. REFORMATION LEGACIES

MEMORY AND HISTORY

Irena Backus, *Historical Method and Confessional Identity in the Era of the Reformation (1378–1615)* (Leiden, 2003)

David Cressy, *Bonfires and Bells: National Memory and the Protestant Calendar in Elizabethan and Stuart England* (London, 1989)

A. G. Dickens and J. Tonkin, *The Reformation in Historical Thought* (Oxford, 1985)

Simon Ditchfield, Katherine Elliot van Liere, and Howard Louthan (eds), *Sacred History: Uses of the Christian Past in the Renaissance World* (Oxford, 2012)

Bruce Gordon (ed.), *Protestant History and Identity in Sixteenth-Century Europe* (2 vols, Aldershot, 1996)

TOLERATION, PLURALISM, AND PATRIOTISM

David R. Blanks and Michael Frassetto (eds), *Western Views of Islam in Medieval and Early Modern Europe: Perception of Other* (Basingstoke, 1999)

Tony Claydon and Ian McBride (eds), *Protestantism and National Identity: Britain and Ireland, c.1650–c.1850* (Cambridge, 1998)

Willem Frijhoff, *Embodied Belief: Ten Essays on Religious Culture in Dutch History* (Hilversum, 2002)

Molly Greene, *A Shared World: Christians and Muslims in the Early Modern Mediterranean* (Princeton, 2000)

Ole Peter Grell and Roy Porter (eds), *Toleration in Enlightenment Europe* (Cambridge, 2000)

Ole Peter Grell and Bob Scribner (eds), *Tolerance and Intolerance in the European Reformation* (Cambridge, 1996)

Jonathan I. Israel, *European Jewry in the Age of Mercantilism, 1550–1750* (Oxford, 1989)

Benjamin J. Kaplan, *Divided by Faith: Religious Conflict and the Practice of Toleration in Early Modern Europe* (Cambridge, Mass., 2007)

John Christian Laursen and Cary J. Nederman (eds), *Beyond the Persecuting Society: Religious Toleration before the Enlightenment* (Philadelphia, 1998)

Keith P. Luria, *Sacred Boundaries: Religious Coexistence and Conflict in Early-Modern France* (Washington, 2005)

Gerald MacLean and Nabil Matar (eds), *Britain and the Islamic World, 1558–1713* (Oxford, 2011)

William S. Maltby, *The Black Legend in England: The Development of Anti-Spanish Sentiment, 1558–1660* (Durham, NC, 1971)

John Marshall, *John Locke, Toleration and Early Enlightenment Culture* (Cambridge, 2006)

R. Po-Chia Hsia and Hartmut Lehmann (eds), *In and Out of the Ghetto: Jewish–Gentile Relations in Late Medieval and Early Modern Germany* (Washington, 1995)

R. Po-Chia Hsia and H. F. K. van Nierop (eds), *Calvinism and Religious Toleration in the Dutch Golden Age* (Cambridge, 2002)

Thomas Max Safley (ed.), *A Companion to Multiconfessionalism in the Early Modern World* (Leiden, 2011)

Stuart B. Schwarz, *All Can be Saved: Religious Tolerance and Salvation in the Iberian Atlantic World* (New Haven and London, 2008)

Jesse Spohnholz, *The Tactics of Toleration: A Refugee Community in the Age of Religious Wars* (Newark, Del., 2011)

Alexandra Walsham, *Charitable Hatred: Tolerance and Intolerance in England, 1500–1700* (Manchester, 2006)

Ruth Whelan and Carol Baxter (eds), *Toleration and Religious Identity: The Edict of Nantes and its Implications in France, Britain and Ireland* (Dublin, 2003)

WORK AND PLAY: THE REFORMATIONS, ECONOMIC RELATIONS,
AND THE RHYTHM OF EVERYDAY LIFE

John Brewer and Roy Porter (eds), *Consumption and the World of Goods* (London, 1994)

Jan de Vries, *The Industrious Revolution: Consumer Behavior and the Household Economy, 1650 to the Present* (Cambridge, 2008)

Craig Muldrew, *The Economy of Obligation: The Culture of Credit and Social Relations in Early Modern England* (Basingstoke, 1998)

Ulinka Rublack, *Dressing Up: Cultural Identity in Renaissance Europe* (Oxford, 2010)

Simon Schama, *The Embarrassment of Riches: An Interpretation of Dutch Culture in the Golden Age* (London, 1987)

R. H. Tawney, *Religion and the Rise of Capitalism* (Harmondsworth, 1926)

Brodie Waddell, *God, Duty and Community in English Economic Life, 1660–1720* (Woodbridge, 2012)

Max Weber, *The Protestant Ethic and the Spirit of Capitalism*, trans. Stephen Kalbert (Los Angeles, 2002)

MATERIAL CULTURES AND ENVIRONMENTS

Marta Ajmar-Wollheim and Flora Dennis (eds), *At Home in Renaissance Italy* (London, 2006)

D. A. Brading, *Mexican Phoenix: Our Lady of Guadalupe: Image and Tradition across Five Centuries* (Cambridge, 2001)

William Christian, *Local Religion in Sixteenth-Century Spain* (Princeton, 1981)

Will Coster and Andrew Spicer (eds), *Sacred Space in Early Modern Europe* (Cambridge, 2005)

Marc R. Forster, *Catholic Revival in the Age of the Baroque: Religious Identity in Southwest Germany, 1550–1750* (Cambridge, 2001)

David Gaimster and Roberta Gilchrist (eds), *The Archaeology of the Reformation 1480–1580* (Leeds, 2003)

Tara Hamling, *Decorating the Godly Household: Religious Art in Post-Reformation Britain* (New Haven and London, 2010)

Howard Louthan, *Converting Bohemia: Force and Persuasion in the Catholic Reformation* (Cambridge, 2009)

Simon Schama, *Landscape and Memory* (London, 1996)

Jeffrey Chipps Smith, *Sensuous Worship: Jesuits and the Art of the Early Catholic Reformation in Germany* (Princeton, 2002)

Andrew Spicer and Sarah Hamilton (eds), *Defining the Holy: Sacred Space in Medieval and Early Modern Europe* (Aldershot, 2004)

Alexandra Walsham, *The Reformation of the Landscape: Religion, Identity and Memory in Early Modern Britain and Ireland* (Oxford, 2011)

DISENCHANTMENT, SCIENCE, AND ENLIGHTENMENT

Robin Bruce Barnes, *Prophecy and Gnosis: Apocalypticism in the Wake of the Lutheran Reformation* (Stanford, Calif., 1998)

Euan Cameron, *Enchanted Europe: Superstition, Reason, and Religion, 1250–1750* (Oxford, 2010)

Stuart Clark, *Thinking with Demons: The Idea of Witchcraft in Early Modern Europe* (Oxford, 1997)

Lorraine Daston and Katharine Park, *Wonders and the Order of Nature, 1150–1750* (New York, 1998)

Mordechai Feingold (ed.), *The New Science and Jesuit Science: Seventeenth-Century Perspectives* (Dordrecht, 2003)

Sarah Ferber, *Demonic Possession and Exorcism in Early Modern France* (London, 2004)

Andrew Keitt, *Inventing the Sacred: Imposture, Inquisition and the Boundaries of the Supernatural in Golden Age Spain* (Leiden, 2005)

Sachiko Kusukawa, *The Transformation of Natural Philosophy: The Case of Philip Melanchthon* (Cambridge, 1995)

Brian P. Levack, *The Witchhunt in Early Modern Europe* (London, 1995)

Peter Marshall and Alexandra Walsham (eds), *Angels in the Early Modern World* (Cambridge, 2006)

John O'Malley et al. (eds), *The Jesuits: Cultures, Sciences, and the Arts, 1540–1773* (Toronto, 2000)

R. W. Scribner, 'The Reformation, Popular Magic and "the Disenchantment of the World"', *Journal of Interdisciplinary History*, 23 (1993)

R. W. Scribner, *Religion and Culture in Germany (1400–1800)*, ed. Lyndal Roper (Leiden, 2001)

Jane Shaw, *Miracles in Enlightenment England* (New Haven, 2006)

Philip M. Soergel, *Miracles and the Protestant Imagination: The Evangelical Wonder Book in Reformation Germany* (Oxford, 2012)

Keith Thomas, *Religion and the Decline of Magic: Studies in Popular Beliefs in Sixteenth- and Seventeenth-Century England* (Harmondsworth, 1973)

Gary K. Waite, *Heresy, Witchcraft and Magic in Early Modern Europe* (Basingstoke, 2003)

Alexandra Walsham, *Providence in Early Modern England* (Oxford, 1999)

Alexandra Walsham, 'The Reformation and the Disenchantment of the World Revisited', *Historical Journal*, 51 (2008)

CHRONOLOGY

1378–1417	Great Schism between rival papal claimants
1384	Death of John Wyclif, English critic of papacy and inspiration for Lollard heresy
1409	Council of Pisa
1414–18	Council of Constance
1415	Execution of dissident priest Jan Hus sparks protest in Bohemia
1419	Start of Hussite wars
1423–4	Council of Pavia–Siena
1431–49	Council of Basel
1438	Pragmatic Sanction of Bourges limits papal control over Church in France
1439	Council of Florence achieves temporary reconciliation between Orthodox and Latin Churches
1453	Fall of Constantinople to Turks
1455	Printing of Gutenberg Bible
1480	Founding of Spanish Inquisition
1483	Birth of Martin Luther
1484	Birth of Huldrych Zwingli
1485	Accession of Tudor dynasty in England
1491	Conversion to Catholicism of the King of Kongo
1492	Spanish Conquest of Granada from Moors; expulsion of Jews from Spain; Columbus discovers America
1492–1503	Pontificate of Borgia Pope Alexander VI
1494	Treaty of Tordesillas: Alexander VI divides known world between Portugal and Spain; German humanist Sebastian Brand publishes satirical *Ship of Fools*
1497	Jews expelled from Portugal
1498	Dominican preacher and reformer Girolamo Savonarola burned for heresy in Florence
1505	Luther becomes Augustinian friar at Erfurt
1506	Work begins on new basilica of St Peter in Rome
1507	Jetzer Case: four Dominicans executed in Bern for faking apparitions of the Virgin Mary
1509	Birth of John Calvin; accession of Henry VIII in England
1516	Concordat of Bologna gives Francis I of France right to appoint bishops and abbots; Erasmus publishes new Latin and Greek version of the New Testament
1517	Luther posts Ninety-Five Theses in Wittenberg; Franciscans arrive in India
1518	Luther debates with Cardinal Cajetan in Augsburg
1519	Luther debates with Johannes Eck in Leipzig; Charles V becomes Holy Roman Emperor
1520	Luther excommunicated and burns papal bull; publishes core ideas in three treatises: *The Babylonian Captivity of the Church*; *The Freedom of a Christian*; *To the Christian Nobility of the German Nation*
1521	Luther defies Emperor at Diet of Worms and is hidden by Frederick the Wise at Wartburg
1522	Luther's translation of New Testament; Zwingli presides over Lent sausage meal in Zurich; Luther reverses Karlstadt's innovations in Wittenberg

1523	Two Augustinian friars burned in Brussels: first Reformation martyrs; arrival of Franciscan friars in Mexico
1523–6	Reformation in Zurich
1524	Luther and Johan Walter produce first Protestant 'hymn book'
1524–5	Peasants' War in Germany
1525	Luther marries Katharina von Bora; Erasmus breaks with Luther over freedom of will; Conrad Grebel performs adult baptism in Zurich
1526	Turkish victory at Mohács in Hungary; William Tyndale's English New Testament printed
1527	First Anabaptist executed by reformers (at Zurich); Gustav Vasa of Sweden declares independence from Rome
1529	'Protestatio' at Diet of Speyer gives its name to 'Protestants'; failure of Luther and Zwingli to agree over Eucharist at Colloquy of Marburg; first religious war in Switzerland
1530	Augsburg Confession supplies Lutheran statement of faith
1531	Lutheran League of Schmalkalden against Charles V; death of Zwingli in second Swiss religious war
1532–5	Henry VIII breaks with Rome and becomes 'Supreme Head' of Church of England
1534	Affair of the Placards and crackdown on Protestants in France; Calvin flees to Switzerland; Ignatius Loyola founds Society of Jesus; Kildare Rebellion in Ireland
1534–5	Anabaptist kingdom of Münster
1536	Publication of Calvin's *Institutes*; beginnings of Calvinist reformation in Geneva; Lutheran Reformation established in Denmark; Pilgrimage of Grace against Henry VIII
1540	Society of Jesus recognized by pope
1542	Establishment of Roman Inquisition
1543	Luther publishes *On the Jews and their Lies*
1545–7	First session of Council of Trent
1546–7	Schmalkaldic War
1547	Death of Luther; defeat of Lutheran princes at Mühlberg; death of Henry VIII and Protestant regime established in England under Edward VI
1548	Augsburg Interim re-imposes Catholicism in Empire
1550	Rights of Amerindians debated at Valladolid
1551–2	Second session of Council of Trent
1552	Death of Francis Xavier in Macao
1553	Burning of Servetus in Geneva; Mary I restores Catholicism in England
1555	Peace of Augsburg: *cuius regio eius religio*
1556	Abdication of Charles V
1558	Death of Mary I and accession of (Protestant) Elizabeth I in England
1559	Death of Henry II of France; Calvinist National Synod in Paris; papal Index of forbidden books
1559–60	Religious revolution in Scotland inspired by John Knox
1560	Inquisition established at Goa
1562	Outbreak of religious civil war in France (continues intermittently to 1598); de facto religious toleration in Poland; persecution of Christian 'back-sliders' in Yucatan, Mexico
1562–3	Third session of Council of Trent
1563	Frederick III establishes Calvinism in German Palatinate; first edition of John Foxe's *Book of Martyrs*
1564	Death of Calvin; birth of Shakespeare; birth of Galileo
1565	Archbishop Carlo Borromeo begins reform programme in Milan
1566	Iconoclasm in Netherlands

1567	Start of Dutch Revolt against Spain
1568	Mary Queen of Scots flees to England; revolt of the *moriscos* (converted Muslims) in Spain
1570	Pope Pius V excommunicates Elizabeth I; establishment of Inquisition in Mexico and Peru
1571	Naval victory of Christian forces against Turks at Lepanto
1572	St Bartholomew's Day Massacre in Paris
1577	Formula of Concord reunites German Lutherans
1579	Philippe du Plessis-Mornay's *Vindication Against Tyrants* justifies overthrow of ungodly rulers
1582	Gregory XIII reforms the calendar
1582–3	Third Council of Lima ('The Trent of the Americas')
1584	Huguenot Henry of Navarre becomes heir to French throne; Reginald Scot publishes sceptical *Discovery of Witchcraft*
1589	Assassination of Henry III of France: Henry of Navarre succeeds as Henry IV
1593	Henry IV converts to Catholicism
1598	Edict of Nantes declares limited toleration for Huguenots in France
1600	Scholar Giordano Bruno burnt for heresy in Rome
1603	Death of Elizabeth I and accession of James I, uniting Scottish and English crowns
1605	Gunpowder Plot to blow up English parliament
1609	Expulsion from Spain of the *moriscos*
1610	Canonization of Carlo Borromeo
1616–17	Intense witch persecution in bishopric of Würzburg
1618	Outbreak of Thirty Years War
1619	Synod of Dort (Netherlands) condemns deviations from Calvinism
1622	Establishment of papal congregation *Propaganda Fide*; canonizations of Ignatius of Loyola, Francis Xavier, Teresa of Avila, and Filippo Neri
1629	Ferdinand II's Edict of Restitution bans Calvinism in Empire and provokes entry of Sweden to Thirty Years War
1631	Jesuit Friedrich Spee's *Cautio Criminalis* critical of procedures in witchcraft trials
1633	Galileo condemned for heresy by Inquisition; Vincent de Paul and Louise de Marillac found Daughters of Charity
1638	National Covenant in defence of Reformation signed in Scotland
1639	Bishops' War between England and Scotland
1641	Catholic rebellion in Ireland
1642	Outbreak of Civil War in England; Pope Urban VIII radically trims number of holy days
1648	Treaty of Westphalia ends Thirty Years War and enacts religious toleration in the Empire
1649	Execution of Charles I of England
1660	Restoration of Charles II and re-establishment of Anglican Church
1670	Publication of Benedict Spinoza's *Tractatus Theologico-Politicus*: banned by both Catholic and Protestant authorities
1678–9	'Popish Plot' in England
1685	Louis XIV revokes Edict of Nantes
1688–9	'Glorious Revolution' deposes Catholic James II in Britain and Ireland; toleration for (Protestant) non-Anglicans
1691	Dutch pastor Balthasar Bekker attacks belief in witchcraft and supernatural in *The Enchanted World*
1692	Witch persecution in Salem, Massachusetts
1702–11	Huguenot rebellion in France
1704	Papal prohibition of 'Chinese Rites'

PICTURE ACKNOWLEDGEMENTS

90   akg-images
94   Iconographie Calvinienne by Emile Doumergue (Lausanne, 1909) pp. 161–162
95   Ecole Nationale Superieure des Beaux-Arts, Paris, France/Giraudon/The Bridgeman Art Library
100   akg-images
101   Collection Rijksmuseum, Amsterdam
103   IAM/akg
105   The Granger Collection/Topfoto
106   Carloe Eire
108   © Nudelman Numismatica
110   IAM/akg
112   Centennial Library, Cedarville University
113   akg-images
122   Universität Bern, Zentralbibliothek: ZB Hospinian 7:2
124   © Zentralbibliothek Zürich, Ms. B 316, f. 182v
125   akg-images
127   Mennonite Historical Library, Goshen College, Goshen, IN
129   Photograph courtesy of Mennonite Historical Library, Goshen College, Goshen, IN
130   Photograph courtesy of Mennonite Historical Library, Goshen College, Goshen, IN
132   Courtesy of the Schwenkfelder Library & Heritage Center, Pennsburg, PA
134   IAM/akg-images
136   Photograph courtesy of Bijzondere Collecties, UvA
138   Photograph courtesy of Mennonite Historical Library, Goshen College, Goshen, IN
140   IAM/akg-images
141   Photograph courtesy of Mennonite Historical Library, Goshen College, Goshen, IN
142   Photograph courtesy of Mennonite Historical Library, Goshen College, Goshen, IN
144   Photograph courtesy of Mennonite Historical Library, Goshen College, Goshen, IN
145   Photograph courtesy of Mennonite Historical Library, Goshen College, Goshen, IN
149   Private Collection/The Bridgeman Art Library
153   akg-images/Paul Koudounaris
155   © The Field Museum, #A114604_02d. John Weinstein
155   Twenty-six Martyrs' Museum, Nagasaki.
157   © Victoria and Albert Museum, London
158   Photo: Courtesy Saint Joseph's University Press
159   Archivum Romanum Societatis Iesu (ARSI), Jap. Sin. 43 f. 74v
166   akg-images/Andrea Jemolo
167   akg-images/Gilles Mermet
170   Private Collection/Ken Welsh/The Bridgeman Art Library
174   The Bodleian Library, University of Oxford. E.4.6.Th
180   © Richard Schofield
180   © Hans Roegele, architect & designer
182   © Richard Schofield
182   Evonne Levy
191   © Richard Hoare and licensed for reuse under this Creative Commons Licence
192   © The British Library Board. C. 70.g.14, image 56. Image produced by ProQuest as part of Early English Books Online. www.proquest.com
195   akg-images/British Library
198   Yvan Travert/akg-images
202   akg/De Agostini Picture Library

INDEX

Aachen 26–7
Abbas the Great, Shah of Persia 160
Abbeville 99
Aberdeen 190, 193
Acapulco 154
Acontius, Jacopo 237
Acosta, José de 162
  Historia natural y moral de las Indias 162
  De Procuranda Indorum Salute 162
  Tercero catecismo y esposición de la doctrina Cristiana por sermones 162
Adams, John 110
Afghanistan 163
Africa 153, 158, 163, 185, 226
Agra 154
Agricola, Johannes 59
Agricola, Rodolphus 16
Aikenhead, Thomas 267
Akbar, Emperor (Mughal) 154
Albrecht of Mainz 43, 45
Alcalà, Diego of 173–4
Aldrovandi, Ulisse 263
Alfonso I (of the Kongo) 158
Allstedt 57
Altötting 250
American Colonies 72, 77, 96
  Connecticut 106, 233, 251
  'Great Awakening' 267
  Massachusetts 233
  New England 104, 108, 226, 233, 251
  Pennsylvania 226
  Protestantism in 150–1
  Revolution 98
  Rhode Island 226
  Virginia
  see also United States
Americas, the 158, 163, 168, 185, 230, 237
  Latin 181, 229, 236, 250
  Meso 159
  North 100, 104, 176, 232
  South 159, 161–2, 183
Amsterdam 233–4, 243, 266
Anabaptists 65, 76, 96, 99, 104–6, 116, 118, 123–4, 126–7, 129–30, 132–40, 142–9, 231, 234, 237; *see also* Radical Protestantism
Andrews, Lancelot 223
Angers 99

Anglicanism, *see* England, Church of (Anglican)
Anglo-Saxons 160
Anhalt, 72, 104
Anjou, Duke of 213
Anne of Denmark 223
Antwerp 15, 143, 155, 253
Aquinas, Thomas 13, 166
  Summa Theologica 15
Aragon 12
Argentina 160
Arians 235
Aristotle 13, 15, 162, 262
Armenian Monophysites 106
Arminianism 109–10, 147–8
  The Remonstrance 109
  see also Remonstrants
Arminius, Jacob 109, 223
ars moriendi books 32
Arthur (English Prince) 187, 192, 196
Asia 160, 168, 181, 185, 226, 230
  East 158, 161
astronomy 262
atheism 265, 267
Augsburg 9, 16, 43, 45, 47, 51, 53–4, 59, 173, 247
  Peace of 74, 158, 231
Augustine of Canterbury 160
Augustine of Hippo 84
  City of God 252
Augustinianism 13, 45, 47–8, 51, 75; *see also under* religious orders
Auslauf 231
Austerlitz Brethren 130, 142
Australasia 226
Austria 26, 123, 163
  Protestantism in 129
Auxerre 99
Avignon 6, 176
Ayala, Don Pedro de 186–7
Ayutthaya, Bishop of 160
Aztecs 159, 162–3

Bacon, Sir Francis 214, 265
Bake, Alijt 30–1
  Four Ways of the Cross 30
Balbín, Bohuslav
  Epitome historica rerum Bohemicarum 178
Bale, John 94
Banbury (Oxfordshire) 246

Band of the Lords of the Congregation 210–11
banking 15
baptism 121, 123–4, 137, 145
Baptists 147–8, 226
Baronio, Cesare 172–3
  Acta sanctorum 178
  Annales ecclesiastici 178
Barrow, Henry 147
Bartoli, Daniello
  Istoria della compagnia di Gesù 178
Basel 6, 8, 11, 17, 24, 32, 44, 65, 81, 105, 135, 143
  Council of 8–9, 12, 15
Batenburg, Jan van 135
Batenburgers 135
Battle of Bosworth 187
Battle of Flodden 188, 205
Battle of Frankenhausen 126–7
Battle of Landside 212
Battle of Pinkie 205
Battle of Solway Moss 200
Battle of the White Mountain 139
Bavaria 153, 178, 239
Bayeux 99
Beaton, James 195, 201–2
Becket, Thomas 188
Beckum, Maria van 140
Beckum, Ursula van 140
Bede:
  Ecclesiastical History 162
Behold the Man (woodcut) 4
Bekker, Balthasar:
  The Enchanted World 265
Belgium 261
Berger, Georg:
  Contrafactur der Osnabrückschen Bischofe 134
Bern 18, 28–9, 87, 143
Berze, Jasper 152
Bernardino of Siena 21–2
Besse 235
Bethlen, Gabor 108
Beza, Theodore 145
Bèze, Thèodore 93, 112
  The Rights of Magistrates 98
Biberach 231
Bible, the 45, 61, 64, 77, 83–4, 89, 97, 103, 111, 114, 117–20, 126, 131, 196, 205, 230, 252–3, 262, 265

Bible, the (*cont.*)
  debates about 18
  Douai 172
  Gospels 87, 91, 120–1, 123, 126, 142
  Gutenberg 9, 11
  interpretation of 15, 22, 117, 120, 123, 126, 133
  King James version 221
  pocket versions of 24
  reading of 197
  translations of 23, 75, 112, 194, 205, 207
  work on 17
  Wyclif 23, 38
bigotry 229; *see also* intolerance
Biondo, Flavio 11
Blaurock, Georg 121, 129
Blois 81
blood purity laws 236
Bodin, Jean 231
Bodmin 205
body 75
Bohdisattva 154
Bohemia 35, 48, 130, 178
Bohemian Brethren 106
Boleyn, Anne 196–7, 199, 209
Bolivia 182
Bologna 169, 263
  Concordat of 12
Bond of Association 213
Book of Common Prayer 103, 203, 205, 210, 214, 221, 224–6
Book of Discipline 211, 240; *see also* Second Book of Discipline
books 255
  banning/burning of 195
  culture of 254, 256
  of Hours 5, 21–2
Bora, Katharina von 62–3
Borgia family 6
Borgia, Francisco 154
Borromeo, Carlo 178–83
  Acta ecclesiae Mediolanensis 178–9
Bosch, Hieronymus
  Garden of Earthly Delights 1
Bossuet, Jacques-Bénigne 246
botany 263
Botero, Giovanni 175, 178
  Della ragion di stato 159
Bothwell, Earl of 212
Bourges 80, 99
  Pragmatic Sanction of Bourges 11–12
Bouvais 99
Bouwens, Lenaert 137
Bowes, William de 19
Boyvin, René:
  Portrait of Calvin 80
Brady, Tom 49

Braght, Thieleman Jans van:
  Martyrs' Mirror of the Defenseless or Baptism-Minded Christians 139–40
Brahe, Tycho 262
Brancati, Francesco 183
Brandenburg 105, 173
Brant, Sebastian 13, 16
  Ship of Fools 12, 26
Brederode, Reinhard II van 5
Brethren of the Common Life 29
Briçonnet, Guillaume 179
Bristol 194
Britain/British Isles 152, 186–7, 189, 192, 193, 200, 223, 224, 232, 233, 248–9, 253
  Great 188
  see also England; Wales
Brown, Norman O. 72
Browne, George 200
Browne, Robert 147
Bruges 15
Brugge, Johann van 136
Bruno, Giordano 262–3
Brussels 137
Bucer, Martin 64, 87, 204
  De Regno Christi 87
Buchanan, George 200, 212
Buchelius, Arnoldus 236
Budapest 13
Buddhism 160
Bugenhagen, Johannes 69
Bullinger, Heinrich 186, 204
Bünderlin, Hans 130
Burgundy 163
Burnett, Amy 57
Butler earls of Ormond 188
Byzantium 9; *see also* Constantinople

Cadbury family 241
Caen 99
Cajetan, Cardinal 43, 47
Calvin, John 40, 76–7, 93, 104, 116, 142, 186, 237, 256
  The Ecclesiastical Ordinances 87
  On fleeing the illicit rites of the ungodly 91
  The Institutes of the Christian Religion 81, 83–5, 87, 97
  The Inventory of Relics 79
  actions of 88, 112, 204
  ideas/theology of 80, 83–5, 91–2, 94, 97, 109, 111, 114, 116, 147, 209, 221–2, 253
  influence of 95–6, 114
  life of 79–81, 87
  portrayals/reputation of 80, 94, 110–11
Calvinism 76, 94–5, 97, 100–1, 104–5, 108–9, 166, 174, 223, 240, 242, 247, 265

American 106, 109
  Dutch 79, 104, 109, 137, 233, 239, 247, 261
  English 101, 103, 109, 223, 261
  French 104
  German 104–5, 107–8
  Hungarian 105–6
  Polish 108
  Scottish 247, 261
  Swiss 104, 247
  see also under Reformed Protestantism
Calvinists 98–9, 105, 108–9, 112, 114, 148, 214, 219, 231, 236, 243, 258
Cambridge 194, 204, 209
Campion, Edmund 215
Canada 160, 226
  Quebec 184
Canterbury 19, 26, 196
  Archbishop of 197, 206–7, 209, 220, 223
Capac, Huayna 159
capitalism 229, 240–2
Capuchins 179
Carcassonne 176
Caribbean 162
Carpaccio, Vittore:
  Pope and Saint 10
Casas, Bartholome de las:
  In defence of the Indians 237
Castellio, Sebastian 96, 145, 150
  Advice for a Desolate France 96
  On the Art of Doubting and Believing 97, 145
Castile 12
Castle Acre Priory (Norfolk) 198
Cathars 119, 176
Catherine (daughter of Isabella and Ferdinand) 187
Catherine of Aragon 196, 206, 212
Catholic Reformation 118, 152, 163, 171, 177–80, 201, 206–7, 229, 231, 239, 246–7, 250–1
Catholicism 160, 173, 184–5, 197, 207, 229, 239, 241, 244, 250, 253, 255–6, 259–60
  global 152, 162–3, 165
  recusant 221
  Reformed 175
  Tridentine 168, 178, 181, 236, 246, 253; *see also* Trent, Council of
  see also Church, the: Catholic
Catholics 108, 125, 131, 150, 166, 223, 226, 237, 240, 248, 252
  in opposition to Calvin 93–4
  in opposition to Luther 46
Caussin, Nicolas 181
  La Cour sainte 181
Cauvin, Gerard 77
Cavalleriis, Giovanni Battista de:
  Ecclesiae Anglicanae Trophea 215

Cecil, William 210–11, 213
chantries 33–4
Charenton 236
Chariots of Fire (film) 246
charity 32
Charlemagne 26
Charles I (of England) 101, 104–6, 117, 148, 221, 223–6
Charles II (of England) 104
Charles V (Holy Roman Emperor) 11, 49, 53, 55, 120, 123, 171, 196, 204, 230
Charles VIII (of France) 12
Charles of Guise 169
Chaucer, Geoffrey 1, 35, 40
Chicago:
    Field Museum 154
children 61, 64, 89, 131, 183–4, 235, 254, 259–60
China 153–5, 157, 159–63, 166, 183
    Hizen Province 160
Christology 144
Christoph von
    Württemberg, Duke 93
Church, the:
    Catholic 115, 117, 119, 142, 176, 178, 231, 239, 242–3, 248, 255, 261; *see also* Catholicism
    bureaucracy of 75
    criticism of/opposition to 57, 66, 82, 90, 120, 123, 126, 146, 150, 221, 257, 259
    defense of 130
    doctrines of 161–2
    re-Catholicization 140, 162
    relationship with the state 76–7, 114, 150, 183, 192–3, 197, 235
churches 25
    building 190
    design/style of 79
Clare of Montefalco 262
clergy 20, 35, 203, 209, 214, 256
    hostility towards 18, 35, 190
    living conditions 18
    reputation 18, 256
    role of 21, 103
Coburg Castle 43
Cochinchina 161
Cochlaeus, Johannes 46, 48–9, 59, 70
Colet, John 19
Colgan, John:
    Acta sanctorum hiberniae 178
Collegium Germanicum-
    Hungaricum 173
Collinson, Patrick 220
Colmar 1
Cologne 10, 152, 155, 176, 184, 194
Colonna family 6
Columbus, Christopher:
    Book of Prophecies 162

community 130, 137, 192, 242, 259, 268
    perfectibility of 77
Conciliarism 11, 48, 171
Confession 21
confessionalization 116
Congregation of the Doctrine of the
    Faith 175
Congregation of the Holy Office, *see*
    Inquisition, the: Roman
Congregation of the Oratory 172
Congregation of Propaganda
    Fide 171, 177, 181
Congregation of Sacred Rites 174
Congregationalists 109
consistories 105, 247; *see also under*
    Geneva
Constance:
    archbishopric of 18
    Council of 6, 15, 38, 48
Constantine (Roman Emperor) 157
Constantinople 12
convents 61
conversion 157–8
Coornherts, Dirk 91, 150
Cop, Nicholas 81
Copernicus, Nicholas 262–3
Coppe, Abiezer 148
Coptic Church 163
Corporacque (Peru) 180
Corpus Christi:
    Feast of 25
    Processions 38
Corsica 161
Cortés, Hernan 159
Counter-Reformation, *see* Catholic
    Reformation
Coventry 194
Cranach, Lucas 44, 54, 56–7, 62, 69–72
Cranmer, Thomas 196–7, 199, 201, 203–4, 206–8, 219, 226, 250
Cromwell, Oliver 104, 148, 199, 233
Cromwell, Thomas 197, 201
Cuhna, Rodrigo da:
    *Historia ecclesiastica da igreja de
    Lisboa* 178
culture 268
    reading 254, 256
    and religion 114
Czechs 39

Dante 32
Dartmouth Butterwalk (Devon) 254
Daughters of Charity 184
Davidites, *see* Jorists
Davidjorists, *see* Jorists
Dax, Leonhard 139
Day, Richard:
    A book of Christian Prayers 211

De Profundis 33
death 33–4, 261
Decalogue, the 246
decrees:
    Frequens 6
    Haec Sancta 6
Dedham (Essex) 220
Denck, Hans 130, 132
Denmark 204, 232, 259
    people of 262
Derricke, John
    The Image of Irelande 217
Descartes, René 265
Diggers 148
Dionysius the Areopagite 13
diversity 230, 240
divorce 12, 61, 88, 196, 204
Doering, Christian 56
Dominicans 65, 153; *see also under*
    religious orders
Dordrecht (Dort):
    Synod of 109–10, 223
Douai 214
Dublin 188, 200
    Archbishop of 214
    Trinity College 214
Duchetti, Claude:
    *General Congregation of the
    Council of Trent* 170
Dudley, John (Duke of
    Northumberland) 201, 204, 206
Dugdale, William:
    Monasticon Anglicanum 248
Dundee 201
Duns Scotus 13, 28
Dürer, Albrecht 24
    'Foolish teachers and foolish
    students' (woodcut) 12
Dvořák, Anton 39

Eck, Johannes 13, 47–8, 127
Edinburgh 211, 267
economics 23, 111, 123, 127, 177, 229, 241–3, 257, 267
Edward IV (of England) 12, 203
Edward VI (of England) 101, 103, 117, 200–1, 203–4, 206–7, 210, 226
Edwards, Jonathan 267
Edwards, Thomas:
    Gangraena 148, 233
Egypt 163
Einsiedeln 27
Eisenach 51
Eisleben 59, 69, 250
election 85, 113, 126
Elizabeth I (of England) 103, 117, 143–4, 147, 209–14, 219–21, 226
Elphinstone, William 193

England 77, 100–1, 105, 109, 143,
148, 187–8, 190, 195, 201–2,
211, 217, 239, 248, 250, 253,
257–8, 261
    Act of 1689: 235
        Reversal of 235
    Act of Appeals 197
    Act of Supremacy 210
    Act of Uniformity 210
    Buckinghamshire 204
    Catholicism in 103, 197–9, 204,
        206–9, 212–16, 235, 248
    church in 12, 18–19, 235
    Church of (Anglican) 101, 104,
        115, 117, 147–8, 186, 196–7,
        209–10, 221, 223, 235, 247
    Civil War 101, 104, 118, 146, 148,
        221, 225–6, 230, 233, 243
    Cornwall 188, 204–5
    Devon 204, 254
    Dispensations Act 197
    dissent within 35, 38, 104, 235, 241
    Elizabethan settlement 219
    Forty-Two Articles 210
    Glorious Revolution 235
    Gunpowder Plot 183, 216, 239
    Instrument of Government 233
    Kent 199
    Norfolk 204
    Oxfordshire 204
    Parliament of 225
    people of 94–5, 98, 162, 183–4,
        199–200, 212, 215
    Popish Plot 235
    Protestantism in 97, 135, 146–9,
        177, 186, 194, 197, 199–200,
        203–4, 207–13, 215–16, 219,
        221, 223–5, 235, 241, 244–5,
        253, 255, 261
    Republic/Cromwellian
        Protectorate 146, 148, 233
    Restoration (of the monarchy) 104,
        106, 233, 244
    Revolution 131, 134, 146–8,
        150, 246
    Royal Society 265
    Shropshire 224
    Thirty-Nine Articles 210
    Wars of the Roses 12, 187
    Warwickshire 213
    Yorkshire 204
English College 173
Enlightenment, the 84, 229, 235,
    237, 239, 256, 262, 267
Entfelder, Christian 130
Episcopalians 226
Erasmus, Desiderius 13, 16–18, 26,
    81, 131, 186–7, 194, 196, 207
    Novum Instrumentum 17
Erfurt 48, 51, 58, 60
Erikson, Erik 72

Young Man Luther 72
Esslingen 62
Estonia 32
ethics 111, 242–3; *see also* morality
Ethiopia 163
Europe 238
    Eastern 206
    states of 3
evangelism 66, 83, 201, 239
    English 194–5, 197, 208
    French 91
Evora 176
excommunication 87, 219

Faber, Georg 62
faith 84, 111, 117, 121, 142, 207
family 254
Family of Love 143–4, 147–8
Farel, Guillaume 85, 87
Fawkes, Guy 216
Featley, Daniel:
    The Dippers Dipt 148–9
Febvre, Lucien 72
Ferdinand I (Archduke) 130
Ferdinand and Isabella (of Spain) 12,
    177, 186–7
Ferrara 16
Ferrero, Marco 157
Fessner, Michael 51
festivals/holidays 219, 244, 246
Fifth Monarchists 148
Fincelius, Job 257
Fisher, John 193, 199
Fitzgerald, Thomas 199–200
Fitzgerald earls of Kildare 188
Flanders 15–16, 28, 99, 137–9, 154
Flensburg 132
Florence 1, 13, 16, 183
    Council of 8
    Duomo, the 8
Fox, George 148, 260
Foxe, John:
    Acts and Monuments 103, 208
France 23, 32, 40, 77, 81–2, 91–4,
    99–100, 176, 186, 188, 200–2,
    206, 211, 213, 217, 223,
    235–6, 248, 257
    Brittany 161
    Catholicism in 178, 231–2, 246,
        250, 257
    Edict of Fontainbleau
        99–100, 232
    Edict of Nantes 99, 231–2
        Revocation of, *see* France, Edict
        of Fontainbleau
    Franche-Comté 176
    kings of 12, 169, 239
    language of 87, 89, 111
    nation of 83
    Protestantism in 104, 232
    Revolution in 119

Wars of Religion 93, 96–7, 169,
    230, 236, 257
Francis I (of France) 80–1, 83, 171
Francis II (of France) 212
Francis (dauphin of France) 206
Franck, Sebastian 131
Frederick III (Holy Roman
    Emperor) 11
Frederick the Wise of Saxony 42–3,
    47, 51, 53, 73, 120, 228
free will 147
freedom 58, 119, 121, 151, 231,
    233, 237
freethinkers 108
'Freewillers' 147
Friesland 138–9, 141
    East 137
Froben, Johann 17, 24
Fromm, Erich 72
Fugger:
    family 9, 45
    palace 47
Fulda 173
fundamentalism 259

Gabrielites 130
Gaelic (language) 188, 214
Gaismair, Michael 126
Galenism 262
Galilei, Galileo 262
Gansfort, Wessel 15
Gardiner, Stephen 199, 201, 205
Geneva 40, 85–7, 99–100, 104–5, 116,
    204, 206, 209, 211, 229, 247
    Academy 93, 104
    Church 88
    consistory 88–9, 91, 240
    under Calvin 88–96, 111–12, 145
Geneva Psalter 111–12
George III of Anhalt 72
George, Duke 47
Germany 9, 23, 31, 33, 39, 54, 67–8,
    74, 77, 100, 107, 116, 119, 169,
    176, 194, 228, 235, 248, 250
    church in 18
    'Grievances of the German
        nation' 11
    language of 53, 65, 75, 120, 133
    nation of 16, 48
    Peasants' War 58–9, 116, 119–20,
        123, 125–9, 133–4, 146, 204
    people of 58, 65, 97, 204, 257
    princes of 11, 67–8, 231
    Protestantism in 104, 108, 118,
        121, 123, 126, 129–31, 146–8,
        150, 204, 227, 247, 261
    reformers of 76
Gerson, Jean 13
Giesingen 248
Glanville, Joseph:
    Sadducismus Triumphatus 264

Goa 152, 154
  College of St Paul 152
Godinho, Manuel 154
Golden Age of Sacred
    History 178
Goodman, Christopher 209
  *How Superior Powers Ought To Be
    Obeyed* 98
Gordon earls (of Huntly) 217
Gordon riots 236
Göttlicher Schrifftmessiger 228
Goulart, Simon 257
grace 45, 84, 97, 117, 142, 147
Graf, Urs:
  *Two Mercenaries and Women with
    Death in a Tree* 34
Graham, Billy 168
Granada, Emirate of 2
Granada, Luis de:
  Rhetoricae Ecclesiasticae 166
Gratian 39, 153
Great Schism, the 6, 11
Grebel, Conrad 121, 129–30
Greece 8–9, 97
  language of 80
Greek College 173
Greenwich 190
  Treaty of 201
Gregory the Great 160
Grey, Lady Jane 206
Grey, Lord 200
Grindal, Edmund 220
Grote, Geert 29–30
Grünewald:
  Crucified Christ 1
Guanyin 154
Guildford (Connecticut) 106
Guise family 200
Gutenberg, Johann 9
  press of 15, 22; *see also* printing
    press
Gutenberg Bible, *see under* Bible

Haarlem:
  St Bavo 79
Haemstede, Adriaen van 137
Haestens, Heinrich von:
  *Greuwel der vornahmsten
    Hauptketzeren* 144
Hamilton, Archbishop 206
Hamilton, James (Earl of
    Arran) 200–1, 206
Hamilton, Patrick 195
Hampton Court Conference 221
Hapsburgs, the 16, 105, 108, 130,
    137, 139, 163, 232,
    239, 253
healing 219
health, 241
Hebrew (language) 16, 80
Heidelberg 13, 104–5, 109

Heidelberg Catechism 104
Henri IV (of France) 99, 231
Henrietta Maria (wife of Charles I) 223
Henry II (of England) 188
Henry VII (of England) 186–8, 192–3,
    206, 213
Henry VIII (of England) 12, 101, 147,
    192–3, 196–7, 199–203, 205,
    207, 212, 226, 244
Henry Whitfield House 106
heresy 35, 38–9, 89, 169, 187, 195,
    197, 201, 207–8, 248, 263
  combatting 48, 130, 176, 200, 206
heretics 81
Herp, Hendrik:
  A Mirror of Perfection 30
Hesse 64, 75, 104
Het Offer des Heeren 137–9
Hielists 143–4
Hindus 163
Hobbes, Thomas 265
Hoffaeus, Paul 156
Hoffman, Melchior 132, 142
Hogarth, William:
  'Credulity, Superstition and
    Fanaticism' 266
Hogestraten, Jacob von 13
Holbein, Hans:
  Erasmus 16–17
Holy House of Loreto 250
Holy Roman Empire 11, 23, 119, 163,
    169, 230
  Imperial Diet 53, 55
Holy Spirit, the 130–1, 140, 147
Hondus, Hendrik:
  Pyramide papistique 90
Höngg 121
Hooker, Richard 223
Hornung, Wolf 64
House of Neophytes 173
Howard, Thomas 198
Hubmaier, Balthasar 127, 129–30
Hugenots 92–4, 98–100, 231–2,
    235–6, 241, 257
humanism 11, 13, 40–1, 66, 193, 196,
    250, 261
Hume, David 84
Hungary 14, 77, 97
  Protestantism in 105–6
Hunne, Richard 193, 196
Hus, Jan 38, 48, 53
Hussites 35, 38–9, 119
Hut, Hans 130
Hutter, Jacob 139
Hutterites 130, 135, 139–40,
    142, 146

Iberia 230, 236
  La Convivencia 2
  reconquest of 2, 177
  see also Portugal; Spain

iconoclasm 99, 101–2, 211
identity 223, 268
  confessional 206, 243–4, 253
  group 136–7, 256
  individual 256
  national 239
  social 229
idolatry 80, 82–4, 90, 93, 97–8, 118,
    160, 201, 247–8, 252
Illingworth, Elizabeth 255
images 203, 253, 256, 264
  use of 56–7; *see also* propaganda
  see also symbolism
Incas 159, 161–3
independence (religious) 231
India 152, 154, 157–8, 160, 163
individualism 242, 256
indulgences 45, 47
Ingolstadt 127, 129
Inquisition, the 176, 239, 261
  Portuguese 175
  Roman 88, 173, 175–7, 247, 266
  Spanish 2, 88, 175, 247
Institute of the Blessed Virgin Mary
    (Institute for English Ladies) 184
intolerance 230, 238–40; *see also*
    bigotry
Ireland 178, 186, 188, 190, 194,
    199–200, 205, 214–15,
    217–18, 223, 225–6, 236
  Church of 223
  Donegal 217, 248
  Kilkenny 205
  Nine-Years War 215
  Ossory 205
  Protestantism in 205, 215
  Rebellion 233
  St Patrick's Purgatory 248
  Ulster 215
Iserloh, Erwin 42
Isfahan, Bishop of 160
Isidor the Farmer 173
Italy 2, 6, 15, 23, 161, 166, 169, 178,
    193, 229, 241, 252
  Catholicism in 178
  invasion of 12
  people of 97, 135

James I (of England) 117, 226
James II (of England) 235
James III (of Scotland) 200
James IV (of Scotland) 186–8, 192
James V (of Scotland) 200, 206, 226
James VI (of Scotland) 217, 219, 221,
    223–4; *see also* James I (of
    England)
Jansen van Barrefelt, Hendrik 143–4
Janzoon Saenredam, Pieter 79
Japan 154–7, 160, 162
Jefferson, Thomas 110
Jena 57

Jerome, St. 16–17, 24
Jerusalem 163
Jesuits 30, 108, 152, 154, 156–8,
    160–1, 163, 165–6, 168, 173,
    178–9, 181, 183–4, 200, 213,
    215–16, 240, 250, 255,
    260–1, 263
Jetzer, Johannes 28–9
Jews/Judaism 2, 12, 39–40, 65–6,
    106, 123, 150, 175–6, 230–1,
    234, 236, 251, 265–6
    anti-semitism 37, 39–40, 66–9, 236
    Cabbala 16
Joachim of Brandenburg 64
John (King of England) 197
John the Baptist 190, 246
Jonas, Justus 42
Joris, David 135–6, 143
Jorists 136
Josel of Rosenheim (Rabbi) 66
Jost, Lienhard 132
Jost, Ursula 132
Julian of Norwich 13

Karlstadt, Andreas Bodenstein von 47,
    54, 57, 59, 120–2
Karsthans 59
Kaufmann, Thomas 49
Kempis, Thomas á:
    Imitation of Christ 30
Kennedy, Archbishop 14
Kepler, Johannes 262
Ket's Rebellion 204
Kiel 132
Kiffin, William 148
Kirchner, Athanasius 263
    Mundus Subterranus 263
Knipperdolling, Bernhard 133–4
Knox, John 94, 97–9, 202, 206,
    209–12
    *First Blast of the Trumpet Against
    the Monstrous Regiment* 209
Kongo, Kingdom of 158
Koran, the 65
Kramer, Heinrich:
    Hammer of the Witches 40
Krechting, Bernd 133–4

La Rochelle 99
Lalaing, Yolande de 5
Lambeth Council 21
Lamists 150
Landgrave, the 64
Landini, Silvestro 161
Laneau, Louis 160
Lang, Johannes 64
Lanzenstil, Leonhard 139
Lasco, John á 97
Lateran Councils:
    Fourth 21
    Fifth 171

Latimer, Hugh 197, 250
Laud, William 223–5, 233
    'Beauty of Holiness' 148
Laudianism 148
Lausanne 98
Lauterbach, Anton 62
Law:
    canon 18, 62, 185
Layerthorpe (England) 19
laypeople 29, 241, 244, 256, 267–8
    resentment of priests 18
    views of 60
Lazarists 179
Le Mans 99
learning:
    classical 10–11, 15, 80
    see also humanism
Lederlein, Jacob:
    Five Calvinist Articles 95
Lefèvre d'Étaples, Jacques 13, 81, 85
Leiden:
    University of 104
Leiden, Jan Beukels van 133–4
Leipzig 44, 47–9, 55
    debate 54
Leith 211
Leslie, George 166
Lettres édifiants et curieuses 166
Leunis, Jean 181
Leverton (Lincolnshire) 235
L'Hopital, Michel de 231
Libertines, The 89, 93, 96
Liège 184
life 244, 256, 268
Liguori, Alphonsus de 168
Lima 162, 179
    Third Council of 179
Lindemann family 51
Lindsay, Sir David 200
Lisbon 176, 178
literacy 229
Lithuania 173; *see also* Poland-
    Lithuania
liturgy 204, 233
Livingstone, David 163
Locke, John 98, 237
    Letter Concerning Toleration 237
logic 15
Lollards, the 23, 35, 38, 119,
    192–5, 208
Lombard, Peter:
    Sentences 15
London 188, 193, 204, 236, 241, 267
    Bishop of 194, 196
    Charterhouse 194
    St Paul's Cathedral 19
    Society of Antiquaries 228
    Spitalfields 241
    Tower of 215
    Victoria and Albert Museum 155
Longobardo, Niccolò 157

Louis XI (of France) 12
Louis XIII (of France) 181
Louis XIV (of France) 99–100, 231
Louth (Lincolnshire) 191
love 32, 247
Low Countries 4, 15–16, 29–30, 132,
    137, 144, 184, 213, 232; *see
    also* Belgium; Flanders;
    Netherlands, the
Loyola, Ignatius 165, 173, 255, 261
    Spiritual Exercises of Ignatius
    Loyola 255
Lübeck 32, 132
Lucca 176
Luder, Hans 51
Ludolf of Saxony 30
Lufft, Han 73
Lund 13
Luther, Martin 13, 68–9, 73, 116,
    122, 125, 127, 151, 163, 172,
    186, 192, 237, 250, 254
    'Appeal to the Christian
    Nobility' 48
    actions of 42–3, 54, 120
    allies of 59
    'apology' of 53
    character of 71, 73
    correspondence 44, 67
    ideas/theology of 45–9, 53,
    58–60, 64, 66, 76–7, 84,
    116–17, 123, 194, 207, 257
    influence of 59, 69–70
    life of 50–1, 55, 60–2, 70–2, 201,
    227
    portrayals of 55–7, 63, 70–2, 228
    works of 70, 73, 137
Lutheranism 69, 71, 87, 105, 115,
    117–18, 150, 169, 174, 176,
    187, 195, 197, 201, 231, 240,
    247, 253, 261
    and Calvinism 93, 95
Lutherans 73, 76, 83, 96, 106, 133,
    143, 146, 204, 230–1, 239, 262
    Pietists 30, 240, 267
Luyken, Jan 139–40
    *The Flight of the Hugenots from
    France* 100
Luzón 160
Lycosthenes, Conrad 257
Lyons 96, 99

MacSweeny clan 217
Madonna of St Luke 154–5
Madonna of the Snows 154, 156
Magdeburg:
    Bishop of 43
Mainz 9, 45
Maitland, Richard 219
Malaysia 152
Manila 153–4
Manohar (school of) 155, 157

Manuel, Niklaus 18, 28–9
  Totenfresser 18
Mansfeld 51
Mantz, Felix 121, 129
Manutius, Aldus 16
Marburg Colloquy 76
Marcourt, Antoine:
  *Articles veritables sur les horribles
    grandz et importables abuz de
    lamesse papale* 81
Margaret (daughter of Henry VII) 187
Marianism 53, 147, 181, 208, 239
Marie de l'Incarnation 183
Marillac, Louise de 184
Marnix Sainte Aldegonde, Philips
    von 97
Maronites 173
  of Antioch 163
Marot, Clément 112
Marpeck, Pilgram 142
marriage 60–2, 64–5, 75, 88, 183,
    187, 197, 203, 219
Marseille 99
Marshall, William:
  *The description of the severall Sorts
    of Anabaptists in Daniel
    Featley* 149
Marteville 79
Martin, Gregory 172
Martin, Marie Guyart 184
martyrs 70, 129, 137, 139, 141, 152,
    173, 214, 226–7
Marx, Karl 242
Mary I (of England) 97, 101, 103,
    198, 200, 203, 206–10, 226,
    240
Mary (Queen of Scots) 200, 206,
    209, 212–14, 226
Mary (daughter of Henry VII) 187
Mary of Guise 206, 209–11
Mary of Lorraine 200
mathematics 263
Mathesius, Johannes 70
Matthijs, Jan 133
Maximilian I (Holy Roman
    Emperor) 16, 53
Meaux 91, 99, 179
Mechelen (Belgium) 261
Melaka 152, 161
Melanchthon, Philip 42, 56, 64,
    69–70, 92, 254, 262
Melchiorites 133, 135, 142–3
Mellitus, Abbot 160
Melville, Andrew 219
Mendoza, Juan Palafox y 179
  Direcciones pastorales 179
Mennonites 135–9, 141–2, 146, 150
Mercurian, Everard 156
Merian, Matthias
  View of Geneva 86
Merici, Angela 183

Methodism 109, 240, 267
Mettrie, Julien Offray de la 84
Mexico 154, 166, 179
  Provincial Synod of 167, 179
  Puebla 179
Milan 178–80, 182, 246
  S. Fedele 182
Milton, John 150
mind 75
Ming dynasty (China) 163
minorities 200–1, 204–5, 221
Missal, the 22
Modena 176
modernity 256, 267
Mogrovejo, Toribio de 179
monasticism/monasteries 29–30, 61,
    190, 248, 250
  rejection of 53, 197–9
  see also convents; religious orders
Montepulciano (Tuscany) 252
Morales, Ambrogio de:
  La coronica general de España 178
morality 246–7; *see also* ethics
Moravia 97, 105, 127, 129–30, 135,
    139–40, 142, 146, 173
Moray, Earl of 212
More, Thomas 195, 199, 205, 207
Morone, Cardinal Giovanni 170
Morroco 163
*Moses with the Ten
    Commandments* 11
Muggletonians 233
Munich 184
Münster 65, 119, 133–7, 146
  Anabaptist Kingdom of 116
  St Lambert Church 133–4
Müntzer, Thomas 57, 65, 126–7,
    130–1
  'Prague Manifesto' 126
Muslims/Islam 2, 12, 65–6, 167, 230,
    236–7, 251
  Moors 175
Myrc, John:
  Instructions for Parish Priests 21

Nadal, Jerónimo da 158–9
  Adnotationes et meditationes 158
  *Evangelicae Historiae
    Imagines* 156–7, 182
Nagasaki 154
Nahuatl (language) 161, 167
names 89
Naples 176, 184
nationalism 99, 106, 227, 237
Native North Americans 160–1,
    167–8, 184–5, 237
nature 256–7, 259, 268
Nayler, James 148
Neoplatonism 13
nepotism 11
Neri, Filippo 172–3

Netherlands, the 77, 98–102, 109,
    204, 232, 235, 239, 241–3,
    248, 253, 257–8, 265
  Catholicism in 248
  Dutch Republic 137–8, 150, 232
  Dutch Revolt 138, 230,
    239, 258
  people of 15, 79, 97
  Protestantism in 104, 110, 133,
    135, 141, 146–7, 150, 233,
    244, 247, 261, 266
  Spanish 214
Neuchâtel 82
New England, *see under* United States
New France, *see* Canada
New Haven (Connecticut) 252
New World, the 2, 95, 154–5, 161–3,
    166–8, 179, 185
Nicea:
  Council of 144
  Second Council of 171
Nicholas of Cusa 9, 13, 19
  De Concordantia Catholica 9
  De Docta Ignorantia 9
Nicholas of Lyra 15
  Postilla Litteralis 15
  Postilla Moralis 15
Niclaes, Hendrik 143–4
Nicodemism 91–2, 142, 208–9, 214
Nikolsburg 127, 129
Ninety-Five Theses, the 42–5, 77,
    227–8
  criticism of 47, 54
Nominalism 13–14
Nonconformism 226, 235, 241
Norfolk, Duke of 199, 201
Noyon 40, 77, 79, 81
Nuns:
  Poor Clare 184
  Ursuline 184
Nuremberg 16, 22, 44, 51, 259
Nzinga a Nkuwu 158

Oberman, Heiko 45–6
Ochino, Bernardino 97
Oecolampadius 186
Oemle, Nicholas 51
Olevianus, Kaspar 97
O'Neill, Hugh 215
Oporinus 65
Orcadians 190
Orlamünde 121
Orléans 80–1, 99
ornithology 263
Orthodox Church, the 8–9, 106
Otomi (language) 167
Ottoman Empire 8, 105, 108, 163,
    230, 237, 241; *see also*
    Turks, the
Our Lady of Guadalupe 250
Our Lady of Walsingham 192

Oxford 250
  University 38, 148, 187, 194, 204
    Cardinal College 187
    Constitutions of 23

Pacher, Michael 27
Padua 16
Paesi Novamente Ritrovati 166
Palatinate, the 97, 104–5, 153, 168,
    239, 261
Palestine 250
Panvinio, Onofrio 152
papacy, the 178, 216, 227
  antipathy towards 119, 236–7, 256
  authority of 6, 9, 11–12, 170–1
    challenges to 45, 120, 196–7,
      210, 256
    limits to 47
  as corrupt 1
  divided, *see* Great Schism, the
  finances of 6
  loyalty to 199
  responsibilities of 169
  as weak 193
papal bulls:
  burning of 54
  Pastoralis Romani Pontificis 184
  Periculoso 183
Papal States 6–7, 178
Paracelsus, Theophrastus 143, 262
Paraguay 160
Paris 12, 14, 22, 81, 94, 99, 246
  Bishop of 179
  Collège Royal 80
  Louis de la Salle 181
  Mont Valerian 250
  Parlement 92
  Sorbonne 13, 80–1
Parker, Matthew 209–10
Parkyn, Robert 207
Passau 37
Passeri, Bernardino 158
patronage 60
Paul (Apostle) 13, 15, 46
Paul, Vincent de 184
Pavia 16
peasants 58–9, 61, 66
Peasants' War, *see under* Germany
Peasholme, St Cuthbert 19
pedagogy 23, 157–8
Pellegrini, Tibaldo 180
Pellizzone, Giovanni Andrea 180
Peña, Francisco 174
  Directorum Inquisitorum 174
Percy earls of Northumberland 188
Pérez, Juan 97
Perkins, William:
  A Golden Chaine 222
Perrin, Amy 89, 93
Perrin family 89
persecution 35, 240

of Catholics 104, 166, 225
of Protestants 81, 101, 130, 133,
    137, 207–8, 239–42
Perth 190
Peru 154, 162, 179–80
Perugia 184
Peter (Apostle) 132
Peter of Ghent 167
Peter of Spain 15
Petrucci, Pietro Jacopo 167
Pettegree, Andrew 54
Peutinger, Konrad 16
Philip II (of Spain) 99, 155, 177, 209,
    214, 237, 257
Philip of Hesse 64, 75
Philipites 130
Philips, Dirk 136–7
Philips, Obbe 136
Philippines 153–4, 160, 166
Picart, Berhard:
  Inquisition Torture Chamber 239
'Pilgrim Fathers' 226
pilgrims 2, 10, 26, 192, 199, 219, 250
Piombo, Sebastiano del 207
Pirckheimer, Willibald 16
Pizarro, Francisco 159
Placards, Affair of the 81–2
Plantin, Christophe 143
Plantin printing house 155
Platonism 143
plays 23
Plessis-Mornay, Phillipe du:
  Vindiciae contra Tyrannos 98
pluralism 151, 267
Poland 77, 97, 108, 135, 150, 179, 231
  people of 262
Poland-Lithuania 106, 108, 144, 157
Pole, Reginald 199, 205–7, 209
Ponet, John 209
Pontoise 99
Popes:
  Alexander VI 1–2, 9, 11–12
  Boniface IX 35
  Callistus III 12
  Clement VI 47
  Clement VII 196
  Clement VIII 156
  Cyriac 10
  Eugenius IV 8, 11
  Felix V 8
  Innocent III 6
  Innocent VIII 9, 177
  Julius II 9, 171
  Leo X 9, 228
  Martin V 6
  Nicholas V 9, 11
  Paul IV 207, 236
  Pius II 11
  Pius IV 169, 180
  Pius V 154, 172, 185, 213
  Pius X 185

Sixtus IV 9, 11
Sixtus V 173, 247
Urban VIII 246
Ponet, John:
  *Short Treatise on Politicke
    Power* 98
Portugal 12, 154, 161, 163, 176–7,
    185, 230, 236
  people of 265
Pozzo, Andrea 163
  The Apotheosis of St Ignatius 165
Prague 38
  Charles Bridge 251
predestination 84–5, 109, 147,
    221–3, 240
Presbyterians 100, 109, 148, 217,
    219–21, 233, 246
Pressburg 184
print (medium of) 53, 55–7, 255–6
printed material:
  broadsides 227
  pamphlets 54, 70, 257
  prints 155
printing press, the 15, 22, 54, 56, 166,
    254–5; *see also* Gutenberg:
    press of
progress 229
propaganda 73, 213
  Catholic 94
  Protestant 56–7, 66, 75, 90, 208
protests 49
psychology 72, 240
puritanism 89
Puritans:
  American 106, 226, 252
  English 30, 95, 104, 146–8, 219,
    221–4, 233, 243–4, 246, 254
  Scottish 219–20

Quakers 148, 150, 226, 233, 235,
    241, 243–4, 260
Quechua (language) 161
Quedlinburg, Jordan of 30

Rabus, Ludwig 50, 70
Rader, Matthäus
  Bavaria sancta 178
Radewyns, Florens 29
Radical Protestantism 115–21, 125–6,
    131, 133–4, 137, 140, 142,
    144, 146–9, 194; *see also*
    Anabaptists
Ranters 233
Realism 13–14
reason 111, 229
Rebstock, Barbara 132
Reformed Protestantism 104, 115,
    117–18, 143, 146–7, 150
  Dutch 137–8, 143, 244
  English 103–4, 117, 147, 203–4
  Calvinist 97

Hungarian 106
Swiss 87, 143
see also under Calvanism
Reinicke, Hans 51
Reit, Berhard 62
Reiter, Paul 46
relics 26
religions of the world 164
religious orders:
 Antonine 1
 Augustinian 51, 159–60, 261–2
 Benedictine 111, 127, 184,
  190, 198
 Carmelites 160
 Carthusians 194, 199
 Cistercian 153
 Cluniac 198
 Dominican 18, 28–9, 159–60
 Franciscan 15, 18, 28–30, 152,
  159–62, 167, 173, 184, 190
 Piedosos 152
 Redemptorists 168, 179
 see also under Nuns
Remonstrants 109; *see also* Arminians
Renee of Ferrara, Duchess 85
Reublin, Wilhelm 121
Reuchlin, Johannes 16, 39
Rheims 173
Rhineland 30
Ricci, Matteo 154, 157
Richard III (of England) 187
Ricoldus 65
Ridley, Nicholas 250
Riedemann, Pieter 139
Ries, Hans de 137, 139
Rinuccini, Giovanni Battista:
 Il Cappuccino scozese 166
Ripon (Yorkshire) 183
Rocha, Giovanni da 157
Rocha, Juan de:
 Annunciation 159
Rochester:
 Bishop of 193, 199
Roegele, Hans 180
Roerer, Georg 42
Rome 2, 9–10, 16, 27, 53, 152–3,
  158–9, 171–3, 181, 184–5,
  213–14, 229, 247, 262
 Borghese chapel 155
 Capitoline hill 250
 Jewish Ghetto of 236
 as location of the papacy 6, 11–12,
  43, 48, 157, 170, 178, 181,
  196–7, 199, 209–10, 239, 243,
  248, 255, 257, 261
 papal palace in 1; *see also*
  Vatican, the
 Protestant 91
 S. Bartolomeo 181
 S. Ignazio 163, 165
 S. Maria Maggiore 154–5, 170

St Peter's Basilica 9, 45, 172,
  177, 250
Rothmann, Bernhard 133
Rouen 81, 99
Roussel, Gerard 91
Rovere family 11
Rowntree family 241
Ruusbroec, Jan van 30

Sabbath, the 245–6
sacraments 20–1, 25, 47, 58, 132,
  168–9, 181, 210–11, 255
 The Sacrifice unto the Lord
  138, 141
St Andrew 190
St Andrews 13–14, 195, 201–2, 206
 Holy Trinity Church 220
St Anna 51
St Balbina 28
St Bartholomew's Day Massacre 236
St Columba 190
St Cuthbert 188
St Derfel 190
St Elisabeth of Thuringia 42–4
St George 188
St Gerasima 152
St Hildesheim 26
St John Nepomuk 251
St Leger, Anthony 200
St Magnus 190
St Nicholas of Tolentino 261
St Ninian 192
St Priscilla 152
St Salvators 14
St Ursula 10, 152
St Wolfgang 26–7
Saint-Omer 184
Sainte-Marthe, Scévole de:
 Gallia cristiana 178
Salazar, Domingo de 153
salvation 109, 126, 142, 223, 237;
 see also soteriology
Salzburg 126
Salzkammergut 26–7
San Eliseo, Juan Tadeo de 160
Sattler, Michael 127, 129–30
Savonarola, Girolamo 1, 13
Savoy 85
Savoy, Duke of 8; *see also* Popes:
 Felix V
Saxony 30, 47–8, 51–2, 59–60,
  121, 143
 Elector of 45, 54, 69
 Lower 26
Scandinavia 204, 247, 261
Schammer, Georg 62
Scheurl, Christoph 44
Schilling, Heinz 49
Schleitheim Articles 127
Schmalkaldic League 204
Schmalkaldic Wars 230

Schön, Erhard:
 Saviour of the World 36
Schwenckfeld, Caspar 131–2, 142
Scholasticism 166
science 229, 262–5
Scientific Revolution 256, 262
Scot, Reginald:
 The Discovery of Witchcraft 260
Scotland 11, 77, 99–100, 186–8,
  194–6, 201, 205, 209–12, 247
 Aberdeenshire 217
 Ayrshire 194
 Bishops' Wars 224, 233
 Catholicism in 199–200, 206, 217
 Church of 109
 Fife 211
 Highlands of 188, 214
 kings of 193
 Kirk of 101, 211, 217, 219, 221,
  224, 240
 National Covenant 224
 Orkney 188
 Parliament of 224
 people of 94, 97–8, 163, 215, 246
 Protestantism in 200–1, 219–20,
  233, 261
 Reformed Kirk of 99–100
 Shetland 188
Scribner, Bob 56–7
Second Book of Discipline 219
secular:
 rulers 49, 59, 75, 98, 175, 177,
  231, 237
 authority of 62, 65, 84, 197, 212
 society 248
secularization 256
Segneri the Elder, Paolo 168
Sens 99
sermons 22
Servetus, Michael 96, 135, 145, 229
sex/sexuality 31, 60–1, 64–5, 148,
  219, 243, 246–7
Seymour, Edward (Duke of
 Somerset) 201–2, 205
Seymour, Jane 201
Shakespeare, William:
 Twelfth Night 243
Shanghai 183
Sichem Arnhemius, Christoph van:
 *Historische Beschrijvinge ende
  offbeeldinge der voorneemste
  Hooft Ketteren* 127, 129,
  136, 145
Sicily 176
Sienna 22
 Duomo, the 11
 Piccolomini library 11
Sigismund (Holy Roman Emperor)
 6, 38
Sigismund, Elector John 105
Silesia 131 n. 2

Simons, Menno 136–8
sin 77, 84
Slovakia 139–40
Smyth, John 147
society 117, 123, 127, 148, 151, 175, 248, 267
  and the church 114
  early modern 242
  fragmentation of 236
  hierarchy of 115, 148
  processes of 85
  unrest in 119
  welfare and 242
Socinians 150, 265
Solari, Aurelio 180
Solari, Ludovico 180
soteriology 109, 147; *see also* salvation
soul, *see* spirit/soul
South Africa 100, 232
Sozzini, Fausto 135
Spain 12, 99, 138, 153–5, 160–3, 167, 169, 176–7, 185–6, 215–16, 229–30, 232, 236–7, 239, 250, 257
  Armada of 214, 237
  people of 96–7
Spalatin, Georg 47, 53
Spangenberg, Cyriacus 70
Spee, Friedrich 260
  Cautio Criminalis 260
Spinoza, Baruch (Benedict) 150, 265–6
  Tractatus Theologico-Politicus 266
spirit/soul 32, 75, 130–1, 140, 142–5, 233, 241, 255
Spiritualists 96, 108, 132, 140, 142–3
Stahl, Andreas 51
Stanford in the Vale (Berkshire) 203
state, the:
  building 187
  relationship with the Church 76–7, 114, 150, 183, 192–3, 197, 235
Staupitz, Johann von 13
Stewart, Henry 212
Stewart, Matthew (Earl of Lennox) 201, 217
Stockholm 132
Stoeckel, Wolfgang 55
Stokesley, John 196, 199
Strafford, Earl of 225
Strasbourg 16, 59, 64, 85, 87, 132–3
Streicher, Helena 131
Stumpf, Simon 121
Sucre (Bolivia) 182
Summenhart, Conrad 13
supernatural, the 257, 260–1, 268
Swabia 231
Sweden 14, 204, 232, 248
Swiss Brethren 123, 129–30, 137
Switzerland 18, 76–8, 81–2, 87, 92, 98, 100, 119, 121, 232, 235
  Protestantism in 123, 126, 130

symbolism 25, 247, 251–3
syncretism 250

Tacitus:
  Germania 16
Tainos 162
Tamerlane 163
Tarascan (language) 167
Tauler, Johannes 30
Taurini, Giacomo 182
Taurini, Gianpaolo 182
Taurini, Giovanni 182
Tawney, R. H. 240
Technochtitlán 159
Temple, Sir William 243
Teresa of Avila 173, 261
Tetzel, Johan:
  counter-theses 54
The Hague 243
theocracy 77, 87
theologians 38, 83
theology 20, 45–6, 92, 226, 235
  Protestant 103, 111, 114, 116, 123, 241–2, 253, 258
  reformed 81, 94, 104, 147
  study of 15
Thirty Years War 139, 153, 168, 230–1, 248
Thomann, Heinrich
  Die Thomann-Abschrift von Bullingers Reformationsgeschichte 124
'Thomas' Christians 163
Thomism 47; *see also* Aquinas, Thomas
Thuringia 126
Tintern Abbey 249
Tlaxcala/Tlaxcallan 159, 167
To the Assembly of the Common Peasantry 125
Toland, John 266–7
  Christianity not Mysterious 267
toleration 108, 226, 233, 237–8, 240; *see also* intolerance
Toulouse 176
Touraine 99
Tours 81, 99, 184
Transylvania 105, 108, 135
Treaty of Tordesillas 12
Trent:
  Council of 168–71, 173, 177–81, 183, 185, 204, 206–7, 262
Trier 184
Trinitarianism 144, 229
  Anti- 96, 135, 145, 263, 265; *see also* Unitarianism
Trinity, the 262
Tübingen 262
Tunis 163
Turks, the 65–6, 69, 139, 192, 230, 237, 241
Tunstall, Cuthbert 194–5, 205
Turner, Joseph Mallord William:

Tintern Abbey 249
Twelve Articles of the Upper Swabian Peasants 123
Twisck, Peter Jans:
  True History of the Witnesses of Jesus Christ 141
Tyndale, William 194–5, 197
Tyrol, the 123, 126

Ughelli, Ferdinando:
  Italia sacra 178
Ulm 131
Ultraquists 38
Unitarian Socinians 106
Unitarianism 144, 265
United States 109–10, 150–1, 226, 241; *see also under* American Colonies
universities 190
Utrecht 30, 236

Valadés, Diego de 166–8
  Rhetorica Christiana 166–8
Valencia 12
Valla, Lorenzo 17
Valladolid 214
Vatican, the 9; *see also* papacy; Rome
Venice 93, 172, 176, 247
Vermigli, Peter Martyr 204
Vicars, John:
  A sight of ye trans-actions of these latter years 225
Vico, Giambattista 84
Vienna 65, 173, 184
Vingle, Pierre 82
Viret, Pierre 98
Virgil 11
Voltaire 237, 267
Voragine, Jacobus de 10

Waldensians 35, 38, 119
Waldshut 127, 129
Wales 187–8, 190, 194, 198, 201, 214
Wallington, Nehemiah 241
Walpot, Peter 139
Wan-li dynasty (China) 154
Warburton, William 235
Ward, Mary 183–4
Ward, Samuel:
  Deo trinuni Britanniae bis ultori In Memoriam classis 216
Warham, William 197
Wartburg 49
  Castle of 120, 122
Waterlanders 137–9, 147
Weber, Max 111, 114, 240–1
  The Protestant Ethic and the Spirit of Capitalism 111
Wesley, John 109, 267
Westminster:
  Abbey 109
  Synod 206

Westminster Catechism 109
Westphalia 119, 260
  Treaty of 171
Wettins of Saxony 48
Weyden, Roger van der 16
Weyer, Johann 260
Whitfield, Henry 106
Whitgift, John 220–1
Whithorn (Galloway) 192
Wiericx, Hieronymus 158
Williams, Roger 150, 237
Wilsnack 26
Winchester:
  Bishop of 199, 209
Windesheim 29–30
Winstanley, Gerrard:
  The New Law of Righteousness 148
Winthrop, John 95
Wishart, George 201
Witches/witchcraft 25, 40, 176,
  259–60, 265

Witikon 121
Wittelsbach dukes of Bavaria 153,
  168, 184, 239
Wittenberg 42, 47, 51, 54, 57–8, 61,
  67–9, 116, 120, 123, 126, 132,
  152, 227, 262
  All Saints Church 43–4
  Elstertor 49
  monastery of 250
  University of 59, 122
Witz, Konrad:
  Christ on Lake Geneva 8
Witzel, Georg 60
Wolsey, Thomas 193
women 61–2, 64, 131–2, 140, 166,
  183–4, 205–6, 209, 230, 243,
  254, 259, 261
Word of God 25, 116–21, 123, 126,
  130, 133, 145–7, 150–1, 196, 254
Worms 194
  Diet of 49–50, 55–6, 125

  Edict of 120
Württemberg 143, 262
Wyclif, John 38, 194
Wycliffite Bible, *see* Bible, the: Wyclif

Xavier, Francis 152, 157, 168,
  173, 261
Xavier, Jerónimo 157
'Xavier-Water' 168

York 19, 23, 193, 200

Zacharias, Andreas 48
Zahir ud-din Babur 163
Zionists 150
zoology 263
Zurich 105, 116, 120–1, 123–4,
  126–7, 129, 204, 209
Zwickau 60, 131
Zwingli, Huldrych 77, 83–4, 116,
  121, 123–5, 186, 201, 204, 256